COMMUNIST RESISTANCE IN NAZI GERMANY

COMMUNIST RESISTANCE IN NAZI GERMANY

ALLAN MERSON

LAWRENCE AND WISHART
London

Lawrence and Wishart Ltd
39 Museum Street
London WC1A 1LQ

First published 1985

First published in USA in 1986 by
Humanities Press International, Inc
Atlantic Highlands, New Jersey 07716
ISBN 0-391-03366-2

Photoset by Type Practitioners, Sevenoaks, Kent
Printed and bound in Great Britain by
Oxford University Press

Contents

Illustrations

Illustrations are taken from the following books:
Geschichte der Deutschen Arbeiter Bewegung Vol.5 (9)
Klaus Mammach, *Widerstand 1933–1939* (1, 2, 3, 6)
Margot Pikarski and Günter Uebel, *Die KPD Lebt!* (7)
Karl Schabrod, *Widerstand Gegen Flick und Florian* (4, 5)
Valentin Tomin and Stefan Grabowski, *Die Helden der Berliner Illegalität* (8)
Erich Weinert, *Das Nationalkomitee 'Freies Deutschland'* (10, 11)

For the countless German Communists, known and unknown,
who gave their lives in the struggle against fascism

Foreword

The aim of this book is comparatively modest: to give a clear account, to English-speaking readers, of the resistance which the German Communists offered to the Nazi dictatorship. I have tried at once to sketch the development of the Communist Party's ideas and activities, and to convey something of the feel of the period.

It was a period of bitter class struggle, fought underground until 1939, when it merged into open war between nations. Everything about it was, and still is, controversial, and the historian cannot, any more than the people of that time or the reader today, easily remain neutral. Dr Duhnke, the American author of a *magnum opus* on this subject, wrote in his foreword that although his outlook might fairly be described by Marxists as 'bourgeois', he hoped to do justice to the subject 'in all truth and conscience'. That is my aim, too, and I believe that the Marxist approach which I have adopted will help me to render a truthful account.

No one who has studied a subject as long as I have this can fail to have accumulated debts. I could not have undertaken the study without the facilities provided by the Wiener Library and by the History Departments of Southampton University and of the Humboldt University at Berlin, as well as by the Institute of Marxism-Leninism (Central Party Archive) at Berlin, the *Hauptstaatsarchiv* of North-Rhine-Westphalia at Düsseldorf, and the Düsseldorf office of the *Vereinigung der Verfolgten des Nazi-Regimes*; to all of them I record my thanks.

I am also indebted to the respective librarians who allowed me to consult papers in the West German Federal Archive at Koblenz; in the *Oberlandesgericht* at Hamm in Westphalia; and in the Berlin Document Center and the *Geheime Staatsarchiv der Stiftung Preussischer Kulturbesitz*, both in West Berlin.

Of many individual debts, some – for oral testimony – are acknowledged in the Appendix at the end of this book. In addition I am grateful to many friends and scholars for help and advice, notably to Professor Wolfgang Abendroth, Dr Richard Bessel, Jack

Cohen, Nicholas Jacobs, Professor K-H. Jahnke, Alfred Jenkin, Dr Ian Kershaw, Professor Jürgen Kuczynski, Dr Bruno Löwel, Dr David Morgan, Dr Ehrhard Moritz, Dr Gerhard Nitzsche, Dr Detlev Peukert, Dr Margot Pikarski, Dr Gerhard Rossman, Andrew Rothstein, Heinz Schumann, Professor Wolfgang Schumann, Werner Sterzenbach, and Dr Ziegahn of the Hauptstaatsarchiv, Düsseldorf, and not least to Jeffrey Skelley and Stephen Hayward of Lawrence and Wishart.

I owe special thanks to Aurel Billstein of Krefeld, tireless Communist veteran and local historian; to Professor J.S. Bromley of Southampton for constant encouragement and patient criticism; to the late Friedrich Fränken and Berta Fränken, who made me at home at Düsseldorf and introduced me to many of their fellow veterans of the Resistance; to the late Karl Schabrod and Klara Schabrod, who, besides much other help, put the records of the Düsseldorf VVN fully at my disposal. I owe thanks, too, to Professor Ernst Hoffmann and Ursel Hoffmann for much stimulating discussion and practical help, and to Professor Gerhard Schilfert and Gertraude Schilfert for help and hospitality too various to itemise. Finally, I must not forget to thank my wife for her patience and encouragement at difficult moments.

I know that those who have helped me may not agree with everything I have written. They are, of course, in no way responsible for it.

1985 Allan Merson

CHAPTER I

Introduction

For twenty years or so after 1945 the nature and extent of resistance to the Nazi dictatorship by Germans was a question as much of current politics as of history. At first, in the brief period of the early war-crimes trials, the prevailing atmosphere was such that those who had been associated with the Nazi régime were subject to suspicion, or even to prosecution, until they had undergone the process sometimes oddly described as 'de-nazification'; while those who had plotted to assassinate Hitler or to overthrow his rule were accorded a somewhat grudging recognition. But this soon changed. With the onset of the Cold War, rehabilitated Nazis began to resume a political role in the Western zones, while former *émigrés* and anti-Hitler plotters found themselves pushed on to the defensive.[1*] In the Federal Republic of the 1950s, in which the Adenauer-Globke régime represented a partnership of those who had served Hitler and those who had plotted against him, anti-Nazi resistance was an embarrassing and divisive topic.

In the late 1950s and early 1960s several serious studies of German Resistance appeared in the Federal Republic, written by academic historians who had had experience either of imprisonment or of exile; some of these touched on the Communist Party's activities. Gerhard Ritter, for instance, in his study of Carl Goerdeler and his circle,[2] gave a brief account of the Marxist intellectual group known as the Red Orchestra, and referred to other Communist resistance in terms which implied that the Communist Party maintained a continuous and highly organized activity throughout the period of the Third Reich; but this was only to explain why he had omitted this activity from his book, bluntly declaring Communists to have no place in a history of the German Resistance.[3] The treatment of Communist activity was much the same in Hans Rothfels's *German Opposition to Hitler* and in most other Western works of that period.[4]

Ritter's and Rothfels's books were translated and British writers generally followed them, though often failing to include their

*See Notes on pp. 313ff.

reservations about working-class opposition and so giving a different impression: the impression, that is, that there had been no significant anti-Nazi resistance before about 1937, and that it had then come almost exclusively from a small minority of churchmen, aristocrats, generals and other conservatives. This resistance was, moreover, variously judged by British writers. Some, like Wheeler-Bennett, regarded those opponents of the Nazis as nationalists who shared the aims if not the methods of the Nazis and had justifiably been viewed with distrust by the Western powers.[5] Others, such as David Astor, preferred to think of them as forerunners of democracy whose treatment by the Allies had been both a shameful betrayal and a grievous mistake.[6]

Both schools were united, however, in believing that the labour movement in general, and the Communist Party in particular, had played no significant part in such resistance as there had been. Alan Bullock declared in the 1950s that the German Communist Party collapsed in 1933 with little resistance,[7] and its role was passed over silently or briefly and disparagingly by Shirer,[8] Wheeler-Bennett[9] and Grunberger,[10] as well as by Terence Prittie in his book *Germans Against Hitler*,[11] published in 1964 with a commendatory foreword by Hugh Trevor-Roper. Professor Geoffrey Barraclough's was a lone voice among British historians when he suggested, in a critical review of Prittie's book, that the churchmen and army officers with whom it mainly dealt might prove to be only a small part of the Resistance when the activities of working people came to be investigated.[12]

The slowness of Western historians to investigate the anti-Nazi activities of working people was not due to lack of prompting. A rough but extensive compilation of evidence which pointed to the importance of the opposition activities of Communists and Socialists was published in 1953 by the West German writer and concentration-camp victim, Günther Weisenborn, under the title *Der lautlose Aufstand* (The Silent Insurrection).[13] Unfortunately, however, it was not adequately followed up in the West. In the (East) German Democratic Republic, however, from the 1950s onwards, numerous books and articles were published in support of the contention that the Communist Party had organised resistance throughout the period of the Third Reich. This contention was not so much disproved as ignored. Of 89 works listed in Prittie's bibliography, for instance, only one was published in the GDR.[14]

This self-censorship reflected a dogma, widely accepted by Western writers in the Cold War period, to the effect that Communist activities, whatever the facts about them, did not deserve to be classified under the honourable title of Resistance. On that basis many non-Marxist historians of German Resistance thought themselves justified in ignoring GDR work until far into the 1960s.

The account which GDR historians gave of the German anti-Nazi Resistance was very different from that given by Prittie and other British writers. Very little of the GDR work was published in English translation and even those British scholars who took the trouble to consult it seem to have been little influenced by it in practice. They were put off by the Marxist terminology employed and unwilling to accept the conclusion drawn: that the true heirs of the anti-fascist Resistance of 1933–45 were the Socialist Unity Party and the German Democratic Republic. In recounting the heroic deeds of the Resistance, the Communists of the GDR were conscious of tracing their pedigree and demonstrating their political and moral legitimacy more simply and directly than the Federal Republic, with its ambiguous origins, could hope to do.

The Marxist historians of the GDR have their problems, but they do not believe that these can be solved by completely separating history from politics or approaching it with a completely open mind; and if they have made their mistakes, they have also made distinguished contributions to the historiography of the Third Reich and the Resistance. These are listed in their standard bibliographies[15] and ably summed up in their standard textbook of German history, published in 1969.[16]

In the late 1960s there was a lessening of tension between the two German states, marked by Willy Brandt's *Ostpolitik*, and this was reflected in the historiography of the German Resistance. In the GDR more attention began to be paid to bourgeois and Social Democratic resistance.[17] More strikingly still, historians in the West at last began to concede that the activities of Communists, both individually and as a party, had played a major role in the German Resistance and could not honestly be omitted from the historical record on the argument, hitherto current, that they represented another form of 'totalitarianism' comparable to that of National Socialism itself. A growing number of regional and biographical studies were published in West Germany by the left-wing Röderberg-Verlag. At the same time a number of historians associated with the Social Democratic Friedrich-Ebert-Stiftung at Bonn published studies of local resistance in particular cities which, though anti-Communist in tone and conclusions, recognised clearly that resistance had begun, not in 1937 but in 1933, and that in the first years it was mainly Socialist and Communist.[18] In 1971, again, an American historian, Horst Duhnke, in a full-length study of the KPD in the period 1933–45 (on which the present writer has drawn heavily) introduced what might be described as a running criticism of GDR work (which he accuses of distortion and falsification) by conceding that 'the scope, significance and effectiveness of Communist Resistance have been unduly neglected in the West'.[19] Similarly the British historian, T.W. Mason, in his pioneering work on labour in the Third Reich, assigned a major role to the resistance of the Communists, though he criticised GDR accounts of it.[20]

Mason's work opened up new fields by exploring the economic background of working-class attitudes and discontents in Germany during the 1930s. His work has been followed up in the West by a new generation of scholars, probing into further aspects of German society under Hitler and throwing light on many social and psychological factors related directly or indirectly to opposition and resistance, including public opinion (Kershaw)[21] and unrest among youth (Peukert).[22] These new sociological approaches have also greatly widened the scope of regional studies, of which there has been a rich crop, notably the multi-volume collective project on Bavaria,[23] with a section on 'Persecution and Resistance of Communists'; and Dr Peukert's striking study of *The KPD in the Resistance on Rhine and Ruhr*, from which the present author has learnt much.[24]

It was not only in West Germany that the 1970s and early 1980s saw a great increase of historical research and publication about the Third Reich and the Resistance to it. In the GDR, too, many new volumes of memoirs were published, and useful bibliographical works such as Rudi Goguel's bibliography of works in German on anti-fascist resistance and class struggle published between 1945 and 1973.[25] The Institute for Marxism-Leninism in Berlin has also published in its bi-monthly journal many documents from the KPD Archives, whose contents are thus gradually becoming more accessible.[26] The material recently published includes selected correspondence between the Central Committee and the Districts in the years 1933–37[27] and a magnificent selection of 240 clandestine leaflets in facsimile covering the whole twelve years of the Third Reich.[28]

Since the 1970s, then, Western historians of Nazi Germany have generally come to recognise Communist resistance as a significant phenomenon, needing to be put in its historical place. What that place is has varied with interpretations of the Third Reich itself. Those who see the Nazi régime as essentially a form of aggressive capitalist imperialism will seek, as Communists do, to draw a line between those opponents who represented a fundamental challenge to aggressive imperialism as such and those who sought no more than to pursue similar aims by more cautious, more realistic, more effective means. Hence the technical term 'anti-fascist resistance', used by Communists to describe all those whose opposition went to the lengths of rejecting Nazi imperialist aims altogether. Those, on the other hand, who see the essence of the Third Reich as 'totalitarianism' still seek to draw some kind of line which excludes from Resistance those like the Communists who are said to aim at replacing one form of totalitarianism by another.

Whatever judgment may be made of the alternative which the Communists offered to the German people, there can be no doubt that they did aim at the political overthrow and replacement of the Nazi régime. But what of critics and opponents of Nazism whose aims and actions fell short of that? The Social-Democratic ideologist Richard Löwenthal has recently distinguished two such categories: on the one hand what he calls *Verweigerung* (nonconformity), that is, a refusal to fit into the social pattern dictated by the state, such as refusal to give the Hitler greeting; and secondly *weltanschauliche Dissidenz* (ideological dissidence), meaning a non-acceptance of the National-Socialist world outlook.[29] To count all such attitudes as Resistance – to include everyone who failed to give whole-hearted support to National Socialism and to assume that the demands of Nazism were absolute – would be to reach the totalitarianism-concept by another route. In practice the Nazi leaders were too realistic to suppose that they were likely to convert the entire population to their views in any near future. What they concentrated on, therefore, was to isolate and deprive of influence those active revolutionary elements which tried consciously to mobilise popular discontent against the government; and it is to these revolutionary elements that the term 'Resistance' refers in this book. The mass of those whose discontent on economic and similar grounds was waiting more or less passively to be mobilised has been called by Dr Mason 'Opposition' as distinct from 'Resistance'; and the distinction is a useful one.[30] 'Resistance' implies activity.

Ever since the relaxation of international tension in the 1970s, the accessibility of public archives has increased, though tending to fluctuate with the state of East-West relations. For the purpose of the present study the most important archive – that of the KPD itself – has continued to have the status of a private archive, to which access is controlled by the Socialist Unity Party through its Institute for Marxism-Leninism in Berlin and is not completely unrestricted.[31] In the present state of East-West relations this is not surprising and is true of many public and private archives in the West as well. The present writer can do no more than record that he has enjoyed every reasonable facility at the Institute, and much personal help.

The increased accessibility of party records and other source-materials has led in recent years to a big increase in research into the position of the working class in the Third Reich. This has not, of course, solved all problems concerning the history of the anti-fascist Resistance in Germany; but it has enabled some of them to be formulated with a new clarity. One such question is whether the fall in the number of arrests and prosecutions of Communists after 1935 reflected reduced activity or only more success in eluding the police? More generally, by what criteria can the extent and effectiveness of resistance be measured? In the case of the KPD, how much emphasis deserves to be placed on the activities of members working illegally within Germany as against those living in exile abroad? And, in that connection, were the Communists' illegal activities, whether in Germany or in exile, effectively controlled and directed by the Central Committee or its Political Bureau? This is now one of the main points of controversy between contemporary historians of East and West. Duhnke, for instance, asserts that the policies of the exiled Communists 'had no great influence on the German history of the period', and might have had little importance 'had the German Communists not been able to establish their state in eastern Germany after 1945'.[32] The Marxist historians of the GDR, on the other hand, have sought to correct the anti-Communist bias of their bourgeois counterparts by emphasising, and sometimes overemphasising in an almost ritual manner, the leading role played in the anti-fascist resistance by the Central Committee of the KPD. With regard to the later socialist state in eastern Germany, some may say – and it is one of the arguments of this book – that it was, in part at least, the Communists' role in the Resistance, and the lessons they learned from it, which enabled them after 1945 to take advantage of the possibilities that arose for establishing a socialist state.

Some of the historical problems of the Resistance arise from the nature and inherent bias of the sources available. People engaged in underground political activity learned to put little in writing, except flimsy leaflets whose occasional survival in police files may not provide a true measure of the quantities circulated or the effect produced. Moreover, the diminishing quantity of such evidence which survives after 1936 may in part reflect a shift from written to oral methods of propaganda, rather than a decline of activity as such. In general, too much importance may have been attached to certain categories of evidence which do survive, such as police and court records. It is necessary to bear in mind when appraising the mass of factual detail contained in those records, that the Communists and the Gestapo were engaged in a ceaseless battle, in which mutual deception and deliberate misinformation played a part. The Situation Reports compiled by central and regional Gestapo headquarters may also have been less objective than they appear to be at first sight, for the police had an interest in making sure that the magnitude of their task was appreciated and the necessary resources provided. Records of political trials also present problems of interpretation. Accused Communists were sometimes prosecuted collectively in a large group trial, for administrative convenience, although the underground organisations to which they belonged were not in fact closely connected; and the description given in court of an accused's illegal activities might be directed to proving specific charges rather than to giving a complete or balanced picture.

Other main sources for the history of Communist Resistance are the resolutions and policy documents issued by the exiled Party leadership, more of which have come to light in the past fifteen or twenty years.[33] Professor Duhnke describes his account of the KPD's history during the years 1933 to 1945 as containing two separate stories: that of Communist activity within Germany, and that of the development of KPD policy, mainly worked out by *émigrés*, the two stories running parallel and only occasionally overlapping. In his view, the latter aspect – development of policy – had previously been neglected.[34] His own book, on the other hand, gave most of its attention to policy documents and has been criticised for failing to bring out the human side of the story.[35] The treatment of the same period by GDR historians in volume 5 of their *History of the Working-Class Movement*, published in 1966, has also been criticised by a British reviewer for adopting 'too formal and bureaucratic an approach' and giving little impression of the human realities of the struggle.[36]

To do justice to these 'human realities' is now easier for the historian in at least one respect than it was in the immediate post-war decades. The personal testimony of survivors has become available on a much greater scale, in the form both of published memoirs and of interviews collected either by practitioners of 'oral history'[37] or by institutions set up to help victims of Nazi persecution to obtain compensation.[38] In and after 1945 those survivors who were not physically and mentally shattered by their experiences, and anxious only to forget, were usually involved in intense political activity of a day-to-day kind. This continued to be true in the 1950s, although the situation and preoccupations of active Communists developed on very different lines in East and West Germany. By the later 1960s, however, many of these men and women were reaching the age of retirement and had more time to reflect about the past. They began to be keenly aware, too, that a generation had grown up for whom the experiences of the anti-fascist struggle and the lessons to be drawn from it were a closed book; and their own instincts were reinforced by the promptings of historians keenly aware that valuable evidence was daily being lost through the death of important witnesses. Now more than ever, survivors were urged to put their recollections on paper or on tape as a political as well as a historical duty owed to succeeding generations.

Communist memoirs published in the 1970s were not only more numerous. They gradually changed in character as the political pressure eased and the position of the Socialist Unity Party became firmer, permitting more open discussion of past weaknesses. Not all memoir-writers were equally quick to adopt the frankness which now became possible. Some, with a lifetime of service as Party officials, found it hard to escape from the deeply rooted habit of official reporting, with its accompanying jargon. Others, however, like Karl Mewis, Bruno Retzlav-Kresse and Jürgen Kuczynski, and many more, have been able to combine a politically orthodox approach with a lively and personal style.[39]

Almost all accounts published in the GDR of Communist

resistance to the Nazi tyranny estimate its effectiveness and significance much more highly than do most Western historians. They differ, too, in assessing much more positively the degree of control which the KPD leadership actually exercised over illegal activities in Germany. One British historian has also accused GDR authors of underestimating the extent of Communist resistance in the first years (1933–35), while overestimating its extent in the following years, thus concealing a virtual collapse in 1935–36.[40]

Anyone who tries to understand the history of the German Communist Party in the 1930s faces a number of problems which arise from the fact that the Party was, both in theory and in practice, not an independent organisation, but a section of an international party. This meant that the decisions of the KPD's Central Committee were subject to the overriding authority of the Executive Committee of the Communist International (ECCI). It did not necessarily follow from this, in theory at least, that the interests of the German party were automatically subordinated to those of the Soviet state, as expressed in its foreign policy. But it did mean that the interests of the world Communist movement as a whole took precedence over the interests of individual sections. In the early years after 1917, when proletarian revolution was expected to spread throughout the world, the victory of the revolution in Germany was not necessarily to be regarded as less important than the survival of the Soviet régime in Russia. But as the prospect of revolution in Europe receded, during the 1920s, the International came to regard the USSR as the 'fatherland of the international proletariat', whose defence as a state was given priority over the revolutionising of further capitalist societies. This principle of international strategy was to confront the KPD with difficult decisions at times, notably during the period of the German-Soviet Non-Aggression Pact of 1939–41.

The aim of this book is to sum up in simple terms what is known at present about German Communist resistance to the Nazi régime, and to indicate some of the more important questions arising. The main emphasis is placed on what actually happened in Germany, because it is on that that most new light has been shed by current research, rather than on policy discussions and polemic among *émigrés*, of which many detailed accounts have been given. The author's first concern has been to ask for how long, and in what ways, the German Communists acted against the Nazi régime after

1933, and to assess what effect their activities really had.

To understand what was involved in anti-fascist resistance – its possibilities and its limitations, its successes and failures, its victories and defeats – it is necessary not only to stand back and take in the picture as a whole, but to step forward and examine some of the detail close up: to consider what happened in a particular locality, on a working-class housing estate, on a group of allotments, in a street-corner pub, on the shop-floor of a factory, in a works canteen, at a labour exchange. And it is necessary to observe the actions and experiences, not only of classes and organisations, but of families and individuals, including those of the 'rank-and-file', without whose support the activities of leaders would have been impossible or meaningless. It is for this reason that some attempt, necessarily inadequate, has been made in Chapter 6 to give life to the generalisations by taking a closer look at the Communists and their struggle in one particular place: the city of Düsseldorf on the Lower Rhine. It cannot be claimed that Düsseldorf was in any way typical of Germany at that time: no one place was that. But its history during the Third Reich is more than usually well documented both by police records and by recent local studies, and a closer look at it may help to give a deeper understanding of what resistance really meant in a city which had been one of the strongholds of the Communist Party.

Although the main aim of this book is to tell what happened, it inevitably raises questions of explanation; and some of these questions will be broached here, though not always answered. Why above all, the reader may ask, were the Communists not able to take advantage of the failure and ultimate defeat of the Nazi régime to put themselves at the head of a broadly popular and patriotic resistance movement, as happened in Italy? This question is not so easy to answer as might seem at first sight. And why was the unity of the working-class movement so difficult to achieve in Germany after 1933? In some ways the very passage of time makes it necessary to review our judgement of people and events. Can we continue to see the history of the KPD as a collapse, a record of failure, now that the socialist state to which it contributed so much has developed and progressed for 35 years? The lessons which the KPD's leaders drew from the disaster of 1933 came too late to be used with decisive effect in the overthrow of the Third Reich, but the course of German history since 1945 owes not a little to those lessons, and for that reason alone they surely deserve reassessment.

Transition to Illegality 1933

CHAPTER 2

The German Communist Party

Before 1933 the German Communist Party was the largest outside the USSR. Rooted in the Marxist tradition of the pre-1914 German socialist movement, its formation in 1919 and enlargement in 1920 had represented a protest by the revolutionary sections of the working-class against what they saw as betrayal by a reformist leadership, in 1914 and again in 1918. For these events had produced on the left of the labour movement a long-term reaction of anger and disappointment which was sharper in Germany than in almost any other country. It was accompanied, not surprisingly, by a corresponding reaction of enthusiasm and admiration for the Russian Bolsheviks who were seen to have stuck to their principles by opposing war in 1914 and turning military defeat into proletarian revolution in 1917. In 1919 left-wing socialists in Germany, as in most other countries, welcomed the establishment of the Communist International as a means of applying on a world scale the lessons of 1917.

There was however, a brief hesitation on the part of the German Communists who were at first inclined to follow the view of Rosa Luxemburg, recently murdered, that an international would be premature. But the KPD soon joined and became one of the main sections of the Comintern.

It did not seem likely at first that the Bolsheviks would be able to hold on to power in Russia unless they were supported by socialist revolutions in one or more of the advanced industrialised countries. In this connection it was natural to think of Germany, where the bourgeois state was shaken by military defeat and confronted by a large, well-organised and experienced working-class movement. For some years after 1918 the outcome of the world-wide struggle between capitalism and socialism appeared – to both sides – to depend on the success or failure of the German Communists.[1] Until 1923 'a German 1917' seemed to be a real possiblity. The bourgeois régime set up at Weimar was still unstable, both economically and politically, and the defeat of the revolutionary attempts in 1918–19,[2] 1920[3] and 1921[4] could be attributed with some plausibility to unpreparedness on the left rather than to unfavourable objective conditions. It was not until the collapse of the Communist-led uprisings of 1923 that it became clear that the post-war revolutionary situation had passed for the time being and that capitalism had entered a period of stabilisation both in Germany and on a world scale.[5]

This meant that the Russian workers' state was faced with the problem of survival in a hostile world and that the International was likely to be faced, in varying forms, with the question of whether or not the defence of the socialist state should take precedence over the immediate interests of the movement in other countries, in case of a clash between the two. Such conflicts were expected at first to be no more than short-lived and to be swept aside by the next crisis of the world capitalist economy, which it became a major preoccupation of the International to foresee.

After four years of relative economic stability, the Communist International forecast the approach of a new crisis in 1928 and adopted a political line designed to enable Communist parties to take advantage of the expected leftward movement of the masses.[6] This was the policy of the Third Period, the ultra-left line, the policy of revolutionary offensive. In Germany, as in other countries, the Communist Party saw its task, more than ever, as that of winning the leadership of the working masses and equipping itself, ideologically, organisationally and politically, to be the instrument for the conquest of power. It was during the years of the world slump that followed (1929–32) that the German party, under the leadership of Ernst Thälmann and his close associates, took on the character it was to have when Hitler assumed power in January 1933.[7]

It was a party whose membership and leadership were drawn overwhelmingly, apart from a thin sprinkling of artists and intellectuals, from the manual working class.[8] This was not true only of the main industrial centres. In the West-Prussian town of Schneidemühl (now Pila in Poland), to give but one example, where the KPD's membership records for the years 1929–33 have come to light, no less than 92 per cent of members were 'blue-collar workers'.[9] In the Party as a whole white-collar workers and members of the lower-middle class were rare among the members;

state officials, including teachers, were even rarer, partly no doubt because of discrimination in appointments: the equivalent of the modern *Berufsverbote.* Working-class members, moreover, tended to be drawn disproportionately from certain industries – notably those, like the heavy industries of the Ruhr, which had experienced mushroom growth and mass immigration in the era of industrialisation, and in which employers' tyranny had hindered the development of normal trade unionism and promoted revolutionary militancy. As a result of these factors, the Party's membership was heavily concentrated in particular areas, in some of which – so-called 'red citadels' – the Party was capable on occasion of achieving an absolute majority on factory or town-councils.

The most important areas of Communist strength were: Berlin; the Ruhr basin and the adjacent Lower Rhine district; the Halle-Merseburg industrial region of Saxony (*Mitteldeutschland*) and neighbouring Leipzig; followed by Stuttgart and Hamburg. In these areas the Party had a solid, apparently unshakeable basis of support. Much has been made by some historians of the fluctuating element, which came and went within a short time. There was such an element, and the huge influx of recruits into the Party, especially in the crisis years 1931 and 1932, was partly offset by a continuous exodus, so that a high proportion of the 360,000 members registered at the beginning of 1933 had been in the Party for only a very short time. Nevertheless the fluctuation was in the long run perhaps less significant than the existence of a solid core who were bound not only by conviction, but by strong bonds of personal loyalty and neighbourhood ties, both of which were to prove to be important features of the resistance to National Socialism after 1933.[10]

Even before 1914, the Social Democratic workers' movement in Germany had comprised, not only a political party and a majority of the trade unions, but what recent historians have called a 'camp' (*Lager*):[11] that is, a whole cultural world set apart from and against the 'camp' of the bourgeoisie, subject only to the influence of state education and compulsory military training, and to that of the church in the Catholic areas. After 1918 this socialist 'camp' embraced still greater numbers of people and of institutions, in most of which the Communists represented at first a left-wing or revolutionary tendency. But as the conflict between Communists and Social Democrats sharpened, especially after 1928, the division between the two parties was reproduced in the 'mass organisations' and there came into being a 'red', 'revolutionary camp' set apart not only from that of the bourgeoisie, but also from that of Social Democracy.

There was the Revolutionary Trade Union Opposition (*Revolutionäre Gewerkschaftsopposition* or RGO), whose aim was to transform the General Federation of Trade Unions from within, and there were, in some branches of industry, separate 'red' unions which had come into being either through expulsions from the 'Federation' or by way of a local 'leftist' deviation from the official KPD line. An important role was played, too, by the Communist paramilitary defence organisation, the Red Front Fighters League (*Roter Frontkämpferbund* or RFB), and, after its banning in 1929, the League of Struggle against Fascism (*Kampfbund gegen den Faschismus* or KgF) which often seems to have represented simply an illegal continuation of the RFB. Another Communist subsidiary organisation was the Communist Youth League (KJVD) which, though comparatively small and largely confined to members of Party families, was important as a recruiting ground for the next generation of Communist cadres. An essential part, too, was played in the class struggles of the 1920s by a number of defensive organisations such as Red Aid (RH), International Workers' Aid (IAH), the Workers' Samaritan League and the International League of Victims of War and Labour (IBOKA), all of which mobilised financial and other support for imprisoned workers and their families.

Besides economic and political associations, the Communist camp included a network of workers' leisure-time organisations. There was a multitude of workers' sports clubs, many of them affiliated to the Communist-led Community of Struggle for Red Unity in Sport, commonly known as *Rotsport*, which was a federation of clubs, some combining many branches of sport, others specialising in a particular sport, such as cycling or mountaineering. There was a similarly wide range of cultural organisations. To combat the influence of the church – in Protestant areas almost exclusively a bourgeois institution – there was the Proletarian Free-Thinkers' League. There were, too, workers' libraries, lecture societies, Friends of Nature and Workers' Esperanto. There were workers' bands and orchestras, choirs and theatre or cabaret groups, whose performances enlivened political meetings. There were workers' chess and radio clubs. And many of these organisations, like the Party itself, produced their own publications, local and regional as well as national.

This network of institutions constituted a whole revolutionary cultural world, confronting its bourgeois counterpart and, to a certain extent also that of Social Democracy. It had the effect of binding its adherents together by a multiplicity of social ties and personal loyalties beyond those of Party membership as such; and this was to prove an important source of strength in conditions of illegal struggle. However, it also involved a process of self-isolation and tended to raise local as well as national barriers to working-class unity.[12]

These societies and movements were conceived in Communist circles as 'mass movements', through which the Party could reach out, influence and mobilise millions of workers beyond its own membership. But in fact many of these 'mass movements' never extended far outside the circle of Party members and their families and friends. At the end of 1931, for instance, when the Party had 246,525 registered members, the RGO and Red Unions together had 312,555, Red Aid 307,971, the Free-Thinkers' League 162,618, the League of Struggle against Fascism 99,207, IAH 55,635, while *Rotsport* counted 113,542 individual members and 3,003 affiliated clubs.[13] At the same time the effort to give these organisations something more like a genuine mass character – for which the Party leadership never ceased to call – imposed a severe strain on the time and energies of Party activists, especially as most of these organisations had a complex hierarchical structure similar to that of the Party itself.

The Communist Party was, compared to the Social Democrats, a party of youth. Its members represented the generation of 1895–1905 and their average age in 1933 was about thirty.[14] Many of them had experienced the First World War, at least in its final stages, and had taken part as very young people in the revolutionary events of 1918; many of them had been unable to find work afterwards. Their experiences of war, revolution and unemployment had made them deeply disillusioned with social-democratic gradualism and put them in a mood to embrace more extreme solutions like the Marxist doctrine of proletarian revolution and the Leninist doctrine of the revolutionary party. Some aspects of the German Communist Party of that time which may strike readers today as doctrinaire and bureaucratic appealed to the sense of order and discipline which were a legacy of the militarism they had rejected, as well as part of the tradition of the German labour movement. And, indeed, the style of leadership which came to prevail under Thälmann and Schehr was popular with the rank and file just because it did not sound bureaucratic, but struck a note of working-class shop-floor idiom, as befitted prospective leaders of a proletarian revolution. Typical of the anecdotes which contributed to 'Teddy's' (i.e. Thälmann's) charisma was the comment he is said to have scrawled on the draft of an article submitted by the economist, Jürgen Kuczynski: 'Too much cyclical crisis, not enough broken lavatory seats.'[15] When he visited his home town of Hamburg, as another veteran has recalled, before going to the Party office he would drop into a dockside pub to chat with the workers in local dialect.[16]

The Communist Party and the Social Democratic Party had one thing in common. Both proclaimed socialism to be their aim, but neither could hope to achieve it without the support of a united working class following its lead. The path to socialism was visualised by reformists and revolutionaries alike as a path of struggle for the unity of the working class under its leadership. Throughout the period of the republic (1919–33) the struggle between the two went on, with ups and downs, depending on the fluctuations of the capitalist economy and the willingness of capitalists to moderate the treatment of employees in such a way as would foster reformist illusions and keep discontent within bounds. It was a struggle which took place on many levels – in the factories and mass organisations as well as in local and national politics. In the trade unions, for instance, the revolutionaries tried to remain within the movement while retaining the maximum degree of independence of action. Both there and in other mass organisations the contest between the two working-class camps involved much bitterness and hostility, despite many examples of local fraternisation. Communists could not forget or forgive Noske's collaboration with the Free Corps in suppressing the revolutionary workers in 1919,[17] nor numerous subsequent occasions when Social Democratic ministers and police chiefs in coalition governments had used their powers in similar fashion. During the greater part of the republican period, indeed, the Social Democratic Party had formed part of the Establishment, while the Communist movement existed in various degrees of semi-legality, pursued by notoriously biased courts of law and harassed by a police force which was quite often under Social Democratic control.[18]

In these conditions it was difficult for Communists to envisage a union on equal terms with Social Democratic leaders whose anti-Communism was deep-seated and of long standing. Yet proletarian revolution was equally difficult to envisage except through a united working class. The answer could only be to win over the Social Democratic rank and file to accept Communist leadership, and this was the conclusion to which the Communists moved steadily in the 1920s. The consequent leftward trend in the policy of the German Communists was further confirmed by economic developments both in Germany and in the world as a whole. As another capitalist crisis approached, the bourgeoisie could be expected to resort to more dictatorial forms of rule, all of which now tended to be subsumed under the umbrella term 'fascism'. And just as reformist Social Democrats had previously adapted themselves to various forms of bourgeois rule and helped to give them a democratic disguise, so they might be expected, as the theorists of the Communist International now began to say, to lend their support and participation to a new variety of fascism: 'social fascism'. This vague concept was to be a source of confusion and of disastrous political errors. Yet there was more than a grain of truth in it, as was to be shown by the attempts at collaboration with the Nazi régime which were made by some trade union and Social Democratic leaders during the first months of Hitler's rule. It was a logical enough conclusion to draw from a doctrine which saw only two possible lines of development of society, so that those who did not take the path of proletarian revolution must necessarily follow in the wake of bourgeois reaction.

The economic crisis in the capitalist world, the onset of which the Communist International had foretold in 1928,[19] broke out at the end of 1929. In the following three years unemployment in Germany rose to unprecedented heights until, by late 1932, some one-third of the labour force was out of work and another third was working part-time. The big business interests and their political parties insisted on drastic reductions of wages and social benefits and the economic basis of coalition government involving co-operation of bourgeois with Social Democratic parties ceased to exist. The last such coalition at Reich level broke up in March 1930 and a form of bourgeois dictatorship by presidential emergency powers took shape. For the Communists the most immediate result was a flood of applications for membership. From about 120,000 in 1928 the numbers rose to some 287,000 in March 1932 and to an estimated 360,000 at the end of that year, of whom 287,180 were paying dues.[20] The rapidity of the growth posed serious organisational problems and on 25 July 1932 admissions had to be limited for the time being to long-standing and active members of the labour movement.[21] Some of the new members did, in fact, represent a movement over from Social Democracy; some, though not many, were disillusioned Nazis.[22] Many were probably manual workers who had not previously been organised, or who were driven to desperation by the experience of unemployment and the hopelessness of their prospects. The growing revolutionary mood which the KPD sensed was genuine enough, but it did not bring so great an accession of strength to the Party as the increase of numbers suggested, for the proportion of unemployed in the membership rose in those years from some 50 or 60 per cent to almost 90 per cent.[23] These unemployed members might, and often did, devote most of their time to political activity and helped to swell the size of demonstrations, not only for the Party itself, but for its associated mass organisations, which thus showed a level of activity which was in a sense artificial.

Another striking, and as events were to show more decisive, result of the crisis was the sensational growth of the National Socialist movement. Those who flooded into the fascist organisations after 1929 included workers, but the social composition of the National Socialist movement as a whole was very different from that of the Communist Party, and the movement between them was much less than has often been alleged. The Nazis recruited largely from the lower middle-class, from minor officialdom, and from sections of workers who had not been drawn fully or effectively into the labour movement, such as white-collar workers and agricultural labourers. One of the conclusions which the Communist Party drew from the rise of National Socialism was the need to expand its own social basis and to pay more attention to the interests of those sections of the working population. The recognition might have been important, but it came too late.

Following the ultra-left line which had prevailed in the Communist International since 1928, the German Party leaders saw the political situation in terms of a straightforward struggle between the working class and the bourgeoisie ('class against class'), which the crisis was steadily transforming into a choice of revolution or counter-revolution. They thought events were moving towards a revolutionary situation and found confirmation of this in the steady increase of their membership and voting strength. Time, it seemed, was on their side. By the end of 1932 they already had the support of a majority of the organised working class in some of the key industrial centres and were gaining ground in the others. In Berlin itself, in the Reichstag election of November 1932, the KPD polled 37.7 per cent of valid votes cast, as against the Social Democrats' 23.8 per cent.[24] It was thought, too, by friends and enemies alike, that the KPD was technically prepared for the seizure of power in the sense of having some units with elementary military training, some stores of arms, and a disciplined and politically educated apparatus much bigger than that which had been able to take power in Russia in 1917.

In the event the KPD's preparations were to prove unsuited to the conditions of Germany in 1933 and utterly inadequate; and some have concluded that the Comintern's doctrine of revolution was out of date. The West German historian Dr Peukert argues, with the benefit of hindsight, that the Party's Leninist organisation was too bureaucratic: able to lead a well-planned campaign, but not flexible enough for the new conditions of the rise of fascism.[25] There was, he suggests, a contradiction in the KPD's policy between proclamations of imminent revolution in theory and a tendency in practice to wait for numbers to increase, much as the Social Democrats had waited before 1914 for the supposedly inevitable maturing of revolution.[26] He attributes this to another contradiction, between the interests of the German workers demanding revolution, and those of the Soviet state which, though desiring to have a strong, radical working class in Germany, wanted no trouble in Central Europe while industrialisation in the USSR got under way.[27] Or it may perhaps simply be that the KPD, like others before, had been preparing for the last revolution and had not sufficiently appreciated the fact that the ruling class had also learned from its historical experiences.

As for the rise of National Socialism in the years of the world crisis, the KPD saw it as only one form of fascism, alongside 'Brüning-fascism', 'Papen-fascism', 'Schleicher-fascism' and, increasingly, 'social-fascism'.[28] They were very conscious of the inherent instability of the Nazi movement and thought that if it disintegrated, the revolutionary forces might gain ground. This, as it turned out, did not happen, though at no time had it seemed more of a possibility than at the end of 1932, when the Nazi Party was in deep crisis.

The rise of National Socialism and the decline of Social Democracy during the years of world crisis can be seen in retrospect to have faced the German Communists with an important choice. They needed to decide, either to concentrate their strength on barring the road to National Socialism, even if that involved some form of co-operation with the SPD leadership, or to give priority to winning the rank and file of the working class for the revolutionary path, in effect treating the Nazi danger as a secondary problem. This was a question to which the Party took a long time to find an unambiguous answer.[29] It meant reaching clarity on the nature of fascism and on the extent to which a revolutionary situation was really imminent. On several occasions the KPD leadership appeared to have decided to give priority to the Nazi-fascist danger, as for instance in the period from April to July 1932, when they made a number of gestures expressing readiness to enter into agreements for joint action with the SPD at top level as well as locally. There were, as a result, some impulses towards united action locally, but no co-operation was achieved at leadership level. This was partly because of the bitter anti-Communist feeling which prevailed among the right-wing SPD leaders and partly because the KPD was not prepared to suspend all public criticism of the historical record of the SPD, as its Executive demanded. In July the emphasis in KPD policy shifted back to the insistence on 'unity from below'.[30]

In the main, the KPD kept its eyes firmly fixed on what it saw as the maturing conditions for proletarian revolution in Germany, the crucial point being the winning over of the majority of the working class; and that meant, in part at least, winning them away from the influence of Social Democracy. Every increase in the Communist vote was interpreted as a further stage in the development of a revolutionary situation; and although Communists did not ignore the much more rapid growth of the Nazi vote, they were slow to realise that it was symptomatic of a radical change in the situation to which they should have reacted (as they were later to recognise)[31] by a thorough revision of their whole strategy.

They did not so react because they overestimated their own

strength. This was due in part to an excessive concern with quantitive as against qualitative criteria. Rising voting and membership figures were deceptive when an increasing proportion of the individuals concerned were unemployed and when the Party's factory cells were declining in size and influence.[32] In view of these objective trends, it may well be that the growing strength which the KPD felt itself to have at this time was more apparent than real. Thälmann himself emphasised the urgent need to improve the Party's work in the factories at an all-Reich conference held in October 1932, after which Party work in some of the biggest factories was placed directly under individual members of the Politburo.[33] Simultaneously, the bourgeoisie also overestimated the strength of Communism and the imminence of revolution and became convinced of the need for its own kind of unity and for redoubled efforts to isolate the KPD.[34]

At the same time the Communists failed to grasp the full significance of the meteoric rise of the Nazi movement and remained blind to some of its novel features; their analysis of the world situation as a whole was also unclear.[35] There were undoubtedly divisions within the Party leadership, the full story of which may not become known until the Party's archives are more fully open than they are now.[36] From the researches of GDR scholars it would appear that an extreme ultra-left, adventurist line was taken in 1932 by Heinz Neumann, but that Thälmann and Schehr were groping their way tentatively toward some form of better relations with Social Democracy and the trade unions associated with it. Neumann's view, of which no adequately documented account appears to have survived, was strongly criticised in the Party press until, in the autumn, he was finally ousted from the leadership and sent by the Comintern on a mission outside Germany.[37] As for Thälmann and Schehr, their line was not free of inconsistencies. In their public speeches, such as that which Schehr made at the Lower Rhine District Congress at Wuppertal in November 1932, they struck a note of optimism and spoke of a coming revolutionary offensive. The present Congress, Schehr told the District delegates, amid scenes of enthusiasm, was 'the last legal Congress before the Party's seizure of power'. They would 'fight their way from illegality to power'.[38]

If revolution was on the agenda, the Communists' preparations for it can only be described as inadequate.[39] Insofar as the Party had made any preparations for a violent struggle, they were mainly of a defensive character. The *AM-Apparat* (the Party's underground organisation), which had once had the character of a military branch of the movement, had become essentially an intelligence agency;[40] and the Red Front Fighters' League (RFB), though it had continued to exist illegally since its banning (by a Social Democratic minister) in 1929, was armed and organised to repel Nazi street terror rather than to fight a civil war or to seize power by an uprising. Some Western historians have taken the view that the KPD made preparations for an armed uprising in 1932, and the Ministry of the Interior appears to have thought so too. The contrary view is taken by most recent historians and is borne out by the fact that no attempt was made at any such uprising.[41]

But although the Party did not seriously attempt to seize power, it did make many preparations for the event of a ban on its activities, the possibility of which had been talked about from time to time since 1929.[42] The Red Front Fighters' League, which had been banned at that time, had continued its activities in a disguised form ever since, and the fact that it was able to do so deluded the Party into thinking that it too would be able to function illegally by similar methods. Already in May 1932, at a meeting of the Central Committee, Thälmann had urged that a reorganisation be carried through with a view to illegality, and Pieck was asked to make proposals;[43] and again in June 1932 the Secretariat appointed a commission (Dahlem, Schehr, Ulbricht) to review the plans which had been made for illegal working, not only of the central Party apparatus, but also of the Districts and the 'mass organisations'.[44] The measures of reorganisation which emerged were intended to achieve a simplification, by reducing the number of departments at each level, but in some other respects increased the complexity of the apparatus. New stages were added to the organisational hierarchy. Instructors (*Instrukteure*), that is non-elected commissioners, were appointed by District Committees to supervise groups of Sub-districts. Similarly, in December 1932, the 28 Party Districts were grouped into eight regions (*Oberbezirke*), each of which was to be supervised by a Regional Adviser appointed by the Central Committee and responsible to it. At the same time the number of basic units was increased by the division of some Districts and Sub-districts.[45]

These changes were already being put into effect by the end of

1932 and represented preparations for a transition to semi-legal working. At the same time clandestine quarters and contacts were prepared for full-time Party functionaries at the Centre and in the Districts,[46] and alternative presses were arranged, both within Germany and abroad.[47] During the autumn, too, a small group of Party functionaries was sent to live in Denmark, with the help of the Danish Communist Party, and similar arrangements may have been made in other neighbouring countries.[48] New rules were laid down, too, for the admission of new members, partly no doubt for security reasons; Party schools and lecture courses were arranged for existing members, in order to train them in the 'rules of conspiracy' and other aspects of political work in conditions of illegality.[49]

It is difficult to be sure how seriously the KPD prepared for the revolutionary situation which it envisaged, or how near it felt it was to that situation at the end of 1932; or, indeed, whether the approach of that situation was thought of as increasing or diminishing the need for an alliance with the Social Democratic movement. There was in the KPD's own attitude a certain ambivalence which tended to be covered over by ironical or semi-jocular remarks, as when Thälmann told comrades that they should not be afraid to talk to Social Democrats for fear of 'blotting their copy-book' with the Party,[50] or when Party members referred wryly to the 'Uprising Plan' which was in fact nothing but a collection of reports on the state of the Districts.[51] The 'Uprising' was an essential part of the vision of a German 1917 and was necessary to the morale of the Party. Yet even the world slump of 1929–32 did not create the conditions required for it. This was the inescapable conclusion to which a sober examination of the situation led. The problems facing the movement called for a theorist of the calibre of Lenin, but, with the possible exception of Gramsci, who was in prison, the Third International now lacked such a theorist.

The need for a correct analysis of the situation was especially crucial in Germany, where the reaction of the Communist Party to the formation of the Hitler government was to be shaped in large part by the belief that the economic situation was still worsening and that the Nazi-Nationalist coalition would be unable to master it.[52]

The German Communists had long been warning against the danger of a fascist dictatorship, yet when it came, it came in a form that took them by surprise. They did not, it is true, share the illusions of the Social Democrats, whose leaders advised their followers to wait and see whether the Hitler government appointed on 30 January 1933 would observe the constitution.[53] But the Communists failed, none the less, to see Hitler's accession to power as the ominous turning-point which it can be seen in retrospect to have been. They had been expecting further reactionary dictatorships: clerical-fascist, military-fascist, conservative-fascist, popular-fascist, perhaps even social-fascist. Hitler-fascism had been viewed as only one of the possiblities, and not necessarily the most probable or the most dangerous; and, even if it came, it might well be short-lived, as the others had been.

Besides underestimating the popular elements in National Socialism, the Communists overestimated their own strength. From a distance they looked like the powerful revolutionary vanguard which they proclaimed themselves to be; but when looked at more closely, the claim needed some modification. The result was that when faced with the Nazi assumption of power, the Communist Party was not strong enough to attempt an individual action, yet was too isolated to be able to act in concert with others.[54]

CHAPTER 3

Defeat and Recovery February-June 1933

The formation of Hitler's government was announced at about midday on 30 January 1933. Within a few hours protest meetings, marches and demonstrations were taking place in many German cities: in Stuttgart, in Frankfurt-am-Main, in some of the towns of the Ruhr and Rhineland and of Thuringia, and a wave of strikes spread among the dock-workers of Hamburg and the Northern ports.[1] The movement was organised for the most part by the Communist Party, though not without an element of spontaneity and some participation of other workers.[2] But the movement was patchy; the demonstrations were easily dispersed by the police and no attempt was made to develop them into armed uprisings. The Communists had no foothold in the army or the police and, more crucially still, they had less organised influence in the factories than they had once had.[3] The chance of any effective action to forestall the incipient counter-revolution therefore depended on whether the other sections of the working-class movement could be brought into united action with the Communists. In the hope of achieving this, the Party's Central Committee on the same day addressed an appeal to the three main trade union federations and to the Social Democratic Party.[4] Declaring that the new cabinet 'of open fascist dictatorship' was preparing to ban the Communist Party as the first step of an attack on the working class as a whole, it called for a united response in the form of 'Strikes; Mass Strikes; General Strike!'

The Communist appeal was issued in leaflet form and reprinted in many German cities.[5] Though addressed directly to the working masses, it did not contain direct criticism of the Social Democratic or trade union leaders and was not couched in terms of an appeal over their heads direct to the rank and file. It has none the less often been dismissed as unrealistic on the ground that its call for united action of the working class came much too late. This is true in the obvious sense that the divisions and enmities between the parties of the left proved to be too deeply rooted to be overcome in a short time. But this is not to say that the position of the new régime was so firmly entrenched from the start that it could not have been shaken and the course of events altered if the working-class parties had in fact joined together in vigorous action. There are signs that Hitler was nervous about that possibility in the first days, and events were to show that even after five weeks of ferocious persecution and hysterical propaganda, almost one-third of the electorate were prepared to cast their vote, under the eyes of storm troopers, for either the Communist or Social Democratic Party, disunited though they were.[6]

The appeal of 30 January evoked a response from local trade union and Social Democratic organisations in a number of industrial centres, and there were joint discussions about the possibility of united action. At Leipzig, for instance, Social Democrats were invited to a meeting with the KPD District Secretary, Fritz Selbmann, on 1 February and were later offered time for a speaker at public meetings on 3 and 19 February.[7] At Stettin, where the Social Democrats had arranged a public meeting, the KPD rallied its members in support.[8] Generally it was the younger Social Democrats and the socialist youth who were most militant and inclined to united action. The leadership, on the other hand, especially the central Executive Committee, rejected or ignored the KPD's advances and forbade its local organisations, on pain of expulsion, to co-operate with Communists. There were some brief local strikes and sit-ins, but for the most part the non-Communist workers followed the advice or instructions of the trade union or Social Democratic leaders, who urged them to distance themselves from the allegedly provocative actions of the Communists and to give the new government a chance to show whether its assurances were sincere.[9] No action should be taken against it unless it should break the law or itself resort to violence. To many workers the wisdom of this policy seemed at first to be confirmed when the cabinet proceeded to dissolve the Reichstag and to arrange for a general election. The Communist Party was not banned and its warnings appeared, on a superficial view, to have been unnecessarily alarmist. With more reason it might have been said to have been outmanoeuvred, isolated, and made to appear relatively powerless.

Later in retrospect, the Communists were to recognise that their inability to mobilise resistance to the formation of the Hitler government was a major defeat, revealing the failure of the ultra-left line of the previous years.[10] But the Party's immediate reaction was quite different: it was rather to confirm that line. The Nazi dictatorship was alleged to be fundamentally unstable and likely to be of short duration.[11] As the capitalist crisis deepened and the contradictions of the régime sharpened, it was thought that it would become more vulnerable to mass strikes and demonstrations and would become liable to revolutionary overthrow. This refusal to acknowledge defeat, these optimistic illusions about the fascist régime, were the basis on which the Party was able to reorganise itself and continue the struggle in the short term.[12]

The Communists' first attempt to come to terms with the new situation was made at a secret meeting of the Central Committee and other leading officials in the neighbourhood of Berlin on 7 February. In a four-hour speech, of which only extracts have been preserved, Ernst Thälmann, the Party Chairman, rebutted the legalistic illusions with which the Social Democratic leaders had sought to justify their passivity in face of the new government, and reiterated the call for a united front of the working class.[13] He emphasised that the new régime would stop at nothing in its treatment of opponents; yet in the main he struck a confident note. The Party's failure to mobilise effective opposition on 30 January, he said, was a result of its failure to overcome the influence of Social Democrats and Christian trade unionists on the workers; but the Communists were now gaining ground and the revolutionary crisis was maturing. In an interesting passage, of which much was later to be made, Thälmann insisted that while there could be no way of ending the Hitler government other than its revolutionary overthrow, this might not necessarily be the same thing as the proletarian revolution. This has been interpreted as foreshadowing the Popular Front strategy of subsequent years, though the words in themselves amount to no more than a passing thought, a call for flexibility of tactics or for not letting any dogmatic preconceptions hinder the struggle against fascism.[14] Whatever the remark implied, the general tenor of the speech was clear: the fight must continue and there were no grounds for pessimism.

In the event, the Party was not immediately banned, but remained nominally free to hold meetings, to publish newspapers, and to carry on a campaign for the general election set for 5 March. To have refrained from taking advantage of such legal possibilities as existed would have been unthinkable. Yet at the same time the requirements of public political activity hampered the process of going underground, which had already begun, and prevented the Party from making the necessary transition of outlook as well as of organisation. Meanwhile Party leaders continued to call for a united front of the working class. But the call was not unconditional or without ambiguity. 'We are prepared for every kind of united front,' Wilhelm Pieck was to declare at one of the Party's last public meetings in Berlin, on 23 February, 'but it must be a unity of struggle. We will not undertake to abstain from criticism of those Social Democratic and trade union leaders who, by their "wait and see" slogans, make it easier for fascism to consolidate its power.'[15]

During February 1933 conditions varied from place to place, and the freedom which the Communist and other left-wing parties nominally enjoyed to conduct a political campaign was in practice drastically curtailed by the arbitrary interference of the police, on whom new powers were conferred by a presidential emergency decree issued on 4 February.[16] The Communist daily press, too, which had already been banned for a period under the recent Schleicher régime, was subjected to further bans, culminating in a two-week ban from 14 February;[17] in addition, many of the Party's outdoor public meetings were either forbidden altogether or interrupted by police intervention. Above all, a new atmosphere existed when the last pretences of impartiality on the part of the police were abandoned. Typical of the new position of the police was an incident, trivial in itself, which occurred at Düsseldorf as early as 1 February, when a policeman was subjected to severe disciplinary action on the insistence of the Nazi *gauleiter*, because he had entered the premises of the local Nazi newspaper in order to take particulars of a stormtrooper who had been involved in an incident in the street.[18]

The battle of the streets and housing estates became fiercer, and the open enlistment of the police on the side of the Nazi terror bands was soon formalised and generalised. Goering, who now controlled the police throughout Prussia (which included two-thirds of Germany) issued a directive on 17 February requiring them to proceed with the utmost ruthlessness against the government's opponents and to use their firearms when in doubt;[19] and on 22 February he arranged for the enrolment of some 50,000 Nazi stormtroopers and nationalist 'Steel Helmet' militia as auxiliary police.[20]

The Communist Party was now up against an enemy with an overwhelming superiority of physical strength. Yet it was reluctant to abandon the concept of a 'revolutionary offensive' as the basis of its strategic thinking. Thälmann tried to relate current strategic formulae to the new circumstances by calling for 'higher forms of mass emergency defence',[21] though making clear that this did not include 'individual terror'. At the same time Communists continued to appeal to the Social Democratic Party and the trade unions to join them in warding off Nazi attacks. But these approaches continued to meet only occasional local response, especially as the Nazis concentrated their attacks in the main on the Communists, so as to encourage constitutional illusions among the Social Democrats.

On the whole the Communists pursued a somewhat uncertain course, at times laying the weight of their emphasis on the need for united working-class action, on other occasions on the importance of winning over the majority of the workers to the revolutionary path.[22] Meanwhile, throughout February, the Central Committee's Secretariat in Berlin organised conferences at Regional and District level, at which Instructors from the Centre criticised the local Party leaderships for not having adapted their methods effectively to the new situation created by Hitler's accession to power. They were said to be still suffering from 'legalistic illusions' encouraged by the election campaign, at a time when the Party was likely to be banned at any moment and ought to be making urgent preparations for going underground.[23]

Despite the harnessing of the state to the Nazi cause and a great increase in violent acts of revenge and provocation by the stormtroops, the left-wing parties did not collapse and, as the elections approached, it looked increasingly doubtful whether the National Socialist party would obtain a simple majority on its own or even in conjunction with its Nationalist allies, let alone the two-thirds majority necessary for constitutional change. It was at that point, on the evening of 27 February, that the whole situation was changed by the Reichstag Fire: the first of those sensational acts of staged violence which, like the *Reichskristallnacht* pogrom of 1938 and the Gleiwitz incident of 1939, were to become characteristic of the political style of the Nazi leadership. The Fire was a highly imaginative act of provocation which was used to whip up a wave of panic and of anti-Communist hysteria and so to obtain acceptance of presidential emergency legislation suspending the constitutional rights of the individual. The Fire also provided occasion and excuse for a surprise attack on the Communist Party, the raiding of its premises, the closure of its presses and the arrest of its leading members throughout Germany.

The Fire fitted so conveniently into the political needs of the Nazis at the time and was so characteristic of their methods, that on the argument *cui bono* alone – and that was only one of many arguments – few people outside Germany doubted at the time, or for 25 years afterwards, that the Nazis were responsible. Then, in the late 1950s, in the context of the Cold War, the theory became popular in the West that the Nazis had not designed the Fire, but had merely exploited the unaided work of the Dutch anarchist, Van der Lubbe, for their own purposes. This theory is not accepted by Marxist historians in the GDR, nor by some of the most reputable non-Marxist historians in the West; nor does the present writer accept it. But to argue the question adequately would require a fuller treatment than there is room for here.[24] Suffice it to say that the Fire, and the actions of the government in the days following, constituted in effect that banning of the Communist Party which its leaders had so often foreseen.

Despite many warnings from the Party Centre, the Communists were nevertheless taken by surprise to some extent, and unprepared for a blow in which machiavellian cunning and unrestrained violence were closely combined. On the night of the Fire, and in the days following, some 1,500 Communists were arrested in Berlin and an estimated 10,000 in Germany as a whole.[25] Among those seized were a high proportion of middle-rank functionaries, full-time officials of District and Sub-district leaderships, including many of those who had been designated as reserves in the event of a ban. The top leadership escaped (apart from Ernst Thälmann himself, who was arrested on 3 March, probably through betrayal), perhaps because they had already begun to live and work clandestinely. So also, at first, and for the same reason did the key figures in some of the Regions and Districts, such as Lambert Horn, political secretary of the Lower Rhine District and Hans Beimler, political secretary of the South Bavarian District.[26]

In all the towns and cities of Germany, while official and unofficial organs of propaganda blared forth reports of a supposed gigantic plot against the state, prisons and improvised detention centres overflowed with prominent local figures of the Communist movement, most of them well-known for their public activities, as well as from police files. Many were dragged from their beds or seized at their place of work, before they had understood the full significance of the Fire or received any political guidance about it. There was undoubtedly a good deal of confusion, both ideological and organisational. Street cells, factory cells and local branches found themselves cut off from contact with their leaders and responsible committees and deprived of the Party newspapers on which they normally relied for political news and guidance. The simplest facts of the situation were unclear, for while Communist Party membership was being treated as sufficient ground for taking people into 'protective custody', no formal ban had been pronounced. Moreover, at the Reichstag elections on 5 March the Communist Party's electoral list appeared on the ballot papers and at some places Communist functionaries went openly to the poll, though elsewhere they were being arrested. In the published results, too, the Communist Party was allocated 81 seats.

These uncertainties were of short duration. They arose from tactical considerations on the part of the Nazis, designed to clothe the impending assumption of dictatorial powers by the cabinet in the disguise of a constitutional act passed by a two-thirds majority. Virtually all the activities of the Communist Party were declared illegal on 6 March, and on 9 March its parliamentary mandates were cancelled. When the newly elected Reichstag met on 23 March, the places of the 81 Communists were vacant. Not even the Social Democrat's chairman, Otto Wels – the only opposition voice – uttered a word of protest. In the ensuing weeks active Communists continued to be relentlessly hunted down.

There is no doubt that the Communist Party had been dealt a shattering blow. In some places the whole leadership of a branch or of a Sub-district was arrested and had to be replaced more than once in a very short time. Some well-known local functionaries left their homes for a time and took refuge with relatives elsewhere; but economic pressures and family obligations prevented most from escaping in this way. It was a true reign of terror, exercised mainly by storm troops acting without police restraint in an orgy of sadistic violence and of revenge for incidents in the street battles of previous years. The Brownshirt bands were not really out of control, as was pretended by the apologists of the régime, but were given free rein by a policy which, though directed primarily against the

Communists, was also designed to intimidate other political opponents of the Nazis and even their conservative allies. In the hunt for fugitives, hidden arms, concealed typewriters, duplicating machines and anti-Nazi literature, whole working-class suburbs were sometimes sealed off in military-style operations by strong forces of Brown and Blackshirts and police, and searched from attic to cellar with brutal destruction. The aim was to intimidate and demoralise the working class as a whole by invading its strongholds, as if with a conquering army, showing them that they were finally, after so many years, no longer capable of defending themselves. Sometimes these terror operations assumed the scale of a one-sided civil war, as in the Berlin suburb of Köpenick in June 1933, when a week-long orgy of bestial atrocities left seventy dead, most though not all of them Communists.[28] The authorities usually claimed to have found evidence that the Communists had made preparations for armed uprisings and civil war. But, although such searches did in fact bring to light arms which had been hidden by the Red Front Fighters' League since it had been made illegal in 1929, they were on a very small scale and were hardly consistent with anything more than purely defensive purposes.

The main aim of the Nazis' campaign of terror following the Reichstag Fire was to knock out the Communist Party without hope of recovery. By the beginning of April many well-informed officials, including Goering himself, were confident that this had been achieved. But the judgement was premature. In rural areas and small towns, it is true, the comparatively small numbers and consequent conspicuousness of Communists made it virtually impossible for them to resume political activity. In the main industrial centres and large cities, however, their influence was more difficult to counteract, rooted as it was in the class consciousness of the industrial workers. This became apparent in the surprising results of the Reichstag election of 5 March 1933. The election took place six days after the Fire, amid nation-wide anti-communist hysteria, when the Party was unable to hold meetings or to publish its press and had in effect been driven underground. Yet its candidates obtained no fewer than 4,847,939 votes, 12 .3 per cent of those recorded, representing a decline of no more than 18.9 per cent from the peak vote the previous November.[29]

The loyalty of the Communist voters was emulated by that of many of the Party's members, as began to become apparent after the first shock. Many, it is true, who had only recently joined, during the rapid growth of the winter, fell away and did not renew contact with the movement. But the solid core of longer-standing members showed an impressive degree of attachment to the Party. T.W. Mason estimates that the number who 'bounced back' into political activity after the initial shock amounted to fully one-third of the membership.[30] At Düsseldorf, according to a report of Hugo Paul, the KPD Instructor there, a quarter continued, or resumed, organised political activity, while another quarter continued to pay membership dues and receive literature.[31] The number who went over to the National Socialists was very small. In Düsseldorf, for instance, desertions have been estimated at 60 out of a membership of about 6,000.[32] There were also a few long-standing police spies who emerged and did immense harm; in addition, a few individual members, under pressure of torture or of threats against their relatives, were induced to enter the service of the police as spies or *agents provocateurs*.[33] But as far as can be seen from the files of police and law courts, in Düsseldorf at least, such cases were remarkably few. The strongest impression conveyed by these records – an impression shared by the authors of many internal police memoranda – was the high degree of cohesion, loyalty and discipline among Communist Party members.[34] It has often been alleged that the disciplined structure of the Party on the pattern of democratic centralism weakened its members' ability to cope with the unforeseen turn of events in 1933, by depriving them of the habit of initiative. This is a doubtful generalisation and one that is difficult to test. It has to be remembered, too, that the habit of discipline, of conscientious reporting and carrying out of orders, had advantages as well as disadvantages in a period of crisis. It was perhaps in recognition of this that even at this dangerous time a sympathiser would occasionally apply for membership or an inactive member become active.[35]

Wide as was the gap torn in the Party's ranks by the mass arrests of March 1933, the wound was not fatal. The greatest losses were in Sub-district and city, ward or branch leaderships, among Communist town councillors and similar public figures. At national and District levels the losses were at first less, mainly because the process of going underground had already begun in the previous month or two, involving moves by full-timers to clandestine living-quarters, evacuation of offices, and also much transfer of personnel,

Ernst Thälmann in the exercise yard of the Moabit Prison, Berlin 1934

often in connection with division of Districts and Sub-districts.[36] The ten members of the politburo, except for Thälmann, escaped arrest altogether, perhaps because they had already taken to living and working on a clandestine basis from about the middle of February, though also, by a coincidence which turned out fortunate but might have proved disastrous, they happened to be gathered together at a politburo meeting at the time of the Fire, and so could be warned of the danger. The District Secretaries and the newly appointed Regional Advisers also largely escaped arrest during the first weeks. Hans Pfeiffer, the Adviser for the Western Region, for instance, was sent to Düsseldorf at the beginning of April to supervise the reorganisation of the three Districts for which he was responsible. That included the transfer of the political secretary of the Lower Rhine District, Lambert Horn, to Berlin (to take the place of Walter Ulbricht, hitherto Political Secretary there) and his replacement by Erich Glückauf, the editor of the Communist newspaper in the Lower Rhine District. Other examples could be given to show that the Party was able, to a considerable extent, to regroup its leading cadres amid the confusion of the first two or three months.

This reorganisation involved many transfers of full-time leading functionaries to towns and districts which they did not know and in which they were themselves not known. Their first task, therefore, after providing for their own lodging and subsistence, was to make contact with reliable local members who had so far escaped arrest, either because they had been out of the public eye for some reason, or because they had been content to remain rank-and-file members, holding no responsible position. This required an ability to make good and quick judgements of people and an ability to inspire them and win their confidence. Such a man was Josef Wagner, a leading Communist from Augsburg, who is said, from his hiding-place at this time, to have displayed 'feverish energy';[37] and another such man was Hugo Paul, newly appointed Instructor for Düsseldorf and Neuss, who showed memorable ability to choose good men and women and to persuade them to take on greater responsibilities than they had been accustomed to.[38]

Although the rebuilding of the Party involved some decentralisation, this was only a matter of detail. The essential character of the organisation was not changed, since its aims and policies were not changed. The first task in rebuilding it, therefore, was to fill key positions in a familiar structure; to find comrades prepared to carry on in new circumstances routines with which they were at least broadly familiar, both for the Party itself and for its many subsidiary bodies. First there was the routine of dues collection and card stamping, handing over and accounting for the money collected, both for the dues and for the basic 'literature' that was bought by members through their dues collectors. Because these routines and the organisation built around them were so widely familiar, it was comparatively easy to rebuild the shattered apparatus, especially in view of the high level of conscientiousness and of basic literacy and numeracy of the German working class. Again and again the records give evidence of cell treasurers and literature-sellers who, when they were cut off from their Party contacts in March or April 1933, retained money in hand and accounted for it carefully later, when they had re-established contact with the Party apparatus.

Thus the rebuilding of the shattered Party after March 1933 seemed to the leadership to require as first priority the filling of vacant positions in the structure and the picking out of those comrades who were willing and able to take on higher responsibilities. However, if the familiarity of the structure made this easier in one way, it had the disadvantage that it enabled the police to keep track more easily of the Party's activities.

The first task of those who, at this crisis, took on leading positions at whatever level, whether in the Party or in its subsidiaries, was simply to ensure the survival of the organisation, of its structural hierarchy and of the finances necessary to maintain it. This was considered to be of supreme importance in itself, even if nothing more was possible for the moment, for the analysis on which Communist policy was based presupposed the imminence of a revolutionary crisis, whose outcome would be largely determined by the existence of the revolutionary party.[39] The second task was to show the Party's face, whatever the cost; to continue the struggle, whatever the odds. By this was understood, not the occasional sensational *coup*, but patient, systematic 'mass work'. For Communists at this time revolutionary work meant keeping in touch with the masses, avoiding isolation, trying continually to bring new sections of the people into political activity. The Party leadership continually issued leaflets attacking and exposing the Nazi government, in many thousands of copies, which local groups were to distribute. Most effective were locally written leaflets rebutting some local Nazi lie or commenting on some Nazi atrocity. Such were the leaflets written by Hugo Paul in Düsseldorf in May 1933 which will be described later;[40] telling blows, written in working-class idiom, but essentially defensive. Nothing more might be possible at the time; yet more was demanded and expected, and not always in vain. Directives from the Party Centre called for more initiative, for a more offensive tactic, for mass petitioning, for mass deputations to the Justice Department, for sit-downs and strikes. Sometimes young members, with more boldness than calculation, answered by scaling factory chimneys with a paint brush or cutting slogans in the grass of a public park – or even engaging with foolhardiness in a last street scuffle with Brownshirts. Bruno Retzlaff-Kresse recounts such an episode at Stettin, where, as late as the end of May 1933, young Communists responded to a provocation by members of a local SA unit by counter-attacking them and putting them to flight.[41]

The types of political action called for by the Communist leadership were all within the framework of conventional democratic politics, but now suicidally costly. Yet at this stage the Communist Party had many members with the heroism, the optimism, the illusions, to undertake such actions.

The sort of 'mass actions' for which the leadership called could not hope to succeed without unity on the left. After the Emergency Powers ('Enabling') Act of 23 March perhaps they could not be expected to succeed even with that unity. Yet the attitude of the trade unions and of the Social Democrats gave no hope of any such united action. The unions were busy detaching themselves from socialist politics in the hope of buying a place in the Third Reich while the Social Democratic Party was disintegrating week by week, the different factions having in common only the desire to avoid any connection with Communism. At the local level, it is true, many Social Democrats were in a mood to reject the whole legacy of reformism and to go back to the revolutionary Marxist traditions of the past, but not many of these were prepared to join the Communist Party unconditionally. In this situation the Communist Party showed uncertainty, making some overtures to the Social Democratic Party executive, as on 1 March and again on 14 March,[42] but then taking their rejection as evidence that united actions could in practice be hoped for at most on the local level. For a time, too, there seemed to be ground for hoping that the demoralisation of Social Democracy would bring a significant increase of numbers to the Communist movement.

That the reformist trend in Social Democracy had suffered an overwhelming defeat and was politically bankrupt was becoming ever clearer in the first months of the Third Reich. But what of the Communist movement? What was the extent of its defeat and of its recovery?

It can hardly be denied that the Communist movement suffered a defeat of historic proportions in 1933. If we wish to measure the extent of the defeat it may be true, as a recent historian has observed, that the Reichstag election statistics are less significant than the results of the Works Council elections in March and April, which revealed a serious decline in the strength and influence of the Communists in the factories.[43] Indeed, it has been argued on the same lines that the failure of the Communist-led Revolutionary Trade Union Opposition (RGO) to attain a sizeable influence before 1933 pre-determined the failure of the Communist opposition to National Socialism.[44] Yet, though the Communists suffered a major defeat, they refused to admit the fact. Perhaps the historian is right who suggests that this obstinacy is to be explained by the very heroism of the resistance they subsequently put up to the tyranny, and the losses incurred in it, which made them feel that such sacrifices could not have been in vain and must have brought victory within reach.[45]

But though defeated, the Party was not destroyed in 1933, as the Nazi authorities first thought and as some more recent historians have asserted.[46] Though many recent recruits may have fallen away, a solid core of established members remained loyal and 'committed itself to the underground resistance struggle in the specific form chosen by the leadership – that of trying to maintain a mass illegal organisation and a high level of semi-public activity'.[47] This assessment is broadly confirmed for the Ruhr and Rhineland by Dr Peukert, who finds that 'passivity and depression had only affected the periphery';[48] the solid core was in a fighting mood and proceeded to display, in Dr Mason's words, 'ingenuity, courage, recklessness'.[49]

By May 1933 Goering himself admitted that his previous assessment that the KPD had been destroyed was mistaken. In a confidential circular addressed to senior administrators and police chiefs on the 27 May, he informed them that 'during the past month a quite extraordinary increase in the illegal organisational activity of the Communist functionaries has been noticeable', and that 'the activity of the Communists has resulted in incidents'.[50]

On the whole, the overriding impression left by the evidence for the first six months is of the staunchness and loyalty of a significant proportion of the Party's rank and file, as well as of most of the leadership. The first test of this loyalty was willingness to continue payment of party dues and purchase of party literature in circumstances in which these actions had become dangerous. The maintenance of this routine activity on a considerable scale in these months was more than an instance of good discipline: it was a significant political fact. For although the continuance of an illegal organisation might not have much immediate effect, it was nonetheless feared by the Nazis as a potential danger. As long as the Communists maintained an organisation, they might still be able, in the event of a change in the situation – a political setback or governmental crisis – to move the working class into action.

The spirit of the illegal Communist Party, its strengths and weaknesses, are well expressed in a political letter which was addressed to Party members by one of the District leaderships about the beginning of June 1933. It is worth quoting in full:[51]

> Dear Comrade,
> The heroic struggle of our party against the Hitler dictatorship is already beginning to bear fruit. We have succeeded, in spite of the bloody fascist terror, in spite of the arrest and striking down of tens of thousands of our finest comrades, in pulling the party together, closing the gaps and steeling our bolshevik cadres by applying the decisions of the Comintern and of the CC of our party. Now, in the difficult conditions of the fascist dictatorship, our truly bolshevik cadres are growing into courageous, resolute, clear-sighted leaders of the masses.
>
> Our bolshevik party forms the basis of the mass struggles now beginning to develop again. After 4 months of Hitler dictatorship we find the estimate of the situation which was given us by the 12 ECCI Plenum brilliantly confirmed. We recall, too, the words of Comrade Schehr, the closest collaborator of Comrade Ernst Thälmann, at the Wuppertal congress of our District organisation:

'This is the last legal congress before our
seizure of power; we shall organise the
revolution from illegality right on to victory.'

We are at present preparing our party organisation for the study of the latest resolutions of our CC, in order to forge the keener weapons with which we can alone lead the constantly growing numbers of the hungry and discontented into victorious struggle against the capitalist starvation dictatorship.

Comrades! You yourselves can observe in your daily work how the conditions are becoming more favourable for new anti-fascist mass struggles. Hitler's catastrophic policy is leading of necessity to an upsurge of anti-fascist feelings. Our task as a party is to organise these feelings in factories, labour exchanges, in the countryside and among the disillusioned middle strata, and to lead them into direct battle-actions.

Many comrades have in recent weeks given heroic examples of BOLSHEVIK loyalty and fighting spirit, both in detailed [inner-party][52] work and in the factories, trade unions and labour exchanges. These comrades deserve our bolshevik recognition, for they set an example to those who still stand anxiously aside, waiting on events.

Comrades! The rapidly sharpening economic crisis and the threat of disastrous wars demand a more all-round arming of our party. The last party comrade must be mobilised in factory-cell and street-cell! New fighters must be brought into the party of the coming victorious revolution. The best Social Democratic workers and trade unionists belong with us!

More material must be brought out! Our newspapers, pamphlets, leaflets, have a hundredfold effect. But to bring out literature it is necessary to raise money! All comrades must be brought within the scope of dues collection. With every new dues-paying comrade it becomes possible to issue better, more comprehensive material. Every additional penny collected in dues, every mark contributed, every party member harnessed to party work strengthens the anti-fascist assault-battalions and helps to put them in readiness for the decisive struggle.

Comrades! Our bolshevik honour demands the highest watchfulness and ever heightened courage on the part of all Communists.

OUR PARTY IS FIGHTING IN THE MOST DIFFICULT CONDITIONS! THE HARDER THE STRUGGLE THE TOUGHER WE SHALL BECOME AND WITH JOYFUL HOPE WE SAY: THE SOONER OUR VICTORY COMES, THE FINER IT WILL BE!

RED FRONT!

District Leadership of KPD, Lower Rhine

No one can fail to recognise, and to admire, the fighting spirit, the *élan* and resolution expressed in this letter. The Party functionaries at the head of the Lower Rhine District, it is clear, had emerged from the disastrous setbacks of February and March with morale and determination unimpaired. The lead they gave was vigorous and clear: a call to battle, free of any trace of doubt, disillusion or defeatism. Nor, as we have tried to show, was this the mood only of a few full-time committed Party officials. It was the mood of a considerable core of loyal, disciplined rank-and-file members, and it inspired much individual heorism in these months.

But if there was a spirit of heroism in the words of this letter, there was also a certain unreality, a note of revolutionary romanticism. The constant repetition of the word 'bolshevik', while serving as a reminder, to writer and reader alike, of the Russian revolutionaries of 1917 who had triumphed over all dangers and difficulties, tended at the same time to strengthen the illusion that the situation in Germany in 1933 was similar to that in Russia sixteen years earlier. If the German Communists had not been broken by the shattering experiences of the first half of 1933, they had not drawn any far-reaching new conclusions from them either. Their analysis of the political situation was still fundamentally similar to the analysis they had made in the autumn of 1932. Now, as then, they saw the future in the perspective defined by Schehr at Wuppertal: early crisis, seizure of power, Soviet Germany. And now, as then, they called for all-out mass struggle, not of a defensive character, but as an offensive along the whole front.

This analysis, as the future was to show, was incorrect and unrealistic and the offensive strategy based on it was to lead the Party to further heavy losses and defeats in the protracted struggle of the next two years.[53] It would be wrong to underestimate the gravity of this lost battle: it was to involve the loss, not just of thousands of the best members of one generation, but of the confidence of a new generation, which would not easily be regained. But it would be equally wrong to conceive it as a battle lost without a struggle. If the German Communist Party had collapsed as suddenly in 1933 as some historians have alleged, it could never have regained the confidence of that new generation.

In reality the battle was more protracted, more heroic, more tragic. The immediate crisis of February-March 1933, serious though it was, was relatively quickly overcome. While many weaker brethren, fellow-travellers, recent recruits, fell away in the confusion, a firm basis – tens of thousands of class-conscious Party members – emerged steeled for the struggle and prepared for heavy sacrifices.

The German Communist Party could not have overcome the initial crisis of 1933 in this way if the errors and misjudgements of 1928–35 had simply been imposed on it by Stalin and the Comintern. In fact, the sectarian isolationism, the over-optimistic assessment of the revolutionary workers' strength, the belief that the socialist revolution was imminent, the feeling of contempt for the petty bourgeoisie and of hatred for social democratic reformism – all these attitudes and moods were intensely characteristic of the revolutionary section of the German working class at this time. They represented, in a sense, the reverse side of its most positive qualities. The defeat of February-March 1933 brought out both the negative and the positive aspects in sharper definition. The revolutionary party, isolated and forced to struggle for survival, came out in full fighting spirit; but at the same time it waged the fight with outdated weapons and tactics and in a traditional spirit which combined heroic valour with misjudged optimism. The very success of the Communist leaders in rallying the membership served in part to confirm them in their reluctance to probe deeply into the causes of defeat.

CHAPTER 4

State and Opposition

The National Socialist State

The fascist state which was rapidly taking shape in Germany in the Summer of 1933 rested on social forces not essentially dissimilar to those which had supported the republic and the empire before it, but it differed in the relationship of state and ruling class and in the methods of rule employed. In the world-wide ecomomic crisis of 1929–32 German monopoly capitalists had begun to fear – whether rightly or wrongly – that their internal authority and their external aspirations were being gravely endangered by the weakening of their influence over the mass of the people and the resurgence of revolutionary socialism. Their ill-defined and probably exaggerated fears became acute at the end of 1932, when the Nazi mass movement showed signs of disintegration and further radicalisation, and of getting out of control. The monopolists and fascist leaders thereupon came to terms. The dictatorship which resulted represented in one aspect a re-shuffle within the bourgeoisie itself: not just a personal alliance of fascists and monopolists, but a concentration of power in the hands of the representatives of the biggest and most aggressive monopolies, whose organisations came, in course of time, to be more and more intimately merged with those of the state. This aspect of German fascism is vital to a correct assessment of it;[1] but more immediately relevant in the present context – for understanding the conditions in which the opposition worked – is the alteration in methods of rule.

The combination of ideological influence and repression by which most states have secured the acquiescence of the masses was given a new shape by the Nazis: both propaganda and repression were intensified but at the same time made to reinforce one another in a complex interaction. The most crucial change was the complete destruction of the labour movement that had been built up in the course of a century of struggle. The very conception of class struggle was no longer to be current, nor that of separate class interests, nor indeed that of classes; for the Nazis, all that existed were the common interests in a classless 'people's community'. This fictitious community of interests was expressed firstly and most fundamentally in the 'Works Community', in which the interests of the 'Works Leader' and those of his 'Followers' were merged in the interests of the firm. To make this a reality, a gigantic new organisation was founded: the German Labour Front, combining the inheritance of trade unions and employers' associations in an effort to supersede the tradition of class struggle.[2] In reality, however, capitalist relationships and the conflict of interests arising from them continued undiminished and even the Labour Front and the Nazi Party organisation within it (NSBO)[3] could only achieve minimum credibility; what small degree of support it won was by taking some account of workers' interests. As a result, in many firms, especially in smaller ones, friction was endemic between the Labour Front and NSBO on the one side (backed at the top by the Nazi Party organisation), and, on the other the employers, whose now established right to determine wages and conditions of work was supported by the authority of Labour Trustees appointed by the Reich Chancellor and answerable jointly to the ministers of Labour and Economics.[4] Such frictions within an outwardly totalitarian structure made small cracks through which discontent might have been, and sometimes was, expressed until the police intervened.

Powerful and sophisticated as the propaganda machinery of the Third Reich was, its success depended in the last resort on an equally powerful and sophisticated machinery of violence. In the first months, as has already been observed, there was no sophistication about the repression. It was a campaign of terror, carried out by brown and black-shirted storm troopers against every working-class organisation and against working-class residential areas. It was designed to produce a situation in which workers could not feel safe in their homes, streets, sports clubs, places of employment or anywhere else in the town in which they lived. It was designed to isolate the activists of the labour movement and to make others afraid to be seen with them. It was a terror in which the storm troops could rely on the help of the police, whose own prisoners might be handed over to the local storm troopers for further 'interrogation'.

By the summer of 1933 the lawless terror and sadistic paying-off of old scores of the first months had served its purpose and was becoming a nuisance to the Nazi leadership. Professional administrators complained of the interference with orderly government, and reported that liberal circles were not only beginning to sympathise with some of the victims of the terror, but were also concerned that the continuing instability was keeping alive notions and hopes of further revolution.[5] Thus the anarchic elements of the Nazi movement, represented above all by the Brownshirts (SA), began to be brought under firmer control. In Prussia, for instance, they were deprived of their auxiliary police powers from August 1933.[6] and in the following months their private concentration camps were gradually brought under Goering's control as Prime Minister.[7] Repression now assumed a more regular, 'administrative' aspect and its organs began to be integrated into a system which continued to expand and develop throughout the life of the Third Reich.

At the centre of the system was the Secret State Police (*Gestapo*). The Gestapo originated in the political police sections which had formed a relatively small branch of the state and city police forces of the Weimar Republic (like the British 'Special Branch'). The term 'Gestapo' applied at first, strictly speaking, only to the political police branch in Prussia, which in 1933 was greatly expanded and made autonomous under Goering; but by the spring of 1934 the equivalent branches in other States (*Länder*) had been effectively if not yet formally united with it in a single organisation under control of Himmler, head of the SS. At the same time the original staffs of professional policemen were now joined, and often commanded at district and regional level, by new personnel drawn from the Nazi Party's own police, the black-shirted SS, and its security branch, the SD. The SD, too, continued to exist and to function independently of the Gestapo, and to duplicate some of its work.

The systematisation of the machinery of repression by the Nazis after 1933 was no more than a tendency, never fully realised. In this, as in other spheres, the Nazis adapted old methods and old institutions, reinterpreted old rules and made *ad hoc* additions and innovations. The result was a jungle of overlapping competencies and inadequately co-ordinated institutions in which the traditional legal and constitutional principles and practices were neither consistently recognised nor consistently rejected.

The Political Police

Before 1933 the political police in German cities and county governments were a comparatively small body of (mainly) anti-Communist specialists within the broader organisation of the criminal police; they constituted Section 1A of a city police department which, like the rest of the city administration, was subordinate to the county government. In the first year or two of the Nazi régime two major developments took place. Control of the police passed, often after a short struggle between the local SA and SS, into the hands of the latter; then the political branch of the police gradually separated out and became a virtually independent arm of government in the shape of a State Police Office responsible for a whole administrative county. This office, though nominally part of the county government and subordinate to the county prefect (*Regierungspräsident*) was in reality an independent organ, often housed in separate premises, or even in a different town, and directly responsible to a newly instituted central Secret Police Office (*Gestapa*) in Berlin. At the same time the *expertise* and personal knowledge of the professional anti-Communist hands of Section IA remained indispensable in many counties, and the more experienced of them, if they were not politically compromised beyond hope of redress, might sometimes become conspicuous figures in the new Gestapo, making up for any previous democratic or Social Democratic associations by an especially ruthless zeal in the hunting down of opposition.[8] Despite the expansion which county Gestapo forces were to undergo, a small core of anti-Communist specialists with personal knowledge built up over the years often continued to play a central role in them. The mass arrests and interrogations of the years 1933–35, with the laborious assemblage of evidence for the state prosecutors, often strained the Gestapo's resources and, incidentally, no doubt strengthened the tendency to resort to the short cuts of violence and torture. When a major operation was planned, it was usually necessary to call upon the greater resources of the criminal police to help in the routine tasks of raiding premises and arresting suspects;[9] in addition, the Gestapo, which had no representatives stationed in village or suburban police stations, could always call upon the services of the local police.

Besides the expansion of the political police and its transformation into the Gestapo, the establishment of the Nazi régime also conferred official status on the Nazi movement's own police forces, which came to supplement and overlap with the Gestapo. The least inefficient of these Nazi Party organisations was the Security Service of the SS (*Sicherheitsdienst* or SD), which had an office at each SS regional headquarters. These offices maintained their own networks of informers and tried, with the help of their sometimes rather scrappy reports, to keep in touch with the development of Communist and other opposition activities. In the first months of 1933 it was still possible for the SD to take some initial action on the reports it received, such as making arrests and interrogating suspects; but before long all executive action was reserved for the Gestapo, to which the SD sent reports, receiving Gestapo reports in return.

The SD, like the Gestapo, was a comparatively high-level body of specialists. To spy on and control the revolutionary movement where it was strongly rooted in working-class life required in addition an organisation at the level of the street and the housing estate. This was the role allotted to the Nazi mass organisations, especially the brown-shirted SA, each unit of which had long had its intelligence branch. In the period 1933–35 Gestapo files often contain reports derived from these intelligence branches, so well placed for observing individual Communists in their daily life and work. In the main, however, Storm Troop Intelligence Units seem to have been amateurish and unreliable, pouring out information which was inaccurate and muddled: typical informer's stuff, mixing genuine observation with imagination and spite; and it is noticeable that their reports were not always acted on by the Gestapo. Nevertheless, they were useful for petty acts of spying or provocation, and they occasionally produced an enthusiast with a real gift for playing this despicable role.

Another source of information for the Gestapo was the Nazi Party itself, each of whose local branches had an intelligence officer whose task was to recruit political informants and to collect information about opposition activities. It was at this level that ex-Communists were occasionally induced by pressure or blackmail to supply information about illegal political activities, but such information did not always prove to be reliable. Nevertheless, it was useful for the Gestapo to be able to refer the names of local individuals released from concentration camps to such local Nazi Party groups or to Labour Front officials, who would keep an eye on them. Indeed, the effectiveness of the Gestapo was in part due to the abundance of unpaid, unsolicited assistants who put themselves at its disposal; these ranged from employers reporting workers who abstained from giving the Hitler greeting, to sports club chairmen who submitted membership applications to the Gestapo for screening.

The Gestapo was remarkable, not only for the variety of its sources of information, but even more for the wide range of its political interests, which far exceeded those of a conventional police organisation. In course of time its offices came to have a highly complex structure, with specialist sections devoted not only to such major preoccupations as the Communist or 'Marxist' movements, Catholicism or the Jews, but to almost every aspect of economic and social life, not to mention numerous more recondite topics such as Germans returning from the Soviet Union or the French Foreign Legion. The monthly situation reports of the district offices dealt broadly with the current economic and political situation in all its aspects, and often recommended positive political action, sometimes directly, sometimes by suggestions and hints. The Gestapo was capable also of taking direct political initiatives over a wide field, beyond the mere detention of opponents. It could ban meetings or publications, dissolve organisations, intervene in appointments or issue warnings which were not meant to be ignored. Its opinion about individuals, confidentially sought by and given to employers, could result in arbitrary dismissal, even when an alleged offence was still *sub judice*.

Of the methods employed by the Gestapo to combat political opposition, some were traditional police procedures, such as the interception of telephone calls or the opening of letters, and underground organisations were sometimes uncovered in this way. Some information came in through gratuitous denunciation: by neighbours, for instance, of a worker who went off on unexplained errands on his bicycle; by a middle-class housewife of her charwoman after a wage dispute; by an estranged wife seeking divorce; or, especially in later years, by children in the Hitler Youth of their parents. Much more than on all these sources, however, the Gestapo relied on regular informers – *V-Leute* or *Vertrauensmänner*.[10] Some of these simply kept watch in places of work or blocks of flats, handing in illegal leaflets, reporting gossip and rumours and observing fellow-employees or neighbours who had a left-wing past or who had been released from prison or concentration camp. Other *V-Leute* were deliberately planted in illegal Communist or other organisations. They might be in the service of one of the Nazi Party's own units; or they might be employed directly by the

Gestapo. Particulars of the Gestapo's informers were kept in separate files, and these do not seem often to have survived; but evidence suggests that, while such 'V-Men' must have existed at almost every place of work or residence, and must have totalled a huge number, those who had effectively penetrated anti-Nazi underground organisations were relatively few and therefore of great individual significance.[11] Indeed, most of the mass arrests and trials by which the Gestapo broke up successive clandestine Communist Party organisations were probably the work of a few such individuals in each area.

Gestapo penetration of the Communist underground was in 1933 sometimes due to the presence in the Communist Party of long-standing police agents, sometimes, at a humbler level to individuals who defected to the Nazis when they came to power, but were instructed to remain ostensibly members of the KPD. Occasionally, too, the police were able to get on the track of illegal groups simply by leaving a known Communist at liberty and having him carefully watched. Once the pattern of the underground struggle had become established, however, the penetration of clandestine organisations was usually achieved by the Gestapo in one of two main ways: by inducing arrested Communists, as price of their release or by threat of ill-treatment, to agree to resume their illegal contacts in the role of a police informer; or by getting a real police agent to pose as an underground Instructor sent from a higher leadership to reorganise a local underground organisation. Sometimes both methods were employed. What is remarkable is not that such betrayals by individuals under torture or blackmail, or perhaps by threats to their families, occurred in the illegal Communist organisation, but that so few cases of it can be found. Most of the big trials of Düsseldorf Communists in the years 1934–35, for instance, can be traced to betrayal by a very few individuals who were therefore highly valued by the Gestapo and preserved from exposure for as long as possible.[12] They preferred, if possible, not to have to produce such a renegade as a witness at the subsequent trial, which might put an end to his or her usefulness. In some cases, informers might be included among the accused at the trial, in order to preserve their cover. On occasion, indeed, the Gestapo was capable of arranging the release of a Communist from a concentration camp, even without any specific undertaking on his or her part, simply on the calculation that he or she would prove amenable to pressure to become an informer. Some of the informers were, of course, unreliable and had only agreed to act in the hope of tricking the police or of escaping abroad. The Gestapo, for its part, had a system of enlisting unreliable informers and keeping them under observation.

Gestapo 'V-Men' were used in a variety of ways. Illegal leaflet finds might be referred to them for investigation. More important was their role as *agents provocateurs*, of which numerous examples occur in trial records, some sophisticated, others quite crude. The most difficult to combat were the rare cases in which the Gestapo agent was a trusted KPD member who, after a short period of arrest, could plausibly claim to have lost contact and to be justifiably asking former Communist acquaintances to put him in touch again.[13]

The most important function of this type of informer was to enable the Gestapo to break into an illegal organisation and to obtain such an extensive knowledge of it that arrests, when it was finally decided to make them, would reach into all branches of the organisation and not stop short of the leadership. For this it was important that even though the information supplied by the informers might be far from complete – as was nearly always the case – it would be enough to enable the police interrogators to pretend a complete knowledge and so bring maximum pressure to bear on the first suspects to be arrested. When information of this sort was lacking, the Gestapo sometimes arrested Communist suspects more or less at random and tried to bluff them into making extensive admissions by pretending more knowledge than they really had. The more experienced resisters, however, learned to recognise and counter this tactic.

Leading functionaries living an illegal existence could only carry on political work through contacts living legally. Branch meetings, or committee meetings of the traditional kind, were no longer safe; but the attempt was made to continue the practice of collective leadership in a modified form by regular consultations of a few, at District or Sub-district level. At first such meetings might be held in the flats of supporters in middle-class suburbs, where they were less likely to attract attention or to be overheard, or in the garden allotment huts which so many German workers had. In the end, however, bitter experience convinced the Party that anything like a formal meeting was dangerous and that the least insecure form of consultation was an apparently chance encounter of individuals in a public place such as a square or street, from which one member might follow the other to a café or park bench. This type of meeting, arranged in advance for a precise time, was called a *Treff*, and the first concern of the Gestapo when they arrested a political suspect, was to induce him or her to divulge particulars of any appointments of that sort which had been made for the immediately following days. In other cases an arrested leader was taken on a supervised walk through key places, such as shops of an important factory, or cafés likely to be used as rendezvous, in the hope either that he could be induced to point out any of his contacts who came into view, or that these would betray themselves by some unguarded reaction. Even if a prisoner were compelled to reveal an appointment and to keep it, under police supervision, he or she might still thwart them by pretending not to recognise the other partner, or by giving some slight warning signal. Another familiar trick was to put a stool-pigeon in the same cell as an arrested activist in the hope of inducing confidences and also of obtaining 'independent' witnesses.

Crucial in the operations of the Gestapo, once arrests had begun, was of course the interrogation of those arrested. Two kinds of interrogation may be distinguished: immediate interrogation, aimed at securing, by 'shock treatment', information about forthcoming *Treffs* and long-term, protracted interrogation in which the most varied forms of pressure would be brought to bear and all human weaknesses explored and exploited. In questioning arrested opponents the Gestapo had two distinct and sometimes conflicting aims. They wished to obtain such information about the prisoner's contacts and associates as would enable them to uncover and track down the still unknown parts of the organisation; but they also needed to extract admissions which would help the public prosecutor to obtain a conviction against the accused or others when the case came up for trial.

The methods of interrogation by which the Gestapo pursued these aims have often been described by surviving victims and witnesses. That torture continued to be practised as a regular and recognised technique, long after the initial 'spontaneous' atrocities in SA cellars, is only too well attested. Indeed, the practice was ultimately institutionalised, and recognised by the Ministry of Justice in a formal agreement with the police, under the name 'intensified interrogation' (*verschärfte Vernehmung*),[14] which included deprivation of sleep, exhausting exercises, and beating. The maltreatment was usually of such a kind as to leave no very clearly recognisable marks when the victim finally came up for trial, but this represented no serious check on the brutality of a treatment which not infrequently resulted in the prisoner's death from 'heart failure'. Expressions of the philosophy underlying these methods can easily be found in Gestapo files. In one case, for instance, in which for some reason restraint had been exercised, the writer of an internal office minute observed discontentedly that, 'the existence of a unified organisation could not be established, and gaps remained which would certainly have been filled in if one or more of the arrested persons had been handled more toughly'.[15]

Torture, frequent though its use was, was not the only method. Indeed, the 'professionals' of some Gestapo offices prided themselves on their sophistication and psychological insight. In dealing with an intellectual they might adopt a flattering, ingratiating approach, airing their knowledge of literature in the tone of a friendly fireside chat and making their questions sound like an expression of genuine personal curiosity. However, equally they were capable of a sudden *volte face* if they thought that an act of personal humiliation might break down the defences of a respectable middle-class official.[16] In appropriate cases they would use promises of early release to extract confessions. Sometimes, though all their pre-trial interrogations had elicited nothing, they would decide much later, perhaps on some hint in a prison governor's report of a change in the prisoner's attitude, to visit the prison and renew their questioning.[17]

In obtaining evidence for production at a subsequent trial what mattered was the deposition which the interrogated prisoner could be induced to sign. At the end of prolonged interrogation it often happened that a prisoner, overcome by exhaustion, could hardly muster the strength to risk renewal of the torture by raising objections to particular phrases; but at the trial itself such a prisoner not infrequently withdrew parts of his or her previous depositions on the ground that a signature had been obtained by violence or threats of violence.[18]

Effective though the Gestapo was, with its large resources and extensive freedom of action, there were limits to its efficiency. In its early days its district offices seem sometimes to have inherited from the old political police section an irrational rancour against particular individuals, whose real importance might be comparatively small.[19]

In deciding whether to apply for preventive detention orders against individuals due for release from prison they relied, at least in some cases, on files which contained little but a few prejudiced statements originating in pre-1933 rumours and informers' gossip constantly repeated since then. In the police, too, as elsewhere, expansion might mean dilution and arbitrary power breed carelessness. To counter such tendencies the heads of the service attempted to develop an *esprit de corps* and an image of the Gestapo-man as a 'political soldier' engaged in exceptionally difficult and dangerous work which called for the dedicated involvement of the whole man in a day-and-night struggle against a cunning and determined enemy.[20] The training ultimately came to include discussion about religion and the study of the history of the political police from Ancient Egypt onwards.[21]

The Courts of Law

The political police had acquired, under the presidential emergency decrees of 4 and 28 February 1933, the power of holding political opponents in so-called 'protective custody' (later, and more accurately, termed 'preventive detention') without charge or trial for an indefinite period of time. They made extensive use of this power from that time onwards, holding in concentration camps thousands of Communists who had been arrested after the Reichstag Fire but could not plausibly be charged with breaking any law then in force. After the first disorderly months, however, the Gestapo usually preferred, or was expected, to bring arrested political opponents before the courts for trial. Under laws hitherto in force, a suspect arrested by the police could not be held in custody for longer than twenty-four hours unless an examining magistrate[22] issued a warrant and undertook a preliminary enquiry, which itself must culminate within a definite time in a decision either to drop the case for lack of *prima facie* evidence or to proceed on a specific charge to a formal judicial enquiry. This procedure was drastically modified by successive changes after February 1933. Police arrest ceased to be limited to twenty-four hours, and the preliminary judicial investigation[23] was soon dispensed with, an indictment now being drawn up by the state prosecutor, largely on the basis of reports, depositions and other material supplied by the police, without prior judicial sifting.

The choice of charge to be brought, and therefore, of the court before which the accused would be tried, rested with the State Prosecutor's branch. An almost infinitely extendable range of political offences involving violence or instigation to violence, infringement of government decrees, or even 'malicious criticism' of the government, could be made the subject of charges under the 'Reichstag Fire decree' of 28 February 1933 and the 'malicious opposition' (*Heimtücke*) decree of 21 March 1933.[24] Such charges would be brought before one of the Special Courts[25] which had been set up by another emergency decree of 21 March specifically to try political offences by a summary procedure.

This Special Court procedure was used against many people who had manifested dissent, criticism or opposition, but it was not usually applied to those whose offences consisted in helping to continue the Communist Party's activities by buying (or selling) illegal literature or paying party dues. The course chosen in almost all such cases by state prosecutors – no doubt on directions from the Ministry of Justice – was to construe the Communist Party's activities as a conspiracy to 'change the constitution of the German Reich by force' and to bring against its members a charge of 'preparation of treason'.[26] Treason, including preparation of treason, was a matter for the Reich Court or, after April 1934, the newly instituted People's Court;[27] but these courts, or the Reich Prosecutor attached to them, were empowered to delegate the hearing of the less serious cases to one of the Higher Regional Courts (*Oberlandesgerichte*). For convenience in coping with the large numbers involved, the accused were commonly tried in groups, ranging from half a dozen to a hundred or more persons who were supposed to have acted jointly. Sometimes, however, the persons indicted together had really little or no connection, except that they had all come to the notice of the police during a particular stage of an investigation.

Although the law itself was made increasingly elastic, and although the standard of proof was progressively lowered by changes in court procedure, it was still necessary, in 1933–35, for judges to adduce some grounds for finding accused persons guilty of an infringement of the law. At first sight the simplest way of dealing with Communist Party activities might seem to have been to apply the law of 14 July 1933, which had forbidden the formation or continuation of any political party other than the National Socialist

Party, on pain of up to three years hard labour, and, indeed, this was occasionally used.[28] But this law could not be applied to Communists arrested before 14 July 1933, nor in fact to very many of those arrested later, whose membership activities could only be proved for some period before July 1933. The state prosecutors therefore chose in most cases to try to persuade the judges that membership of the Communist Party had been treasonable before 14 July 1933. This doctrine was accepted by the courts and embodied in judgements which stand today as monuments of tortuous and dishonest 'reasoning'.

The awkward fact was that the KPD had not, before 14 July, been banned by any specific law of unquestionable validity. Its candidates had been allowed to stand and to be elected to the Reichstag on 5 March, and the banning of its press and the cancellation of its parliamentary mandates later in the month had been effected by administrative action resting on a highly dubious constitutional basis. The doctrine expressed in numerous judgements of Higher Regional courts – that the KPD was already illegal and membership of it treasonable before March 1933 – was therefore also of very dubious legal validity. In many cases the argument advanced was that the treasonable nature of the Communist Party was a fact of common public knowledge after the Reichstag Fire of 27 February, so that no other proof of it was needed by the court and anyone who had participated in the Party's activities after that date could be assumed to have been conscious of the treasonable nature of his or her actions.[29] Sometimes a different twist was given to this sophistry by the argument that because the Hitler government's emergency legislation of February–March 1933 had deprived the Communist Party of all possibility of achieving its aims by parliamentary or constitutional means, its continuation after that must necessarily be aimed at 'changing the constitution of the German Reich by force', and must therefore be construed as treason.[30] In course of time the judges increasingly adopted the simple doctrine that the Communist Party could be taken, without need of proof, to have become illegal at the time of the 'transfer of power' of 30 January 1933.[31] Occasionally, indeed, the courts threw historical fact as well as legal integrity to the winds by accepting the implication that anti-Nazi activity even before 1933 had been treasonable.[32]

In the assessment of sentences, too, legal considerations were increasingly outweighed by political arguments. The penalties prescribed for preparation of treason were sharply increased, extending in some cases to life-imprisonment or even death, by a law of 13 October 1933 and another of 24 April 1934. The courts, however, retained considerable discretion. It was here that some judges expressed their personal reservations about Nazi barbarity by seeking out technical grounds for mitigation, if not acquittal;[33] but increasingly an opposite attitude can be observed. Severity was justified in one case, for instance, on the ground that the acts of political opposition of which the accused had been guilty had been committed after the plebiscite of 12 November 1933: 'that is, at a time when the whole people had already made its profession of faith (*Bekenntnis*) in the Third Reich'.[34] In another case a harsh sentence was justified on the ground that the acts were committed between May and August 1934, 'a time when, from a political point of view, peace and calm had long reigned in Germany and the blessings conferred by the measures of the national government were apparent to every citizen. . .'[35] In still another case Communist propaganda was judged to deserve a severer sentence because it was directed at youth.[36]

It was not only in the interpretation of the law and the awarding of sentences that political pressure and political fanaticism distorted the practice of the courts after 1933. Old liberal standards of fairness and impartiality in the conduct of the proceedings and the assessment of evidence – never very conspicuous in political trials – were now still further debased, though not without some protests from a tiny minority of liberal lawyers. Occasionally, at the beginning, there was overt political intervention, as happened, for instance, during the trial of a group of Red Front Fighters (RFB) in September 1933 for the alleged murder of an SS man at Düsseldorf in 1932, when the local SA leader stood up in court before judgement was pronounced and demanded the acquittal of two of the accused who had since joined the SA.[37] More often, both then and later, the careful reader of the judicial records will find signs of friction between courts and police and expressions of *malaise* felt by judges when presented with the uncorroborated testimony of police informers or with 'confessions' which had patently been extorted by ill-treatment. At first it occasionally happened that such evidence was rejected by a scrupulous and courageous judge.[38] But such manifestations of the 'independence of the judiciary' were soon ended by political pressure exerted through the Ministry of Justice and by changes in the method of allocating judges to particular types of case, if not by more drastic measures.[39] If nevertheless, as sometimes happened, an accused Communist (usually contrary to the advice of the defence lawyer) withdrew in open court admissions which had been made in interrogation, on the grounds that they were untrue and extorted under duress, any scruples felt by the judges were likely to be expressed in a very indirect way. If the testimony so withdrawn was the only evidence against an accused, they might in exceptional cases register an acquittal on grounds of inadequate proof.[40] More often, however, they merely noted that the circumstances of the interrogation could not be elucidated, and based their conviction on other evidence. This was all the easier in that the courts seem to have had no hesitation, in political cases, in giving full credence to the unsupported evidence of police informers and *agents provocateurs*, and to have accepted hearsay evidence.[41]

While it is true that in the early years the Gestapo was sometimes irritated by the lingering scruples of judges and their concern with legal technicalities, the courts were soon brought into line. Friction seems to have lasted longest in the initial stages of political cases, in which, as the Düsseldorf Gestapo was still complaining in its Situation Report for September 1934,[42] the judges – partly because of constant changes of personnel – showed insufficient understanding of the workings of the Communist Party, so that they sometimes failed to issue a warrant for arrest or even gave bail to a prisoner accused of preparation of treason. As far as the Higher Regional Court was concerned, it soon came to a tacit acceptance of the practice of Gestapo torture and the use of *agents provocateurs*, and steadily put behind it the now out-of-date attitude of judicial impartiality, at least where political opposition was suspected.

Although Nazi legislation provided for extremely summary trial of political offenders, particularly by the Special Courts, this was applied mainly to individual actions. Participants in organised Communist opposition often suffered, on the contrary, a long-protracted martyrdom of pre-trial detention and interrogation.[43] Even in quite ordinary cases this interval between arrest and trial might last several months; in the case of important functionaries who had served in different areas it was liable to involve several transfers from one interrogation centre to another and to last for six or seven months or even one or two years. The outcome was likely to be a sentence of imprisonment with hard labour in a penitentiary,[44] the period spent in pre-trial custody being usually counted against this. In the first year of the Nazi régime the hard labour sentences imposed on Communists for 'preparation of high treason' generally ranged from six months to two years or, at most to two-and-a-half or three years.[45] By a law of 13 October 1933, however, the distribution of treasonable literature was made punishable by death or by hard labour for life or for a period of up to fifteen years;[46] and corresponding sentences began to be imposed on Communists whose organised activities were 'proved' to have been committed after that date.

Prisons and penitentiaries, which usually continued to be run by the old professional governors and warders, might afford a certain immediate relief from the grosser forms of politically motivated torment. But imprisonment did not necessarily put an end to police persecution. The Gestapo might at any time visit the penitentiary to re-interrogate a prisoner or might obtain his removal to a police prison in connection with current enquiries.[47] It was not unknown for statements made by prisoners to the prison doctor about tortures they had previously suffered to be reported to the Gestapo for any action it might consider appropriate.[48] Above all, completion of the sentence signified, not release, but the return of the prisoner to the jurisdiction of the Gestapo.

Regional Gestapo files afford innumerable examples of the procedure which was followed when a Communist serving a sentence in a prison or penitentiary became due for release. The prison authorities had to give several weeks notice to the Gestapo and furnish a report about the prisoner's conduct and attitude, indicating in particular whether his or her political outlook had undergone any modification. On the basis of this report, and of the recommendations of the appropriate Gestapo outpost (if any) in the prisoner's home town, the county Gestapo office would recommend to the Gestapo headquarters in Berlin (which had the final say) whether the prisoner should be taken into protective custody or released on certain conditions. An adverse recommendation from the county Gestapo was rarely if ever overruled by Berlin, but a favourable report on some individual might still be disregarded in the light of some change in central government policy towards Communists.

Of the Communists condemned in the early period, many of whom became due for release between 1934 and 1936, those who were judged to have been broken, and to be unlikely to resume political activity, were released on condition of reporting regularly to the Gestapo. But the better known or more resolute who had refused to renounce their political principles while in prison were sent to concentration camps, where the treatment was infinitely worse than in an ordinary prison.[49] The systematic ill-treatment of the prisoners in these camps and the consequent high mortality rate have often been described. Few even of those who survived emerged from them without permanent damage to their health and a shortened life. What is perhaps not always realised is that even in concentration camps Communists continued to be involved in a direct political battle with the Gestapo. Their conduct and conversation were continuously observed from a political point of view by the camp authorities and reported to the Gestapo in periodic reviews of their case in which, again, the recommendation of the county office was referred for decision to Berlin. In every case a political judgement was decisive: release was unlikely unless prisoners were thought to have undergone 'conversion' or at least to have lost their spirit and renounced previously-held political principles, though even here discreet conduct combined with resourceful canvassing by relatives and friends occasionally turned the tables.[50] Release, even if finally achieved, was at first provisional, conditional on regular reporting to the police and subject to secret observation by police informers and employers.

The struggle between the Gestapo and the working-class resistance was on no small scale. According to a Gestapo report of 10 April 1939, 162,734 men and women were then held in concentration camps for political reasons and a further 139,801 in prisons or penitentiaries awaiting trial or serving sentences on political charges.[51] Between the accession of Hitler to power and the beginning of war in 1939 there were 86 mass trials and many smaller ones, at which some 225,000 people were sentenced to 600,000 years in prison for political offences. During the same short period it has been estimated that as many as a million Germans suffered, for a shorter or longer time, the tortures and indignities of the concentration camps.[52] Among them were tens of thousands of Communists, some of whom were never released, others released only to be seized again by a cruel 'cat-and-mouse' procedure.

The Character of the Illegal Struggle

The German Communist Party had had much experience of illegality in the early 1920s, and again more recently in the case of its affiliate, the Red Front Fighters' League, which had been banned in 1929 and had functioned semi-clandestinely ever since. The Party itself, too, had been expecting illegality and making preparations for it.[53] It was not without organisers trained in the traditional techniques of underground political struggle, and some others were actually at Moscow at the beginning of 1933, attending the Comintern's Lenin School, whence they later returned clandestinely to take up key posts in the illegal Party in Germany. Even apart from these highly trained cadres, most full-time functionaries, and no doubt many others too, were familiar with the general notion of 'rules of conspiracy'; that is, with procedures for circumventing bans and proscriptions, frustrating interrogators and avoiding self-incrimination, with the use of aliases and false papers, the detection of police informers, and so on. In addition the Party had a special undercover branch, the *AM-Apparat* (or simply *Apparat*) with representatives at all levels down to Sub-district, whose tasks included – or now began to include – the detection of police spies, the warning of those in danger, arrangements for emigration, and other aspects of security and counter-intelligence. Before 1933, too, as noted above, steps had been taken to hide typewriters and duplicating machines, to put aside sums of money, to appoint reserve leaderships and to bring into being other prerequisites of illegal activity.[54]

Yet the KPD proved to be ill-prepared in some respects for the conditions in which illegal struggle was to be conducted under fascism. This was partly due, of course, to the inherent vulnerability of a mass democratic party of 360,000 members and the impossibility of transforming it suddenly into a clandestine cadre organisation suited to the needs of a long underground struggle – a difficulty accentuated by the paradoxical circumstances of February-March 1933. But the German Communists' subsequent difficulties were not all due to the problems of this transition. The Party succeeded in surmounting the defeat of February-March 1933 and in mobilising its forces to continue the struggle. Yet for two or three years after that it conducted the struggle against the Nazi state by methods which were in certain respects unrealistic and tragically costly in proportion to the results achieved.

The immediate reason for this was that the KPD's preparations for illegality had been based on examples and on past experiences which were seriously misleading. The Gestapo was less inefficient and corrupt than the Tsarist secret police had been, and it did not observe the same legal and practical limitations as the German police during the Weimar republic. Warnings of what was to come had been given by Thälmann and others, but it is easier to issue warnings and even to introduce new schemes of organisation than to change the established habits of mind and modes of operation of a mass party. The German workers, too, with their talent for organisation, perhaps lacked the gift, as well as the tradition, of 'conspiracy'.

The comparative slowness of the KPD to adapt its methods of struggle to the new situation was not, however, due only or even mainly to the inertia of large organisations. It was due even more to a mistaken assessment of the situation and to a consequent misapprehension about the strategic aim which the struggle could achieve. For the German Communists continued to believe that the situation was ripe for proletarian revolution, and in some ways more ripe than ever, now that the bankruptcy of social democratic reformism had been so unmistakably revealed. Despite all the defeats of 1933 the German Communists continued to 'live in an intoxication of optimism',[55] looking forward to the imminent breakdown of Nazi policy, to great class battles immediately ahead, to a final revolutionary crisis. This, in the main, was the Party's view as late as the summer of 1934. What was needed, it seemed to follow, was not the patient building up of a long-term underground cadre organisation or persistent experiments in the use of legal opportunities within Nazi organisations like the Labour Front,[56] but the urgent mobilisation of the masses to overthrow and supersede fascism. *Mass* work, *mass* organisations remained the keywords; and as long as Communists continued to see the situation in this perspective, it was difficult for them to revise their traditional methods. The organisation remained heavy and inflexible, slowed down by too many mechanical routines and exposed to detection because of an over-complex structure with too many interconnections, leading to too many meetings. It continued, too, to be highly centralised. District leaderships received a constant stream of Party directives and publications as well as visits from representatives of the underground centre in Berlin. Detailed guidance made for discipline and unity, but it also produced an accumulation of paper, with consequent problems of storage and disposal, and it may have worked against the growth of local initiative and creativity.[57]

Yet bureaucracy was not the whole story. There were not a few examples of local initiative and quick reaction to events, while the talents of individuals and the improvisations of small groups produced the most imaginative and effective underground propaganda. The excessive complexity of organisation was modified by the introduction of the three-member-group system during 1934. Nonetheless, throughout the first years there was a tendency to reckless bravery, reflecting the short-term perspective of imminent revolution. Too many arrests were traceable to neglect of the accepted 'rules of conspiracy'. At Düsseldorf in 1934, to give one example out of many, a Communist's dwelling was being used simultaneously for three different illegal purposes; and in another, even more disastrous crossing of wires, a representative of the Party's Reich Publications Chief (*Reichstechniker*), who came from Berlin to the Lower Rhine to use a printing works there, employed a local Communist who was already working illegally for the District leadership, enabling the Gestapo to break into both organisations simultaneously.[58] Some arrests occurred because clandestine functionaries did not resist the temptation to use their sleeping quarters for an occasional meeting or failed to dispense with written notes and drafts.

Even the greatest caution, the most meticulous observance of security rules, could not eliminate risk. Political action necessarily involved risk, and precautions could scarcely ever reduce the frequency of disaster, though they could diminish its extent and its repercussions when it happened. The new strategy adopted in 1935 (which will be discussed later) brought with it a more patient, far-seeing approach to underground political activity and a more consistent emphasis on the observance of precautions. Less emphasis began to be placed on literature and more attention to be paid to oral propaganda, such as the spreading of rumours. But sooner or later, if a broad anti-fascist front was to be built up, it was necessary to make a direct personal approach to individuals, with the inevitable risk of denunciation or betrayal. The tactic of working in Nazi mass organisations and using the legal opportunities they presented, which was more insistently recommended by the Party leadership

a) 'Down with Hitler' slogan on the Königsbrücke, Breslau 1933
b) 'Free Thälmann' slogan on fence, 1935

after 1935, also brought new dangers as well as new opportunities, increasing the difficulty of unmasking traitors and renegades.

Before criticising those who took mistaken short cuts in illegal activity, it is necessary to visualise the appalling difficulties under which they worked. Not least of these was acute poverty and often real hunger, which accentuated the constant strain of danger and uncertainty and undermined all but the strongest constitutions. Most active Communists in these years were unemployed, living on the pittance of welfare payments, unable to afford tram fares and forced to walk long distances to carry out any political assignment. If they were married, they inevitably involved their families in the privations and dangers of illegal work and sometimes suffered the additional anguish of marital estrangement or a clash of loyalties.[59] For clandestine organisers, living in a strange environment with a false identity and only fleeting contacts with other human beings, the strain was of a different sort, but certainly no less. Often it meant spending something like twelve hours each day away from one's lodgings, yet without attracting attention by staying long elsewhere; hours spent largely on foot, broken only by a limited number of *Treffs* and political discussions and by periodic encounters with police patrols checking papers or raiding cafés. Every such organiser lived in a tightening net which experience showed would be drawn close in a matter of months at most.[60] One of the most insidious moral and psychological dangers was 'spy-psychosis', for it was hard, when a wave of unexplained arrests occurred, to keep mistrust and suspicion within rational bounds, to resist panic and consequent paralysis of activity.

Communists who participated in the Party's illegal activity faced the virtual certainty of being caught sooner or later, and were well aware of the treatment they could expect at the hands of the Gestapo. All of them must have considered, and some discussed with others, how they should try to behave in face of the notoriously brutal methods of police interrogation. Some thought it would be impossible to resist Gestapo tortures indefinitely and that the main aim could only be to hold out long enough for the alarm to be given. It was the fear of betraying comrades which was one of the most insidious, inescapable pressures on the clandestine activist; and though most of the reported suicides of prisoners in police custody were probably really murders, some were the voluntary acts of men or women who had decided in advance to take this step if it seemed to be the only means of escaping irresistible pressure to betray comrades. Even those whose suicide followed a moment of weakness were not necessarily acting only from remorse; the lives of accused anti-fascists might be saved by the absence from court of a key witness against them. Some, though they might not have thought in advance that they would be able to hold out, in fact told the Gestapo nothing, mentioned no names, and persisted in this silence through years of prison and concentration camp. Each case was different and the full circumstances will never be known, so that historians lack the means, even if they had the right, to pass judgement on the conduct of individuals. What they can say, on the evidence seen by the present writer, is that the morale of the illegal Communist Party was high and that it fought the Gestapo with the cohesion of an army in which class consciousness nourished a stubborn sense of duty and loyalty.

To pretend betrayal in the hope of tricking the Gestapo was a dangerous expedient, not to be recommended. Yet it succeeded in some cases. In others, experienced and resourceful Communists were occasionally able to discover gaps in the prosecution evidence and to exploit these to obtain an acquittal. Others acquired through experience an adroitness and sixth sense which enabled them to live year after year under observation, yet to exert an anti-Nazi influence in ways which were difficult to pin down.[61] But all these were exceptions. The overwhelming majority of those who contributed to the Communist Party's clandestine activity came, sooner or later, to the police cells, to the Special Court, Higher Regional Court or the People's Court, then to prison and concentration camp. Many were broken in health by ill-treatment and died prematurely; some were executed, some murdered.

The Strategy of Revolutionary Mass Action 1933–35

CHAPTER 5

The Underground Struggle

Policy

Before considering the structure and activities of the German Communist Party from the summer of 1933 onwards, it will be useful to glance briefly at its 'general line' or overall strategy. For organisation and activity were determined in the last resort by the Party's aims, expressed in its political line, and some of the inconsistencies and apparent confusions in the 1933–35 period can only be understood against the background of a prolonged and complicated process of policy revision.

In subsequent years the KPD was to recognise that although it had won the immediate battle for survival in the early months of 1933, thanks to the loyalty and discipline of a significant part of its membership, it had nonetheless suffered a major defeat, calling for fundamental reassessment of the situation. But the Party's immediate reaction – with some individual exceptions – was quite different. It was to reaffirm that the conflicts within capitalism were sharpening, foreshadowing a final revolutionary crisis, for which the Party must prepare. The dissolution of the trade unions and the break-up of the Social Democratic Party were seen as creating conditions favourable to the winning of the leadership of the working class by the Communist Party; and the Party leaders called on the members, not to examine past mistakes, but to persevere in a struggle against what can now be seen to have become overwhelming odds.[1]

Hitler's seizure of power had not caused the Communist leaders to abandon their belief that Germany was near to the brink of proletarian revolution. They interpreted the establishment of the Nazi dictatorship, not as a major defeat of the working class, but as a final, desperate move of the monopoly bourgeoisie to stave off the growing threat of the workers' revolutionary movement. The result, it was argued, was likely to be, not the postponement of the final crisis of capitalism, but its hastening by exposing alike the illusions of Social Democracy and the inability of the Nazis to solve a crisis which could only become rapidly worse.[2] Disillusioned workers from the camps of social democracy and national socialism could be expected to turn to the Communist Party as the crisis deepened.[3]

The conclusion drawn was that it would be wrong to make any serious compromise with social-democratic reformism and that the Communist Party must maintain its whole apparatus ready for the seizure of power, meanwhile seeking to exploit the basic instability of the Nazi régime by an offensive strategy. This line, which was in effect a continuation of that of the Twelfth ECCI Plenum of September 1932,[4] was reaffirmed in two ECCI statements on the German situation on 5 March and 1 April 1933.[5] Illustrations of its application in practice can be found in the correspondence which has survived between those Politburo members who had remained in Germany in the spring of 1933 and those who had emigrated to France, as well as in the instructions given by the Berlin leadership to District Committees.[6] For instance, in a letter sent by the central leadership in Berlin to the leadership of the North Bavarian, i.e. Nuremberg, District on 4 August 1933, concerning preparations for Communist activity at the forthcoming Nazi Party rally, the task of winning over working-class Nazis was said to presuppose the most vigorous, principled fight against Social Democratic policy, and Communists were called upon to recruit Social Democratic workers into the Revolutionary Trade Union Opposition (RGO).[7] Again, in a letter from the Berlin leadership to the *émigré* secretariat at Paris a few weeks later, concerning a proposed Party school to which clandestine activists were to be sent from western Germany, it was proposed to spend no less than four days on the study of the ECCI statements of September 1932 and March 1933 and on a KPD resolution based on them.[8] It is noticeable that the term 'social fascism' was still used in the letter with reference to the development of the KPD's own strategy and tactics.

It followed from this continued ultra-left analysis that the Party must maintain its centralized organisation and intensify its activities. Any recognition that the Party had suffered a defeat, and therefore any attempt to explain the causes of the defeat, was denounced as defeatism or even cowardice.[9] For members and leaders alike, Soviet Germany still seemed to be within reach, dependent only on the courage and readiness for self-sacrifice of the revolutionary workers.

The underground leadership did, it is true, during 1933, arrange courses and schools and produce memoranda designed to develop Party policy.[10] But the content was on traditional lines, and though some attempts were made to stimulate new thinking in a spirit of self-criticism, this seems to have remained within the broad context of the expected proletarian revolution and a Soviet Germany. Schehr, for instance, in asking two fellow-members of the inner-German leadership on 1 August 1933 to produce a memorandum on the Party's agricultural policy, stressed that this was essential for the development of the anti-fascist offensive, in other words, for winning support in the countryside.[11] Self-criticism was of detail within the general concept of an offensive, of 'mass work'.

Only one member of the ten-man Politburo, the top leadership, is known to have urged an attempt to draw the workers into armed struggle in 1933, in order to prevent the new government from consolidating its position. This was Hermann Remmele, who was subsequently ousted from the Politburo.[12] All the others, as far as is known, judged that the Party lacked both the industrial strength and the political allies, as well as the paramilitary potential for such an attempt, and rejected the proposal as 'adventurist'. But their own view of the relation of forces was hardly less unrealistic, for they still did not concede that the workers had suffered a defeat or that there was any need for a serious reconsideration of their Party's policy.[13] There had been, it is true, a suggestion of new policy initiatives and a hint of rethinking. Already on 30 January 1933, and several times in the subsequent three months, the KPD leadership made direct approaches to the Social Democratic Party executive for joint action against the new régime; but when these approaches were ignored or rejected, they quickly reverted to denunciation, not only of the right-wing Social Democratic leaders, but also of their left-socialist critics, as 'social-fascists' playing the role of 'social support of the bourgeoisie'.[14] Meanwhile, on the theoretical plane, the hint in Thälmann's speech of 7 February, that the immediate aim of the struggle against the National Socialist dictatorship might be something different from the proletarian revolution, was not repeated or developed. On the contrary, as the struggle sharpened in the following months, the Communists continued to insist that the Nazis were running into deepening crisis and that the bankruptcy of social democracy would leave the way open for the Communist Party to carry through the proletarian revolution.

Why did the German Communist Party take so long to recognise the events of 1933 as a serious defeat, to assess realistically the situation resulting from them, and to draw appropriate conclusions?

Critics such as Edinger have attributed the delay to the international ties of the Party, pointing out that the KPD had to conform to the general strategy laid down for the movement as a whole: in this case the 'class against class' line which had prevailed in the Communist International since shortly before its Sixth World Congress in 1928.[15] And it is obvious that a fundamental strategic reorientation on the part of a world-wide movement was likely to take time to carry through. These factors alone cannot, however, explain the slowness of the KPD to adapt itself to the new situation of 1933. For although the reorientation of the International was a slow and complicated process, taking over two years to complete, the German party in no way took the lead but rather tended to lag behind. The Executive Committee of the International did not hinder the KPD from drawing the lessons of 1933 but, on the contrary, ultimately intervened at several crucial stages to induce the 'leftist' majority of the KPD leadership to abandon its opposition to the new strategic conception which had been pioneered in other countries. The main source of the delay must therefore be sought in the conditions and traditions of the movement in Germany itself.

The new situation of illegality and terror made it virtually impossible for the German Communist leadership after February 1933 to conduct a fundamental policy debate in the party, or even to make a detached, informed, far-reaching review of the rapidly changing situation. This was all the more so after the arrest of Thälmann, who alone might have had the authority necessary to initiate a revision of policy. It is likely, though, that he would have felt, as many of the other leaders apparently did, that the crisis of survival, when it was necessary to mobilise the whole membership against an attack of unprecedented savagery, was not the moment for contentious arguments about policy. Later in the year, when the Party had overcome the immediate threat to its existence and when the outlines of the situation had become clearer, new considerations arose to reinforce the disinclination for a major policy review. For it now seemed clear that if the Communist Party had only just, with a supreme effort, survived, the Social Democratic Party had suffered a disaster, revealing the complete bankruptcy of reformist socialism. The time seemed to have come, long expected by the left, when the majority of the working class could be won to follow the revolutionary lead – if not immediately, then as soon as the failure of National Socialism had become plain. This argument was all the more compelling in Germany because the bitter hostility between reformist social democracy and revolutionary communism between 1914 and 1932 had run so deep there. Numerous anguished memories reinforced the reluctance of the Communist leaders to make an agreement with the Social Democratic leadership on any terms which would inhibit them from continuing the debate against reformism or from accepting recruits from the ranks of social democracy, especially as it continued to be assumed that the Nazi régime would soon break down.

Throughout 1933 and far into 1934 the 'leftist' strategy adopted in 1928 continued to guide the activities and organisation of the KPD. The establishment of the Nazi tyranny was still not viewed as a major defeat for the KPD, nor as having brought about a fundamental change in the situation.[16] Crisis, leading to a revolutionary situation, continued to be expected from month to month. Consequently the Party's attitude to social democracy also changed little. Appeals for united action were constantly being made to active Social Democratic groups, but, after March 1933, not to the leadership (in Germany or in exile) for well over a year. The idea that social democracy was 'the chief social support' of bourgeois rule was not seriously reconsidered, despite the comparative difficulty of applying it to the Third Reich.[17] Consistently with that conception, Communist groups in factories continued to be instructed to form – or to revive – 'independent class trade unions', which meant unions committed to revolutionary politics. In conformity with the same assessment of the political situation, the clandestine party organisations were built as fighting units whose tasks were defined in terms of 'mass struggle' and preparation of the conditions for revolutionary uprisings.[18] By 1933 the KPD was like a political army, committed to a strategy of continuous offensives against an enemy holding all the advantages. Its secret circulars resounded with calls for 'mass action', for the building of 'mass organisations', and for true bolshevik heroism.[19]

This persistent over-optimistic adherence to the ultra-leftist assessment and to the line of policy derived from it did not go altogether without questioning, as appears from some memoirs published years later. But the strict discipline which had been observed in the KPD, especially since 1925, tended to keep disagreements private, so as to give an impression of unanimity in public; and the conditions of the Hitler terror led to a still keener sense of the need for such discipline and unanimity. It is thus impossible, from the sources now available, to know for certain when the demand for a revision of the ultra-left strategy first began to be voiced by a section of the top leadership. Walter Ulbricht, who later came forward as the chief protagonist of a change of policy, wrote a number of articles after he left Germany in the autumn of 1933, which were marked by a noticeably sober estimate of the weaknesses of the KPD's work – for instance in the factories – and by an emphasis on the need to make full use of the legal opportunities offered by Nazi institutions, which thus foreshadowed certain features of later policy. These emphases may, as is now stated by some GDR historians, have reflected an argument behind the scenes as early as 1933;[21] but if they did, it was long before the challenge was made public and explicit. To all outward appearances the effect of the establishment of Hitler's dictatorship had been to confirm the German Communists in their leftist line.

Meanwhile striking developments had been taking place in the German Social Democratic movement. The setting up of the Third Reich, which had confronted the KPD with a serious crisis both in practice and in theory, had brought about a virtual collapse of social democracy. Abandoned by its bourgeois allies and faced with the exposure of its gradualist illusions, the SPD had split into fragments. Those Social Democratic leaders, whether trade unionists or parliamentarians, who persisted to the last in trying to earn a place in Hitler's Germany, had forfeited all respect and political significance, whether their career ended in a Nazi prison or in pensioned retirement. A high proportion of the rank and file fell out of activity in disgust, but among those – especially of the younger generation – who remained active, there was a sharp reaction against the whole reformist tradition and against the elderly leaders who represented it, combined with an active search for a new revolutionary path. Some of these activists joined the Communist Party or at least made contact with its underground groups. But others were not ready to do so unconditionally, feeling that the KPD too had in some ways failed and needed to revise its conceptions. Of these latter among the Social Democrats there were some who envisaged the foundation of an entirely new revolutionary socialist party;[22] others preferred to think in terms of an SPD transformed by a left-wing leadership and seeking united action and eventual union on equal terms with the Communists. One thing at least was clear. After June 1933 the remnant of the old leadership now in exile had little chance of maintaining control of the surviving Social Democratic groups, whether these were in Germany or abroad, whether active or merely waiting, unless they were seen to abandon reformism and return to revolutionary Marxism, and unless they co-opted representative figures from the socialist left.

So compelling was this situation that it led, not only to the inclusion of a number of 'leftists' in the Executive Committee in exile (Sopade),[23] but to what looked like a miraculous and total conversion of the right-wing majority. Already on 18 June 1933 the SPD Executive issued from its exile in Prague a manifesto entitled 'Break the Chains!' which, in the words of Dr L.J. Edinger, a leading historian of German social democracy, 'in the language of revolutionary Marxism . . . pledged the exiled leaders to fight against the reactionary dictatorship of monopoly capital and its Nazi cohorts and for the establishment of the rule of the working class in Germany'.[24] In the following January the Executive, in what has become known as the Prague Manifesto, developed this conception more fully, renouncing the whole theory of reformism which had guided the practice of the SPD since 1914. Dr Edinger describes the first of these two manifestoes – and the comment applies even more to the second – as 'an extension of the previous efforts of the SPD leadership to control their own dissatisfied left-wingers and combat Communist efforts to capture the Social Democratic rank and file . . .'. Even so, the *émigré* leadership only just succeeded in retaining control of the movement.

These developments in social democracy might seem to have presented an opportunity for the KPD, not just to win over disillusioned followers of the SPD, but to achieve new results in the campaign for a united front. The view of the KPD leftists, however, still prevailed in the Politburo, and while it did not preclude approaches to SPD leaders, it made their success unlikely. They insisted on a view of the Social Democratic left as insincere and dangerous and required as the price of unity humiliating admissions of error and recognitions of Communist hegemony which the new trends in social democracy were unwilling to concede.

The leftist line of the KPD leadership received its final

endorsement at the Thirteenth Plenum of the Executive Committee of the Communist International in December 1933.[25] This supreme body of the movement (between world congresses) reiterated the full approval which the Praesidium of ECCI had already expressed in April for the political line pursued by the German party before and at the time of the Nazi assumption of power.[26] Declaring that 'social democracy continues to play the role of the main social prop of the bourgeoisie also in countries of open fascist dictatorship',[27] the Plenum called on all sections of the International 'persistently to fight for the realisation of a united militant front with the Social Democratic workers, in spite of and against the will of the treacherous leaders of Social Democracy'.[28]

In the same month as this reaffirmation of the ultra-left line, unambiguous if tentative propositions for a new line were voiced in the last place from which they might have been expected – the Reich Supreme Court in Berlin, where Georgi Dimitrov delivered his closing speech in the Reichstag Fire trial on 16 December 1933. In a passage evidently addressed to the working-class movement outside the walls of the court, Dimitrov dwelt on the importance of a united front of the working class against fascism and declared that the Communist International expected the Communist parties of the individual countries to approach the leaderships of the corresponding Social Democratic parties with proposals for a joint action programme, as well as attempting to reach local agreements for joint action. These remarks handled the question of a united front with a distinctly different emphasis from that of the statements issued after the recent Thirteenth Plenum, in which the exposure of social democracy continued to be regarded as the main aim of any joint action proposals to its leading bodies. When in subsequent months events in France, Austria and Spain helped to stimulate a process of new thinking in the International, it was again Dimitrov, after his arrival in Moscow on 27 February 1934, who seems to have taken the lead in the working out of a new strategy. His triumph at the Reichstag Fire trial had given him a unique prestige throughout the world Communist movement; but he was to some extent preaching if not to the converted, at least to the half-converted. The decision taken soon after – in April or May 1934 – to call a new World Congress of the International and to entrust the main political report to Dimitrov presumably already reflected a growing conviction of the need for a major revison of strategy.

Organisation[29]

The German Communist Party had about 360,000 members in January 1933.[30] A high proportion of these were recent recruits and their absorption into the formal structure of the party represented in itself a formidable task, so much so that only 287,180[31] had as yet been reached by the local dues-collecting apparatus and further recruitment had had to be suspended, except for long-standing sympathisers.[32]

The KPD, like other sections of the Communist International, was organised on the principle of democratic centralism, which aimed at combining the discipline of a revolutionary vanguard with a mass membership. There was a formal democratic structure, with a Central Committee elected by periodic National Congresses and twenty-eight District Committees elected by District Congresses. In practice, especially since 1925, this democratic constitution had functioned in such a way as to put the central leadershp in an almost unchallengeable position, through the growing infrequency of National Congresses (the last had been in 1929) and the ability of the leadership to arrange and control the proceedings. At District level, similarly, the elected leaderships were increasingly overshadowed by the full-time secretaries, who were virtually nominated from above and responsible to the Secretariat of the Central Committee. At both national and District levels, too, elections managed on the 'panel' system favoured continuity and made it difficult for opponents of the current leadership to get a foothold.

The power of the central leadership in Berlin was further increased by the fact that the KPD was subject to the overriding authority of the Communist International. It is true that the International itself had a formal democratic constitution; its workings, however, were inevitably strongly influenced by the fact that most of its sections had to work in conditions of illegality, and therefore of secrecy, giving the International as a whole the character of a general staff of world revolution. Moreover, once the hope of an early world revolution had receded, in the early 1920s, the existence of the Soviet state came to be of key importance for the International, and in the last resort, this gave the Soviet government a *de facto* supremacy which deeply modified the working of the whole International.

One such modification was the growing infrequency of World Congresses, which had originally taken place annually. By 1933 there had been no World Congress since the Sixth in 1928, with the result of a growing centralisation of authority in the International's Executive Committee (ECCI) whose headquarters were in Moscow. Several members of the German Party leadership were members, or candidate members, of ECCI and attended its plenary meetings where, nominally at least, they carried considerable weight, owing to the size of their Party and to the crucial role which it was expected to play in the coming world revolution. Day-to-day relations were maintained by the residence in Moscow of a member of the German Politburo, Fritz Heckert, while Thälmann and his colleagues could also consult with the International's Secretary for Western Europe, Georgi Dimitrov, who lived clandestinely in Berlin until his arrest on 9 March 1933. After the banning of the Party in the same month, its leaders kept in touch with the International by correspondence, or by an occasional personal visit, but it was not, except during the Congresses in 1935, from Moscow that they directed the underground struggle in Germany.

Subject to the overriding authority of ECCI, power in the German Party between Congresses lay with a Central Committee which consisted at this period of 38 members and 25 candidate members and had hitherto met monthly. One of its functions was to elect a Political Bureau (Politburo) of ten full members and five candidate members who met weekly to decide major policy questions, and a Secretariat of five members to deal with day-to-day administrative matters. This system of collective leadership conformed to democratic principles, but in practice, as happens in many other democratic organisations, there had been a tendency for meetings of the National Congress and of the Central Committee to become less frequent and for power to become concentrated in the hands of the central Party administration, notably the Secretariat, whose members were usually also members of the Politburo. The most influential of this inner group was Ernst Thälmann, who had been Party Chairman since 1925 and whose popularity both with the rank and file and with Moscow put him in an almost impregnable position. A definitive assessment of his political career, however, remains to be made.

The centralisation of the Party inevitably increased still further in the conditions of illegality after March 1933. But power remained concentrated in a small collective: no one inherited Thälmann's personal position. Of his close political associates John Schehr, who shared some of Thälmann's qualities, seems to have played an outstanding part in directing the clandestine work of the Party within Germany during 1933, but he was arrested in November and murdered by the Nazis on 1 February 1934.[33]

The situation at the Centre was to some extent reproduced in each of the 28 Party Districts, in which leadership was exercised by an inner group of three full-time secretaries (for politics, organisation, and agitation and propaganda respectively), expanded on occasion by the addition of the editor of the chief Party newspaper in the District, the heads of other District departments, such as education, finance, trade-union affairs, etc., and the leaders of the most important Sub-districts who were normally also paid, full-time functionaries. Here again, the political secretary or 'District Leader'[34] might acquire an authority which was difficult to oppose.

Below District level there were about a thousand Sub-districts (*Unterbezirke*), comprising 8,210 cells, of which about 6,000 were street cells. It had been party policy for some years, following the current doctrine of the International, to go over to an organisation based on factory cells, but the growth of unemployment among members had thwarted all endeavours in that direction and only some 11 per cent of the members were as yet organised in that way.[35] The attempt to strengthen the Party in the factories continued to be given a high priority: Party groups in important factories were placed directly under the District Party Committee, and even, in the case of some especially vital enterprises, under a member of the Politburo. In December 1932, for example, Wilhelm Florin had been made personally responsible for the factory cells in the Hamburg docks, Wilhelm Pieck for the giant chemical plants of IG-Farben, and John Schehr for the Siemens electrical works, as well as for the Berlin railway works and Krupps and other Ruhr works.[36] In the important chemical works in the South West – Höchst and Badische Anilin and other constituents of the IG Farben empire – a special system of Instructors was established, linking the works cells directly to the Regional Adviser and the Central Operative Leadership.[37]

Below the Sub-district were town branches (*Ortsgruppen*) and city ward branches (*Stadtteile*), with their street cells and works cells, each having its treasurer and literature and education secretaries and perhaps other functionaries as well. So complex was the structure that it has been said of one District (Lower Rhine), that as many as half of the members were 'functionaries', that is, office-holders of some sort.[38] Some of these might be responsible in some degree to the equivalent functionary at the level above, as well as to the collective leadership at their own level. A special degree of autonomy was enjoyed, necessarily, by the functionaries of the *Apparat* or *AM-Apparat* at each level, who were concerned with secret work in the police and the army, and with counter-intelligence and security. It was the latter aspect, particularly the detection of police spies and the timely warning of endangered comrades, which became the main function of the Apparat in and after 1933, though attempts were made to influence policemen or storm troopers through specialised leaflets or personal contacts.[39]

Complex as was the structure of the Party, it was only the central pillar of the Communist edifice, alongside numerous other institutions of the revolutionary left, and the KPD's policy in the years 1933–35 allowed no withdrawal from these outlying sectors, but demanded a continuous effort to develop them in conditions of illegality as constituent parts of the revolutionary mass movement which it was the Party's task to build up. Some of these mass organisations were to play a significant part in the underground resistance.

Among these was the Young Communist League (KJVD), some of whose branches not only displayed an impressive initiative and self-sacrificing enthusiasm, but seem to have been especially successful in making contact with non-Communist groups: not only Social Democratic, but nationalist and Roman Catholic as well. 'Red Aid', too, not only helped the Party's struggle in general by relieving active resisters of some degree of anxiety about their dependants, but at times played a more directly political role by acting as representatives for the Communist movement in unity talks with other socialist or Social Democratic groups.[41] Because it was not formally a Communist Party organisation, Red Aid may have been accepted more readily as a negotiating partner in unity talks by Social Democrats who genuinely wanted negotiations, but did not want to infringe their party leadership's ban on working with the Communist Party. Dr Hetzer, in his study of Bavaria in the Nazi period, states that the KPD Sector-leadership in Switzerland, recognising by the spring of 1935 that efforts to achieve a united front were unlikely to succeed at Party level, sent instructions to the clandestine Communist groups in South-West Germany to use Red

Aid, not only as a means of helping the imprisoned, but also as a broad organisation to gather together all anti-Nazi elements.[42] The same expedient may have been resorted to in other parts of Germany, too, for later in the same year a leaflet was circulated in Berlin under the heading: 'Unity in the struggle against the Fascist Terror! Joint Appeal of the Berlin-Brandenburg District Leaderships of the SPD and Red Aid'.[43]

The Party's paramilitary arm, the RFB, which had already functioned illegally or under cover since 1929, was of course a special target for attack by the Nazis in 1933 and must have been almost entirely destroyed. Yet as long as the Communist Party's policy envisaged a seizure of power, there was a reason for trying to preserve at least the material resources hidden away by the RFB. How far that was achieved must remain a matter of conjecture and topic for research.

As resources became scarcer, it was inevitably the mass organisations which were drained of personnel. In the Ruhr, according to Dr Peukert, none of them had anything like a network covering the whole District by the end of 1933.

In June 1932, when a ban on the Party was thought to be imminent, a three-man committee of Politburo members had been set up to review the organisation of the Party and of its subsidiary movements, with special reference to their ability to adapt to changing conditions; and the committee's recommendations began to be put into effect in December 1932.[45] The process took an unexpectedly long time because of the uncertainties and ambiguities attending Hitler's take-over and the period of semi-legality that followed, and it was not until about April 1933 that the reorganisation was in any sense completed.

The changes were intended to introduce more simplicity and efficiency into a structure which involved the direct subordination to the Centre of 28 Districts and to each District of up to 20 Sub-districts. In future the Districts were to be grouped in eight regions (*Oberbezirke*), in each of which a Regional Adviser (*Oberberater*) appointed by the Secretariat of the Central Committee would ensure close liaison between the Centre and the Districts concerned, spending part of his time in Berlin and part in the Districts allocated to him, and reporting regularly at each end. A similar function was to be performed by Instructors, who could be appointed by District leaderships to take charge of a group of Sub-districts. During the following year or two, experience of underground struggle gave rise to a tendency to divide the larger Districts, and sometimes also the larger Sub-districts, with a view to limiting the repercussions following the arrest of key functionaries. By the end of 1934, according to one source, the number of Districts had been increased from 28 to 48.[46] Some of these measures, however, may have increased the vulnerability of the organisation by increasing the number of levels and the temptation to take short cuts. Between November 1933 and March 1934, for instance, the KPD records[47] show that despite the existence of the Regional Advisers, the central underground leadership at Berlin maintained direct contact with the most important District leaderships, while some of these in turn had direct contact with a frontier post in a neighbouring country.[48]

From 1933, too, as secret printing facilities became scarce, the Technical Branch, headed by a chief (*Reichstechniker*) at Berlin, and later at Saarbrücken, with subordinates at Regional and District levels, arrogated to himself a certain autonomy and caused complaints in some Districts by carrying out printing operations there without prior consultation with the District functionaries concerned.[49]

It was impossible, in conditions of underground struggle, to consult the members at branch or cell meetings, or to hold regular congresses and elections; inevitably, the importance of nominated Instructors increased. Yet as far as possible the bureaucratic structure was maintained, with its comparative inflexibility, both in the Party itself and in the mass organisations. The hierarchy of ranks and the lateral divisions of area and function were as clearly defined as those of an army and could not be fundamentally changed in the midst of battle. It was to take something approaching the destruction of the movement to force a radical revision of its organisation and methods of struggle. Meanwhile, the traditional forms, familiar to members, gave them something to base their practice on, to adapt and to rebuild. The cells, which had grown in size during the period of expansion, were now broken down into five or even three-member groups, in which only one of the members had contact outside the group. This meant that a break through by the police was easier to seal off, though it also meant that the arrest of the key member might isolate the group for a time.

In a party as centralised as the KPD, the quality of its top leadership was of crucial importance, especially when it was exposed to the severe test of illegality in conditions which differed in many respects from what had been foreseen, and when it became impossible to hold regular meetings of the Central Committee at which the leadership could render account and policy be reviewed. The last such meeting was that of 7 February 1933, already mentioned,[50] but that had to be broken off for security reasons before Thälmann had concluded his long opening address, and therefore before there could be any discussion. The chief significance of the occasion, despite a passing hint of new thinking, was probably to give the stamp of Thälmann's authority to the prevailing leftist line, and to make any radical revision of it more difficult in the years that followed.

Following accepted practice the leadership of the Party in the months ahead rested in the hands of the ten full members and five candidate members of the Politburo. Of these the Chairman and undisputed leader of the Party, Ernst Thälmann, had been arrested on 3 March 1933. It has been shown recently that some degree of political contact or consultation was subsequently maintained with him in prison through the permitted visits of his wife and daughter;[51] but it is not likely that this amounted to more than obtaining his general approval of policies that were being followed. Of the other Politburo members, Remmele, who had apparently stood out for a more vigorous reaction to the Nazi assumption of power, was summoned to Moscow to explain his views to ECCI and did not return to Germany or play any further part in the leadership of the Party,[52] while Heckert continued to reside in Moscow as the KPD's liaison with the International, and Merker was apparently in the shade at this time. Thus from March 1933 the direction of Party work in Germany rested in the hands of a small group of seven or eight Politburo members: Dahlem, Florin, Pieck, Schehr, Schubert, Schulte, Ulbricht, and possibly also Merker. All these men remained in Germany and it is a tribute to the security arrangements of the KPD that none of them was betrayed or discovered by the police, except for Schehr, who fell into their hands in November 1933.

At the end of May 1933, however, the Politburo decided that the presence of almost all its members in Germany had become too dangerous. It therefore divided itself into two sections: a Home Leadership (*Inlandsleitung*) in Berlin, led by Schehr, together with Schubert, Schulte and Ulbricht; and an External or *émigré*

Leadership (*Auslandsleitung*) led by Pieck, together with Dahlem and Florin, with their base in Paris.

From May 1933 the Home Leadership at Berlin directed the underground struggle within Germany with the help of eight Regional Advisers and a skeleton 'technical' staff dealing with the dispatch and reception of Instructors and couriers, the arrangement of lodgings and meeting places, finance and propaganda. Of the 28 Party Districts, the Home Leadership is known to have been in regular contact with 18 in November-December 1933, and in irregular contact with eight others. In addition, Schehr sent a regular information report to Pieck at Paris.[53] The External Leadership, for its part, published the Party's central organ, *Rote Fahne*, and other material, made arrangements for the escape from Germany of those who were in danger, negotiated with other *émigré* groups, and developed the Frontier Posts into a well-organised system for smuggling both people and literature in and out of Germany.

This division of the Politburo was only a temporary arrangement. By the autumn of 1933 the position of those of its members who had remained in Germany had become so precarious that it was decided that they too should emigrate. The immediate direction of the underground struggle was to be delegated to a new Internal or Home Leadership, composed of three or four experienced Party functionaries who had proved themselves in illegal work as District Secretaries or in other responsible positions, but were not members of the Politburo. Following this decision Schubert, Schulte and Ulbricht left Germany in the late autumn of 1933. Schehr was to follow as soon as he had completed the task of working in the new Internal Leadership. In the event both Schehr himself and the newly installed Home Leadership were arrested on 13 November in circumstances which do not seem to have been fully clarified. What is clear is that the Nazi government, drawing its own conclusions from the Reichstag Fire trial, then in its final stages, had them murdered without trial. A new Internal Leadership was meanwhile chosen and installed. It was responsible directly to the reunited Politburo at Paris, but in February 1934 Franz Dahlem, a member of the Politburo, returned to Berlin to act as an intermediary between the Internal Leadership and the Politburo. His role seems to have been to keep an eye on the situation in Germany and to report independently to his colleagues abroad, rather than to take part in the day-to-day work of the Internal Leadership. He stayed until July

1934, when it was apparently intended that Schubert should take his place, but it is not certain that he did so, and there is a possibility that the supervision of the underground work may have been passed to Merker, or to Dahlem and Ulbricht in Czechoslovakia.[54]

From the autumn of 1933 the KPD leadership was in emigration, striving, from its places of refuge in neighbouring countries, to exert effective control and direction over the underground struggle within Germany through the Internal Leadership in Berlin and by occasional direct contacts with the frontier posts and with the main underground functionaries in the areas near the frontier. As far as the exiled Politburo had a base, it was Paris, the seat of its Secretariat, except in the period 1935–36, when the events surrounding the Seventh World Congress of the International drew most of the Party's leaders to Moscow.

The Internal Leadership at Berlin (also known as Central Operative Leadership) worked throughout 1934 as a team, with occasional replacements. Its members divided their responsibilities partly by region, partly by subject, and directed the work of Party organisations throughout Germany to some effect. In June 1934, to give one example, they reported to the *émigré* Secretariat that they were trying to induce Party Districts to pay more attention to increasing their influence in important industrial concerns. They had recently sent a special Instructor to the 'chemical region of the South West', who was working with the Regional Adviser there, though directly paid by and answerable to Berlin, and they were about to send further Instructors to important factories in that region.[55]

On 27 March 1935 the Central Operative Leadership suffered a severe blow when a new team, which had just taken over from its predecessors in Berlin, was arrested at its first meeting. Partly because of the comprehensive scope of the arrests and partly because of the preparations then being made for the impending World Congress of the International, the building up of a new Central Operative Leadership was at first postponed and finally abandoned. From that time the Politburo sought to direct the struggle in Germany, not through a centre in Berlin, but through a number of 'frontier secretariats', later known as 'Sector Leaderships' in the neighbouring countries, supervised by a small sub-committee of the Politburo (Dahlem and Ulbricht), based first on Prague and then, after October 1936, on Paris. The Western Sector, for instance, directed from Amsterdam, seems at first to have included the three adjacent Party Districts, Ruhr, Lower Rhine and Middle Rhine, though the Middle Rhine District was later placed separately under a Sector Leader in Brussels. The Southern Sector, directed from Zürich, included North and South Bavaria, Baden and Würtemberg. Most extensive was the Central Sector, directed at first from Czechoslovakia and, after 1938, from Sweden, which included not only Berlin and Saxony, but most of eastern Germany as well.[56]

The KPD frontier-crossing organisation reached a high degree of efficiency, especially in mountainous areas. The Sector Leadership at Prague, for instance, in 1934 disposed of eleven frontier posts, which controlled a constant two-way traffic with Silesia, Saxony and Thuringia. According to a statement by one *émigré* Communist (Bruno Retzlaff, who was first smuggled out of Germany over this frontier and subsequently crossed to and fro on many clandestine missions), over a thousand crossings were made in one section of the Czech frontier in the years 1933–36 without a single loss.[57] This was perhaps exceptional, yet there is no doubt that the record was impressive, even in the Sudeten areas. One Communist woman, Minna Fritsch, once a school cleaner, made no less than forty illegal journeys to Germany. A contributory reason for the relative success of the KPD's activities on this frontier was that they were assisted by the Czech Communists, and that here, as elsewhere, they were supposed to be kept quite separate from the affairs of the exile community in the host country, whether or not those affairs involved an element of illegality.

The KPD suffered crippling losses in its clandestine operations in 1933–35, but it survived them, thanks to the self-discipline and loyalty of its members. Historians commenting from a hostile point of view have made much of complaints against *émigré* leaders for issuing calls from positions of comparative safety for what were virtually suicidal actions. Such complaints would not be unusual in the history of political emigration, but they are unfair in this case. The Politburo members had undertaken their share of dangerous missions in 1933 and would have been irresponsible if they had continued to expose themselves unnecessarily. Their task was not only to direct the underground struggle, but to preserve the continuity of the Party. They were to face a severe test in this latter respect in 1934–35, when a serious division of opinion arose among them over basic issues of strategy and tactics.

Other organisations which opposed the Nazis, notably the Social Democratic Party, aimed to build a clandestine movement of restricted scope and with strictly limited functions. The Communist Party differed from them in aiming to build a mass movement capable of overthrowing the Nazi régime. But how strong was the illegal Communist movement in fact?

The numerical strength of a clandestine resistance organisation can hardly, in the nature of things, be measured exactly. Estimates made by the organisers on the one hand and by the police on the other may be taken to provide some indication of outer limits. In the Lower Rhine District, according to a report which has already been quoted, some 50 per cent of the pre-1933 membership was still in contact, that is, paying dues, in the middle of 1933, and half of these were still politically active in some way.[58] The report by the Secretary of the same District, Otto Hertel, of a dues-paying membership of about 10 per cent of the 1932 figure in any one month of the first half of 1934 can probably be taken as a minimum, if only because the Secretary's wage came out of the dues so accounted for. These apparently varying estimates (apart from the different periods referred to) are roughly reconciled in Dr Peukert's conclusion that '[the KPD] remained in existence, despite waves of arrests, until about 1935 and embraced at times up to 10 per cent of the membership of 1932. Altogether, every other one of the 300,000 Communists may have taken part, for a time, more or less intensively in illegal activities.'[59] In Berlin, too, according to the recollections of Anton Ackermann, who was a member of the underground leadership in the city, there was a stable Communist Party organisation of some 5,000 members, which issued over a hundred illegal papers and periodicals during most of 1934 and the first half of 1935.[60] Whatever the limitations of Communist resistance, by however much it fell short of being a 'mass movement' in the literal sense, there can be no doubt that in the years 1933–35 at least, it involved some thousands of active members – a much higher proportion of the previous membership than was active in any other party.

The maintenance of the extensive network of illegal institutions of which the Communist camp was composed required a formidable organisational effort. The first condition of stability of these illegal organisations, and indeed of their very survival, as both the Communists and the authorities believed, was the development of an effective, working system of dues payments and the attendant routines of card stamping and regular accounting. These functions were performed, at least during the first two or three years, with exemplary German thoroughness, and provided the funds from which the living expenses of a much reduced number of paid full-time organisers were met, leaving a surplus towards the expenses of the Central Operative Leadership in Berlin, and, occasionally, a contribution to one of the 'mass organisations'. The familiar suggestion that the underground activities of the illegal KPD in Germany were being financed mainly from Moscow is not borne out by the surviving Party accounts, at least in 1934. It would appear from Dr Peukert's study of the Western Districts, for instance, that in February–March of that year the Lower Rhine District collected in dues and literature sales a total of 1,488 Reichsmarks, of which 1,116 were spent on nine people's wages and on travel, printing and sundries, leaving a surplus of 372 Reichsmarks, i.e. 25 per cent. In July 1934 the surplus was 40 per cent of receipts and was sent to the 'Central Committee', that is, presumably, to Berlin. It would thus appear that at that period the income of the central Party authorities (Reich Treasurer) was still mainly derived from collections within the country, with some supplementation from outside sources.

At first the extent to which the new conditions of illegality had increased the vulnerability of the Party, and the need to study the implications of that, were much underestimated. The traditional procedures for registering members and collecting their regular dues payments continued to be followed, the payments carefully recorded and accounted for and acknowledged by the issue of a stamp; money payments attested the renewal of a lapsed membership or the enlistment of a new recruit. A key figure of each Party unit, from the three or five-member group upwards, was its treasurer, while the first test of an effective organisation continued to be a balanced budget.

The careful keeping of accounts at each level made the Party vulnerable and provided evidence for many prosecutions, and has therefore often been criticised as showing lack of realism. But finance was only a means to an end. As long as the KPD persevered in the aim of building mass organisations financed by the contributions of their members, it could hardly dispense with the keeping of exact accounts and other formal records traditional in the German labour movement. To question the practice implied questioning much else besides.

The money collected was passed up to the District treasurer and used to meet the living and working expenses of a small number of District functionaries who lived illegally and occupied a key position in the underground organisation. If there was any surplus, it would be passed on to the treasurer of the Central Operative Leadership at Berlin and used to cover a deficit in other Districts or towards the expenses of the central organisation.

The collection of membership dues was combined with the distribution of locally produced party literature and the collection of payments for it, a traditional system which provided all too many clues for the police and evidence for the courts. The same was true of the filing of reports and other written records, a practice which was so deeply embedded in the tradition of the German labour movement that it continued to be followed in defiance of the 'rules of conspiracy' and in spite of much bitter experience. Already in June 1933 an archive filling three suitcases, accumulated by the Regional Adviser for the West and kept on a chicken farm belonging to one of his secretaries, had provided evidence for the prosecution of nearly a hundred people as well as the Adviser himself.[62] A year later, in a case already referred to, a report on the work of the Lower Rhine District of the Party during the first half of 1934 was seized by the police together with the remainder of the 'archive' which had accumulated in the lodging of the District Secretary.[63] This was not mere personal carelessness, for the central leadership itself had, at the end of June, sent out to all Districts an exhaustive questionnaire, asking for information about every aspect of the situation in Germany. This was only one of many instances of the bureaucratic style of work which may well have been one of the strengths of the Party in legal conditions, but was proving to be one of its weaknesses in conditions of illegality. To obtain so much paper was already a problem; to dispose of it afterwards was a still greater one.

The key posts in the underground Party were filled by paid functionaries, most of whom had had previous experience as full-time party organisers or editors, some only in their home Districts, others in several parts of Germany. The going underground of the Party had meant at first a reshuffling of posts within Districts, but soon security considerations and the need to make the best use of the shrinking reserve of cadres made it necessary to move experienced organisers to new Districts. Some gaps were filled by graduates of the Comintern's Lenin School in the USSR, some of whom returned to Germany towards the end of 1933 or in 1934, after a training lasting a year or more.

These key functionaries lived clandestinely, under false names and with forged papers. As they were increasingly often strangers to the Districts in which they worked, it would have been difficult for them to exist, and quite impossible for them to have developed significant political activity, without the support of a large number of local activists who could find them lodgings, act as couriers, arrange contacts for them, and keep them informed about the changing situation around them. The fact that most Party members were still unemployed was superficially an advantage, since it enabled them to devote much of their time to political activity; in reality, however, it was a disadvantage, since it limited the Party's influence in industry.

Many lessons were learned in the first years of the Communist Party's underground struggle, though at heavy cost. In the field of organisation, experience led to measures of decentralisation. In the latter months of 1934 and in 1935, many larger Districts and Sub-districts were divided, and after March 1935 the Central Operative Leadership in Berlin was replaced by a sort of federal system, in which the Party Districts in Germany were combined in a number of groups or Sectors, each of which was directed by a Sector Leadership in a neighbouring country – an acknowledgement, in a sense, that expectations of imminent revolution were no longer realistic. Under the sector system the illegal Party's contact with the German people was more difficult to maintain, but losses were reduced.

Experience showed that organisers living illegally could not expect to elude the police for more than a limited time: six months at the outside, short of exceptional luck or skill. They were therefore moved at intervals to new posts, and in some cases withdrawn from Germany for a time.

The Political Secretary and the few other paid functionaries whom a Party District might be able to afford at any given time lived a life almost unbelievably hard and precarious. Not being registered with the police, they could not apply for public assistance and were altogether dependent on the meagre and uncertain wage provided by the underground Party and on such help from Communist families as considerations of security permitted them to accept. Some were chronically undernourished and kept alive only by taking the occasional meal with a Communist family, at the very real risk of attracting attention. Sometimes they stayed overnight with a rota of local Party members or contacts; sometimes they themselves found a room to rent. In either case they were in danger from curious or malicious neighbours. One expedient sometimes resorted to was to rent a room from a Jewish houseowner, where a lodger was relatively safe from most types of visitor.[64] Even so, the clandestine functionary could not safely remain in his lodging during normal working hours, but was forced to pretend to have some occupation, such as that of a commercial traveller. This meant spending the daytime tramping the streets or sitting in cafés, expecting at any moment to have one's forged papers inspected by a police patrol.

It was a life which involved both a nervous and a physical strain which only the strongest constitutions could stand. Experience showed that the underground functionary, however careful, was rarely more than one step ahead of the police, who would almost certainly catch up within a relatively short time. When the organisation of the underground Party had been reviewed at the time of the setting up of the Central Operative Leadership in November 1933, it had been decided that functionaries living illegally should be moved at intervals of not more than three months. If this could have been strictly observed, there might have been fewer arrests, but the practical exigencies of the struggle and, as time went on, a shortage of cadres, led inevitably to risk-taking and neglect of the rules of conspiracy, and to heavy losses.

Despite all that had been written and spoken about the need to prepare for illegality, the Party was nevertheless in some ways ill-prepared for the conditions of 1933, and was hindered by the rigidity of its own structure from adapting itself quickly. The struggle which developed, if not strictly a 'mass struggle', was one in which many thousands of Communists threw themselves head-on into a fight which was virtually certain to end in arrest, torture, imprisonment and very possibly death. It is difficult not to be impressed by the fact that so many of them – rank-and-file members as well as experienced Party officials – volunteered again and again and often returned to the struggle after being released from a concentration camp on condition of abstaining from political activity. As we have noted, Dr Peukert has estimated that no less than half the 300,000 Communists at the time of Hitler's accession to power took part in some form of illegal political activity.[65]

Clandestine work in Germany was very difficult, and already in 1933 at least one District Political Secretary – Wilhelm Pinnecke, whose Middle Rhine (Cologne) District bordered on Belgium and Holland – found that he could carry out his work more effectively from beyond the frontier.[66] At that time such a move was not acceptable to the Party Leadership, from the broad political consideration that the illegal Party must be as close as possible to the masses, so as to be prepared, and to be known to be prepared, for the revolutionary situation when it developed. Occasionally, however, when a thorough discussion was desirable, as in the winter months of 1934–35, when a change of political line was under consideration, leading functionaries, both 'legal' and 'illegal', might be brought over the frontier for a conference with members of the Politburo. A regional conference attended by some three dozen delegates of the Rhine-Ruhr Districts took place at Amsterdam at Whitsuntide 1935,[67] following several smaller meetings. Earlier the same year Franz Dahlem and Walter Ulbricht had held similar meetings in Czechoslovakia.[68]

The Communists who were active against the Third Reich were in their vast majority working men, many of them qualified craftsmen. The fact that most of them were unemployed in and after 1933 did not distinguish them by class from other workers: indeed, their unemployment was sometimes a direct result of their previous political activities. Some historians have thought it significant that the proportion of women among them was small. But it was almost certain that the proportion of women active in the KPD was as great as that in the trade unions and other socialist parties, and considering their small numbers, women members played a distinguished and in many cases heroic role in the Communist underground. The founders and leaders of the KPD before 1933 had included notable women, and the records of the concentration camps for women (such as Ravensbrück) bear witness to much exceptional courage.[69]

The members of the Communist movement, whether men or women, employed or unemployed, were people who, by 1932, were deeply disillusioned with capitalism, were influenced by Marxist ideas, and were unable to see the way forward to a better life in any other way than by proletarian revolution. It was this general conviction, based on deeply felt experience and inability to see an alternative, that sustained the morale of active Communists. The strength of this morale undoubtedly came as a surprise to the police and threw out the political calculations of the Nazi leaders. Among the many tributes to the high quality of KPD functionaries which can be found in Gestapo records, the following is not untypical:

> . . . Again and again the facts confirm that the KPD has at its disposal a huge staff of functionaries with exceptional tactical and organising ability who, despite the most careful observation, were able by tireless work to rebuild the KPD in the individual Districts . . . partly with good success.[70]

It was partly because of this reserve of politically conscious, experienced functionaries and partly because of the loyalty and conviction of a large rank-and-file membership that the Party was able to recover from the severe shock of March 1933 and to carry on the struggle in increasingly unfavourable conditions.

Some historians, like Mason, have argued that the fact that the subsequent underground struggle was conducted by a 'reconstructed, centralised party bureaucracy' turned it into 'an almost unmitigated disaster'. It was an attempt, Mason says, to 'apply Lenin's principles of organisation, designed to fight the Tsarist police, to an utterly different society'.[71] It is of course true that the democratic centralist organisation of Communist parties had been adopted in part because it had apparently worked so well in Russia, and it is a matter of argument whether this form of organisation was the most appropriate for a revolutionary socialist party in the German republic of the 1920s. The Communists thought it was because they believed that a further revolutionary crisis was imminent and would confront them with the need to work in conditions of illegality. In those conditions, when they occurred in the 1930s, as the experience of the Social Democrats as well as of the Communists was to show, some at least of the features of democratic centralism must necessarily be adopted by any party which wished to continue the struggle in more than a token fashion. In the conditions of 1933, it may be argued that anti-Nazi parties in Germany had a choice of two roads: the road of struggle and the road of 'wait and see'. The former might lead – as it did – to failure in the short term; the latter proved to be a road to disaster in both short and long terms.

Political Activity

By the summer of 1933 it had become clear that the German Communist Party had survived the stunning blow it had suffered during the preceding winter and spring. During the next two years the Party fought back with astonishing determination, incurring new losses and replacing them from hidden reserves of strength. Its avowed aim was no less than the overthrow of the Nazi dictatorship, and this continued to be conceived of as a mass uprising led by a revolutionary party, on the model of 1917 in Russia. From this it followed that the first and most essential task was to maintain the Party itself and its subsidiary mass organisations by the familiar routines of political activity, adapted to circumstances of illegality.

Most members of the underground Communist movement were living legally in the sense of being registered with the police under their own names. In most cases their past connection with the movement was known to the police and they might well be under police supervision, especially if they had served a prison sentence or had been released from a concentration camp. Without the help of such locally-known Communists with their knowledge of the area and its labour movement, the leading functionaries who lived illegally might have found it impossible to make the sort of contacts they needed, or to acquire the sort of information about the situation in the district which they required for their reports. Conversely, of course, it was through locally registered activists that the police had most chance of getting onto the track of the key functionaries living illegally.

Brief *Treffs* and conversations of which no written record was made (except perhaps some points jotted down afterwards) were not always adequate for an organisation in which the habit of formal debate and the recording of decisions was so deeply rooted. Occasionally, therefore, activists in key positions, 'legal' and 'illegal', were brought across the frontier for a consultation with members of the *émigré* Politburo. On several occasions, when preparations were being made for the participation of the German Party in the Seventh World Congress of the International, something like regional conferences were held in neighbouring countries, attended in each case by some twenty clandestine activists and lasting for a week or more.[72] Contact between the underground movement and the exiled leadership was also maintained by occasional Party schools, which were also held in other countries.[73]

A characteristic feature of democratic centralism as practised by Communist parties is the issue of detailed directives by higher Party bodies to guide the activities of the basic units. This practice was maintained to a surprising degree in the conditions of clandestinity, through a network of illegal publications, of which some account will be given later. Some of these publications were specifically addressed to Party functionaries and contained statements of Party policy and organisational material which would in normal times have been filed for reference and for quotation in speeches. Such political directives would have served little purpose if they had not taken account of the actual situation, both in the country as a whole and in particular areas; and in this respect the leadership, both in Berlin and abroad, was now more dependent than ever before on regular and truthful reporting by local and District functionaries. The increased accessibility of the KPD archives in recent years has revealed that the Party leadership did call for and receive comparatively full reports on the situation in Germany. At the end of June 1934, to take a striking example, the Politburo circulated to District Secretaries a detailed questionnaire, calling for returns on many aspects of the situation in the Reich.

It is clear from surviving correspondence that the Party leadership was aware of the danger that reports sent to them might be coloured by wishful thinking, and often insisted on the need for objectivity.[74] How far such warnings were heeded is not easy to judge. The ultra-left line which was current doctrine in the Comintern at that time undoubtedly fostered the illusion that the economic and political situation in Germany was worsening and the conditions for proletarian revolution maturing, and this may well have led senior functionaries in Germany to overemphasise in their reports evidence which tended to confirm those conclusions. To do otherwise might have been seen as an undermining of the morale of the underground Party. By about the middle of 1934, however, a note of realism was becoming apparent in many reports. Here again, it is difficult to judge how far the changing perception in the Districts was a cause and how far a consequence of the change of line at the top.

A developed system of written reports and directives was a necessary feature of a centralised organisation like that of the KPD, and they in turn made necessary a developed system of couriers. Controlled by a section of the Operative Leadership in Berlin, these couriers kept up a weekly or fortnightly contact with the Regional Advisers and District Secretaries, as well as with the Central Committee's Secretariat at Paris and, increasingly, with frontier posts in neighbouring countries.

Another characteristic feature of the comparatively bureaucratic organisation which was carried over from the pre-1933 Communist Party into the period of illegality, was the importance which attached to typewriters, duplicating machines and other office equipment. The concealment of these in flats, roof-spaces and garden huts had been among the Party's most distinctive preparations for illegality. But the use of these machines now had its dangers. It offered too many clues to police investigators because it involved both the bringing in of more individuals, as typists and as technical or secretarial assistants, and the possibility of tracing the source of paper and other supplies. When it came to operating these machines, further complications arose. The typewriter and the duplicating machine might have to be hidden in one place and taken to another place to be used, and the place of storage might have to be changed at intervals. Then there was the problem of obtaining supplies of paper and ink without leaving traces and clues. It can safely be said that, however many precautions were taken, the producers of written or printed propaganda were virtually certain to be traced before long. Moreover, the keeping of written material, whether handwritten, typed, duplicated or printed, inevitably resulted in an accumulation of paper and the growth of an archive which could quickly grow too big to be easily disposed of by a functionary living in clandestinity, even if he could persuade himself to do without it. In more than one case, such a fast-growing, unmanageable archive, piling up in suitcases, was 'inherited' by a clandestine functionary from his predecessor and ultimately fell into the hands of the Gestapo, to whom it not only yielded far-reaching insights into the Party's organisation in the District, and therefore the means of breaking through the defences of suspects in interrogation, but also provided prosecution evidence in a series of trials.

If the maintenance of its own organisation was the underground Communist movement's first concern, the next was to develop a lively political agitation aimed at countering Nazi demagogy and exposing the real aims and interests that lay behind it. The production and distribution of printed and duplicated propaganda material had always been a prominent aspect of the party's work, and its comparative importance was increased, now that it was impossible to hold public meetings. The attempt was made to continue the production of a wide range of publications at all levels, both of the Party and of the mass organisations. These ranged from the central organs of the Party and of the International down to local branch papers and brochures, leaflets and stickers produced by individual cells, and included, though in reduced quantities and uncertain regularity, the continued publication of the District Party newspaper and the District organ for Party functionaries. The content of these papers will be discussed in the next section. Here it may be noted that all these illegal papers – except for purely local stickers and leaflets – were sold, and that Party members were expected to subscribe to some of them and to pay their 'literature' money to their cell treasurer together with their membership dues, as well as to sell copies to others.

The distribution of Party literature in this traditional manner left many clues behind for the police and was ultimately given second place – in theory at least – after oral propaganda, such as group chanting of Red Front slogans in the midst of Labour Front rallies, or the discreet repetition of rumours in public lavatories or in such public houses as were habitually frequented by Communists and sympathisers. There was, as a county prefect in Bavaria remarked in a report of June 1933, a 'shadow world' of ex-Communists, centring on such pubs in solidly working-class districts and engaging in forms of political activity which the police found difficult to pin down. People would be seen standing round in groups in public places, talking seriously in low voices and then lapsing into silence when anyone in authority appeared.[75] The police often knew, or suspected, that such behaviour covered more serious opposition activities, such as collecting money for the families of political prisoners or passing on news derived from illicit listening to foreign broadcasts. They could not always find proof of their suspicions and therefore kept up a constant pressure on workers with left-wing records, pulling them in for questioning and searching their homes on the slightest pretext – or none at all. Sometimes they mistook for a Communist a more or less non-political working man whose exasperation with the petty tyranny of the Nazi authorities overflowed in a Red Front song on his way home at night after a pint or two of beer.[76]

Group radio-listening in garden huts, and the discussion of current news during country rambles were not the only form of political discussion which the underground Communists engaged in. A striking characteristic of the clandestine Communist activists was the importance they attached to Party-political education. In September 1933, for instance, the central Party leadership within Germany planned to send some twenty leading functionaries from the Western Districts to France for a Party school, which was to last for a month.[77] Nothing is more remarkable about the outline syllabus which they devised for the school than the high proportion of the total time to be devoted to basic theory, and the importance attached to the making available of sufficient copies of the Marxist classics.[78]

Another point which emerges from the Party correspondence of the years 1933–35 is that, although no far-reaching changes in policy were made, the underground Party leaders were concerned, despite the pressures of the day-to-day struggle, to clarify and develop the policy of the Party on a number of issues, with a view to overcoming its isolation and winning allies. In the summer of 1933, for instance, John Schehr, head of the Home Leadership in Germany, asked his collaborators to prepare a series of memoranda on such topics as agriculture, civil servants, and tradesmen and artisans; he emphasised that the memoranda were not intended for publication, but to provide a self-critical review of the Party's past work in each field.[79]

The Party's avowed aim of building up its strength could only be achieved by recruiting new members, and the leadership repeatedly called for new efforts in this area. How serious an effort was made is difficult to judge, but in any case it does not seem to have been very successful. Many Social Democrats were disillusioned with the virtual collapse of their party in 1932–33, and there were strong impulses towards unity in some places. But in the main it seems that only a minority of those so affected went over to the Communist Party. The hostility which had accumulated over the years had left a poisoned atmosphere in which anything like co-operation on equal terms was almost impossible to bring about. Most Communists continued to think of unity as simply winning over Social Democrats to repudiate their own party, its history and leaders. The most successful attempts at unity at this period were made by the Communist Youth League, whose Western Districts, at least, had already in the autumn of 1933 entered into serious discussions with Catholic youth leaders at Düsseldorf, and with certain nationalist youth leaders. These discussions, although they were inconclusive at the time, were to have some importance in the long run.[80]

The building up of organisations, the development of policies, the winning of recruits and allies were, of course, only means to an end and served little purpose unless they enabled the Party to conduct a day-to-day and week-by-week political fight against the Third Reich. It has to be asked, therefore, how effectively, if at all, was the Communist Party able to mobilise public feeling against the crimes and repressive acts perpetrated by the Nazis. Was it to any extent able to puncture Nazi demagogy and to open people's eyes to the inevitable consequences of war preparations? How quickly did the Party react to events? Did it ever succeed in capturing the initiative?

It might be thought that to publicise Nazi atrocities against opponents, whether these took the form of judicial murder or of extra-legal terror, was to frighten potential recruits and so to serve the ends of Nazi violence. But that argument, if occasionally mentioned in passing, was immediately dismissed and found no place in Communist thinking. As a rule, the illegal Party at all levels gave the greatest publicity to acts of terror, such as the death sentences which, in several places, were imposed retrospectively on members of the Red Front Fighters League for affrays which had taken place in 1932.[81] In such cases the Communists' response was to call for 'mass protests' by conventional methods such as demonstrations at funerals or collections of money for wreaths, or help to bereaved relatives, or even in some cases signature collection or lightning strikes.

Such protests may have played into the hands of the police by adding to their lists of the politically unreliable, but that does not necessarily mean that they were pointless. The Central Operative Leadership reported in March 1934, for instance, that in some cases storm troopers or members of the Nazi Factory Cell Organisation (NSBO) had joined in protests against political murders or had contributed to wreaths for the victims, and they called on underground District Leaderships to give more, not less, publicity to local murders and executions.[82]

If the Communist leaders had any doubt that the way to react to Nazi repression was to take the offensive against it, all such doubts were removed by the experience of the Reichstag Fire Trial of

September to December 1933. The political defeat which was there inflicted on the Nazi leaders was due to a number of factors, amongst which the evidence produced at the international court of jurists in London beforehand and the personal courage and political acumen of Georgi Dimitrov have usually received the greatest prominence. The 'Dimitrov strategy' however, was to some extent a collective product and it made an impact because the clandestine Communist Party was prepared to follow it up. Already at the beginning of September 1933, the Party's leadership within Germany foresaw that the forthcoming trial would be a political battle of crucial importance and appointed a three-man committee to plan the campaign round it.[83] In a letter of instructions to the committee, Schehr, as head of the Politburo's Internal Leadership, criticised some of the material put out before then as striking too defensive a note. The Party's propaganda, he wrote, should take the offensive, directly accusing Hitler and Goering of responsibility for the Fire, and only secondarily set out the case for the defence.[84]

Following this general line, Schehr gave instructions that the Committee in Berlin and the leaders of the Districts should intensify their activities, so as to build up a powerful campaign round the trial, with street and shop-floor agitation culminating if possible in demonstrations or lightning factory-gate meetings, and in the formation of anti-fascist unity committees and joint Communist-Social Democratic self-defence squads. The campaign committee was urged to feel free to use its imagination and initiative in leading the campaign, though at the same time it was to render a daily report to the Politburo. This characteristically ambitious programme was subsequently promoted by the issue of a twice-weekly (later weekly) press bulletin by the Centre and Districts, containing reports of trial proceedings and texts such as that of Dimitrov's concluding speech. The undoubted impact of the campaign within Germany as well as abroad was heightened by the smuggling into Germany and illegal distribution of many thousand copies of *The Brown Book of the Hitler Terror and the Burning of the Reichstag* and of the text of Dimitrov's speeches and interrogatories at the trial. These famous publications, disguised by titles such as 'Home Heating by Electricity' (*Elektrowärme im Haushalt*), became widely known in Germany and evoked a lively response. Evidence collected by the police shows that in one Rhineland town Communists collected money at their weekly 'skat' (card-playing) evenings to buy the Brown Book, while in another town, in Westphalia, members of a cycling club contributed to sending one of their members to Holland to buy the book.

In campaigning round the Trial, the Communists had to convince Germans that the Nazi allegations that the Fire had been started by the KPD as a signal for an intended insurrection was untrue, even though the Party was avowedly aiming at the revolutionary overthrow of the régime. The Party's propaganda was therefore at this time concerned to explain the reasons for its rejection of 'individual terrorism' and to define the conditions in which insurrection would in its view be justified.[85]

The world-wide publicity which the trial attracted and the acquittal of the accused Communists marked a significant political victory for the Communist Party over the Nazi rulers, and the Party leadership looked forward to building on it a similar, or greater, campaign round the expected trial of Ernst Thälmann which had been repeatedly announced and postponed. After the Fire trial, the Central Operative Leadership reported that 'Thälmann committees' had been formed in some Berlin factories and that in some cases they even included members of the Nazi Factory Cell Organisation (NSBO).[86] District Leaderships were instructed to try to form such committees in factories in their own area, and there was talk of making these committees the basis of United Front activity, or of infiltration inside the Nazi German Labour Front.

The Communists were not alone in drawing conclusions from the experience of the Reichstag Fire trial. The Nazi leaders determined to have no repetition of it, and, to be on the safe side, they postponed Thälmann's trial indefinitely. When Schehr fell into their hands they had him murdered rather than tried. They also put in hand, in April 1934, a drastic revision of the law of treason, with heightened penalties, and at the same time created a new court (The People's Court) to deal with it summarily and without appeal. For the future, political trials in Nazi Germany were to take place in conditions in which the possibility of a major political demonstration in the court room was practically excluded. An accused might occasionally withdraw in court statements which he had previously made under interrogation, or protest against maltreatment; but both attendance at trials and the reporting of proceedings were strictly controlled.

Since the Communists aimed at building an anti-fascist mass movement, they could not afford to ignore the great mass rallies arranged by the Nazis, even if they could manage no more than a crude, locally-produced leaflet. In May 1933, for instance, on the occasion of the Nazis' Schlageter celebration, discussed in chapter six below, Hugo Paul, the KPD Instructor for Düsseldorf, wrote a well-phrased leaflet explaining how the working class was deceived about its real interests by nationalist slogans.[87] Later in the same year, when the Nazi Party's annual rally at Nuremberg was impending, the Communists made earlier and fuller preparations. Already a month before the event, the Central Operative Leadership wrote to the North Bavarian District (which centred on Nuremberg), calling on it to make preparations for a bold agitation both before and during the rally, to draw attention to the continuing mass unemployment and to protest against the terror against the working class, which could be expected to be intensified during the rally.[88] Leaflets on these themes, it was suggested, should be introduced into sleeping quarters occupied by the visiting Nazi 'masses', as well as being scattered along the route of the march from chimneys and tall buildings. Children's balloons and paper dragons bearing anti-Nazi catchwords should be floated. Best of all would be bold, sensational actions such as the painting of slogans on the stadium itself, the planting of red flags, shouting or singing by well-placed chorus-groups. Communists who lived in Nuremberg should not hesitate to take in visiting Nazis as overnight guests, in order to explore their opinions and perhaps influence them, especially if it could be shown that there had been gross favouritism in the provision of accommodation.

In sketching these outlines of a campaign, the Operative Leadership suggested that it might provide an occasion for joint actions with Social Democrats, such as protest strikes against Nazi violence or the setting up of a joint defence and warning service. The whole project, on the preparation of which the District Leadership was to make a report, evidently involved big risks and much boldness. It shows how ambitious (some might say unrealistic) the planning of the KPD's clandestine activities was in the first year of the Third Reich. It remains to be seen how heavy the cost was, and how long the Party could continue to incur the losses involved.

The Nuremberg rallies happened only once a year. More frequent, and from the point of view of the Communists more important, were the activities of the German Labour Front, a truly mass organisation, whose function was to disarm the workers and get them to renounce the struggle for their class interests under the deceptive notion of a 'people's community'. The first instinct of many active Communists was to refuse to join the Front and to boycott its activities. The Communist leadership, however, while providing material for the exposure of the Front as an instrument of the employing class, nevertheless urged workers to make use of such opportunities as it offered for voicing their grievances and championing their interests; not surprisingly, the attempt to combine these two approaches constantly posed difficult tactical problems. Should workers be advised to stay away from the Front's annual 'Spring Festival' (which had replaced the traditional May Day of the labour movement) or to attend and to use the occasion to spread anti-Nazi propaganda by whispering or shouting slogans? Or should they be advised to appear at the beginning of the march (where absence might be checked) but to desert *en route*, so that the ultimate effect was one of failure? Or should an attempt be made to sabotage the whole event by spreading advance rumours that it had been cancelled? Surviving documents of the clandestine leadership of the KPD's Berlin District show that in 1935 instructions along these lines were issued to Sub-districts towards the end of April, and were passed down to street and factory cells. Some of the new tactics, involving the use of 'legal' opportunities, are described in the memoirs of Anton Ackermann, who was a leading member of the Berlin Sub-district in the period from 1933 until 1935, when he became a candidate member of the Politburo.[89]

The election of Councillors of Trust in work-places in the spring of 1934 and 1935 raised similar issues. Since the workers of an enterprise could not nominate their own candidates, they had the choice only of voting for or against candidates put forward by the employer and the Labour Front, or of abstaining or spoiling the ballot paper with some political statement. Here again, the most constructive course open to Communists was to advise workers, when the circumstances were favourable, to vote *for* candidates who had no previous Nazi record and *against* those who had. If, after the election, the authorities published no figures, it could be assumed and whispered that the vote had gone against them, although published figures were not, of course, necessarily correct.

Councillors of Trust had no powers, serving only as liaison between management and workers, but pressure could be exerted on them to take up workers' grievances, and the concern of a

Communist Party cell in a factory was to formulate these grievances and keep up pressure on the Councillors. In the Heliwatt radio works in the Berlin suburb of Charlottenburg, for example, the Communist Party's Sub-district leadership issued a leaflet in April 1935, denouncing the recently elected Councillors as weak, and listing a number of complaints which they ought to take up.[90] These included the allegation that the date of the annual week's holiday had been arbitrarily fixed by the management at a time inconvenient to the workforce and without any consultation, as well as the perennial grievance of compulsory deductions from wages, and non-payment for time which the workers were forced to spend listening to National Socialist speeches. Among the questions dealt with in leaflets distributed by other Communist Party factory cells at that time were a management's refusal to issue proper piece-work contracts, dismissals at short notice or without good cause, failure to provide the customary assistants to skilled craftsmen, and, as so often, the rigging of works elections and lack of consultation about the annual holiday.[91]

Such leaflets usually went on from particular issues to a statement of broader political conclusions, such as the need to keep wages in line with rising prices. Often they proclaimed the need for united action by workers of different political views, for the rebuilding of the trade unions, and perhaps for the immediate election of shop-floor delegates to lobby the Councillors of Trust and the management and the calling of a general works assembly. 'Be bold!' was the keynote of many such leaflets. 'These things have been done elsewhere and have been known to succeed.'[92]

Throughout the 1930s the Communist Party struggled to give effect to the current line of concentrating its activities in factories and workplaces, despite the unfavourable circumstances caused by continuing mass unemployment. In June 1934, to cite one example, the Central Operative Leadership made a special report to the Politburo about conditions in the chemical industry of the South-West Region.[93] There was much economic discontent, they reported, but it had had little political effect because of the lack of organisation, but they were now making strenuous efforts to build cells and develop political activity in the big chemical plants. They had appointed a special, paid Instructor for the Region and several sub-instructors for particular factories, and they had allocated 50 Reichsmarks to pay for the production of literature for two major firms. The Communist cells in these firms, they reported, had made contact with some Social Democratic workers and also with some Nazis. One of the Social Democrats had given the Communists some support, though unfortunately, they added, he had got himself dismissed by foolishly refusing to give the Hitler salute at a works meeting.

So much importance was attached to the extension of the Party's influence in the factories that the Party Secretariat ordered the replacement of the Sub-district leader in the Höchst chemical works, because he favoured the production of one clandestine paper for the whole area instead of separate illegal papers for each major factory; and they insisted that publicity be given (in undergrond circles) to this decision.[94]

Communist resistance to the Nazis met its first major test in the summer of 1934, when the contradictions within the régime came to a head in the Night of the Long Knives. The Communists were shown to have been right in thinking that there was serious discontent among both workers and the lower-middle class, both on economic grounds and from disillusionment with leaders who had failed to implement their promises of social revolution. At the same time, the possibility that the several-million-strong army of radical Brownshirts might form the basis of a new German Army, at a time when President Hindenburg – hitherto the bulwark holding back the 'brown hordes' – was on his deathbed, frightened the representatives of big business and other conservatives. On 17 June 1934, Papen, the political spokesman of the conservative classes, issued an ultimatum to Hitler in a speech at Marburg. The country seemed to be on the brink of civil war. But Hitler overcame the crisis with comparative ease and emerged stronger than ever, having destroyed all those – whether radical Nazis or conservatives – who aspired to share his power. The Communists, however, failed to take advantage of the crisis. They were shown again to have underestimated Hitler and the Nazi movement, to have failed to appreciate the full extent and significance of their own defeat in 1933 and of their consequent inability to win credence as an alternative, despite the widespread discontent.

The Communists' failure was reflected in Hitler's success in the plebiscite of August 1934, which set the seal of popular consent on the new concentration of power in his hands. Even more striking was the Nazi victory in the Saar plebiscite of January 1935. The

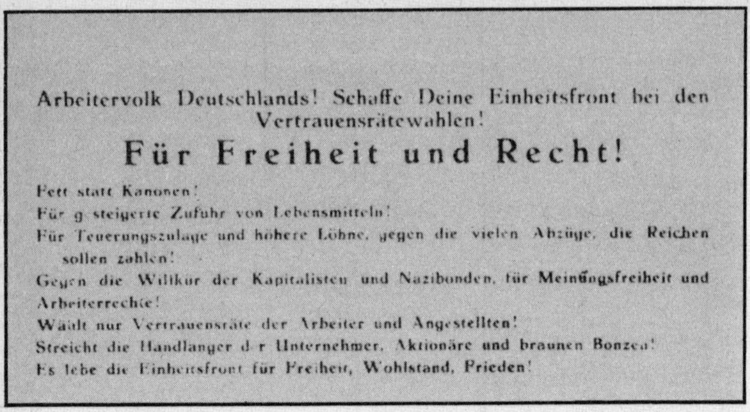

Arbeitervolk Deutschlands! Schaffe Deine Einheitsfront bei den Vertrauensrätewahlen!

Für Freiheit und Recht!

Fett statt Kanonen!
Für gesteigerte Zufuhr von Lebensmitteln!
Für Teuerungszulage und höhere Löhne, gegen die vielen Abzüge, die Reichen sollen zahlen!
Gegen die Willkür der Kapitalisten und Nazibonden, für Meinungsfreiheit und Arbeiterrechte!
Wählt nur Vertrauensräte der Arbeiter und Angestellten!
Streicht die Handlanger der Unternehmer, Aktionäre und braunen Bonzen!
Es lebe die Einheitsfront für Freiheit, Wohlstand, Frieden!

Frauen und Mädchen!

Aus Betrieben und Büros verjagt, auf's Land deportiert, zeigt euren Haß gegen Hitler!

Am 19. August ein entschlossenes

Nein!

1934 Communist Party leaflets; *above*, urging workers to reject Nazi candidates in the Council of Trust 'elections' and *below*, calling on women to vote no in the 19 August plebiscite

Saarlanders, placed under a League of Nations administration by the Treaty of Versailles, had to decide whether they wished to join France, to join Germany or to continue under League of Nations rule. The Communists and Social Democrats and other democratic forces campaigned unitedly for the *status quo*, yet the electorate voted overwhelmingly to join Germany, despite the anti-fascist feeling which undoubtedly existed among the workers of the Saar. Another indication of the contradictory situation was that in the *Vertrauensrat* (Shop Stewards) elections which were held a few months later in German factories, the Nazis had so little reason to be satisfied with the results that they never again held such elections.

The growing power of nationalism in Germany represented in some ways an alternative to social and economic aspirations, and this confronted the Communists with new problems of tactics. One expedient to which they resorted was to try to give an international character to anti-Nazi activity in German industry, by a system of sponsorship, under which the workforce of a foreign factory agreed to help the workers' struggle in a particular German enterprise. How extensive, or effective, such arrangements were is difficult to judge.

As German war preparations developed, the combatting of nationalism and militarism, and the fostering of internationalism played an increasing role in the Communist Party's propaganda. Already in June 1934, the Central Operative Leadership reported that it had made plans for an 'Anti-war Day' in connection with which an address would be circulated and signatures collected both in German factories and in factories across the border in France.[95]

The introduction of conscription in 1935 furnished the occasion for a renewed Communist agitation among youth. In the Berlin suburb of Pankow, for instance, 1,500 leaflets were produced in the name of the Communist Youth League and of a group of the former Free Trade Union Youth. The text contained an argument that conscription was not, as the Nazi alleged, for national defence, but would serve purposes of imperialist conquest and aggression; it concluded by calling for a united struggle for a 'free and socialist Germany'.[96]

Another aspect of Nazi war preparations was the coming into the open, also in March 1935, of a new German air force and the Communist Party lost no time in issuing warning leaflets. When Goering announced the holding of a big air defence exercise on 22 March, the Communist leadership in the Berlin suburb of Pankow produced 400 duplicated leaflets protesting against it. The leaflet ridiculed the exercise as giving a totally false sense of security, and urged readers to sabotage it by non-participation. Then, not untypically of Communist Party propaganda at that time, after having effectively argued along these lines, the leaflet ended by proclaiming that the bombing of Berlin could only be prevented by breaking the fascist yoke and opening the way to a proletarian Soviet dictatorship.[97]

Almost all the activities of the illegal German Communist Party, as its propaganda amply demonstrates, were in the tradition of bourgeois democratic politics. It called for the setting up of committees and the holding of protest meetings, for the collection of signatures and of money, for chalking and leafletting and for whispering campaigns and strikes and the management of factory elections. But methods of terrorism, whether individual or collective, or even of sabotage at this stage, were consciously rejected. Ulbricht, writing to Schehr on 26 August 1933 about the KPD's line on the forthcoming Reichstag Fire trial, said that the Party must explain its rejection of 'individual terror' and also explain the conditions in which it would consider an uprising justified.[98]

It had soon become clear that to fight National Socialism by conventional forms of struggle inherited from the Empire and the Republic was suicidally costly. Yet the Party had no thought of lying low, but continued to insist on the absolute necessity of asserting its presence, whatever the cost, and its directives repeatedly called for more boldness. Dr Peukert criticises such calls as cynical when one considers the high risk attached to such activities as leaflet distribution.[99] In fact, Party leaders and Instructors were not unaware of the dangers and of the extreme difficulty of combining the 'offensive spirit' with the observance of what were called 'the rules of conspiracy', that is, systematic caution. But to the Communists of that time inactivity was unthinkable. Yet to change their Party's traditional forms of struggle would have involved – as it ultimately did involve – a radical rethinking of their whole strategy and tactics.

The conventional democratic forms of struggle to which the German Communist Party continued to confine itself made its clandestine organisations highly vulnerable to pursuit by the Gestapo, especially after the stiffening of the treason laws in April 1934. The Gestapo aimed at destroying, not merely the morale of the Communist Party, but its very existence as a working organisation, by keeping its members isolated from the rest of society until they had either renounced their principles or been utterly demoralised and discredited. To continue Party membership or activity in any form was to be guilty of 'preparation of treason', which was subject to punishment by death or imprisonment with hard labour for life;

those who were still unrepentent at the end of their sentence were usually sent to concentration camps for an unspecified period.

The Gestapo's experts on Communism at each level studied the underground Party and tried to keep in close touch with its activities. They did not always arrest immediately the activists who came to their notice, but often watched them for a time and tried to form a picture of the organisation to which they belonged, or even to infiltrate it. Only when these possibilities were exhausted did they have recourse to mass arrests and interrogations and to trials.

By the end of 1934 the majority of the Party's leading cadres still in Germany were probably already behind bars or in exile. But as the membership moved from freedom to captivity, the struggle itself moved into the courts, prisons and concentration camps. Already before the end of 1933 Dimitrov had set a supreme example of how to fight back from the dock, and the lesson, spread by the Brown Book, was not lost on German Communists, though the Nazis saw to it that little or no publicity was given to any further attempts to use the dock as a platform. Yet, despite all difficulties, some episodes became known and raised anti-fascist morale. One such event was the escape, in September 1934, of a District Secretary, Hermann Matern, and two of his comrades from the prosecutor's prison at Stettin. They were not recaptured and eventually reached Czechoslovakia, despite the fact that a high reward was offered for information and that their escape involved the co-operation of many people, including some who were not Party members.[100]

Mutual trust necessarily played a large part in Communist as in other resistance organisations, especially as members were virtually certain, sooner or later, to be pressed to betray comrades by every inducement, including physical torture. Few if any could be confident that they could resist such pressure to the end (though surprisingly many did) and although most of the reported suicides while in custody were probably really murders, some at least represented the voluntary self-sacrifice of prisoners at the end of their strength. Some leading resisters who survived owed their lives to the suicide of a comrade who was to have figured as the chief witness against them. One of these was Hugo Paul, formerly KPD Instructor at Düsseldorf, who, released in 1939 after six years in prison and concentration camp, was re-arrested and charged with treason in 1943 and might well have been sentenced to death if the prosecution's main witness had not committed suicide.[101]

The organisation of resistance by prisoners in concentration camps was more difficult than any other and constitutes a subject apart. Even here there were a few successful escapes, like that of Hans Beimler, the Communist Party's Political Secretary for South Bavaria, from the camp at Dachau near Munich in May 1933. More frequent were the cases in which Communist prisoners in a camp achieved by co-operation some degree of control of their environment and were able to conduct some form of political activity. Indeed, it was only by organisation among the prisoners that they could hope to survive in the camps, while on the other hand the SS could not run the camps in the long run without some degree of collaboration on the part of the prisoners, in which SS terror and the political consciousness of prisoners each played a part. Usually the camp administration tried to play off the professional criminals against the 'politicals', thus introducing a further element of persecution of the latter. But in some circumstances, especially in the later years of the camps, when economic functions were added to their original penal purposes, the contrast between the corruption of the criminals and the efficiency of the 'politicals' was such that the SS reluctantly entrusted the key prisoner posts to individual anti-fascists who might be virtually elected by their fellows. Such a development called for organisation among the prisoners and this was usually based on a clandestine Communist Party group and opened the way in some cases to remarkable political achievements.

The first stage of resistance in the camps was to survive and to help others to survive. This meant retaining a minimum of physical strength and a basic will to live, and this in turn meant preserving some hope for the future. Many memoirs of survivors show that the ties of comradeship and mutual support of a party group often played a vital role in creating the conditions of individual survival in the camps. In many cases 'political' camp functionaries or Party groups probably saved the lives of newly arrived prisoners who were on the verge of collapse, by providing them with extra food (donated by other prisoners or filched from the SS canteen) or with medicines from the sick-bay, and by securing their allocation to one of the less arduous jobs. Such comradeship also helped to restore the will to live and hope for the future. But acts of solidarity on any significant scale were impossible without organisation. The maintenance of an organisation under the eyes of the SS necessitated an iron discipline, and self-discipline. Those who took office under the SS had to walk a moral and political tightrope if they were to serve their fellow prisoners without attracting the wrath of the camp authorities. On occasion, underground leaderships undoubtedly gave short shrift to the selfish and unco-operative, or, above all, to those suspected of acting as informers.

These basic forms of resistance in the camps inevitably involved co-operation between Communists and others, especially Social Democrats and Christians, who had been political enemies of Communism, and attitudes inevitably changed on both sides. Doctrinal differences loomed less large in face of the common struggle for survival, and the possiblity of co-operation was experienced as a fact. These changes of attitude were undoubtedly one factor in bringing about the rapprochement of the two working-class parties and of other anti-fascist elements after the war. Meanwhile Communists, who in the first years formed the majority of the prisoners in the camps, digested their experiences in many camp discussions, and the trend of their thought was communicated to the Party leadership in Germany and abroad by members who were released. It was not without some influence on the development of Party policy during the first years of the Third Reich.

An important condition of the morale, and therefore of the survival, of political prisoners in the concentration camps, as well as in other prisons, was the assurance that their dependants were being protected from the worst forms of distress. The work of the Red Aid in caring for the families of prisoners was thus an important aspect of the political struggle, and it was an activity which the Nazis therefore treated as 'preparation of treason' and punished with heavy penalties.

The German Communist Party's activities in the years 1933–35 fell far short of its ambitions and expectations. Constantly striving to recover the political initiative and to take the offensive against the Nazi tyranny, the Party was repeatedly forced back with heavy losses on to a defensive struggle to keep itself in existence. Gradually too, its members – leaders and rank-and-file alike, though at different times – were forced to come to terms with the fact that they had suffered a major defeat in 1933, and that the struggle ahead would be a longer and harder one than they had foreseen.

Press and Propaganda

The main weapon of underground struggle in these first years was the written word. The Communist movement in Germany, like the Social Democratic movement before it, had been accustomed to publish a wide variety of newspapers and periodicals. In addition to the Party's central daily newspaper, *Rote Fahne* (Red Flag), there were in January 1933 thirty-five other Communist daily papers of District or regional scope, many of which printed separate editions for particular areas or towns within the District.[102] Moreover, in addition to papers designed to be of general interest, there were others, published weekly or fortnightly, addressed from a Communist point of view to specialised readerships such as party functionaries, trade unionists, youth or those interested in sport.

Most of these publications had never had more than quite small circulations, scarcely reaching beyond the Party membership, but their production and distribution had played a key role in Party life. Their reports and advertisements kept members in touch with the Party's activities and reminded them of their obligations to it, while the delivery of the paper to subscribers, and the collection of their subscriptions, also served the purpose of 'collective organiser' (as Lenin had once put it). The editing of the main regional organs, too, provided a training and livelihood for a not inconsiderable number of leading Party figures. The editor-in-chief, indeed, was often a member of the District Secretariat – the inner political leadership – and might, in the event of a vacancy, step into the shoes of the political secretary himself.[103]

In 1933, when it became impossible, save in very exceptional circumstances, to hold meetings, demonstrations or strikes, the publication and distribution of illegal literature assumed even greater importance. Indeed it is hardly too much to say that the Party saw as its primary task, the main method of putting into effect its current strategy of 'revolutionary mass action', the illegal maintenance of the whole range of its previously legal publications, with as large a print run as its organisation was capable of handling.

The quantity and variety of the illegal literature which is known, or reported on reasonably good evidence, to have been produced by the KPD in the years 1933–35, is remarkable.[104] *Rote Fahne*, after a few weeks of confusion and reorganisation following the Nazi accession to power, reappeared illegally in the middle of March

1933, with a print run, according to a press report, of 300,000 copies, at first in duplicated form and thereafter twice or thrice monthly in printed form.[105] In the more important industrial regions the former District Party newspapers also continued to be published in printed form, either as separate papers or as local editions of *Rote Fahne*. In addition, the clandestine Party organisations in some towns, in Berlin suburbs and in some larger factories, produced their own local papers in duplicated form in quantities varying from 100 copies to 2,000 copies monthly.[106]

The Young Communist League's paper, *Junge Garde*, and the Red Aid paper, *Tribunal*, also continued to be published clandestinely, as was a paper for the Revolutionary Trade Union Opposition; so too were specialised papers, both national and regional, containing organisational and policy material for Party functionaries. Moreover, besides publications which it was intended to issue with some regularity as numbers of an illegal newspaper or periodical, particular documents or texts of speeches were often put out as brochures, printed either in Germany or abroad, in the disguise – as far as the outside cover and opening pages went – of a commercial or literary publication, a city street-plan, a pamphlet on 'Skiing in the Black Forest', and so on.[107]

Altogether a huge quantity of illegal material was produced by the Communist Party. According to a report made by the Party leadership in 1935, the Party had published in the first five months of Nazi rule more than 1,000 local and District newspapers, with a total print run of over 2,000,000 copies.[108] According to another report, the number of District, city, ward and factory papers published by the KPD in 1934 amounted to between 2,000 and 3,000, with a total print run of about 1,200,000 copies.[109] Many of these, of course, were purely local sheets, put out irregularly in duplicated form and often in no more than a couple of hundred copies. Peukert also estimates that the KPD produced over a million leaflets annually, at least up to 1935–36.[110]

Most of these figures are derived from reports made by the Party leadership, who compiled them from the returns of District and local Party units. There seems to be no reason to cast doubt on them as estimates of quantities produced, especially when one considers that not all such publications will have been reported to the Centre. Police reports, too, frequently comment on the high quantities which came to their attention and were confiscated.[111]

The Communists' concern to produce illegal literature in very large quantities, which a disapproving critic has called *Tonnenideologie* ('quantity mania')[112] distinguishes their activity in this field from that of most other anti-Nazi groups, who tended to confine themselves either to specific occasions or topics, or to the circulation of internal party material to a limited number of trusted adherents, to be read and destroyed.[113] How much of the illegal literature which the Communists produced actually reached the readers for whom it was intended is a question which cannot be answered with any certainty. Large quantities of leaflets and pamphlets printed outside Germany were seized by the police at the frontiers: 1,238,202 copies in 1934 and 1,670,300 in 1935, according to police reports;[114] in Duhnke's opinion, these quantities may well represent the greater part of the material produced by the KPD outside Germany.[115] But in considering the effectiveness of this as propaganda, it has also to be considered how many people may have seen each copy. No doubt this will have varied much from case to case. A copy of one of the Party journals containing texts of Comintern resolutions for the guidance of functionaries may have been read by only one person; but some of the disguised brochures, such as the Brown Book, seem to have passed from hand to hand until they became dog-eared.

The task which the Party had set itself, of continuing illegally the whole range of its hitherto legal publicagtions, was a more formidable one than had been anticipated. For the preparations which had been made to provide reserve printing facilities for the event of illegality were often based on a serious underestimation of the difficulties which were in fact to be experienced in the Third Reich. It had tended to be rather näively assumed, for example, that a purely legal camouflage, by the transfer of assets to newly-founded or fictitious companies, would be as effective as it had sometimes been before 1933.

At first every attempt was made to continue producing Party literature within Germany, however great the difficulties, in order to assert the Party's presence and to avoid falling behind events. But since facilities for illegally printing the central organs in Berlin were soon exhausted, recourse had to be had to provincial presses. Since the Party's illegal Regional and District leaderships were likely to know of these and to want to use them for their own District or local papers, conflicts of interests could easily arise between central and

District organisations. There were other reasons, too, which made the production of illegal literature on any considerable scale in Germany inherently precarious. Clandestine printing left too much evidence behind it and the transport of large quantities of paper and other material by road or rail could not fail to attract attention before long.

These and other difficulties eventually drove the illegal party to do much of its printing outside Germany. As early as 20 June 1933 the Internal Leadership at Berlin wrote to the External Leadership at Paris proposing a plan for the distribution to the various Districts of Germany of the KPD papers printed abroad.[116]

It had been recognised from an early stage of the Party's clandestine operations that the production and distribution of illegal literature involved special problems. Whereas the writing and editing of the various publications was essentially a political function, the business of printing and distributing them was regarded as more of a technical matter, requiring specialised skills. For that reason, and also for security reasons, the two functions were as far as possible kept separate, production and distribution being entrusted to a 'technical' branch (*Die Technik*), whose representatives, known as 'technicians' (*Techniker*) enjoyed a certain degree of autonomy at all levels of the organisation from Sub-district upwards. At the top was a *Reichstechniker*, who was established first in Berlin, later at Saarbrücken (before its incorporation in the Reich), with close links with both the Internal or Operative leadership at Berlin and the External leadership or Secretariat of the Central Committee at Paris, and also with a number of Regional Technicians (*Obergebietstechniker*) and District Technicians (*Bezirkstechniker*), as well as having connections, which became more important as time went on, with the frontier posts or Sector leaders in some neighbouring countries.[117]

This rather complicated organisation of the Technical Branch took shape in the course of 1933 and succeeded in bringing out *Rote Fahne* more or less regularly from about the middle of March 1933, first two or three times a month and later monthly. Then, in the spring of 1934, the organisation was broken by the Gestapo. By the autumn, however, it had been rebuilt on a more decentralised pattern.[118] *Rote Fahne* was now printed in a number of regional centres, which included Düsseldorf and Solingen-Ohligs in the Lower Rhine District and, later, at a printing works at Cologne and another nearby at Leverkusen. Towards the end of 1934 a small printer, Georg Haberer at Solingen-Ohligs was printing some 12,000 copies of the paper, of which 5,000 were dispatched to Berlin in crates, while the rest was distributed in the Rhineland.[119] As the average number of copies of *Rote Fahne* printed for each issue during 1933–35 has been given as from 52,000 to 60,000,[120] it is clear that other presses were also being used at that time.

During the winter of 1934–35, after he had printed a total of 300,000 copies of the paper, Haberer's activities were discovered by the Gestapo, though he himself managed, by the skin of his teeth, to escape abroad.[121] Shortly after, the Cologne press was also discovered. As a result of these and other arrests, the main burden of printing *Rote Fahne* and other central Party publications was transferred abroad, with the consequence of much greater delays and a loss of immediate impact. The organisation which had prevailed hitherto could not be revived. Just as the Central Operative Leadership at Berlin was not rebuilt after its destruction at the end of March 1935, so too the Technical Branch was replaced by a sector structure, the most important publications being printed abroad and distributed in Germany through the frontier posts controlled by the various Sector Leaderships.

Production of German Communist literature in other countries, such as Czechoslovakia or France, for smuggling into Germany, involved a need for secrecy and other difficulties, though not of the same kind as production in Germany itself. Not only was a large proportion of each issue probably lost or seized in transit, but what arrived was sometimes out of date and therefore less effective. The most effective material smuggled over the frontier probably consisted of documents whose impact did not depend on speed of retort or sharpness of comment.

In addition to centrally or regionally produced newspapers and pamphlets, local street cells and factory cells produced an astonishing variety of leaflets, sometimes including satirical verse and crude cartoons. The number of copies produced of such a leaflet, though usually quite small – say, between 100 and 1,000 – might on occasion rise to as many as 10,000 or more.[122] In that case, however, both production and distribution raised serious problems. Even quite simple productions might involve the co-operation (and the connivance) of half a dozen people, including perhaps an author, an artist, a typist, the keeper of a duplicating machine, as well as those entrusted with distribution.

The best of the locally produced material was written in a lively and original style, exposing Nazi humbug and addressing itself cleverly to the interests and prejudices of particular readerships. There was plenty of scope for such leaflets to dwell on Nazi corruption and demagogy and to draw attention to such popular grievances as shortages and high price of food and unsatisfactory working conditions. Another type of leaflet was that which drew attention to Nazi atrocities, including not only murders by the SA, but political death sentences and executions. Finally, and the most difficult to express in popular language, there was the Communist alternative, which at this period continued to be expressed in terms of proletarian revolution and Soviet Germany, as witness many resolutions of ECCI and of the Central Committee of the KPD.

The effects of the KPD's propaganda are hard to guage. Was it worth the huge organisational effort which was put into it, and the human risks and losses involved? The sheer quantities of paper and the variety of publications committed to this battle of words were formidable. Yet some have judged that the effort was largely wasted and the effect negligible, and that the regular Party organs in their illegal form, with what has been called their 'affirmative style' and their distribution through Party cells, may have served more to hold the Party together than to win over outsiders, to strengthen the conviction of the distributors rather than that of a wider readership. It seems possible, too, that such wider influence as these papers may have had in 1933 may have begun to wane afterwards, as their predictions of crisis were progressively belied by events.

At national and District level many of the Party's clandestine publications continued to be devoted to a considerable extent to the reproduction of policy statements of the Communist International and of the German Party leadership, expressed in more or less technical Party language which was familiar to the initiated, that is, to Communists of long standing, but may not have appealed to those whose minds were not made up. Much of this argumentation also tended to conclude, not always convincingly, that events were conforming to the current line of the International. Furthermore, by the latter part of 1934, when divisions about fundamental policy issues were developing within the Party leadership, they began to be reflected in an indirect way in the clandestine Party press, just as the ultimate acceptance of a new political line coincided with changes of editorship of the main Party organs.[123]

If an example were needed of the character of the main central publications of the Party in the first year and a half of the Third Reich, it would be found in a pamphlet published in about February or March 1934 under the heading: 'Fight for Soviet Power!' This was the text of a resolution adopted by the Lower Rhine District Leadership of the KPD, expressing full agreement with the resolutions of the Thirteenth Plenum of the Executive Committee of the Communist International in December 1933 and with the subsequent resolution of the Central Committee of the German Party which, the District statement maintained, had correctly analysed the situation in Germany and decided on a correct tactic.[124] These decisions were soon to be repudiated by both the German Party and the International, and it is easy to see in hindsight that they were based on a mistaken judgement of the political situation and had done much damage to the cause of the working class. But because a 'general line' of policy was mistaken, and because the mistakes had been upheld in dogmatic fashion, it does not necessarily follow that the cause would have been better served by mere empiricism, without any 'general line' based on Marxist theory, as some historians assume.

Whatever the role of programmatic documents in the long run, there can be little doubt that two other types of clandestine publication had a more immediate impact. First, there were certain kinds of imported pamphlet which had a news value as well as a programmatic content. Many such texts were hidden within an 'innocent' cover and opening pages. Dimitrov's concluding speech from the dock, for instance, was disguised as a pamphlet on 'Home Heating by Electricity', while the KPD's programme of May 1934 was presented as a 'Cookery Book with 70 Approved Recipes'.[125] The main resolution of the KPD's Brussels Conference of 1935, again, was disguised as a booklet entitled 'The Proper Care of Cactus Plants'.[126]

Another type of illegal publication which made an immediate impact was the locally-produced leaflet rushed out in the heat of the moment, after some Nazi atrocity or local incident, giving a vivid account or making a sharp retort in working-class idiom. Several versions have been found, for instance, of a duplicated, hand-written leaflet which was put out by ward committees in two Berlin suburbs following a disturbance at a market frequented by working-class housewives and street traders.[127] The trouble had arisen from grumbling about food prices and shortages, but the police had surrounded the market and arrested certain 'ringleaders'.

The heavy human losses which the Communist Party incurred in producing and distributing large quantities of 'literature' could be defended as long as a crisis of the régime seemed imminent, for in that event it might be all-important that the Party should be seen to be in full working order and politically active. Since the Party might be called upon to act decisively at any moment, the imprisonment of so high a proportion of its best cadres could be looked upon as likely to be purely temporary, almost as a political education and training for the final battle.

By the latter months of 1934, however, as the prospect of early revolution faded, propaganda, as well as other aspects of Party life and work, began to be viewed in a new light. The human losses inevitably resulting from the drive to maintain a wide range of publications with mass circulation became more difficult to justify, now that the perspective was of a long struggle ahead. From 1935 a more cautious policy began to replace the reckless heroism of 1933–34, and the drive for large circulations gave way to a more selective approach. 'Literature' tended henceforth to be produced in smaller quantities and in a style more suitable for memorising. Though important policy statements continued to be circulated for discussion in the inner circle of the Party, more attention was paid in general to providing the basis for talking points and rumours. This development was to culminate in the acquisition by the KPD of a short-wave radio transmitter (29,8), first in Republican Spain from January 1937, later in the USSR.[128] The emphasis thus shifted from the written to the spoken word, which left fewer traces for the Gestapo – and for the historian!

CHAPTER 6

A Closer Look

No general outline can convey the quality of a struggle so dramatic, yet so closely woven into the pattern of daily life, as was that of 1933–35 between the Communist Party and the National Socialist state. While the chain of events cannot be properly understood except in a national and international context, the character of the struggle can hardly be appreciated without some study in depth. Circumstances, it is true, differed in various parts of Germany and no one place is typical. Yet some attempt must be made, at the risk of misleading the reader, to introduce a local dimension by looking more closely at the Communist Party's struggle in one particular area. I have chosen for this purpose the Lower Rhine District and its chief city, Düsseldorf.

Düsseldorf, with half a million inhabitants, was a big industrial as well as administrative and cultural centre, with radical traditions going back to Heinrich Heine. Many big industrial firms had works and offices there;[1] there was a flourishing opera-house and artistic community and the liberal wing of Catholicism was conspicuously represented. In the working-class movement the Communist Party greatly predominated as far as membership figures and electoral strength went; this trend had culminated in the Reichstag election of November 1932, when the Communists emerged as the strongest party, with 78,340 votes, as against 31,185 for the Social Democrats. The Communist vote in Düsseldorf, in this, the last free election to be held in the German republic, also exceeded that of the National Socialists (63,951) and of the Centre Party (61,771).[2]

In social composition the Communist Party in Düsseldorf consisted overwhelmingly of manual workers, with a fringe of artists, intellectuals and white-collar workers, and it had strong roots in the community, almost all its leaders being local men. But as in other industrial centres, its strength in terms of membership and support in the working-class contrasted markedly with its comparative weakness in the factories and the trade unions.

This contradictory character of the Communist Party's influence in the city was very clearly revealed by the events following Hitler's accession to power on 30 January 1933. Within a few hours of the Nazi leader's appointment, some half-dozen demonstrations of protest were marching from different working-class suburbs towards the city centre. Both the promptness of the reaction and the size of the demonstrations reflected the strength of the Party's following and its ability to mobilise it. Yet the marches appear to have attracted little support outside the ranks of the Communist Party, and to have been easily halted and dispersed by the police and not subsequently renewed. Moreover, the Party's call for a general strike was followed by only one shop of one works in the city.[3] The Party registered its protest, but it did so in isolation. Its attempt to mobilise the workers against the fascist danger was, in the immediate sense, a fiasco.

The Party turned its efforts to the electoral campaign which it pursued during February in face of increasing harassment by Brownshirts and police and the banning of its press for a fortnight. Then, on 28 February, at Düsseldorf as elsewhere, harassment was quite suddenly replaced by mass arrests. Several hundred Communist Party functionaries and locally-prominent members were seized in the city and the Party's offices and presses were closed.[4] Throughout March the hunt went on for the leaders who had managed to escape, while those leaders struggled to put into effect the plans that had been made for conditions of illegality.

The main impression given by police and party records, and by the recollection of survivors, is that the Party in Düsseldorf was stunned but not crippled by the blows it suffered in March 1933. Renegades and turncoats were comparatively few.[5] The top functionaries of the District mostly escaped, for the moment at least, because they had already ceased during February to sleep at home or to use their offices. It was above all the middle-rank functionaries who were arrested, often including the reserve leaderships which had been held in readiness for the event of a ban on the Party. The main effect, therefore, was that numerous minor functionaries, such as branch literature secretaries or street-cell treasurers, found themselves temporarily cut off from the higher functionaries to whom they normally accounted. Some of these dropped out and never resumed contact or activity. But in an astonishing number of cases they simply waited for orders, and often continued to collect

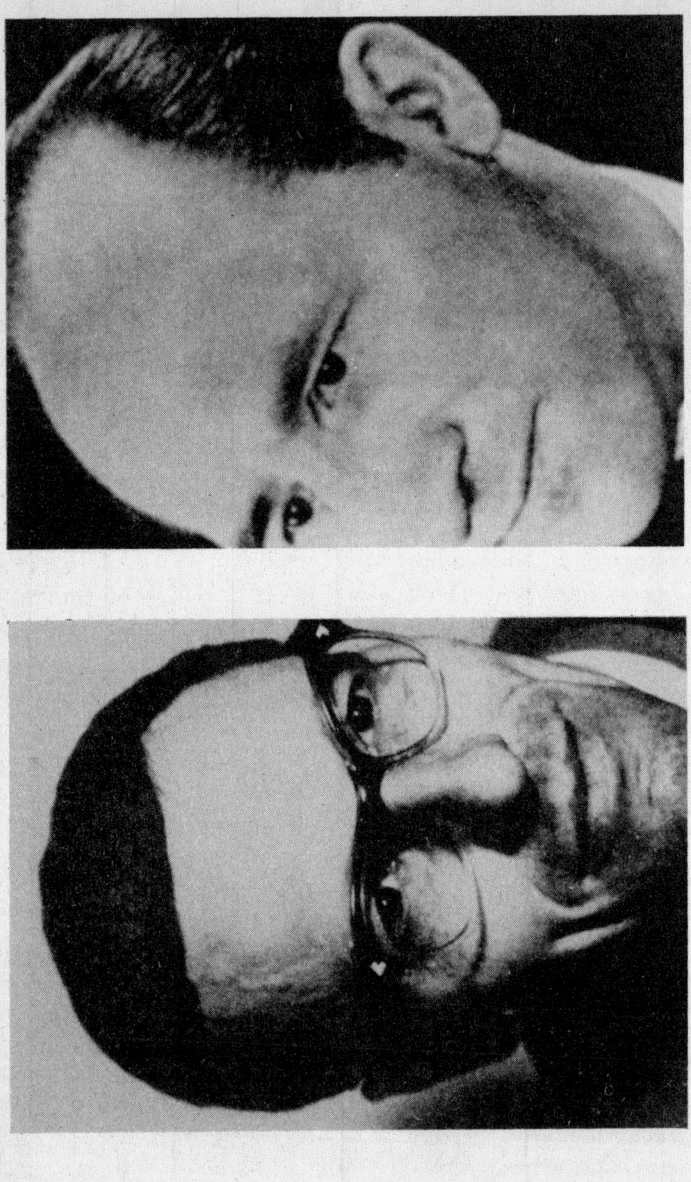

Rudolf Goguel (*left*) and Hugo Paul, Communist activists in Düsseldorf

dues and literature-money and kept it until they could duly account for it.

To renew contact with such functionaries and to incorporate them into a Party organisation again was the first task undertaken by the member appointed to take over the leadership in Düsseldorf. This was Hugo Paul, a man of 27, whose home was in the neighbouring cutlery town of Remscheid, where he had been Sub-district Leader until the end of 1932, when he had been moved to Mönchen-Gladbach as part of the KPD's preparations for the expected ban.[6] Hugo Paul arrived at Düsseldorf at the beginning of April 1933 as 'Instructor' appointed by the District leadership to lead the two party Sub-districts into which the party organisation in the city was divided. He was a man of energy and initiative who lost no time in approaching Sub-district branch and cell functionaries and trying to persuade them to resume activity. One of his first moves was to invite a suitable comrade to take on the post of 'Finance Instructor' for the city, for finance was a key to efficient underground organisation, determining how many Communists would be able to lead a fully clandestine existence. Others, especially those who were unemployed (as most still were) might be able to carry out illegal political activity on a more or less full-time basis for a time, but the obligation to register with the police and the need to draw unemployment benefit set limits to their clandestine activity.

During April and May, Hugo Paul worked hard, trying to reorganise the Party and to fight back against the Nazis. He was a good judge of people and knew how to appeal to their sense of loyalty to class and party. Many who may have been hesitating were won over by him to resume the struggle and, in many cases, to take on more responsible posts than they had previously held, in order to fill the gaps left by those who had been arrested. The most striking thing, indeed, about the reaction of the Communist Party in Düsseldorf to the disaster of those first weeks is the almost automatic, unquestioning way in which so many members took for granted that the fight would continue.

If the first task for Hugo Paul was reorganisation, the second was to fight back against the Nazi offensive in some political way. And that could only mean, in the circumstances of that time, with the weapon of the written word. Of the seven or eight major leaflets which were distributed by the Communist Party in Düsseldorf in May or June 1933, at least two were certainly written by Hugo Paul, and both give clear evidence of the quality of his political leadership and his ability to rise to the occasion. Each was an answer to a major action of the Nazis in the establishment of their dictatorship at Düsseldorf.

First of these was the 'raid' (*Razzia*) on Gerresheim on 5 May 1933. Gerresheim, on the Eastern outskirts of Düsseldorf, was one of the most solid of working-class suburbs, in which neither the arrests after 27 February nor the taking over of the trade unions on 2 May had been able to break the influence and organisation of the Communist Party. On 5 May, therefore, the Nazis surrounded the workers' quarters there with a combined force estimated at 3,500 men, drawn from the SA, the SS, the *Stahlhelm* and the auxiliary and regular police and, on the pretext of searching for hidden arms, ransacked hundreds of flats from cellar to attic, maltreated many workers and detained a number given officially as fifty, but in reality probably nearer six times as many.[7] It was of great political importance that a Communist comment on the raid was distributed within a few days, in thousands of copies. The pamphlet, of fourteen duplicated pages, was written in a vigorous, vivid style, with many details drawn from the fresh experience of those affected, with a withering exposure of Nazi deceptions, and not without a cutting wit, expressed in working-class idiom. At the same time the description of Nazi cruelty and terror was firmly harnessed to a political argument. The pamphlet was aimed, not only at strengthening the confidence of the organised workers in their ability to defeat the Nazi attack, but at opening the eyes of the proletarian and lower-middle class supporters of the Nazis – including those in the SA and the SS – and winning them to see that their interests were the same as those of the 'class brothers' whom they had been duped into attacking.[8]

The main instrument used by the Nazis in this deception was nationalism, and it was with a view to whipping up nationalist feelings among the masses that they built up the cult of Leo Schlageter, who had been condemned by the French for sabotage during the Ruhr occupation of 1923 and shot on Golzheim Heath on the outskirts of Düsseldorf. On 26 May 1933, the tenth anniversary of Schlageter's death, this cult reached a climax in a weekend festival attended by high Nazi leaders and by an estimated 300,000 supporters from other parts of Germany. To expose the real meaning of this cult was an important political task, especially in

Düsseldorf, and that is what Hugo Paul attempted in another pamphlet, 'The Cross on the Heath', which was distributed both in the city and the surrounding region in connection with the Schlageter celebrations. The pamphlet described Schlageter as 'a man who had hopelessly lost his way, having failed clearly to recognise either the real enemy, big capital, or his true friends, the workers in their struggle'. 'Today's youth,' the pamphlet continued, 'rather than tread the same path, or actually join the Nazi party in defence of big capital, should throw in its lot with the working class.'[9]

Hugo Paul was a leader who inspired confidence and who made the same heavy demands on himself as he made on others. By June 1933 he had rebuilt the party in Düsseldorf into an effective organisation. Then the blow fell. In the course of a few weeks, some 90 members, including Hugo Paul himself, were arrested and subjected to the now familiar process of violence and interrogation, ending in a mass trial. A study of the evidence collected for his trial makes clear that the arrests were virtually inevitable in the then state of security precautions. The arrest of Hugo Paul himself resulted from two main circumstances. First, the Gestapo had been put on his track through the capture of the entire archive, which filled three suitcases, kept by Hans Pfeiffer, the Regional Adviser for the three Western Districts, who followed a thorougly bureaucratic routine, keeping copies of letters and minutes of meetings, etc. Secondly, the paper used for Hugo's leaflets had been traced to the firm of Gestetner, from whom it had been stolen by an employee; and this clue had led, through the carelessness of a Party member appointed to keep watch, straight to Hugo Paul himself. He was arrested when he came to the house of a small, self-employed printer who had been printing Hugo's leaflets, and others, the text of which had been composed by the District leadership and conveyed to him for processing.[10]

The mass arrests of June–July 1933 tore wide gaps in the Party's illegal organisation at Düsseldorf. Nevertheless, the steadfastness in the face of police brutality of many of those arrested – including not a few women – prevented the uncovering of many parts of the structure. Of the two Sub-districts into which the party organisation in the city was divided, one (Gerresheim) escaped almost intact and continued to operate for another year. In the other Sub-district, in which both the Sub-district leadership and that of many of the ward branches had been destroyed, replacements were quickly found, either (in the case of some top posts) by transfer of functionaries from neighbouring cities, or by 'promotion from the ranks'. In some of these branches the replacements themselves were soon arrested and replaced and arrested again in rapid succession; in other cases the new team maintained a stable organisation for a year or eighteen months. The outcome depended partly on the political instinct of the new leaders; partly on the quality of their teamwork, their ability to sense danger, to act without panicking and to seal off gaps where the enemy had penetrated. But it depended also on the character of the local community. In wards in which the proportion of class-conscious, organised workers was low, informers proliferated; but where it was high, and solidarity against the police traditional, as it was on some housing estates, the police might have to rely on a few spies and agents who could be recognised in time and neutralised.

The gaps that had been torn in the KPD's organisation on the Lower Rhine were successfully sealed off after July 1933. A new Regional Adviser took the place of Hans Pfeiffer, who had been arrested on 10 June on his return to Düsseldorf after a visit to Berlin. The Political Secretary of the Lower Rhine District, Lambert Horn, had been sent to Berlin in May to replace Walter Ulbricht as Political Secretary there, his place at Düsseldorf being taken by Erich Glückauf, the editor of the Party's District newspaper, *Freiheit* ('Freedom'); and Glückauf remained in charge of the District until November 1933, when he was safely transferred elsewhere. From the summer of 1933 until the summer of 1934, the KPD's clandestine organisation at Düsseldorf enjoyed a certain stability. Small groups were arrested and put on trial or sent to concentration camps, but the top leaders were transferred in and out without disaster, and the illegal organisation in the city as a whole maintained its strength.

This temporary stability is clearly shown in the confidential report which Otto Hertel, who had been acting as Political Secretary since March or April 1934, prepared for the Central Operative Leadership at Berlin in August 1934. Hertel was due to be transferred to the political secretaryship of another District, and this was a final report on his work in the Lower Rhine.[11] It may have also have served as a reply to the exhaustive questionnaire which the Politburo had addressed to Districts at the end of June.[12] The report referred to the work of the Party District during the first six months of 1934.

According to Hertel's report, the authenticity of which seems to be well established,[13] the KPD in the Lower Rhine District had maintained stability, with only minor fluctuations of membership, finance and quantities of literature distributed. During the six months covered, the paid-up membership of the Party in Düsseldorf itself varied between 556 and 717 and had tended to rise slightly. In the District as a whole membership stood at some 10 to 12 per cent of the 1931 figure. The report drew attention to certain weaknesses in the underground Party's work. The local, Sub-district leaderships, it was alleged, did not, with certain exceptions show enough initiative, and they had not made much progress towards solving two key tasks: the building of groups in the factories, and the making of unity approaches to other socialist parties. Nevertheless, there were said to be cells in three of the most important Düsseldorf industrial works: Mannesmann, Rheinmetall, and Phönix Steel Tubes.[14] The District had aimed at producing its own paper (*Freiheit*) weekly, and its journal for Party officials (*Der Revolutionär*) monthly, and had managed to achieve the latter aim. The production of *Freiheit* had been somewhat irregular for financial reasons. The most recent numbers had been produced in 4,000 to 5,000 copies. Another achievement of the District had been to send four members away (presumably abroad) on an education course at the end of June.[15] This must have been a course of some duration for the four had apparently not yet returned at the time of writing, in August.

Of the so-called mass organisations the most active, according to the report, were the Revolutionary Trade Union Opposition and *Rotsport*. Red Aid was also being built up. A rather surprising fact is that there was a full-time clandestine official for cultural organisations – though he was not provided with any income and was only being saved from starvation by subsidies out of local Party funds, which the District could ill afford.[16] The trade-union work was also led by one or two full-time functionaries, the source of whose pay is not clear. Their arrival, in the summer of 1934, was probably the Central Operative Leadership's first answer to the criticism that not enough attention was being paid to Party work in industry. The efforts of the new functionaries proved, however, to be short-lived: they were arrested in September 1934, only a few weeks after Hertel himself.

An unusually clear picture has survived of the illegal Communist organisation in the Friedrichstadt ward of Düsseldorf.[17] This was a small, mainly residential area near the city centre, in which a working-class population was closely packed into five or six-storey blocks of flats. A clear view can be obtained primarily because the underground organisation in the ward was not broken up in stages, but succeeded to a surprising degree in adapting itself to conditions of illegality in the first months of 1933 and then functioned for about a year and a half with the same personnel. It was then largely broken up in a single round of arrests and a single trial, whose records supply an unusually complete and consistent picture, the study of which makes it possible to appreciate some of the strengths and potentialities of the underground Communist Party which caused it to be taken seriously by the Nazi authorities.[18]

Friedrichstadt was, up to the Nazi seizure of power, an area of Düsseldorf in which the Communists were relatively strong. The ward Party there, like other Communist organisations, was temporarily thrown into disorder in the days following the Reichstag Fire, when its leader, Willy Breuer, and three or four others of its leading members were taken into 'protective custody'. But here, at least, recovery was remarkably quick: so quick, indeed, that it was later possible for a member to say in retrospect that the transition to illegality was made without any interruption of the branch's political activity.[19] Already before the end of March Breuer's place had been filled, at the invitation of a member of the District leadership, by Hermann Hermanns, a 25-year-old motor mechanic, who had hitherto been an ordinary member, holding no office, but now agreed to take on the political secretaryship and to try to re-form the branch. His first step was to choose as his ward organiser the 26-year-old mechanic Peter Fahron, and as ward treasurer and third member of the new leadership, the 42-year-old compositor, Robert Bauer. These proved to be excellent choices, particularly that of Fahron, with whom Hermanns worked closely for the next year and a half, discussing all major decisions. Bauer, for his part, though he felt obliged to resign the treasurership early in 1934, did so in such a way that a successor could be found and worked in.

The first task of the new leadership must have been to take stock of the loss of members through resignations and drifting out, and to re-form those that remained into a working, dues-paying organisation. Hitherto the ward branch (*Stadtteil*) had consisted of a number of street cells, each composed in turn of five-member groups. Total membership in the ward has been estimated in one subsequent recollection as 150 at the time of the Nazi take-over. According to the same source, about 80 dues-paying members remained in the branch after that date and of these, 30 could be counted as politically active. That these estimates are probably not far from the truth is indicated by the fact that when the branch was finally uncovered by the police at the end of 1934, proceedings were begun against 26 persons and a further 20 were mentioned but not proceeded against because they were either 'in flight' or unidentified.[20] Of those included in the indictment, apart from the branch officers, two were described as 'street-cell treasurers' and three as 'group treasurers'; and of three others mentioned in the final police report, though not actually indicted, one is described as a 'street-cell leader', another as a 'five-man-group treasurer' and a third as a 'ward courier'. The picture which emerged at the trial, though incomplete, suggested an efficient working organisation which had succeeded in adapting itself to changing circumstances and in overcoming a number of crises and problems in the course of its eighteen months of underground struggle. One street cell in particular, of which the fullest picture ultimately emerged, consisted of three groups totalling fourteen dues-paying members. The member who had been treasurer of the cell before January 1933 was still holding the office on 7 November 1934, the day before the arrests began, when he paid over six Reichsmarks to the ward treasurer at a *Treff* in the Alexanderplatz.

The Friedrichstadt organisation would not have lasted as long as it did if its leaders had not been able to overcome occasional crises. One of these occurred quite early on, when two of the active members were arrested while taking part in a leaflet action. Both must have withstood the police tortures, for they were tried individually without involving others, and the gap was successfully sealed off without apparently affecting the work of the branch.[21] Another potentially dangerous problem arose when the ward-branch treasurer, Robert Bauer, began to succumb to the strain of the responsibilities he bore, with its attendant risks, and asked to be relieved. Hermanns, however, showed himself able to seek just enough and not too much advice, and to make a good choice of persons. Luise Sauer, a 30 year-old shorthand-typist whom Hermanns had known as a member of the legal Party before 1933, who had continued as a dues-paying illegal member, and was spoken of favourably by her street-cell leader, was approached personally by Hermanns and persuaded to take on the ward treasurership in April 1934. The choice proved a good one and the transition was smoothly made, thanks to Hermanns's tactful handling and the loyalty of Bauer, who continued as an ordinary dues-paying member. Other, lesser personal problems were also smoothly solved. When, for instance, one of the group treasurers, Peter Becker, was prevented from continuing to perform his duties because he got a living-in job at an inn, he was succeeded by his brother.

The ward branch appears to have had, in addition to a treasurer, a literature secretary who obtained copies of the Party's central organ, *Rote Fahne*, and of the District papers, *Freiheit* and *Der Revolutionär*, for distribution to cell and group treasurers, who in turn distributed them to members and collected the money accruing, accounting for it together with other receipts. At first, groups were apparently expected to take about three copies of these publications per member, but by the later months of 1934 only *Freiheit* was being regularly distributed, and of that, too, regular sales had fallen. As for the technique of selling, one method of which the police depositions offer a glimpse was for the member to approach a sympathiser in the toilet of a public house in which both were drinking.

Besides selling papers obtained from a higher Party level, the ward branch itself produced leaflets and distributed them free of charge, either by putting them through letter boxes after dark or by scattering them from tall buildings by means of a simple mechanism called a *Knallfrosch* ('snapfrog'). According to the post-war recollections of a survivor, these leaflets were mostly written, either by Hermanns or by Josef Barth, a gifted young student journalist, at the rate of about one leaflet per week. The buildings used to scatter them included the central railway station, the principal theatres and cinemas, and the Königsallee, the 'Piccadilly' of Düsseldorf, where the main banks and richest hotels were. Some of these local leaflets produced in Friedrichstadt were prompt and witty, such as the one which was distributed immediately after the Röhm massacre of 30 June 1934, written by Barth. Even SA men remarked, as Peter Fahron later recalled, that the Communists had been quick off the mark.[22] The leaflet was headed: 'The Beginning of the End of the

Nancy-Boy Government', and it is said that about 1,000 copies were distributed in Düsseldorf. Among other leaflets of this period which were attributed to Barth in the indictment at his trial were several issues of a local paper, *Die Wahrheit* (The Truth), bearing the headline 'Hands up those who are better off in Hitler-Germany!'[23]

By the autumn of 1934 the central leadership of the Communist Party was beginning to review its general line and, in particular, its relations with the Social Democrats. In this connection, early in November, Hermann Hermanns was asked by his contact with the District leadership to build up factory contacts with former Social Democrats, and an appointment had been made for him to discuss this problem with a 'District specialist'. But before the meeting took place, Hermanns was arrested on 10 November.

On the previous day the rounding up of the Friedrichstadt branch by the Gestapo had at last begun. As is often the case, it is difficult to be sure from the surviving evidence how much they had known, and for how long, and why they decided to draw a line at this point. It seems fairly clear, however, that until shortly before this time they had found it difficult to penetrate the branch. The arrest of two members engaged in a leafleting action, in which others were certainly involved, had, as has been noted above,[24] failed to break into the organisation in the early months, and the same may have happened again in the summer of 1934 when the sale of a sixteen-page Communist brochure to a worker in the ward on 1 May led to police enquiries culminating in the arrest of two Communists who lived there.[25] They were probably members of the underground branch, but neither the police interrogators nor the subsequent trial furnished evidence to that effect. What does seem clear is that the Friedrichstadt ward was, even at this time, a closely-knit community in which many people were prepared to close their eyes to opposition activities, and in which police spies did not find such ready support as in some other suburbs. The three brothers Becker, for instance, long-standing Communists and among the most active in illegal work, had as brother-in-law a certain Heinrich W., who was in the SA. They showed him some of the illegal papers which their branch was distributing, and he read them; but although he urged them (or so he afterwards maintained) to abandon their Communist connections, he refrained out of family loyalty from reporting them to his superiors.[26]

By the end of the summer of 1934 the position of the underground

Friedrichstadt branch had become more precarious than perhaps even its leaders were aware. In August and September the greater part of the District leadership and almost the entire underground Party organisation in the neighbouring Altstadt (Old Town) ward had fallen into the hands of the police, and it was by that route that they seem to have found an opening into the Friedrichstadt branch. Three waves of arrests between 9 November and 12 December destroyed the branch and laid the basis for the trial which was initiated by an indictment of 20 March and concluded by a judgement on 27 June 1935.[27]

Exactly how the Gestapo acquired the knowledge necessary to break into the Friedrichstadt branch is not fully clear in the documents of the trial, but such evidence as there is, and the unanimous opinion of survivors, points to betrayal by the renegade Communist, Wilhelm Gather. Gather, who had been a clandestine functionary, had been arrested in the middle of 1934, but released after a short period of detention. He had then proceeded to renew his contacts with Communists in the Altstadt ward and had introduced to them an unknown 'Heinrich', with the result that some 60 arrests had been made and the clandestine ward organisation destroyed. When this happened, Gather had been able, with police connivance, to assume the appearance of having escaped and gone into hiding; and a little later he approached one of the Becker brothers and asked to be put in touch again with the underground Party organisation in Friedrichstadt, with which he said he had lost touch. Of the events that followed, the most probable account runs that a warning against Gather was conveyed to the branch leadership, but that it arrived too late. The arrests of November and December 1934 embraced the whole of the branch leadership and the greater part of the active membership. If, out of almost 50 arrests, the indictment finally included no more than fifteen names, this was partly for lack of legal proof in some cases and in others for fear of exposing police spies, whose evidence would be necessary to prove a charge.

The Friedrichstadt branch must be considered to have been one of the most effective ward organisations in Düsseldorf. It made a relatively smooth transition from legality to illegality in March 1933 and continued its activities for over a year and a half without a serious break and under the same leadership. Moreover, it did not confine itself to collecting dues and distributing literature on behalf of the higher leadership. It produced its own propaganda and seems to have exercised a degree of initiative, and its members held together with a high, and indeed exceptional, degree of mutual trust and solidarity. What was the basis of this record? Apart from the accidents of personality and perhaps some good fortune, it is possible to distinguish some other factors. The ward was a small one, in which the population was almost entirely working class, and no doubt conscious of common interests. Of the fifteen branch members finally indicted, twelve were manual workers and probably all without exception socially of the working class; seven of the fifteen lived in one street. The success of the branch undoubtedly resulted to a very large extent from the reliability, the mutual trust and balanced attitude of both leaders and rank and file.

Friedrichstadt, like many other city wards, was a small, intimate community of crowded tenements, in which news passed quickly from flat to flat by way of the local pub and the corner shop: a community in which any change in people's habitual comings and goings and daily routine attracted the curiosity of neighbours who could hardly fail to notice the unaccustomed blare of a radio or rattle of a typewriter and the visit of an unfamiliar guest at meal-times or overnight.

This meant, on the one hand, that Communists who lived in such working-class housing led a semi-public life and could hardly hope to go out chalking or leafleting at night, hold committee meetings in their flats, or give a night's lodging to a passing courier or Instructor without rousing the interest of neighbours or exciting gossip. On the other hand the very closeness and intimacy of working-class life could serve as a wall of defence in certain conditions, in which feelings of solidarity were strong enough to repel the intrusions of outside busybodies and to close the ranks against the police.

The Gestapo worked at regional or city level. For information about illegal activities at ward or street-level it depended either on agents planted within working-class organisations on a long-term basis during previous régimes, or on the ordinary police, or the intelligence sections of local units of the Nazi Party, or the SA or SS. These latter were often stupid and clumsy, but had the advantage of working at grass-roots level, living and working among the people they spied on. At Düsseldorf a significant role was played in the prosecution of several clandestine Communist groups by a certain Hermann Nosbüsch, a cycle dealer who had a shop in the Old

Town, but lived in the working-class outer suburb of Gerresheim.[28] From the beginning of 1933 or possibly earlier he had been an SA man (the equivalent of a private soldier) in the Intelligence Section of the local SA regiment under *Sturmführer* (lieutenant) Hohenscheidt, who also lived in Gerresheim and was responsible for watching the local Communists. Nosbüsch was evidently kept out of uniform and made to pose as an underground Communist. In the summer of 1934 he seems to have infiltrated several Communist groups and later to have given evidence against them. One of them was a small group of four Gerresheim Communists, of whom only one had made any admissions before the trial and these he withdrew at the public hearing. Nosbüsch was the only other witness and it was the accused's word against his. The court found the four guilty on the grounds that there was no reason to doubt Nosbüsch's word.[29]

From that case it would appear that although the Gestapo were, as always, reluctant to destroy the cover of their own confidential agents by bringing them into court as witnesses, they regarded the SA intelligence man as expendable. In the event, however, his appearance in court did not immediately destroy his cover – presumably because of the limitations which were placed on attendance at such trials and on the reporting of them in the press – and Nosbüsch and Hohenscheidt pursued their careers in the Security Service of the SS, to which all other intelligence or security operations of Nazi organisations except for state organisations such as the Gestapo were transferred on 9 June 1934.[30] Indeed, their activities became more ambitious. Nosbüsch, directing his attention to the neighbouring ward of Zooviertel (Zoo Quarter), approached a known Communist there, posing as a clandestine Instructor who had been sent to reorganise the Communist Party, and got him to arrange a meeting of Communists in a neighbouring wood. While Nosbüsch attended the meeting, Hohenscheidt kept watch to identify those who attended. This operation ended in the trial of thirteen Communists on the evidence of Nosbüsch's account of conversations which he claimed to have had with the accused.[31]

These provocateur's methods had been so relatively successful that Nosbüsch and Hohenscheidt aimed higher in the summer of 1935. Using information regarding passwords and pseudonyms which may have been obtained from Gestapo interrogations, Nosbüsch approached a leading Düsseldorf woman Communist and tried to make contact with the underground District leadership.[32] In this case, however, he failed, for the woman put him off until she could refer the incident to the counter-intelligence branch of the Communist Party organisation, which must have confirmed her initial suspicions.

A number of the Düsseldorf Communists who had been taken into 'protective custody' in the aftermath of the Reichstag Fire were released in April 1934. Most of them had been held in improvised camps in the Ems marshland and put to hard labour in conditions in which it seems to have been possible for them to achieve a certain degree of control of their lives and a certain minimum of collaboration with the camp staff. A well-known example of this limited ascendancy which the Communist prisoners were able to assert was the Christmas entertainment which they planned and performed under the guidance of prominent Communists.[33] One of these was Karl Schabrod, who later became Political Secretary of the Ruhr District of the illegal Party. A second was Wolfgang Langhoff, who had been actor and producer at the Düsseldorf city theatre before his arrest and who published an account both of his experiences in general in 1933 and of this incident in particular, after he had been released (on 1 April 1934) and had escaped to Switzerland.

Another Düsseldorf Communist who was interned in the marshes was Rudolf Goguel, a leader of the Communist trade union for white-collar workers. He was released from the Ems camp on 27 October 1933 and he, too, was later to write an account of his experiences.[34] Like many others he was released on condition of giving an undertaking not to take part in any further political activity and of reporting twice weekly at the Gestapo office. Since there was also a possibility that released Communists in that position might be under observation, it was a rule of the clandestine party to avoid renewing contact with them, at least for a considerable time. Goguel relates, however, how one day, as he was on his way to report to the Gestapo, he met another Communist, Ewald Funke, whom he knew well and fully trusted, and who turned out (though Goguel did not know it at the time) to be the Party's District functionary responsible for security, going by the pseudonym 'Heinz'. Funke, after hearing Goguel's account of his position, told him that the Party needed every member to be active and urged him to resume activity, only observing carefully the 'rules of conspiracy'. Goguel agreed, and was then introduced by 'Heinz' to the Political Secretary of the District and was soon engaged in feverish activity.

Goguel's new activity was primarily directed towards the revival of the trade unions. At first, because he had considerable experience, he was asked to take up a full-time, paid organising position in another District, which would have meant living illegally. But he declined, feeling that his knowledge of Düsseldorf would enable him to do more effective work there. And so, while living legally and reporting to the police, he became very busy, writing leaflets and copy for an illegal trade union paper, *Gewerkschaftszeitung*.

In May 1934 a full-time paid Communist trade union organiser for the Lower Rhine District arrived in Düsseldorf. This was Erich Krause, known by the pseudonym 'Franz'. Goguel worked closely with him, trying to build up union branches in the bigger factories. It was a fruitful collaboration. 'Franz' was a Berliner, about 30 years of age and a tailor by trade. He is described by Goguel as an ideal clandestine functionary, with nothing about him to attract attention, yet energetic and a talented organiser. He lacked only local knowledge, and this was supplied by Goguel.

Goguel's post-war memoirs give a good account of the character of Communist activity at Düsseldorf in the summer of 1934, stimulated as it was by the illusion that a collapse of the Nazi régime was imminent. Three numbers of the trade union paper, as well as from half a dozen to a dozen leaflets were typed out by Goguel for duplication in as many as 5,000 copies. The Communists tried to appeal to the discontent in the SA, though without much success, and they issued leaflets addressed to local Catholics, some of whose leaders, such as Adalbert Probst, had been included among the victims of the massacre of 30 June.

The upsurge of Communist activity at this time did not last more than a few months. On 22 August four out of the five members of the District leadership, including the Political Secretary, Otto Hertel ('Rudi'), whose report has been mentioned in a previous chapter,[35] were arrested after a *Treff* in a city park. Only 'Franz' escaped and he went to Berlin on 27 August, to warn the Central Operative Leadership. While he was away, his assistant, Goguel, was in turn arrested, but this turned out to be a mere 'try-out', such as the Gestapo sometimes went in for, without any solid evidence, and Goguel was released again on 14 September. Nevertheless the net was closing. On 10 September 'Franz' had returned from Berlin and as a precaution had gone to new lodgings, with the result apparently that he could not be contacted and warned in time; and he in turn was arrested on 24 September. He was a key figure, having an extensive knowledge of the clandestine party organisation in the District, including its link with Berlin. Much therefore depended on whether the Gestapo could break him down and they were aware of that. Goguel, arrested again on 29 September, was confronted with 'Franz' on the same day in the interrogation room of the Gestapo headquarters. He had been so terribly maltreated that he was scarcely recognisable, Goguel has reported.[36] The same evening, in case he should be unable to hold out further, 'Franz' committed suicide, as others had done before and were to do in future for the same reason. Goguel did not hear of this at the time; but independently, after similar treatment, he threw himself from the fourth floor of the Gestapo building. He cracked his skull but survived, to figure as one of the 71 defendants in a mass trial. Much later, after a chain of almost incredible experiences, he wrote down his recollections.[37]

That Krause's and Goguel's readiness for self-sacrifice was not unusual at this time is indicated by a reluctant tribute to the morale of the Communist militants which was expressed by the Gestapo office of Münster in Westphalia in its Situation Report for October 1935, in these words:

> During the various discoveries of KPD groups which have taken place in recent months, there has repeatedly been occasion to note the self-sacrificing readiness of all the supporters of the illegal KPD who were on every occasion ready to fill any gap which occurred in the ranks and to take the place of comrades who were arrested, without letting themselves be deterred by the high prison sentences. This readiness to make sacrifices for the Communist idea goes so far that convinced Communists again and again sacrifice their lives to avoid having to betray their comrades.[38]

The greatest difficulty which the clandestine KPD seems to have experienced at Düsseldorf was to establish an adequate base in heavy industry. There were, until 1934, small groups of Communists in one or two engineering works, but the two largest work-place organisations were not in industry proper, but in public service and clerical occupations.

The Düsseldorf tramways, which was a privately owned enterprise (*Rheinbahn A.G.*), had a large and active Communist Party branch which had cells in five depots and some 56 members in all, and continued to be active until at least 1935. It produced leaflets and a periodical – *Der Blitzstrahl* (The Flash of Lightning) – which members sometimes placed on the seats of the early morning trams. It held 'schools', too, and was capable, on occasion, of sending members to attend political schools across the frontier, in Holland.[39]

As for white-collar workers, including both shop-workers and clerical and administrative workers, they seem to have had exceptionally strong and active organisations at Düsseldorf, both before and after 1933, and a number of outstandingly able and well-placed members employed in white-collar and clerical work, and in shop-work. Among them (apart from Rudolf Goguel, already mentioned) were Tilde Klose, who was foreign correspondent of the giant industrial firm of Mannesmann, Paul Tegethoff, an industrial chemist; and Lya Rosenheim, who was employed in Tietz, a large store. Particularly memorable among the activities of the group before 1933 had been the 'agitprop company' *Kolonne Stehkragen* (Starched Collar Brigade), whose performances had enlivened many a political meeting. After January 1933 many of them played an outstanding role in the production of clandestine literature and in the organisation of Party education. Some of them – notably Tilde Klose and Paul Tegethoff – were later to die in concentration camps or prison, after many years of detention.[40]

Düsseldorf had been a considerable cultural centre and Wolfgang Langhoff was only one of a number of artists and intellectuals who made a contribution to the KPD's illegal work. One or two of them occupied leading positions in the clandestine Party organisation: Hans Kralik, for instance, who was Propaganda Secretary (*Agitpropleiter*) of the Düsseldorf Sub-district in 1933 and designed and produced Hugo Paul's leaflets, while his wife, Lia Kralik, who was Jewish, played a part in the Communist-inspired 'White Collar Workers' Commission'. Other artists, too, provided drawings and caricatures for leaflets; others, again, offered their flats or houses for secret meetings, or for lodgings, since they were often more secluded and less easily observed.

For most workers the most familiar branch of culture was sport. At Düsseldorf, as elsewhere, all specifically left-wing sports clubs – Social Democratic as well as Communist – were suppressed by the

Nazis and in some cases their equipment was confiscated too. But their members, especially if they were outstanding sportsmen or had equipment to contribute, might be welcomed into 'bourgeois' or non-political clubs. Communists sometimes tried to move over as a body to one of these clubs, hoping to preserve their corporate existence and perhaps to exert some political influence. In other cases they seem to have adopted the policy of scattering in as many middle-class clubs as possible.[41]

The life of an active Communist in the Third Reich, whether living legally or illegally, was one of extreme hardship, both physical and moral. The failure of a comrade to keep an appointment might spread a ripple of questioning through a neighbourhood or a workplace, and the explanation might never be discovered. The 'illegals' in particular, were sometimes penniless and literally starving.[42] On occasion they might be compelled by some unexplained incident to abandon their lodging and sleep rough, and yet be prevented by the rules of security from appealing for help. Moral agonies were no less acute, especially for those who had had to abandon their families, knowing that they were leaving them in grave economic difficulties. One Düsseldorf Communist, Werner Eggerath, who was a member of the party's Central Operative Leadership at Berlin in the winter of 1934–35, has described how difficult, and indeed impossible, he found it to resist the urge to contact his wife and children and how hard it was to bear the estrangement and incomprehension which had grown up between them.[43]

While clandestine resistance activity weakened family ties, it strengthened the ties of comradeship, creating a strong collective spirit, an intense relationship of trust that went beyond the quality of normal friendship. This had both a positive and a negative side, as Jürgen Kuczynski has observed in his memoirs. The illegal struggle, he writes, made the participants into better comrades, better fighters for human progress, but it did not make them more loveable personalities. They gained, if they did not break down, supreme self-confidence, but at the price of a certain crippling, a loss of spontaneity which was inevitable if they were to achieve what was needed by the Party. They became more distrustful in daily life, but more confident in the world at large; more modest about the small joys of life, but with unlimited expectations for the future of mankind. Without such expectations they could not, perhaps, have developed the courage and at the same time the hardness to persevere year after year in a fight against such odds.[44]

From accounts which have survived in Party archives it has been shown that in the Lower Rhine District, and also in the neighbouring Western Districts, Ruhr and Middle Rhine, a stable Communist Party organisation functioned for over a year, from the spring of 1933 to the late summer of 1934, raising from members in dues and literature payments and occasional donations enough money to cover basic costs and to leave a surplus which might be as high as 40 per cent.[45] During that period, in western Germany, at least, the underground Party was not being financed from abroad, but was sending money to support the activities of the Central Operative Leadership in Berlin. For over a year there was a paid-up membership varying from 1,600 to 1,800 in the Lower Rhine District and fom 1,800 to 2,000 in the Ruhr District. Summing up his conclusions, Dr Peukert remarks that the KPD must be credited with the 'astonishing achievement' of having maintained for the better part of three years an underground organisation of some thousands of members.[46]

The arrest of most of the leaders of the Lower Rhine District in August and September 1934 marked the end of a period of a year and a half during which the organisation of the Communist Party's illegal activity in the District had been relatively stable. From that time the Party in that District began to lose ground in terms of membership, finance, and output of propaganda, and the process continued during the following autumn and winter; all attempts to reverse the trend during the next ten years were to be unsuccessful.

What about other Districts: was the same trend visible there too? Was it a national trend?

CHAPTER 7

A Losing Battle

Throughout Germany the pattern of events was similar, though the timing varied. After the initial shock of February to April 1933, when the KPD had been caught off balance, it had been able, in all its main centres, to rebuild its organisation, to fill many of the gaps in its ranks, to renew its traditional activities. It had continued to collect membership dues and to issue Party literature and seemed to have consolidated its position. From the early summer of 1933, for six months or a year in some places, and up to a year and a half in others, the Party had seemed to maintain its strength and to be prepared for the expected revolutionary crisis.

This recovery of strength was in reality illusory; mass arrests and mass trials steadily undermined it, leaving gaps in the organisation which could no longer be filled. That critical point was reached in some Districts in the winter of 1934–35 in others a little later. Whenever it was reached, it marked a decisive change in the situation. In the Ruhr District, for instance, in Dr Peukert's view, the arrest of members of the District Leadership between January and May 1935 virtually put an end to Communist underground activity on any considerable scale;[1] and the arrest of the Central Operative Leadership in Berlin in March 1935 put an end to operations directed from a single centre within Germany.

The KPD's defeat in the long-drawn-out battle of 1933–35 was due in part to changes in the economic situation in Germany. Although the level of unemployment was still high in the winter of 1934–35, it had been falling and it was now clear that the economic crisis was past its worst. Moreover, by the autumn of 1934 the political situation in Germany was no longer as unstable as it had been in the first eighteen months of the Nazi régime, now that Hitler had succeeded in resolving for the time being the conflict between radical and conservative elements among his supporters.[2]

At the same time the apparatus of repression had been expanded and made more efficient. The Nazi Party's intelligence activities had been concentrated in the hands of the Security Service of the SS (*Sicherheitsdienst* or *SD*),[3] which had been made independent of other branches of the Nazi movement and at the same time increasingly co-ordinated with the Secret State Police (*Gestapo*) through the appointment of SS-men to higher police posts. Thus the Gestapo came to combine the expertise of the old political police with the ruthlessness of the SS.

In the autumn of 1934 wave followed wave of arrests, culminating in group trials, large and small. In these trials it was hardly possible for the accused to follow Dimitrov's example, for the Nazis had learned from the Fire Trial. In April 1934 they had established a new court, the People's Court, specifically entrusted with cases of treason or 'preparation of treason',[4] which were to be tried by a bench of five judges, of whom only the President and one other need be qualified lawyers, the other three being usually high SS or Army officers or Nazi Party dignitaries. This court was not likely to, and did not, display the same legal scruples as had tormented the Reich Court judges at the Fire Trial; moreover, there was no appeal from its verdicts. At the same time the law was amended in such a way as to increase the penalties for 'preparation of treason', which was the usual charge brought against Communist Party activists. Instead of imprisonment for a few months, or at most a year or two, courts could, and did, now impose sentences of hard labour (*Zuchthaus*) for up to ten or fifteen years, or even for life; in some cases the death penalty itself was passed. Moreover, the extreme vagueness and elasticity of the law and of the practice of the courts amounted to a form of torture, which could be, and was, used to exert the maximum pressure in interrogation on persons accused or suspected of political activity.

By 1934, too, concentration camps, which had originally been something of an improvisation, had begun to take on the features of a permanent institution. Political prisoners were usually sent to one of them on the expiry of their sentences, unless they gave evidence of having renounced their previous political allegiance. Although no term was set to the prisoner's stay in the camp, each case was subject to review at regular intervals, with reference mainly to any change in political attitude. The increasing numbers of Communists interned in concentration camps were thus inevitably engaged in a continued political confrontation with the representatives of the régime, not only by their own choice but by the rules and practice of the government itself. Both the material and moral conditions in the camps were such that prisoners could only hope to preserve their health and their self-respect, which often meant their life, by co-operation of an organised kind with fellow prisoners.

The political struggle of Communists against the Nazis did not come to an end, but simply entered a new stage, as more and more of them were put in these camps. It was a struggle with its own rules and criteria of victory and defeat, hidden from the gaze of the nation and the world, seen only by fellow-prisoners; and it was a struggle, not only against the Nazis, but for the achievement in new conditions of that united action of anti-fascists which had been spoken of so often but had proved so difficult to realise. Those prisoners who were released from the camps had to give a solemn undertaking not to speak of their experiences, the facts of which were nevertheless made known by many clandestine books and pamphlets.[5]

As the Party's cadres disappeared into the prisons and camps, the human resources which hitherto had always come forward to fill gaps in the ranks began at last to fail and the gaps to widen.

In Bavaria, according to Hetzer, the organisational structure of the KPD at Sub-district and District levels had been largely destroyed by the end of 1934.[6] In Augsburg, he adds, where the Red Aid organisation had survived, its destruction in the late summer of 1935 had a discouraging effect on the remaining supporters of the KPD, so that no organised Communist activity was to be observed there for a considerable time.[7]

In the Lower Rhine District, Peukert concludes, three of the largest Sub-districts then still active (Wuppertal, Düsseldorf-Gerresheim and Velbert) were broken by mass arrests early in 1935;[8] and in the following June, when Waldemar Schmidt arrived to take up the functions of District leader, he found that the District organisation consisted of little more than working branches in three cities, which were traditional Communist strongholds, and a factory cell in the important chemical factory of IG-Farben at Leverkusen.[9] When Schmidt was almost immediately arrested, there followed an interval of some four months before a further report from the District reached the exiled Party leadership.[10]

This decline in active membership was necessarily reflected in the finances of the underground Party, as the resources accruing from members' dues began to be exhausted in the effort to support fugitives and the families of the imprisoned, as well as to maintain the necessary minimum of paid functionaries. In the Lower Rhine District receipts from membership dues, which totalled 680 Reichsmarks in December 1934, had sunk to 240 Reichsmarks in March-April 1935.[11] As a result the District, which had been able to send a surplus to Berlin in the first half of 1934, had now itself to be subsidised, receiving at least three payments of 400 Reichsmarks from Berlin in the first half of 1935, the necessary price of maintaining a minimum apparatus of functionaries.[12] The smaller Districts had already fallen into this position earlier and few if any of the mass organisations had been able to maintain a complete structure, even in those Districts where Communist influence had been strongest.

By 1935, it is true to say, the clandestine Party organisation no longer had anything like a complete structure, but was reduced to semi-autonomous groups and cells in a number of cities and important factories, maintaining precarious contact with the exiled leadership. The members who were still active continued to make almost superhuman efforts and to give many examples of individual and collective heroism. At the same time, however, they became more and more of a conscious élite, increasingly isolated. The aim which they had hitherto pursued – to combine mass organisation with methods of illegal conspiracy of the Bolshevik type – increasingly revealed itself as inappropriate in the conditions of Nazi Germany. There could be no doubt that the Communists had gained many victories in the moral sphere; but were they gaining political victory too?

The Party leaders were slow to admit, or even to recognise, that they had suffered a major defeat in 1933, and that they continued to fight a losing battle in the political sphere. They saw – as the Gestapo also saw – that despite the gradual recovery of the German economy from the worst effects of the world economic crisis of 1929–32, there continued to be widespread discontent among workers, who grumbled about such things as the still high level of unemployment, food prices and scarcities, deductions from the wage-packet and corruption among Nazi officials.[13] The Communists believed, as the Gestapo for its part feared, that these economic grievances might be developed into a wider political opposition; every sign of discontent tended to nourish wishful thinking and to be taken as evidence of the success of revolutionary propaganda.

In reality, however, the Communist Party's attempts to convert economic discontent into a revolutionary political movement had comparatively little success. This was clearly revealed by the events of June–August 1934. At first sight the political crisis which broke out on the Night of the Long Knives might have been interpreted as a sign of the weakening of the Nazi régime, since the proportion of voters who failed to register a vote in favour of Hitler in the plebiscite of 19 August (whether by voting against the régime, abstaining or spoiling their ballot paper) was considerably higher than in the previous plebiscite nine months earlier. When the events of that summer are taken as a whole, however, they can hardly bear that interpretation. It is easier to see them as marking a strengthening of Hitler's position in the outcome, while such widening of opposition as there may have been is not necessarily to be ascribed to the influence of the Communist Party. The Directorate of Police of the Bavarian industrial city of Augsburg reported on 1 September 1934, for instance, that National Socialism had lost ground there since the previous year, as shown by the fact that the proportion of negative votes of all kinds was greater in the plebiscite of 19 August 1934 than it had been in that of 12 November 1933.[14] But the Gestapo – which was, of course, keenly interested in the question – concluded with some relief that of the 25 per cent of the electorate which displayed some kind of negative attitude, only some 10 per cent were motivated by Communist or socialist sympathies; more of the opposition was due, they thought, to Christian discontent. Dr Hetzer, in his study of Bavaria, while accepting this Gestapo comment, remarks that the Communist Party's agitation had not linked up with other discontent. In Peukert's view, the KPD suffered from 'self-isolation' because it spoke a language which only its own members understood.[15] It was a language which made a virtue of necessity, referring to the shrinkage of the movement as 'our policy of concentration'.[16]

We can now see in retrospect that the events of June to August 1934 marked something of a turning-point in the history of the Communist Party's underground struggle as well as in the history of the Third Reich in general. Hitler had succeeded in overcoming the most dangerous crisis of his rule, and the Communist Party had failed to take advantage of it. And, if the lesson was still not clear, it was to be emphasised beyond all doubt by the Nazi victory in the Saar plebiscite of January 1935. By that time, a combination of economic recovery, nationalism, and foreign policy successes began to outweigh economic discontent, and a section of the working class began to manifest a passive acceptance of the régime. Nazi demagogy, though not without its fleeting successes, had no deep or lasting effects: apathy and cynicism were the dominant mood. The elections of Councillors of Trust in places of work in the spring of 1935 confirmed the impression of contradictory feelings among workers, for the results varied greatly from one place of work to another, the only general trend being the frequent rejection of candidates most closely associated with National Socialism. That the results were unsatisfactory from the point of view of the Nazi authorities was shown by the fact that the holding of such factory elections, limited as their scope was, was discontinued after 1935. From that time working-class feelings began to be expressed in new ways, dictated by further changes in the economic situation, which will be discussed in a later chapter.

German Communists did at least draw one conclusion from the evidence of weakness which the events of June to August 1934 furnished. From the autumn of that year they made increasingly persistent efforts to achieve a working alliance with the Social Democrats and other anti-Nazi elements. Some agreements of that kind were reached on a local scale, within Germany: in particular factories, for instance, during the elections of Councillors of Trust in the spring of 1935.[17] On a Reich scale there were exchanges between representatives of the KPD Central Committee in exile and of Sopade during the autumn and winter of 1934–35, but although the Communist representatives pressed for an effective agreement, none was reached.[18] The Social Democratic representatives usually professed to have no authority to conclude one; in effect the majority of Sopade remained unwilling to enter into any binding agreement with the Communist Party.[19]

In some districts in Germany where the local repesentatives of the Social Democratic underground took a different attitude and were prepared for joint action, yet at the same time were reluctant to defy their own exiled leadership, a way round was found by substituting Red Aid for the KPD as the SPD's partner in such an agreement. In January 1935, for instance, a call for joint action was published in the form of a leaflet signed by the Mid and South Baden leaderships of the SPD and of Red Aid respectively, as well as by a body calling itself 'Red Defence League for Baden'.[20] Some months later, on 26

June 1935, another such leaflet was distributed over the signatures respectively of the Berlin-Brandenburg District of the SPD and the Berlin-Brandenburg Praesidium of Red Aid, with a note to the effect that the Berlin-Brandenburg District leadership of the KPD had taken cognisance of the manifesto and agreed with it.[21]

Nevertheless, such co-operation between the Social Democrats and the Communists occurred only in certain localities and was not achieved on a Reich scale. Various reasons have been suggested for this. The main explanation must be that the Social Democratic leadership in exile, when considering how the overthrow of the Nazis could be brought about, conceived increasingly, from 1934, of alliance with the KPD and reliance on the Western powers as alternative paths, and in that perspective was unwilling to go beyond purely exploratory discussions with the KPD. But although the attitude of the SPD was the principal reason for the failure of all negotiations for united action, it may not have been the only one. Social Democratic historians have argued that the failure of the KPD to move any significant body of workers into action during the crisis of the summer months of 1934 may have made them appear in the eyes of other anti-fascists as weak potential allies whose collaboration was not worth paying a high political price for. This explanation, however, tending to exculpate the SPD, puts the cart before the horse. It could more plausibly be argued that the approaches made from the Communist side still took the form of proposed concessions within the general concept of a Soviet Germany, rather than of an attempt to work out a new and more broadly acceptable conception of post-Hitler Germany. There were, it has to be remembered, serious differences among the leaders of the German Communist Party on that question at that time, and these resulted in a certain vacillation and lack of clarity in the Party's policy statements and negotiating positions. This was particularly unfortunate in the trade union sphere, in which promising moves towards a broad anti-Nazi front took place in some parts of Germany – especially in the Ruhr and Rhineland – in the autumn and winter of 1934–35. At the same time it was in the field of trade-union affairs that the ultra-left members of the KPD's Politburo, led by Fritz Schulte, head of the RGO, had most influence.

Certain contacts and discussions with anti-Nazi groups in the Christian churches, which had taken place in 1933 and 1934, also failed to develop beyond preliminary talks, partly because of the

Christians' reluctance to allow their opposition to assume a political character, partly also because of the inability of the two sides to agree on any clear statement concerning what sort of régime should come after Hitler.[22]

Reluctant as the KPD was to admit defeat, the hard facts gradually but inexorably asserted themselves. At local level there were signs of new attitudes, and of new thinking and discussion among clandestine Party activists about the tactics being followed and above all about the doctrine of 'mass struggle' and the heavy losses to which it led. By the end of 1934, after new waves of arrests, doubts about the existing party line became even more pronounced.

This trend was probably promoted by the fact that some of those who now appeared as leaders of ward or factory groups had not been recruited to organised clandestine activity or promoted to positions of leadership in it by the authority of full-time organisers, but had taken the initiative and created their own illegal groups. Such people, as a result of bitter experience, were inclined to be suspicious of individuals purporting to be high-level functionaries sent in from outside, and to insist on conditions for recognising the authority of such functionaries: an undertaking, for example, to make no contacts within the area covered by the local group except through its chosen representatives. When the newly appointed leader of the Lower Rhine District, Heinrich Wiatrek, arrived at Düsseldorf in the autumn of 1934 and tried to restore contact with the remaining underground organisations, he met with suspicion and reluctance to accept his authority on the part of the *de facto* local leadership which still survived.[23] They demanded an assurance that the new District leader would not recruit people to District functions, such as those of courier or printer (*Techniker*), nor use material resources such as presses, except through the City Leadership. This demand was the fruit of experience and its acceptance was probably one reason why, in Düsseldorf, the city's underground leadership was able to function without discovery for a further eight or nine months. Local activists were beginning to suspect that an elaborate organisational structure such as the KPD had been trying to maintain was incompatible with security.

By the beginning of 1935 the Party's central leadership, too, was beginning to doubt the possibility of maintaining the traditional Party structure with all its ramifications. The Lower Rhine District was not the only one in which it was proving impossible to fill gaps in the District and Sub-district leaderships, and sometimes only a fragment of the traditional structure remained in existence. Lack of cadres also resulted in duplication of functions which in turn led to breaches of security and further losses. This happened especially in the sphere of printing, where the central or regional 'technical officers' were compelled by shortage of available facilities to compete with the local 'technical' functionaries, with the consequence of further insecurity, mass arrests, and the necessity of printing abroad, which again led to delays and loss of impact. A clear indication that the resources at the underground Party's disposal were being used up was its inability to rebuild its central technical apparatus (the printing and publishing branch) after the arrest of key functionaries in January 1935. Here, as in the general management of underground work, Sector leaderships in neighbouring countries were to play an increasingly important role.

A turning-point was reached when the entire inner-German leadership at Berlin – the Central Operative Leadership – was arrested on 27 March 1935. It consisted of Adolf Rembte, who had been a member of the leadership since May 1934 and was due to be relieved, Robert Stamm, who had been leader of the Berlin District and Max Maddalena, an expert in the trade-union field. Herbert Wehner was to have formed the fourth member of the team, but had been prevented from leaving Czechoslovakia because the Czech police detained him.

The Central Operative Leadership had already been experiencing increasing difficulty in controlling underground activity outside Berlin. Now, it was not replaced, and for a time the future form of leadership of the Communist underground struggle remained uncertain. Voices calling for far-reaching changes had been becoming louder. There was a growing feeling that new thinking and new tactics were needed; that it was impossible for the Party to go on incurring such losses, and that Hitler's success in stabilising the Nazi régime had altered the whole national and international situation. The decrease of unemployment and the fading of expectations of revolution also contributed to a change of mood among Communists.

These currents of thought and feeling expressed themselves not only, or mainly, at the top of the Party, but above all among the younger underground functionaries, and it was to draw on their experience that a number of frontier conferences were held in neighbouring countries. Representatives of the Western Districts, for instance, were summoned to Amsterdam to take part in such conferences at the end of August 1934 and at Easter and again at Whitsuntide 1935.[24]

These conferences were from one point of view part of the process by which the frontier posts in neighbouring countries were coming to play an increasingly important part in the direction of the Party's clandestine work in Germany. From another point of view they were part of the process by which preparations were made and suitable representatives of the underground Party chosen to go to Moscow for the top-level conferences which were to review the whole strategy of the movement as well as the tactics and organisation required to carry it out.

In the view of some historians the discontinuation of the Central Operative Leadership and the shrinkage of the KPD's District Organisations in 1935, together with the shift of the clandestine leadership from Berlin to centres of emigration, signified nothing less than the collapse of the Communist resistance. This, as will be argued in later chapters, is to overstate the case. The underground army of some thousands of revolutionaries which had maintained a struggle against the Nazi tyranny for two or three years, though it had suffered a defeat, had not disappeared. Nevertheless 1935 marked the end of a stage, an important transition. The active membership outside camps and prisons, which had remained fairly stable for some two years, was now seriously declining, as casualties were no longer replaced, and consequently the belief in a revolutionary overthrow of the fascist government in the near future began to wane. The Communists had to face the fact that the working class had suffered a major defeat, and that sections of it, though not often converted to fascism, were tending to turn cynical and disillusioned, to lose interest in politics and to retreat into private life.

CHAPTER 8

The Crisis of Policy

The immediate effect of the disaster of 1933 had not been to stimulate new thinking in the German Communist Party, but to bring about a closing of the ranks, ideologically as well as organisationally. The ultra-left line, with its definition of Social Democracy as 'social fascism', its underestimation of National Socialism and consequent excessive optimism, and its strategy of a revolutionary offensive, had been reaffirmed; and the break up of the Social Democratic movement had been seen as opening up new opportunities of achieving working-class unity under Communist leadership. Those who had doubts stifled them for the sake of Party discipline.

Yet experience of the underground struggle, as it developed, could not but strengthen existing doubts and raise new ones. The heavy cost and limited achievement of the ultra-left line in practice caused it to be questioned by at least some of those engaged in underground activity, even if slowly and with delay.

One of those who questioned it was the Düsseldorf Communist, Rudolf Goguel, mentioned above in Chapter 6, who played an active role in Communist trade-union affairs in the Lower Rhine District in the spring and summer of 1934, after his release from a concentration camp. Goguel, in conversation with District functionaries, expressed much criticism of the sectarian line which still prevailed in the KPD and in its associated trade-union mass organisation, the RGO; he even briefly contemplated going over to the right-wing Communist break-away group, the KPO,[1] though in the end he did not do so. He disapproved of the maintenance of the RGO as a separate organisation, and suggested that the Communist Party itself should be reduced to small, reliable groups, especially in industry. His views anticipated almost the whole range of policies which were later to be adopted by the Party in 1935, and he set them down in a memorandum to be forwarded to the Central Operative Leadership in Berlin.

In an organisation in which discipline and unity were so important as they were in the Communist Party, a change of direction could hardly be effected unless the initiative were at some stage taken from above. In the course of 1934 criticisms such as those voiced by Goguel were developed into an alternative policy which began to be put forward against the leftist line at the highest levels of the International. Some scholars have emphasised the part played in this debate by the French Communist Party, whose Popular Front policy could be seen as an application of the lessons of January 1933 in Germany as well as of those of February 1934 in Paris and Vienna. Others, especially in the German Democratic Republic, have stressed the part played by a small 'Marxist-Leninist' minority in the KPD leadership, consisting of Wilhelm Pieck and Walter Ulbricht, although it is difficult to find evidence that they took the initiative before the latter half of 1934. Others again, who are accustomed to represent individual Communist parties as no more than instruments of Soviet foreign policy, have seen in the Popular Front line which was gaining strength in the International during 1934 a faithful reflection of a turn in Stalin's foreign policy. The Soviet government, they point out, had previously been inclined to see the chief danger to its security in the Western powers and in their satellites such as Poland, and had therefore sought to protect itself by cultivating relations with Germany, in the spirit of the Rapallo Treaty of 1922. The accession of Hitler to power in 1933 had not at first appeared to involve any great change in these power relationships. But the German-Polish treaty of January 1934 wakened the Soviet government to the danger of the Nazi régime and to the need to build up a new international alliance to check Hitler's plans of aggression.

This change in the international situation was bound to affect the position and policies of the Communist International and therefore of the KPD. But its immediate effect has often been overemphasised. The leaders of the German Party in particular showed no subservient haste to 'turn when Joe turned'. On the contrary, most of them put up a prolonged resistance to a change of line. A comparison of dates, too, hardly confirms the suggestion that the new line originated with the Soviet government. While it is true that the development of the Popular Front line followed close on the heels of the German-Polish pact, the outlines of the new policy, with special reference to Germany, had already been put forward publicly by Dimitrov in his speeches at the Reichstag Fire trial of September to December 1933. These speeches, and especially his closing address to the court in December, have been described as 'the starting point of a new orientation in the Communist International'.[2] Out of these speeches a new analysis of the world situation and a new conception of Communist strategy emerged; and it was to be further elaborated in June 1934 in a letter which Dimitrov wrote to the committee appointed by the Executive Committee of the International to draft the report which he was to make to the World Congress – the first since 1928 – which it was at that time planned to hold later in 1934.[3]

Dimitrov proposed a radical change in the Communists' attitude to social democracy and to the question of a united front of the working class. Social Democracy should no longer be termed 'social fascism' nor be regarded as 'the main social support of the bourgeoisie'. The idea that left-wing social democracy was the most dangerous kind should also be abandoned, and attempts to unite reformist and revolutionary trade unions in countries in which both existed should not be complicated by setting conditions designed to ensure the hegemony of the Communist Party. As for the united front, it should not be pursued only with a view to 'exposing' social democracy, nor only 'from below'; it should be used to unleash a vast mass initiative, unhampered by petty tutelage by Communist parties or general formulas about the treachery of social democracy.

These points were put by Dimitrov in the form of questions and it is evident, if only from the postponement of the proposed congress until 1935, that they were not accepted by the Executive Committee of the International without a prolonged struggle behind the scenes. In this debate the majority of the leadership of the German Party – the Politburo – was particularly firmly wedded to the old ultra-left line; in the very month of Dimitrov's letter they decided to re-issue the 'Programme of Social and National Liberation' of 1930, amended in detail, but still reflecting the old strategy.[4] At some time during the summer or autumn of 1934 two members of the Politburo – Wilhelm Pieck and Walter Ulbricht – apparently began to press within that body for the adoption of what can perhaps be called 'the Dimitrov line'. Exactly when this happened is not altogether clear from the documents which have survived and been published. It does seem clear, however, that the two were at first isolated in the Politburo and that controversy went on in the higher reaches of the Party, barely concealed, during most of the period from June 1934 to the beginning of 1935, not without some inconsistencies in the statements of individual leaders.[5] Because of these inconsistencies, Duhnke and other Western writers have interpreted what took place as a struggle for power between individuals rather than as a major disagreement over policy.[6] But some inconsistencies could hardly have been avoided, for in a Communist Party operating in conditions of strict illegality it was especially necessary to preserve the appearance of unity in public statements. The process of carrying through a major change of policy could therefore only to a very limited extent take the form of open debate, but was bound to take the form, largely, of giving new emphases, new meanings to accepted terms, while maintaining the fiction that the same policies were being applied in new circumstances.

Meanwhile, among underground militants too, doubts about the ultra-left policy were beginning to grow, especially perhaps in the Western Districts, where there may have been more contact with the emigration. The doubts found expression in an increasing reluctance on the part of rank-and-file members to accept unrealistic or sectarian slogans, such as 'All Power to the Soviets' or 'Build Revolutionary Class Trade Unions'. Local Communist groups which made contact with other underground socialists were beginning to recognise that the Social Democratic Party had also in some measure recovered from its collapse of 1933 and at the same time that its right wing was ceasing to feel the need to camouflage itself in the revolutionary language of the Prague Manifesto. They had to recognise, too, that clandestine SPD and SAP[7] groups maintained a real if modest activity in certain places, so that some of the conditions for a united front existed, given a readiness to negotiate on both sides.

Yet if anything so incongruous as an opinion poll could have taken place in the conditions of the underground struggle, it would probably have shown that the KPD's active membership as well as its leadership was divided. The criticisms and reservations of some rank-and-filers such as Goguel were not shared by all, and were only faintly echoed in the reports of full-time functionaries, who tended to be keenly conscious of the need for discipline and had also, in many cases, grown up in the leftist tradition.

Events themselves intervened when the National Socialist régime was shaken by the political upheaval of the 'Night of the Long Knives' of 30 June 1934. That the Hitler state contained the seeds of internal conflict had long been understood in a general sense by the KPD and the development of such conflict had been looked forward to as likely to furnish the occasion for mass revolutionary action; yet the actual event took the Party by surprise. Hitler was able to master the grave crisis without any effective intervention by the Communist Party. Mass revolutionary action, it turned out, was not on the agenda, if only because the KPD had made too little progress in winning over the mass of Social Democratic workers, and was therefore also unable to attract the dissatisfied elements in the Nazi movement. This failure caused grave disquiet among Communists and exposed the need for a deeper analysis of the causes of the defeat of 1933 and for a renewed examination of the KPD's policies and activities since then.

On 9 and 10 July 1934 a joint meeting of the KPD leadership and the ECCI Praesidium considered the position.[8] The conclusions reached were referred at the end of the month to a specially convened meeting of the Party's Central Committee.[9] On 1 August agreement was reached on a resolution entitled 'The Creation of the United Front of the Working Masses against the Hitler Dictatorship'.[10] This was a compromise. It pointed the way towards the adoption of a new line, but went no further than to make a change of emphasis, without any profound self-criticism, showing that the KPD leadership was following reluctantly behind the development of policy in the International as a whole.

The most striking change recorded in the resolution of 1 August 1934 was in the field of trade-union policy. The underground Party was instructed to aim at the revival of a united trade union federation and, where necessary to achieve this, to abandon any surviving 'revolutionary trade unions' or efforts to establish them. In the field of general anti-fascist struggle, however, while party organisations were instructed to make new approaches to any active socialist groups for joint anti-fascist action and to aim at the broadest anti-fascist front, including dissatisfied SA men and Hitler Youth members, and while many instances of local co-operation were reported, nothing was said about new approaches to the Social Democratic leadership. Moreover, the ultimate outcome of any successful joint action with underground Social Democratic groups was still thought of as their adherence to the Communist Party;

indeed, at this very time a united front agreement concluded by the Communists in the Hessen-Nassau District was condemned by the Politburo as 'opportunist'.[11]

The leftist or sectarian view still commanded a decisive majority in the seven-or-eight-man Politburo. Pieck and Ulbricht were still the sole supporters of a new Popular Front line, and the effect of the resolution of 1 August was to give them greater scope in giving expression to this trend, both in policy statements and in organisational reforms. Nonetheless the Party was severely handicapped during the next six months by the disagreement which prevailed in its top leadership, and which came very near at times to a public debate in the *émigré* press. In August and September 1934 Pieck and Ulbricht published articles emphasising the need for approaches to SPD groups to seek common action round broadly based demands;[12] in October the interest shown in this new tendency by the left-wing socialist leaders on the SPD-Executive – especially Siegfried Aufhäuser – produced a dangerous divergence of opinion about what the KPD's reaction should be.[13] Ulbricht insisted that the Communists should set no conditions for joint action, and should seek to extend the debate, while the Politburo majority attacked him and at the same time published denunciations of the left-wing Social Democrats in familiar sectarian language.

This dispute threatened to split the Party and after a stormy session of the Politburo at Paris on 19–23 October, the Political Commission of ECCI intervened on 27 October, coming down decisively on the side of Ulbricht and Pieck.[14] The majority formally accepted this ruling but (except probably for Dahlem) were still not really won over to the new conception. The new relation of forces was reflected in a resolution which the Politburo passed on 30 October 1934, calling on the Party to make preparations for the coming World Congress of the International by initiating the broadest possible discussion not only among Communists, but in all sections of the working class.[15]

It is difficult to imagine how a grass-roots debate on the scale envisaged could have been carried through in the circumstances of the clandestine struggle, even with the help of special conferences and frontier 'schools'; but the attempt was made.

The resolution of 30 October 1934 clearly reflected the contradictions which still existed among the leaders; for while on the one hand it insisted on the need to draw on the experience of the movement, to adopt a new strategy and tactics appropriate to the changed conditions, and to draw non-Party circles into the discussion of these matters, on the other hand it spoke of the 'continuation of our Bolshevik strategy' and posed as the task of a united working class 'the anti-fascist freedom struggle for the establishment of a Soviet Germany'. Thus the fruitful suggestion which Thälmann had put out in his last speech to the Central Committee, that the overthrow of the fascist dictatorship might not coincide with the proletarian revolution, had still not been taken up and developed by the majority of the leadership.

Nevertheless, for the first time the Pieck-Ulbricht group was able to pass to the offensive. Ulbricht sought, and no doubt obtained, the support of Dimitrov – now advanced to the key post of Secretary-General of the International in Moscow – in countering sectarian practices in the KPD on the united front question, and with regard to trade-union affairs (expressed in the slogan 'Mass Walk-out from the Labour Front'); and approaches to other non-Nazi elements were pursued with a new vigour. An appeal issued in the name of the KPD's Central Committee to Christian workers on 8 November 1934, for instance, clearly went beyond the bounds of the old 'leftist' line and represented a real change;[16] so did an Open Letter of mid-November, addressed to all Social Democratic, trade union and Labour Front members.[17] At the same time the Central Operative Leadership, acting on the instructions of the Politburo, set out a detailed programme for discussions throughout the clandestine Party in Germany, and urged that wide sections of the working class be involved in them, 'especially former Social Democratic, trade union and Christian workers'.[18] Then, on 29 November 1934, Ulbricht, in a tone-setting article entitled 'The Way to Unity of Action in Germany' proclaimed the need to combat sectarian tendencies and to make a differentiated estimate of the various trends in Social Democracy.[19]

Before Ulbricht's article could be effectively followed up, the continued stubborn opposition of the Politburo majority needed to be finally overcome. In order to achieve this, the Executive Committee of the International required the KPD's Politburo to call a Central Committee meeting at Moscow in January 1935. At that meeting the non-German representatives of ECCI who were present[20] threw their weight into the scale and a resolution was passed sharply criticising the KPD Politburo majority for its 'sectarian' attitude and approving the line of the minority.[21] It was probably at this time that two influential members of the Politburo, Florin and Heckert, influenced partly by the change of thinking in the International and partly by reports from the clandestine Party in Germany, came over to accept the new policy in essentials, leaving the unyielding protagonists of the leftist strategy, Hermann Schubert and Fritz Schulte, isolated in the leadership. From that time, therefore, the new line was fairly consistently followed, even if all its implications were not yet fully perceived and accepted. It was at this meeting of January 1935, too, that the decision was taken to arrange a Party Conference later in the year in order to draw out the implications of the new policy, to give it greater authority, and to ensure the greatest possible consultation of the underground party organisations. Meanwhile a working party was set up, under the chairmanship of Ulbricht, to supervise the application of the new line in Germany, especially in relation to united front negotiations, the most sensitive area.

By the time the protagonists of the new line had definitely prevailed in the KPD leadership, the conditions were in one way no longer so favourable to the achievement of a united working-class front as they had been a year earlier. The left-wing group on the Executive of the Social Democratic Party, which favoured a re-union of working-class parties on the basis of revolutionary Marxism and was prepared to negotiate with the Communist Party, had been losing ground in the second half of 1934, while the reformist majority had regained strength in terms both of international recognition and of contacts with surviving Social Democratic groups within Germany. The majority, consequently, had soon abandoned even lip-service to the principles of the Prague Manifesto and had reverted both in theory and practice to reformism, including a resolute opposition to serious negotiations with the Communist Party. It was thus particularly unfortunate that such soundings of the KPD's terms as the left-wing Social Democrat leaders made were met with demands for a virtual surrender, or at least with an uncertain reply, right up to October 1934. When, finally, the effective adoption of the new line by the Communist leadership in January was followed by serious formal proposals to the Social Democratic Executive, it proved comparatively easy, in the sharp crisis which resulted within that body, for the reformist majority to assert itself decisively, not only by rejecting the KPD's approaches, but by expelling from the Executive Aufhäuser and Böchel, the main left-wing supporters of unity. It was unfortunate, too, that the biggest united front achievement in western Germany – the development of Communist-Social Democratic co-operation in a trade union of some 400 members at Wuppertal – was smashed by the police with mass arrests at precisely this time.[22] But the coincidence was perhaps no accident, for it happened more than once that as soon as Socialist-Communist talks resulted in joint actions, the police intervened.

The decisive meeting of the KPD Politburo at which the new line prevailed had taken place on 19 January 1935; its formal adoption followed on 30 January, when a session of the Central Committee passed a resolution entitled 'Proletarian United Front and Anti-Fascist People's Front for the Overthrow of the Fascist Dictatorship', which was later published.[23] The resolution emphasised the necessity of a united workers' front as the key to building the broadest Popular Front, and called for a struggle throughout the Party to overcome sectarianism in its various aspects, such as resistance to a united front and to the re-establishment of the federated trade unions, failure to distinguish between right-wing and left-wing SPD leaders, 'pseudo-radical estimates of the situation', in other words exaggerating the difficulties experienced by the Nazi régime, and, finally, inadequate self-criticism.

After the meetings of January 1935, the process of converting the Party to the new line went rapidly ahead. Conferences between the Party leaders – especially those already identified with the new line – and important underground functionaries took place in countries bordering on Germany. Appropriate changes of personnel were made in the leadership of the Districts and in the Central Operative Leadership at Berlin.[24] The conversion of the underground Party to the new line might have taken place more completely if the newly constituted Central Operative Leadership, from which the champions of the leftist line had been excluded, had not been arrested after its first meeting on 27 March 1935. Nevertheless, some of the younger and most successful clandestine organisers were chosen to represent their Districts at a major conference, at which some of them were to be elected to a new Central Committee in place of prominent last-ditch adherents of the ultra-left line.

Meanwhile the resolution of 30 January 1935 had finally and fully cleared the way, from the Communist side, for negotiations with the SPD at the top as well as at lower levels, and on 11 February 1935 the KPD leadership addressed an Open Letter to the SPD Executive, proposing negotiations. On the Social-Democratic side, however, as we have noted, the situation had been developing in a contrary direction. The Executive had been gradually withdrawing its organisational and financial support from active left-wing underground groups, and the left-wing minority on the SPD Executive was more isolated than it had been a year before; and its main representatives, when they tried to exert pressure for negotiations, were simply expelled from the Executive in March 1935.[25] In the following months several further offers of negotiations were made by the KPD leadership, but all were rejected by the SPD Executive, which now increasingly placed its hopes on renewed signs of friction in bourgeois circles in Germany in certain matters such as church affairs.

The February offer had referred particularly to the forthcoming elections of Councillors of Trust in the factories, proposing joint committees to exploit the last remaining institution in the Third Reich which offered some semi-legal opportunities for the expression of working-class opinion. Although joint action at the top level was refused, local co-operation was achieved in many areas. Its success, as has already been noted, may help to explain why the Nazis never again held that type of election.[26]

In the spring of 1935 much consultation took place at District and Regional conferences of the clandestine Communist Party on topics worked out by the Internal Leadership, such as the role of social democracy in Nazi Germany and the objective and subjective conditions for proletarian revolution.[27] Conferences were also held at Amsterdam and other frontier posts between representatives of the Politburo, notably Dahlem and Ulbricht, and leading underground functionaries from Germany, including younger cadres who had recently graduated from the International's Lenin School, where the new line had prevailed earlier than in the KPD. Most of these younger cadres were in favour of the new line and passed relatively self-critical resolutions. It appears to have been through such frontier conferences that delegates were chosen, probably by the Politburo, to represent the underground Party at the national and international conferences which were soon to take place. Of the 30 KPD delegates at the Seventh World Congress, fifteen came from clandestine work in Germany. Hermann Schubert, who continued to stand out for the old line, was later to condemn the frontier conferences of this period as 'an Ulbricht plot', but it is not easy to see in what other way a change of line could have been effected, without a damaging split. It has to be remembered, too, that it was just at this time that the result of the Saar plebiscite brought a sobering shock, to stimulate realistic thinking.

The new Popular Front line was finally and formally adopted for the Communist International as a whole at the Seventh (and last) World Congress which met at Moscow in July–August 1935. Its application to Germany was elaborated at the subsequent 'Brussels Conference' of the German Communist Party in October.[28]

Although those of the KPD delegates at these conferences who came from underground work in Germany may already have inclined to favour the new 'Dimitrov line' through their experience of clandestine work, and may have shown this at the frontier conferences, they were not necessarily fully committed to it, and it is probable that the opportunity for conversation with Party leaders, both German and non-German, brought some of them to a decision. Schubert and Schulte were still pressing the leftist view, which they represented as 'Thälmann's policy', but they were now going against a strong tide and by the time of the conference in October only one or two other delegates supported them.

The 'Brussels Conference', so called for security reasons, though it actually met near Moscow, was treated as having the status of a full Party Congress. It lasted for twelve days. There were 38 voting delegates, of whom 22 came directly from the German underground and the other 16 from the emigration; in addition there were some participants without voting rights, bringing the total to some 45 or 50.[29]

The course of the conference was to a large extent determined by a preparatory commission, on which adherents of the new line predominated. Pieck chaired and effectively directed the proceedings, putting the case for the new line on behalf of what was now the Politburo majority. A strong influence in the same direction was exerted by Palmiro Togliatti, representing the Executive Committee of the International, who strongly criticised the past actions of the KPD.[30] Similar criticisms were pressed by some of the younger men (and women) who had distinguished themselves as clandestine organisers: Wilhelm Knöchel, for instance, who was to play a key role at two periods in the future, argued strongly that the situation in which Party leaders only made a show of accepting the new line, but acted against it, should not be allowed to continue.[31] This view prevailed, and when, at the end of the Conference, a new Central Committee was elected, the last-ditch leftists were excluded from it, and therefore from its subcommittees such as the Politburo. In place of a large committee of some 60 members, there was now to be a much smaller committee of eighteen members (including Thälmann *in absentia*), of whom nine (again including Thälmann) were to form the Political Bureau. Five of these Politburo members were entrusted with the leadership of the Party's underground operations.[32] This new Executive Committee gave increased weight to younger activists with experience of clandestine work, but overall control of policy remained in the hands of older leaders who formed a majority of the Political Bureau.

At the Brussels Conference the German Communist Party, following the lead which the International had given at its World Congress in August, finally recognised that it had made serious mistakes in the recent past. A new analysis was made of the situation in the world and in Germany and the belief that conditions were ripe for proletarian revolution was abandoned, or at least modified. Social Democracy was no longer to be seen as the main social support of bourgeois rule in Germany. In the perspective now adopted, the overthrow of the Nazi régime was envisaged as leading, not to a Soviet Germany, but to a popular democracy. The basis was thus laid – or so it was hoped – for the sort of broad anti-fascist alliance which had hitherto proved unattainable. At the same time new tactics were proposed, involving greater caution and realism, together with a readiness to exploit all legal opportunities which Nazi institutions might provide for defending workers' interests; illegal organisation was to be looser and more flexible.

Delegates who had come straight from clandestine work in such areas as the Ruhr, Hamburg, or Berlin, gave examples at the Conference of local co-operation with Social Democrats and other socialists, involving as a beginning such elementary acts of solidarity as joint support for relatives of arrested members or mutual attendance at each others' funerals. Instances were also cited of more advanced types of co-operation, such as taking turns in producing an illegal paper designed to lay the basis for re-building of a free trade union. Such reciprocity, it was pointed out, might have special advantages, for, while the Communists might have a stronger organisation, individual Social Democrats sometimes retained positions as Councillors of Trust or even, occasionally still, as policemen.

There was clearly no lack of discontent among peasants and the lower-middle class as well as among workers on a variety of economic and social issues, and examples were quoted at the Conference of the ingenious use of Nazi mass organisations such as the Labour Front, the Hitler Youth, the National Socialist People's Welfare League (NSV) and the Air Defence League. But this was an area in which one swallow did not make a summer. Bold or ingenious *coups* tended to put the police on the alert and were for that reason often difficult to repeat.

The 'Brussels decisions' could not be quickly or automatically applied in day-to-day practice. For one thing, some inconsistencies and areas of unclarity remained. The sectarian errors which had been renounced at the Conference tended to be spoken of as if they had been correct in their time, but no longer corresponded to the changed situation; thus, from fear of admitting that the Party could ever have been wrong, the implications of its self-criticism were not fully drawn. Some terms, such as 'Dictatorship of the Proletariat' and 'Mass Organisation' tended to remain current in clandestine literature without the necessary reconsideration or redefinition in the context of the new strategic conception.

Another factor was that although the way should now have been open for the Communists to offer co-operation to Social Democrats or Christian anti-fascists on equal terms, and although many of the younger Communist cadres, especially those coming newly from the Lenin School, did offer co-operation sincerely and with good will, the traditional hostility and mistrust on both sides ran deep and proved difficult to overcome. There were also some among the older Communists who did not find it easy to break with the deeply-rooted ideas and feelings of the ultra-left period. The proposed 'Trojan Horse' tactic, too, was rejected as opportunist by many underground Communists, who feared that it would lead to misunderstandings and accusations of betrayal. In a sense, too, the change of line seemed to have come too late. The disciplined and confident political army which might once have applied it to good effect had by now exhausted its reserves and was no longer capable of a major effort. Some of the delegates who had helped to work out the new policies were unable to return to Germany to give a lead in applying them, while many clandestine activists learned little or nothing of them until 1945.

Thus a certain dichotomy was to develop in the Party between an *émigré* leadership increasingly remote from life in Germany, and the Communists in the factories and prisons there, tending to lose touch with the current political thinking of the Party which they still thought of as theirs.

Why had the adoption of the new policy involved a process of inner-party struggle and debate spread over more than a year? Essentially because what was involved was not simply a change of tactics or of emphasis, but a revision of some fundamental conceptions about the character and stages of the transition to socialism. The desirability of a united working-class front, and even of a broader anti-fascist front, had been evident enough to Communists, in Germany as elsewhere, ever since the danger of fascism had first arisen. But at the same time it was believed that developed industrial capitalist countries had long been ripe, and even over-ripe for socialism, and that the only possible step forward for a society in the stage of imperialism, whether the political system was bourgeois-democratic or fascist, was to the building of socialism under a proletarian dictatorship. In those circumstances anti-fascist unity was understood necessarily to imply the acceptance by social-democratic or bourgeois-democratic partners of Communist leadership and a programme of immediate transition to socialism.

In practice this was to make an unacceptable condition and was equivalent to regarding united-front offers as a tactic aimed simply at exposing the 'treachery' of Social-Democratic leaders. Yet more credible and realistic offers could not be made until the transition to socialism was seen, not as an immediate prospect for which all the conditions already existed, but as a long-term prospect for which some of the essential political conditions would still need to be brought into being in the course of a distinct historical stage, possibly of long duration, of anti-fascist democratic revolution. This was the conception which had had to be worked out, clarified and absorbed before the new Popular Front strategy could be widely accepted. It was the intensity of the struggle over this conception, the difficulty of the re-thinking involved, which must explain the long time-lag in the KPD's adaptation to the new situation of 1933.

If the German Communist Party seems to have been particularly slow in accepting the new line, this was no doubt partly because in Germany more than in any other country the conditions for proletarian revolution and transition to socialism seemed to have fully matured.

The adoption of the new Popular Front line, combined with the accompanying revised estimate of the situation had, of course, many important implications for the activity and therefore also for the organisation of the illegal Party in Germany. It was now recognized that fascism had succeeded, if not in winning over, at least in neutralising the majority of the workers, and that the building of an anti-fascist front must be viewed as a long-term task. Political slogans should not continually call for mass demonstrations or uprisings, but should be more carefully formulated with reference to the current economic grievances of particular sections of the people, and every possible use should be made of the legal or semi-legal opportunities afforded by the Nazi mass organisations. Cadres should be carefully nurtured and not squandered in heroic but reckless actions.

In a sense this change of strategy came too late, since the head-on offensive conducted by the underground KPD against the Nazi dictatorship had involved such heavy losses in the years 1933–35 that the scale of activity was necessarily already greatly reduced. The effect of these losses combined with the new strategic conception to impose a far-reaching reorganisation of the underground party in the period following the Brussels Conference.

No attempt was made to resurrect the Central Operative Leadership at Berlin, which had directed the KPD's underground struggle up to March 1935. Instead, a decentralised system was developed on the basis of the frontier posts which had existed for some years along Germany's borders. The Party Districts in Germany, so far as they still existed, were reduced in size and increased in number, and at the same time were grouped in six Sectors, the work in each Sector being directed by a Sector Leadership (*Abschnittsleitung*) in a neighbouring country.[33]

The Central Sector, which included Berlin, Brandenburg, Lower Saxony, Saxony, Sachsen-Anhalt, Thuringia, and Silesia, was directed at first from Prague, and later (after November 1938) from Malmö or Gothenburg in Sweden. The Southern Sector, including Baden, Würtemberg, Bavaria and Hessen-Frankfurt, was directed from Zürich; the South Western Sector, covering the Middle Rhine (Cologne, Koblenz, Trier), from Brussels; the Western Sector, including the Lower Rhine, the Ruhr basin and Westphalia, from Amsterdam; the Northern Sector, covering Bremen, Hamburg, Schleswig-Holstein, Kiel, Mecklenburg, Stettin, Danzig and East Prussia, from Copenhagen; the Saarland from Paris.

Each Sector Leadership consisted of a political leader, individual or collective, and a small technical staff for such tasks as forging passes, translating and duplicating; and there continued to be frontier posts, from which regular couriers carried materials into Germany and brought back intelligence. Frontier work was especially important and successful in the mountain regions along the Czech-German border (until 1938), on the Baltic shipping routes and the Rhine barges, many of whose foreign seamen were prepared to help with the smuggling through of illegal material.

The operations of the Sector leaderships were as far as possible kept separate from the activities of the Communist *émigrés* in the country concerned, contact between the two being limited, nominally at least, to one person on each side, though in practice individual exiles might be recruited to the Sector personnel for clandestine work in Germany.

At the top of the Party the eight members of the Politburo elected at the Brussels Conference made such arrangements as seemed best suited to achieve a number of aims: the preservation of their own unity; the maintenance through the Sector leaders of contact with the Communist underground; and at the same time the maintenance of contact through a political leader in each centre of emigration (*Emileiter*) with the Communist exiles abroad, so that they might be able to take advantage of any opportunities for fruitful contacts with exiled Social Democrats or other anti-fascists.

The Party chairman, Wilhelm Pieck, and one or two other Politburo members, remained at Moscow, which now came to be regarded as the seat of the Central Committee. At the same time an Operative Leadership was set up under Ulbricht, at Prague, to direct clandestine operations in Germany through the Sector Leaderships. Later, this was transferred to Paris and placed under Dahlem, and in February 1937 it was raised to the status and function of Secretariat of the Central Committee.[34] It appears from correspondence in the Party records that despite the dispersal in subsequent years of the Central Committee members elected at the Brussels Conference, despite the division of authority between the two sections of the Politburo at Moscow and Paris respectively, and difficulties of communication between them, there was enough consultation to ensure that a practical unity was preserved in major matters of policy.

This was true, at least, of the Party leadership, but it may not have been true of all the underground groups. For although the leadership made efforts to consult representatives of the clandestine Party during the long-drawn-out process of revising its fundamental conceptions, and to see that news of the proceedings was made known to underground groups, it cannot be taken for granted that the new policies came to be universally known and accepted by all Communists who continued to be active in Germany.

A New Perspective
1936–39

CHAPTER 9

Changing Conditions

The carrying out of the policies decided upon at the Brussels Conference was made more difficult, not only by the exhausted state of the KPD after three years of clandestine struggle, but by changing conditions within Germany.

The most obvious change was the steady decline in unemployment which resulted partly from the economic recovery of the capitalist world generally, partly from public works programmes inherited by Hitler from previous governments, together with the beginning of an armaments build-up, and partly from the exclusion of many women and young people from the official labour market.[1]

While re-employment was a real enough gain for the millions previously without work, the economic recovery brought few other benefits to workers. The destruction of trade unionism made it impossible for them to exert their potential economic bargaining power and put employers in a position virtually to fix their own wages, supported by Labour Trustees responsible to the Minister of Labour. Prices rose and rising government expenditure led to heavier taxation and other deductions from the wage-packet. Wage-rates tended to fall in real terms and wage-earners were driven to seek overtime. Import restrictions, too, led to some food shortages and low-quality substitute products, while the increasing concentration of government spending on war-related projects resulted in a decline in the quality and extent of social services.

Employers' dictatorship, rising profits and widening polarisation of wealth and income did not pass unnoticed by workers. The older generation in particular noted cynically the Labour Front's attempts to conceal the actual conflicts of class interest behind a pretence of 'German Socialism' with its 'Strength through Joy' excursions, 'Beauty of Labour' competitions, and the like. Yet the Labour Front, for all its demagogy and corruption, did bring some gains to the workers and made some impresson, especially on the new generation, who had no pre-1933 experience of class struggle, but had been brought up in Nazi youth organisations.

By 1936 the economic situation in Germany had come to assume an appearance radically different from that of 1933. Unemployment, though pockets of it might still be found here and there, no longer presented a major problem.[2] On the contrary, the accelerating war preparations to which the government gave priority in all its decisions were beginning to cause acute shortages of labour, and especially of skilled labour, in certain sectors such as the metal and building industries, chemicals, engineering and coal-mining, as well as in armaments production itself. The government shrank from resorting to direction of labour and employers in these industries began to compete for labour by offering higher wages, which the 'cost plus' system of government contracts would enable many of them to pay at the public expense. There was therefore a tendency for workers to move into those industries from lower-paid occupations such as farm work; by 1936 a true 'flight from the land' was taking place and agricultural production was gravely hampered by shortage of labour. Between 1933 and 1938 labour employed in agriculture fell by some 500,000[3] and in the latter years the Ministry of Labour estimated that there was a shortage of 250,000 workers on the land.[4] Yet farmers were not allowed to compete on the labour market by offering higher wages; consequently the drift to the cities continued and already in 1935 the authorities were beginning to fear that food shortages might lead to riots.[5]

It was not only farm workers but also state employees such as office workers and technicians who could often earn more by going into private industry. Most sought-after of all were craftsmen with technical qualifications and experience, and in some cases their scarcity-value outweighed the disadvantage of a left-wing record. For good skilled workers were liable to be former trade unionists, and Socialists or Communists, while storm troopers and police informers, who had often been taken on by employers in 1933, might not be good workmen. Cases are not unknown, indeed, in which directors of engineering and similar firms shielded industrial workmen from arrest, or even procured their release from a concentration camp, because of their skill.[6]

Although the government tried to keep down both prices and wages for fear of an inflation like that of the early 1920s, the forces of the market were too strong. Between 1936 and 1939 the cost of living rose by an estimated 4 per cent.[7] The earnings of wage-earners rose, too, but very unevenly, so that workers in armaments-related industries increased their earnings, though for the most part only by working longer hours. In the consumption goods and allied industries, on the other hand, earnings probably fell, despite the longer hours and overtime.[8] On the whole, earnings were approaching those of the late 1920s, but at the expense of harder conditions.

In these conditions of unprecedented labour shortage, there would undoubtedly have been a much more considerable rise in real wages and earnings, if trade unions had been able to function legally. As it was, the strength of the workers' bargaining position expressed itself mainly in a weakening of labour discipline, in slow working, absenteeism, frequent job-changes and reduced productivity.[9] Reports reaching the *émigré* Social Democratic Party agreed about these trends, but differed as to whether they should be interpreted as passive resistance or as mere tiredness due to overwork.[10] That working conditions were leading to physical and mental exhaustion is a common theme in surviving reports about the mood of the workers in those years, and the speeding up of work and keeping down of piece-rates were frequent causes of discontent. 'The argument', Dr Kershaw concludes in a study of German public opinion in the pre-war years, 'that the working class was to a large extent won over to the régime by higher wages, provision of employment and the advantages of National Socialist social policy, is . . . no longer tenable.'[11] Most reports, including those of Nazi authorities, agreed that there were deep currents of discontent among them, beneath an appearance of indifference and apathy. But if the working class was 'reserved, cautious and sceptical',[12] this was not because it was unpolitical, but out of fear. Even so, there was much grumbling at work places, and it was not unknown for SA men and Nazi Party members to take part in it, at least passively.[13] The Gestapo's methods, too, though effective for the time being, may have tended to broaden the mood of discontent.

Attempts by workers to take advantage of the scarcity of labour took many forms, some of them reminiscent of familiar forms of class struggle in the past. Some reactions were purely individual and spontaneous, as when a worker changed his employer on a promise of higher wages. But there were also collective actions, such as lightning strikes or concerted refusals to contribute to the nominally voluntary Winter Help collection, as a protest against a harsh time-keeper.[14] In the years when unemployment had been heavy, workers with a record of militancy had been dismissed out of hand. But that was now a thing of the past. There were even factories in which the workers were all former trade unionists, presenting a solid front to the management, and there were others in which the Councillors of Trust unofficially sought the advice and guidance of colleagues who had formerly been trade-union representatives on the Works Council.[15]

Whereas in the first years after 1933, the influence of experienced trade unionists had often been weakened by the intrusion into the factories of inexperienced Nazi youth and storm troopers, there was now a different movement. The expansion of arms factories and the building of airfields and fortifications brought together workers from all parts of Germany (and Austria) and resulted in hastily organised actions of protest, which at first the police found difficulty in dealing with.[16]

It is not always easy for the historian, as it was not always easy for the Gestapo, to discover how far the strikes and other protest actions in arms factories and on construction sites in Germany at this period were spontaneous and how far they were organised as conscious political resistance. The Nazi authorities, with their almost obsessional concern with the danger of revolution, were inclined to put the latter, political interpretation on them, suspecting, for instance, that the strictness of a time-keeper who had once been a Social Democrat was deliberately designed to stir up discontent against the régime.[17] The historian with a similar concern about politics and resistance may be tempted to put a similar interpretation on them, though the evidence must often leave the question open. Perhaps it is relevant to ask at this point why, when so many features of the economic situation were favourable to working-class militancy, it was not more widespread and effective than it appears from the surviving evidence to have been? The efficiency of the police is at least part of the answer. Another part, as has been suggested by Dr Peukert, may be that the armaments boom promoted an individualistic mentality and weakened the spirit of collective struggle.[18]

These renewed manifestations of conflicting class interests confronted the Nazis with a serious problem. Rising wages would mean either inflation or a growth in consumer spending at the expense of armaments, or both, at a time when their plans demanded the quickest possible war preparation. Up to about 1936 they had been able to set these preparations in motion by bringing into play the largely unused resources latent in the economy. But now these reserves were exhausted, and the sharply rising demands of the armed forces could only be met, either by redistributing resources from the civilian sectors of the economy, or else by acquiring new resources by conquest. The latter solution was not yet possible and would only become possible if the first solution were successfully applied. Yet the possibilities of internal redistribution of resources were strictly limited. Because of Germany's extreme poverty in strategic raw materials, the arms build-up itself depended on a huge increase in imports of those materials and of fuel, and this in turn required the acquisition of foreign exchange by an increase in exports. Yet exports were not increasing and were not likely to increase at the rate required to pay for a growth of imports on the scale envisaged. Even a lesser increase was only likely to be attained if the export industries were able to outbid their competitors, and this meant keeping wages down. At this time the call-up of men to the armed forces was tending to dry up the pool from which labour might have been drawn.

The shortage of labour and the consequent tendency of wages to rise thus represented a crucial problem for the Nazi war-planners. Various ideas for dealing with it were toyed with from time to time, ranging from the conscription of millions of women to the release from prison of skilled workers, and even, on one occasion, a reduction of the ordinary police, although this measure was probably never carried out.[19] Finally, in 1936, the whole complex of problems centring in the shortages of labour and raw materials was made the subject of the Second Four Year Plan, which Goering was to administer as commissioner.[20]

Goering was put in charge of the Four Year Plan because he seemed to have the weight of authority and breadth of connections required to mediate between the sharply divergent views of the financiers, industrialists and military leaders on the one hand, and the Nazi Party leaders on the other. The conservatives, represented above all by Economics Minister Schacht and the head of the Economics branch of the General Staff, Colonel (later General) Thomas, demanded a ruthless sacrifice of butter for guns, even if that meant drastic cuts in wages, mobilisation of female labour, increased taxation and the cutting down of civilian consumption. The party leaders were not against such measures in principle, but feared the social and political risks of such a ruthless sacrifice of living standards to military preparations, and Hitler shared their fears. Yet it was difficult to avoid the conclusion that a long war of exhaustion like the war of 1914–18 would require a total mobilisation of resources, both human and material. It was to avoid this conclusion that Hitler had evolved the concept of a world-wide war of conquest taking the form of a succession of short blitzkrieg campaigns, in which Germany could advance from strength to strength by isolating and knocking out a succession of states, each time acquiring new resources for the next campaign. The Second Four Year Plan was designed to provide the means to carry out such a succession of campaigns without reducing the people's living standards below a safe level.[21] The plan provided for the production of synthetic petrol and of iron from native ores. Both projects were uneconomic judged by normal standards, but would ensure a short-term self-sufficiency such as would be needed for short campaigns.

Hitler's blitzkrieg strategy was designed to solve two main problems. One was Germany's extreme poverty in raw materials, especially metals, which made her highly vulnerable to blockade and to a protracted two or three-front war. The other difficulty involved in any policy of military expansion lay in the fear and dislike of such a war among the people, and the danger that any defeat would open up the road to collapse and revolution, as in 1918.

There is ample evidence that Hitler himself, as well as other Nazi leaders, was conscious, almost to the point of obsession, of the danger of working-class unrest which might be exploited by Communists and might lead to another 1918.[22] It was a fear which was repeatedly expressed in Hitler's private utterances, and those who knew him best, such as Albert Speer, have testified to its reality. 'A variety of official sources make it evident,' Mason concludes, 'that the régime was constantly concerned about the political attitude of the working class, and this anxiety . . . was not without influence in the whole field of internal, economic and foreign policy.'[23]

The reports of Nazi authorities on the whole concurred with those of their opponents in viewing the attitude of the working class as changeable and precarious. While a majority, so the SPD Executive concluded in March 1938, gave the government credit for curing unemployment and making Germany strong, there was nevertheless widespread dissatisfaction with working and living conditions and equally widespread doubts about the permanence of the régime. That the dissatisfaction did not take the form of fundamental political opposition was due above all to the lack of any perception of a viable alternative. The Nazis did, of course, make ruthless and unceasing use of the Gestapo in the factories and in working-class housing areas. But, while the police might prevent or defeat attempts at working-class organisation, they could rarely make unwilling workers work well and win their active support. For this reason Hitler, despite the demands of war preparation and the continual lobbying of the generals, turned a deaf ear to their many calls for a drastic reduction of wage levels. For similar reasons he could never make up his mind to dispense with political and social projects which used up very considerable resources and slowed down the pace of the arms build-up. In the same month of August 1936, for instance, in which he proclaimed, in his secret memorandum on the Four Year Plan,[24] that absolute priority must be given to the arms programme, he also approved a scheme submitted by Robert Ley, head of the Labour Front, for a competition for the best factory, a scheme which was furiously opposed by the Ministry of Economics and the High Command because of the considerable expenditure which it was likely to involve, and the increase which would indirectly result in the price of armaments.[25]

This was but one of many incidents in a continuous battle between the ministries and armed forces on the one hand and the Nazi Party on the other, in which Hitler pursued a vacillating and inconsistent course until the very end of the Third Reich. In the end, indeed, his unwillingness to make a really ruthless sacrifice of 'butter for guns' had quite fundamental effects on the character of his war preparations. The Second Four Year Plan of 1936 provided for only short blitzkrieg wars in which a limited armaments sector was to be switched from the needs of one campaign to the different needs of the next, successive enemies being defeated without any severe cut in German living standards. In practice, however, it is doubtful whether German resources were adequate even for wars of this type without cuts in consumption and living standards which would have caused dangerous discontent. The result, in Dr Mason's view, was 'a general crisis of the régime', a political crisis in the years 1937–39, the essence of which was that the Nazi leaders could not mobilise the military resources necessary for temporary superiority of the blitzkrieg type without risking dangerous discontent.[26] The fact that they avoided disaster in 1939 and 1940, he thinks, was not due to superior resources, but to better tactics and gambler's luck.[27]

As war approached, conflict between the desire to mobilise all resources and the desire to avoid serious discontent became more difficult to resolve. The government pursued a wavering course, planning, then repeatedly postponing, such crucial measures as the direction of labour and the rationing of foodstuffs. More and more clearly the logic of events was forcing it, if it wished to ensure its ability to make war in the future, to begin war without delay. In the factories, tension mounted between the Nazi authorities and the workers, and, in order to avoid total discredit and retain some remnants of influence, the Labour Front was compelled to go beyond the familiar demagogy of words and make some show of defending the workers' real interests.

Meanwhile the attitude of the great majority of German workers remained vacillating and unclear. Many of them profited – or thought they profited – by the arms boom or by Labour Front measures such as the Competitions of Professional Skill. Many acclaimed Hitler in moments of nationalistic euphoria following one of his triumphs, and many made him an exception to their contempt for Nazi tyranny and corruption. But at heart most of them remained cynical and pessimistic, fearing war above all, but alternating between hopelessness and illusions about it. In the main – and this was ground common to the reports of clandestine Socialists and Communists and those of Nazi observers – the working class remained dissatisfied and alienated from the régime. The Nazis had succeeded by terror and reprisals in neutralising the working class, no more.[28]

With the means of economic pressure now at the disposal of the German workers, it may be wondered that more did not respond more positively to the calls addressed to them by the Communist movement. Police terror was one factor. Another was the difficulty of communicating to the workers in Germany the new ideas adopted by the KPD in 1935. Now that the prospect of an early proletarian revolution had receded, many workers could see no clear alternative to fascism and little possibility of its overthrow except through war. The conception of a road to socialism through the struggle for peace and for a people's democracy was not likely to win conviction without a prolonged political struggle. But despite some new means of communication, such as radio broadcasts from France and Spain, contacts with the underground were becoming more difficult, and it was months, and in some cases even years, before the news of the new political line reached some clandestine groups. There remained a fatal gap between the widespread discontent of the workers in Germany and the political struggle against the Nazi régime.

CHAPTER 10

Resistance in Lower Key

The decisions of the Brussels Conference were a recognition of hard fact. Hitler's unexpected and overwhelming victory in the Saar plebiscite in January 1935,[1] despite a union of anti-fascist parties against him, had dealt the Communists a sobering blow, only partly offset by some expressions of opposition in the elections of Councillors of Trust in the factories in April.[2] Above all, the continuing heavy losses of the best and most militant comrades were tearing wide gaps in the ranks which could no longer be filled.

When the Conference met, in October 1935, Wilhelm Pieck, the acting Party chairman, reviewing the struggle of the previous three years, gave these facts about the 422 men and women who had been leading Party functionaries in January 1933, either at the Party Centre, in the Districts, or in the 'mass organisations':[3]

Arrested and mostly sentenced:	219
Forced to emigrate:	125
Murdered:	24
Left the Party:	42

It emerged further from the statistics cited by Pieck that some 140 of the original 422 were still at liberty in Germany, most of them evidently having been imprisoned but subsequently released. Only 12 had escaped arrest or worse.

Historians in the GDR have estimated, on the basis of admittedly incomplete figures, that of approximately 60,000 who engaged in anti-fascist political activity between the beginning of 1933 and the end of 1935, at least 18,243 were prosecuted in 2,935 trials for continuing the activity of the Party, and that during the same period, in addition to those 'legally' imprisoned in this way, some tens of thousands were held in concentration camps and about 10,000 forced to emigrate.[4] It has to be remembered, too, that of those still nominally free, many were under police supervision or in employment away from their homes. It is hardly too much to say that the Communist movement of previous years, with its complex, nation-wide structure, now existed only in skeleton form, and that although the aim of rebuilding it was never finally abandoned, the cadres needed were lacking, as were the financial means.

Reports which reached the *émigré* leadership in the months following the Brussels Confernce, despite some contradictions, gave a fairly clear picture of the changing character of the Communists' underground struggle in Germany.[5] Perhaps the most striking change was that most of the underground activists were now in employment. As a result they no longer had so much free time for political work, and as a further result their political contacts and conversations tended to occur at their place of work, if they occurred at all in the new environment. Many Party groups and cells which had been based on residential areas ceased to exist. One such group, it was reported, had formally dissolved itself after deciding to pass over the balance of its funds to families of political prisoners.[6] At the same time the formation of new factory groups was reported in some areas. Attempts were made, too, to overcome the disadvantages of the traditional bureaucratic style of organisation by dividing large Districts into several smaller ones.[7] The style of political activity reported still tended to be bold, but too open and risky: lightning demonstrations, for instance, or collections at labour exchanges for the families of political prisoners or for aid to Republican Spain. Some clandestine groups had contact with the exiled leadership, others did not.

From 1935 onwards, the number of Communists who are recorded in Gestapo reports, or can be estimated from those reports, to have been arrested, fell from about 14,000 in 1935[8] to 11,678 in 1936, to 8,068 in 1937 and to 3,800 in 1938 (as against 1,374 Social Democrats in 1936 and 733 in 1937).[9] This decline may of course have been due to greater caution on the part of active Communists, and to the adoption of new types of activity. But it seems likely that any such caution will have been cancelled out by the increasing skill of the Gestapo and that the figures do, in part at least, reflect an involuntary decline in the scale of Communist activity as well as a change in its character.

Among those who survived and continued the struggle, hatred of fascism was undiminished, but tinged with weariness and, occasionally, with disillusion. In some places survivors released from concentration camps struggled hard to rebuild the traditional

Party structure and to resume 'mass activity' of the traditional sort.[10] But for the most part those who wished to continue the struggle had to learn to work in a new way, in informal groups, taking their cue from spontaneous currents of popular discontent rather than issuing general calls for revolution. The task of the underground leadership was to find these groups and to persuade them to accept its lead.

The changed economic and political circumstances which have been described in the last chapter, together with the exhaustion of the Party and the diminished expectations of early revolution gave rise to new forms of organisation and of resistance activity. The tightly organised, disciplined army of revolution of past years was being replaced by small, scattered, loosely-structured groups, some of which had contacts with the *émigré* leadership, while others did not have, and perhaps in some cases did not even seek, such contact. The formalities of Party membership were not in all cases insisted on in these groups, which may have included anti-fascists who were not strictly members of the Party, but simply groups of friends meeting more or less regularly to play skat or to chat in the local inn or municipal park.[11]

As for methods of political struggle, there was perhaps more emphasis on defensive operations, such as the campaigns of Red Aid on behalf of the families of political prisoners and the publicising of trials and executions. With the rapid growth of armament production and other war preparations, the exposure of such preparations assumed greater urgency.

Under the new, decentralised organisation by which clandestine work in Germany was controlled by Sector Leaders and by frontier posts set up by them, an even more important role than before was played by couriers carrying illegal literature over the frontier, but above all by political Instructors. They did not live in Germany, but visited the area allotted to them at intervals of about a month and made contact with a strictly limited number of clandestine activists. They did not usually take with them illicit literature, which was separately distributed for reasons of security, but they would discuss such Party documents and explain current policy. At the same time they would seek information about the situation in the area and the mood of the workers, and about any anti-Nazi activities there, and this would form the subject-matter of the report which they would render to the Sector leadership on their return.

In the years under consideration, after 1935, Instructors seem, in

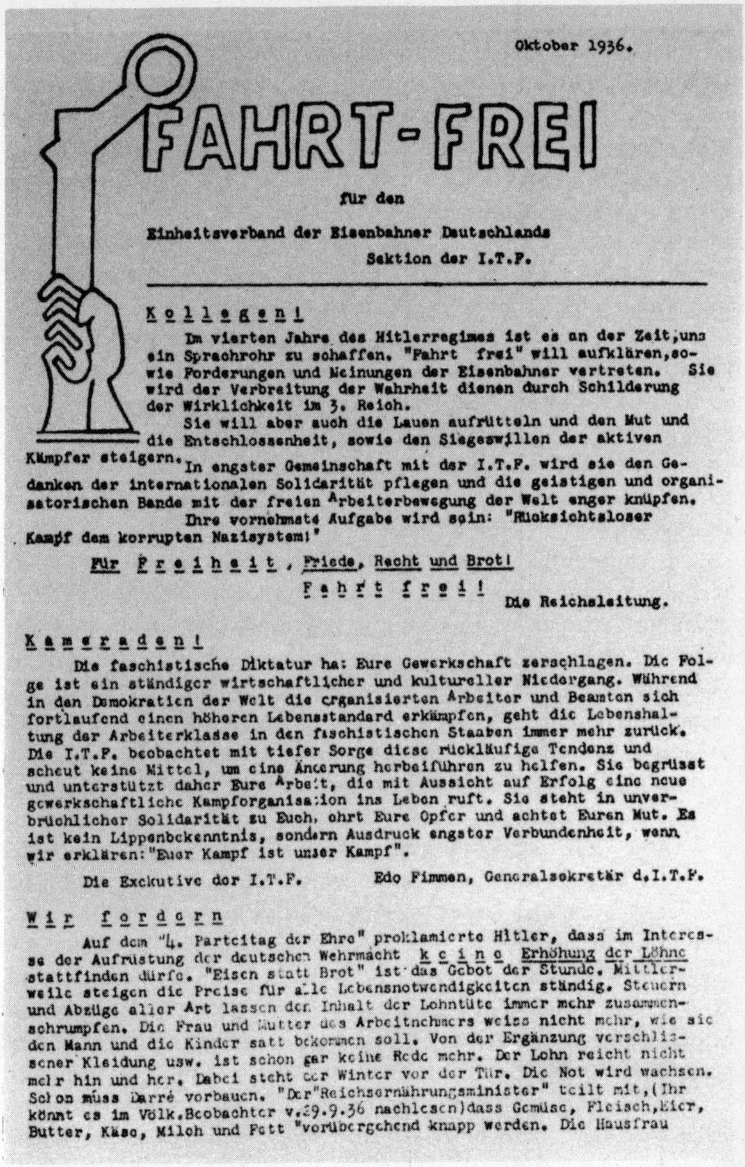

Oktober 1936.

FAHRT-FREI

für den

Einheitsverband der Eisenbahner Deutschlands
Sektion der I.T.F.

K o l l e g e n !

Im vierten Jahre des Hitlerregimes ist es an der Zeit, uns ein Sprachrohr zu schaffen. "Fahrt frei" will aufklären, sowie Forderungen und Meinungen der Eisenbahner vertreten. Sie wird der Verbreitung der Wahrheit dienen durch Schilderung der Wirklichkeit im 3. Reich.

Sie will aber auch die Lauen aufrütteln und den Mut und die Entschlossenheit, sowie den Siegeswillen der aktiven Kämpfer steigern. In engster Gemeinschaft mit der I.T.F. wird sie den Gedanken der internationalen Solidarität pflegen und die geistigen und organisatorischen Bande mit der freien Arbeiterbewegung der Welt enger knüpfen.

Ihre vornehmste Aufgabe wird sein: "Rücksichtsloser Kampf dem korrupten Nazisystem!"

Für F r e i h e i t , Friede, Recht und Brot!

F a h r t f r e i !

Die Reichsleitung.

K a m e r a d e n !

Die faschistische Diktatur hat Eure Gewerkschaft zerschlagen. Die Folge ist ein ständiger wirtschaftlicher und kultureller Niedergang. Während in den Demokratien der Welt die organisierten Arbeiter und Beamten sich fortlaufend einen höheren Lebensstandard erkämpfen, geht die Lebenshaltung der Arbeiterklasse in den faschistischen Staaten immer mehr zurück. Die I.T.F. beobachtet mit tiefer Sorge diese rückläufige Tendenz und scheut keine Mittel, um eine Änderung herbeiführen zu helfen. Sie begrüsst und unterstützt daher Eure Arbeit, die mit Aussicht auf Erfolg eine neue gewerkschaftliche Kampforganisation ins Leben ruft. Sie steht in unverbrüchlicher Solidarität zu Euch, ehrt Eure Opfer und achtet Euren Mut. Es ist kein Lippenbekenntnis, sondern Ausdruck engster Verbundenheit, wenn wir erklären: "Euer Kampf ist unser Kampf".

Die Exekutive der I.T.F. Edo Fimmen, Generalsekretär d.I.T.F.

W i r f o r d e r n

Auf dem "4. Parteitag der Ehre" proklamierte Hitler, dass im Interesse der Aufrüstung der deutschen Wehrmacht k e i n e Erhöhung der Löhne stattfinden dürfe. "Eisen statt Brot" ist das Gebot der Stunde. Mittlerweile steigen die Preise für alle Lebensnotwendigkeiten ständig. Steuern und Abzüge aller Art lassen den Inhalt der Lohntüte immer mehr zusammenschrumpfen. Die Frau und Mutter des Arbeitnehmers weiss nicht mehr, wie sie den Mann und die Kinder satt bekommen soll. Von der Ergänzung verschlissener Kleidung usw. ist schon gar keine Rede mehr. Der Lohn reicht nicht mehr hin und her. Dabei steht der Winter vor der Tür. Die Not wird wachsen. Schon muss Darré vorbauen. "Der "Reichsernährungsminister" teilt mit, (Ihr könnt es im Völk.Beobachter v.29.9.36 nachlesen) dass Gemüse, Fleisch, Eier, Butter, Käse, Milch und Fett "vorübergehend knapp werden. Die Hausfrau

Fahrt-Frei ('Freeway'), an anti-fascist pamphlet appealing to German railway workers, produced in Amsterdam by socialist trade unionists, October 1936

some cases, to have attempted to rebuild the old structure of District and Sub-district leaderships; but in most cases the cadres needed for that were simply not available. The Instructors' own contacts were limited and the advice they gave to these contacts usually was to create informal circles. Sometimes, on arriving in Germany, the Instructor would find that his normal contacts could not be reached because of arrests, and he might have to return to base after one or two days instead of the normal four or five, in order to arrange a new contact.[12] In some cases contact with a local group was lost for as long as a year, and there were some groups which worked more or less independently for years without contact with a Sector leadership and without knowledge of the policy changes of 1935. Moreover, the relatively brief encounters with Instructors were not always enough to put underground activists fully in the picture, and local leaders continued therefore on occasion to be brought over the frontier for conferences or schools, where they could have a fuller discussion with Party leaders.[13]

Such conferences served not only to provide political education for underground activists, but to give Party leaders some idea of the prevailing currents of opinion among those who were actively engaged in the struggle in Germany. According to the report of an Instructor who had visited Würtemberg in February 1936, the younger members tended to agree with the policy line adopted at the Brussels Conference and with the kind of activity which had been recommended there, while older members were more impressed by the losses and defeats of past years and sometimes thought that they were now too weak to do anything more than wait until circumstances offered a new opportunity. 'Mass politics cannot be conducted at present,' they were quoted as saying, 'it only costs needless sacrifices.'[14]

If the new system of contact between the exiled leadership and active Party members in Germany by means of Sector Leaders and visiting Instructors was less effective in terms of 'mass action', it was also less vulnerable than the more formal organisation had been. Dr Peukert has even asserted that in the Western Sector the visits of the Instructors sent in from Amsterdam remained unknown to the Gestapo until the outbreak of war in 1939.[15] This is not likely to have been due to a decline in the efficiency of the Gestapo; it reflects more probably a change in the activities of the underground groups and perhaps a reduction in their size and number.

The membership of such groups as were known to the Sector Leaders in the years after 1935 probably did not amount to any considerable number. The Amsterdam leadership, for example, is reported at one stage to have had contact through its Instructors with no more than 200 or 300 people in the Western Districts of Germany, and had no contacts at all in many industrial towns in which the Party had formerly been strong.[16] The Party organisation at Dresden in Saxony was comparatively strong at the beginning of 1936, with 75 members in street cells;[17] but at Augsburg in Bavaria, another industrial city in which the labour movement had once been strong, the only group of which there is evidence in 1936 was one of 15 people who began meeting in November, but were arrested after a few weeks.[18] As soon as one of these small groups began to grow, or to become really active, it became more vulnerable.

The resistance groups of this period varied considerably in character from place to place and from time to time. Some were not in touch with an Instructor from a Sector leadership; some were not confined to Party members; an occasional one consisted of little more than a well-placed individual. Some idea of their character, and of their variety, may be obtained from the reports presented by Instructors to their Sector Leader, or by the Sector Leadership to the Operative Leadership at Prague or Paris. Extracts from these reports for the years 1933–37 have been printed and it is to be hoped that they will soon be published in full.[19]

The biggest single centre of Communist activity in 1936–37 seems to have been Berlin, where the clandestine groups were sufficiently numerous to prompt a division of the Party District into seven new Districts with Sub-districts of the traditional type.[20] A report made at the beginning of 1936, for instance, spoke of the formation in one of the Siemens electrical engineering works of a Sub-district leadership of three men 'who, after their political suitability had been established, were elected by the comrades of the individual cells'. This was only one of six Siemens works in which there were reported to be Communist cells at this time. In one of these works an individual Communist was even reported to be the top candidate in the election of Councillors of Trust which was due to be held shortly – though in the event it was never held.[21] The illicit Communist paper *Lautsprecher* (Loudspeaker), distributed in the Siemens works, was reported to contain discussion of the Brussels Conference documents 'as a basis . . . for carrying out the tasks of the Party by way of mass work in the Siemens factories'.[22] Both the character of the reorganisation and the concept of 'mass work' were strongly reminiscent of pre-Brussels days. So, too, was a programme which the Berlin District leadership drew up in February 1937. This consisted of an educational course for members of the leadership and its Instructors, a plan for the publication of a variety of political literature, a further plan to renew connections with factory groups by the beginning of April, and finally the holding of a conference at Easter, to which representatives of important factories were to be invited.[23]

An account of Communist activity in another Berlin factory (the Alfred Teves machine and armature factory at Berlin-Wittenau) has been compiled by a GDR scholar from interviews with survivors.[24] The impression is given that Communist cells of some size existed and, by co-operation with Social Democrats, had gained, at least for a time, a certain ascendency in what is described as 'a lively political life',[25] so that they could openly discuss politics with Nazi workers and distribute anti-fascist literature without being betrayed. On one occasion, according to a survivor, when a worker had been arrested, the Council of Trust in the works was induced by pressure from colleagues to sanction a collection for him.[26]

Reports from other Sectors indicated a similar emphasis on the factories. In Dresden, for instance, it was stated in February 1936 that there had been discussions in the Sachsenwerk motor works about the Stakhanovite movement in the Soviet Union, and that Radio Moscow was listened to by workers.[27] Moreover, the preparations for the election of Councillors of Trust had been made an occasion for airing workers' grievances and demanding information. But attempts to start trade-union activity had been discouraged by news of the mass trials at Wuppertal in the Lower Rhine District at this time.[28]

Light is thrown on conditions in Western Germany by a report which was made to the Operative Leadership by Erich Gentsch, when he took over the post of Sector Leader at Amsterdam in May 1937. Contact with the Ruhr and Lower Rhine Districts of Germany was being maintained by four Instructors, he wrote, and a fifth was about to be put into service. Each Instructor, according to the report, had between three and five 'agencies' to visit each month, involving from three to ten days travelling and a busy round of contacts. One, for instance, had to visit not only Essen and Schwelm on the Ruhr, but Mönchen-Gladbach on the western side of the Rhine, as well as some Rhine shipping and a Councillor of Trust in the Labour Front who gave information about conferences of the Front.[29] Yet four or five such monthly rounds, risky and exhausting as they were, could yield no more than a few sample facts. Most of the important Ruhr factories, such as Krupps, still remained beyond the reach of any such visiting Instructor.

A similar report from the Southern Sector Leadership in Switzerland in August 1937 indicates that there, too, the Instructor-rounds were only gradually being built up, or in some cases being rebuilt after an interval. Two Instructors, it was reported, had been sent to Stuttgart and had successfully re-established firm contacts there, while other visits were being prepared to Munich and Karlsruhe.[30] Visits, apparently disguised as holiday excursions from several places in Germany near a frontier were mentioned, and a number of day and weekend schools had been successfully arranged.[31] A noticeable feature of these reports, indeed, is the importance attached to theoretical instruction for cadres who already had highly valued practical experience of clandestine work.

It is not easy in retrospect to judge either how extensive the resistance activities of the German Communists were at this period, nor how far they were effectively directed by the exiled leadership. GDR historians generally insist on the close contact which they believe the exiled leadership of the KPD maintained even at this period with the clandestine groups in Germany;[32] the publication in recent years of much inner-Party correspondence has furnished new evidence to support that view. On the other hand authorities, whether they be Nazi police and courts, or illegal Communist leaders, may have a natural tendency to think in terms of organised, disciplined activity as against spontaneity, and historians need to beware of underestimating the latter. But they also need to treat with caution the contrary tendency of recent writing in the West to play down the organised character of Communist resistance in reaction to the claims made by GDR historians.

It is not disputed that the number of persons arrested by the Gestapo for alleged Communist or Socialist activity gradually declined,[33] after rising to a peak of some 15,000 in 1936, and it is difficult to deny that the Party's clandestine work, for all the persistence with which it was pursued, no longer had the mass character which it had had in the first three years. The significance of figures for numbers of arrests is open to some doubt. Many Communists held back from the sort of 'mass work' which was still liable to be urged on them by Party leaderships, while on the other hand the Gestapo sometimes preferred to keep Communists under surveillance rather than to arrest them, as long as they presented no immediate danger. When the police did strike, however, the blow was liable to be shattering. An Instructor who visited Bremen in November 1936 reported that he had only been able to stay there for one-and-a-half days, instead of the planned five days, because multiple arrests had destroyed all his contacts. Fortunately, he added, the reaction of the comrades had been good: no panic mood or exaggerated talk of spies, traitors and renegades.[34]

Importance continued to be attached to the circulation of printed material, despite the risks involved. An Instructor who had visited Frankfurt reported that comrades there had expressed a desire for more literature, as they were often short of information for discussions with Nazis and of material to lend to Social Democrats.[35]

A report by an Instructor of a meeting with Communists at Munich in June 1937 showed that they were seriously out of touch and knew little or nothing of the Party's new methods of work. Their only contact had been by listening to broadcasts of the transmitter 29,8 (a German-language station in Republican Spain). This must have been inadequate, for they had no good grasp of current Party policy. They conceived of the Party's 'Brussels' line as a mere temporary manoeuvre and they saw no escape from Nazism except through war. Similarly Dr Peukert quotes the remark of the KPD Instructor of the Western (Amsterdam) sector, about an underground Party functionary with whom he had contact as late as March 1939, to the effect that, 'He knows nothing of our present policy, absolutely nothing. He is still living in the year 1933.'[36]

Many cases can be found in court and police records of semi-spontaneous resistance activity by informal groups of friends or workmates who do not appear to have been in regular contact with a Party leadership, and perhaps for that reason sometimes remained active for a much longer time than they would have done if they had formed part of a more formal structure. One such case was that of Karl Düllgen of Düsseldorf and his circle of friends, mentioned in Chapter 4, who remained for years a thorn in the flesh of police and employers.[37] A similar story was reported from Bremen, where a

Communist worker who was released from a concentration camp in 1935 and got employment in the docks, built up a network of resisters, including some SAP and KPO members who argreed to concentrate on the struggle against fascism and to leave disputed issues aside for the time being. The group are said to have been active enough, in the sense of producing leaflets and collecting information, and later, after war had broken out, even carrying out minor acts of sabotage. They did not, however, conform to a traditional pattern of organisation nor work according to any strict plan, but followed their instinct and seized opportunities as they came. Above all, they did not join any larger group or become subordinated to any central leadership; perhaps for that reason, they continued to be active and to escape arrest until 1945.[38]

No sharp line can be drawn between those Communists who resisted in small informal groups and those whose activities fitted into the framework of an organisation directed by representatives of the Central Committee in exile. GDR historians strongly emphasise the role played by the central Party leadership and its Sectors and Instructors, though without denying that independent groups and individuals also played a part. That this part was considerable is suggested by the fact that in the later war years groups of Communists were found to have been conducting some sort of political activity for years, apparently without having had any definite information about the Brussels Conference decisions, as they would have done if they had been in contact with central Party agencies or had received literature issued by those agencies.

Despite its reduced scale, Communist activity was not negligible in these years. In the eyes of the Gestapo, as surviving situation reports show,[39] political opposition was still mainly from the working class, and of workers arrested for political offences, many more (ten times as many in 1937) were described as Communists than as 'Marxists' – a police term for non-Communist socialists; and, although some historians have argued otherwise, the Gestapo *could* tell the difference. They did not regard existing Communist groups as an immediate danger, especially as they believed that many of them had lost touch with their *émigré* leadership, but they were aware of the deterioration that was taking place in working-class living standards and working conditions and feared that Communists might be able to organise the resulting discontent.

The Communist resistance of this period was marked not only by a looser organisation but by a changing type of activity. Traditional methods of political campaigning, such as chalking and leafleting and publication of local papers, were not altogether abandoned, and dues collection (described rather grandiloquently as '*kassentechnische Arbeit*') was continued and further attempts were made to arouse foreign protests against political death sentences and other atrocities; but more attention was paid to radio-listening, individually or in groups, and to whispering campaigns and political discussions based on the broadcasts. In February 1936, to give but one example, an Instructor who had visited Würtemberg reported that the comrades there were dependent on Radio Moscow, but were hampered by bad reception and were in desperate need of more news and 'material', i.e. publications.[40] The evidence of police reports also points to the central importance in those years of 'black radio' listening by small groups of neighbours or workmates, and of the spreading of the news so obtained.[41]

Another activity which attempted in a different way to combat the isolation from which anti-Nazis within Germany suffered, was the day or weekend-school, to which a number of anti-Nazis might be brought together under guise of a holiday, or taken over the frontier – in either case not without risk. The Southern Sector leader reported from Switzerland the holding of three such schools in August 1937,[42] the topics being, respectively: 'Party Policy and Methods', 'The German Economic Situation' and 'Cadre and Organisational Questions'. There had been, he reported, 'a very lively participation of the comrades'.

The loosely-connected Communist opposition groups of this period took their form in many cases from the particular circumstances of time and place. The mountains along the Czech border provided opportunities for the meeting of quite large groups under the guise of mountaineers. On the other hand, the swelling bureaucracies generated by war preparations in the ministries and in industry provided another kind of environment in which political discussion was not only possible but inevitable.

Big factories in the period of accelerated arms production and acute labour shortage could at times give rise to a surprisingly open political life. An example of this is to be found in a report made to the KPD's Central Sector leadership at Prague by the Berlin District Secretary at the beginning of 1936 concerning the position in the Siemens works, which was a major enterprise and in Communist terms a separate Sub-district.[43] It appeared from the report that the Brussels line, and especially the policy of working within Nazi organisations, had been enthusiastically endorsed by the majority of Communists working in the plant, especially by the younger ones, but it was not accepted by the Sub-district leader responsible for the plant. His dissent arose from a more optimistic assessment of the situation, for he thought that the attitude of the workers was such as to make it possible to oppose the Labour Front and to go straight over to setting up free trade unions. It was arranged that both the District leader and the Sub-district leader concerned should visit Prague for a full discussion with higher Party leaders.[44]

Another environment in which a large proportion of German Communists now had to work was the prison system and the concentration camps. Oddly enough, they were by no means the least likely to be well informed about the current policy of the Party or about conditions in Germany and the world. For the new conditions of the late 1930s also affected the struggle between the Communists and the Gestapo. The looser, less stereotyped organisation of the anti-fascist resistance after 1935 made it more difficult for the police to keep track of it. At the same time the Gestapo realised, as the Communists themselves now did, that there was no immediate prospect of revolution. For both these reasons the security authorities tended to modify their tactics. Their chief concern was to keep revolutionary activities under control and to be able to intervene if these reached a dangerous level. A favourite device was to try to control resistance groups by planting police agents in them. In the hope of achieving this, the Gestapo released a considerable number of Communists in the late 1930s, on occasions such as Hitler's birthday in April 1939, and subsequently kept them under cautious supervision. In some of these cases, detecting a weakness in their prisoner, they had made the release conditional on getting a promise that the released person would act as an informant, and in some – though by no means all – such cases, the person concerned had given such a promise with the intention of double-crossing the police. The result was then a sophisticated game of agents and counter-agents, in which the released person occasionally, against all the odds, outwitted the police. More often the game ended in disaster or betrayal. The Party's advice was to refuse to give such undertakings, though it did not discourage anti-fascists from giving the more normal promise to refrain from political activity. Even so, Communists who had obtained their release on such a condition could be assumed to be under supervision and had to expect to be kept at a distance by former comrades for a lengthy probationary period.

By 1936–37 this had become a frequently recurring issue, for Communists released from prisons and concentrations camps now constituted one of the main sources of recruitment to the anti-fascist resistance.

Following the Brussels Conference, and in accordance with its decisions, the exiled Central Committee began, through published statements and visiting Instructors, to advise members who remained in Germany to explore every possibility of legal opposition, not excluding membership of Nazi institutions. Reports coming in from the Sector leaderships subsequently provided many examples of such infiltration into the Nazi framework, especially that of the Labour Front. In one factory a former trade unionist was said to occupy a position in the works fire brigade;[45] another was a *Luftschutz* (Air Raid Precautions) warden or the equivalent of a shop steward in the Labour Front, or a shop-floor representative for *Kraft durch Freude* (Strength through Joy), the Labour Front's cultural branch.[46] These positions, though not in themselves of much political importance, often gave the person concerned the right to visit all the different shops in the factory and so to become acquainted with a wide circle of personnel and problems.

The most important position was that of a *Vertrauensrat* (Councillor of Trust), who, as has been observed above, though having no powers, performed a liaison function between management and workers. They were not elected, but were nominated by Labour Front and Management, subject to a veto by the workers. In practice they would not have served the purpose intended if they had not enjoyed at least a limited degree of confidence on the part of the workers they were supposed to represent, and this became more true in the late 1930s, as full employment increased the potential strength of the workers. Situations then arose which would have been inconceivable a few years earlier. In one works, for instance, an old Social Democrat was actually nominated as a Councillor of Trust by the Nazi Party Factory Organisation (NSBO) in the enterprise, because of his experience in negotiation; and it was reported that he was on good terms with a former Communist who worked there.[47] The most successful political activity, experience showed, was that which began with the day-to-day interests of the workers in the enterprise concerned, drawing attention to the Nazis' failure to apply their own rules.

The Labour Front was not the only organisation in which semi-political activity of this kind could be attempted. Some Communists tried to continue in 'bourgeois' sports clubs the traditions which they had pursued in the disbanded workers' sports clubs. On one occasion, according to an Instructor's report, anti-Nazis who had become members of a House-owners' League managed to embarrass the local Nazi authorities by insistently demanding a lecture on the 'breaking of the bondage of interest' which figured in the original Nazi Party programme.[48]

On the whole, those of the Instructors' reports which have survived and have been published in the GDR give the impression that where the new policies of 1935 became known, they were welcomed, especially by younger activists. This was the case in the Siemens works at Berlin, which has been mentioned.[49] In another case, the anti-fascist workers in a factory, who had previously resigned from the Labour Front, were persuaded by the visiting Instructor to re-join, in the name of the new policy.[50] These were clandestine Communists, who had received news of the Brussels policies either through Party literature or from Radio Moscow, or (in 1937 and after) from one of the transmitters in Republican Spain. It seems likely, however, that a quite high proportion of Communists still active in Germany either did not hear of the Brussels decisions or heard of them only in a brief, garbled version derived from indistinct broadcast reception. Moreover, many of those who did hear of them rejected the Trojan Horse tactic in particular. It went against the grain and was not easily practised by people with a Communist background. It might be difficult, too, for those who did practise it successfully to clear themselves of accusations of 'collaboration with fascism', either then or later.

Broadcasts directed to Germany from beyond the frontiers now played a bigger part in the propaganda activities of the KPD. Up to 1936 the only source of really anti-Nazi broadcasts was Moscow radio, whose German-language programmes, though they reached German listeners, appear to have been difficult to hear in some parts of the Reich. With the outbreak of the Spanish Civil War in July 1936 the situation changed, for broadcasts in German from Madrid,

Valencia and Barcelona were comparatively easily audible in the South and West of Germany. From January 1937 the situation changed once more when the short-wave transmitter 29,8 was placed by the Spanish Republican authorities at the disposal of the German anti-Nazis. Their broadcasts were easily heard in most parts of Germany and played an important role in providing news and comment for underground groups – and indeed, not only for them but, according to some reports, also for Nazi supporters who were interested in getting information about corruption among party and government officials, and other such matters.

Another theme of Communist radio propaganda at this time was, of course, the exposure of the real nature and aims of Hitler's foreign policy and the extent of his war preparations. This involved a double task, for it was necessary to ascertain the facts before they could be revealed. In this period of full employment and shortage of skilled labour, new sources of information were becoming available. There were now a not negligible number of anti-fascists employed in technical and administrative posts in industry or in ministries, who had special knowledge which they were prepared to put at the disposal of the struggle against fascism. Among them were some men and women of middle-class origin but of Communist convictions, such as Harro Schulze-Boysen, who worked as a lieutenant in the Air Ministry, and Arvid Harnack, a senior official in the Ministry of Economics, and his wife Mildred. Each of these, at first independently, later in association, built up a loose but extensive network of anti-fascists including doctors, artists, writers and other professional people, especially in Berlin. Others with special knowledge worked as individuals; one such was Paul Tegethoff, an industrial chemist employed by the armament firm Rheinmetall-Borsig at Düsseldorf, who was regularly visited by one of the Instructors sent out by the Western Sector headquarters at Amsterdam, until his arrest on suspicion of industrial espionage in December 1937.[51]

By 1936 large numbers of German anti-fascists were living as refugees abroad. A high proportion of these were Communists. Most of them were unable to earn a living, either because they were living illegally with false papers, or because they had been admitted to the host country on condition of not taking employment. They were therefore maintained either by funds raised by local anti-fascist committees, or, if they had emigrated with the approval of the

Party, by the International Red Aid organisation. In these conditions the Communist *émigrés* formed a highly organised group. They were normally forbidden by the state which had received them to take part in politics, which meant in practice that their organised activity was mainly concerned with winning local support for the victims of Nazism, including refugees from Germany.

Some of the refugees took part in the clandestine activities of the KPD by re-entering Germany as Instructors or couriers, when the country of their exile had a common frontier with Germany, as had Czechoslovakia, Switzerland, Belgium and Holland. Some exiles made numerous such journeys, at the risk of almost certain death if they were captured, but conditions became less favourable for such journeys after the Nazi occupation of the Sudetenland in October 1938. The clandestine activities carried out by the Sector Leaderships in the border countries were in principle kept strictly separate from the organisation of Communist refugees in the particular foreign country, the *Emileiter* who headed the refugee organisation (on the principle of democratic centralism) being directly responsible to the Central Committee and having only one link with the Sector Leadership.

For many of the exiled Communists the outbreak of the Spanish Civil War in July 1936 represented the opening up of a new front, a chance at last to resume an active part in the struggle. Communists still 'at liberty' in Germany had a similar feeling, and many of those who were physically fit and relatively free of family ties found their way to Spain with the help of the agencies of the Communist International and of fraternal parties such as the French Communist Party, in order to enroll in what became the International Brigades. In doing this they were following the call of the KPD leadership to perform what was regarded as both an international duty and a national duty, for, as Hitler represented the greatest danger to world peace, it was the German anti-Nazis who felt the greatest responsibility for combatting him on the battlefields of Spain.

It was a duty that was very fully and nobly performed. In the years 1936–38 almost 5,000 German anti-fascists served in the Brigades, and of these more than 3,000 gave their lives. Among the 5,000 – the biggest national contingent in the Brigades – the majority were Communists. They included many prominent and experienced Party functionaries, such as Hans Beimler, who represented the Central Committee, and Artur Becker, a leading member of the

Communist Youth League, both of whom were killed. Among the survivors were Franz Dahlem, a member of the KPD's Politburo, and the military commanders Wilhelm Zaisser ('General Gomez'), Heinrich Rau and Heinz Hoffmann, all of them destined later to play a leading part in the foundation and development of the German Democratic Republic.

The Spanish Civil War affected the Communists' resistance against Hitler in other ways too. With the radio transmitter *Deutscher Freiheitssender* (German Freedom Station) it became possible to reach listeners in Germany much more effectively than before, with news and other programmes devised by Communist editors, notably Gerhard Eisler and Kurt Hager, and later, Erich Glückauf and Hans Teubner.[52]

This diversion of some of the most able and energetic cadres of the KPD to Spain may be one reason why the struggle within Germany appeared to lose impetus at this time. The loss of cadres was to some extent a long-term loss, for those who had not been killed or captured in Spain were not able to return to Germany, but were as a rule interned in France after the end of the Civil War, and later in some cases, handed over to the Gestapo by the Vichy government.

The Spanish Civil War had another effect. It produced a revival of concern for anti-fascist unity and further attempts to achieve it. But in Germany, despite the strong impulse towards unity generated by the increasing danger of war, the new approach which had been heralded by the Brussels Conference had disappointing results. In some places discussions were held and a measure of co-operation achieved between Communists and other groups. Elsewhere, however, the full implications of the Popular Front line were not always grasped, while the rooted mistrusts of many years proved difficult to overcome in conditions of underground struggle. These circumstances determined that the battle for a German People's Front would be fought largely outside Germany, and that international events would play a large part in its outcome.

CHAPTER 11

Popular Front Politics

At the Brussels Conference in 1935 the leaders of the German Communist Party had finally come to recognise that war could be prevented and the Nazi régime overthrown – two things which were becoming more and more clearly related – only by the broadest unity of anti-fascist forces, and that this unity could only be achieved round a programme for a new democratic republic, leaving the question of socialist revolution to the future. This new democratic republic was not envisaged as a mere revival of the Weimar republic, with its coalitions of bourgeois parties. Nor were the anti-fascist forces on which it would be based thought of as including those who criticised or opposed the Nazi rulers for their mistakes or their crimes, while sharing their ultimate aims. Much remained to be clarified about the theory and practice of the anti-fascist movement which the Communists now wished to build up, but the first priority was joint activity.

It was not only Communists who were gripped by an acute sense of danger and urgency with the growth of Nazi power and Nazi war preparations in the mid-1930s. Other socialists as well as bourgeois liberals and left-wing intellectuals felt the approach of war and the need for a broad anti-Nazi front.

The central pillar of such an anti-fascist front, as Communists had always believed, must be a united working class in the form, first of all, of a united front of the trade unions and the working-class political parties, above all of the Communist and Social Democratic parties. The events in France in and after February 1934 seemed to confirm the belief that such a united front could halt the advance of fascism and at the same time attract wider support from progressive elements of other classes.[1] The first step, therefore, towards a German People's Front was an approach by the Communist Party in exile to the *émigré* Social Democratic Party. But here the difficulties proved to be greater than in France and were to present the most serious obstacles to the formation of a German equivalent of the

Front Populaire.

The Social Democratic Party of Germany was deeply divided on the question of relations with the Communists. The right-wing majority of the Executive Committee in exile (Sopade), which in late 1933 and early 1934 had shown signs – in the so-called Prague Manifesto – of adopting a radically self-critical analysis of the causes of the disaster of 1933 and of reverting from reformism to revolutionary socialism, had now swung back to reformism and argued that co-operation with the Communists would repel other anti-fascists instead of attracting them, as the left maintained.[2]

In the course of 1935 the KPD addressed no fewer than four unity proposals to Sopade, and pressure from the socialist left was sufficient to force the right-wing leaders to show some willingness to talk with the Communist leadership.[3] The most important such meeting took place at Prague on 23 November, after the Brussels Conference, between the SPD leaders, Hans Vogel and Friedrich Stampfer and two members of the KPD Politburo, Ulbricht and Dahlem. Ulbricht gave an assurance that in the event of agreement the KPD would refrain from all attacks on the SPD.[4] But the outcome was entirely negative. The Social Democratic leaders rejected all the Communist proposals, refused to plan any further meetings or even to issue a communiqué about these talks, which they wished to remain secret. They argued that adherents of their party in Germany were opposed to any co-operation with Communists – an allegation which the Communist leaders disputed, since it contradicted many of the reports reaching them from their Sector Leaders.[5] The SPD leaders also argued that co-operation with the Communists would repel middle-class opponents of Nazism and diminish the chance of coalitions with centre and nationalist opposition forces.

Attempts to form a broad German People's Front were thus hampered from the beginning by the refusal of the Socal Democratic Executive to take part, despite many invitations. The first steps towards the formation of a broad popular movement had meanwhile been taken in the summer of 1935, following an international writers' congress at Paris on 21–25 June. A small preparatory committee was set up under the chairmanship of the writer, Heinrich Mann and, as a result of its work, three conferences were held in Paris in September and November 1935 and in February 1936.[6] Some fifty German *émigrés* took part in each of the first two, and a hundred in the third. The participants included representatives of the Communist Party (about a fifth), a considerable number of individual Social Democrats, some representatives of smaller socialist parties and groups, some Catholics, and a considerable number of middle-class academics and writers, some of whom were associated with the Communist Party.

This informal 'Lutetia Circle', as it came to be called, after the hotel in which it met in Paris, adopted the name 'Committee for the Preparation of a German People's Front' in June 1936 and began to hold discussions aimed at drawing up a platform or programme. The Committee's work culminated in the issue of a proclamation 'For the German People's Front!' on 21 December 1936, signed by 14 Communists, 20 individual Social Democrats, 10 representatives of the SAP and 29 of the 'Intelligentsia'.[7]

The activities of the Paris committee included a number of protests and publications which had international repercussions, such as protests against political executions in Germany, against the remilitarisation of the Rhineland in March 1936, and against the holding of the Olympic Games in Berlin a few months later. They helped also to inspire negotiations during the early months of 1937 aimed at building a united underground trade union movement. In addition they served to inspire attempts to unite Social Democratic and Communist *émigrés* in Spain into a united front.

Yet the discussions aimed at building a German People's Front fell short of the point at which they might have presented a convincing and agreed alternative to the fascist régime. Many of the bourgeois participants wished to give priority to the drafting of a constitution for post-Hitler Germany, which they envisaged as a parliamentary democracy of the Weimar type. Some members of the smaller socialist groups, on the other hand, still spoke of the dictatorship of the proletariat and condemned the Communists' 'new line' as opportunism, as they continued to do as late as 1939.[8] Among those Social Democrats who supported the idea of a People's Front, there were some who shrank from committing themselves to any definite programme, because they wished to leave the door open for the right-wing Executive to join in due course. The Communists, for their part, insisted that joint action should come first, while at the same time they tried hard to persuade their discussion partners that the new line was more than a mere tactical manoeuvre, and that the new democratic republic of which they spoke was sincerely conceived as a distinct historical stage, qualitatively different both from the discredited Weimar republic and from a dictatorship of the proletariat.

These arguments, incidentally, had the effect of stimulating constructive thinking within the Party. After intensive discussions at an extended Politburo meeting in June 1936, in which some underground leaders from Germany took part, a document, 'Guidelines for the working out of a Political Platform for the German People's Front' was drawn up and subsequently discussed with different groups on the Programme Commission, though no agreement resulted.[9]

The People's Front movement among German exiles centred in Paris continued to grow until about the end of 1936 and played a significant role in mobilising world opinion against Nazi war preparations and in support of Republican Spain. But after the beginning of 1937 it lost momentum and ultimately failed to achieve unity round an agreed programme. The most obvious reason for this was that the Executive Committee of the Social Democratic Party in exile continued to hold aloof from the discussions. Since 1934 the Executive had been moving to the right. It had confined its underground activities in Germany to a cautious collection of information and loose contacts with small circles of former party officials, and as these were broken up by the police in the mid and late-1930s, the influences making for militancy in the Social Democratic Party weakened. The Executive ceased to believe in the possibility of a revolutionary overthrow of the Nazi régime and could imagine no other way out than a war ending in the defeat of Hitler by Western capitalist powers. They thought it all-important, therefore, to keep in with the rulers of Britain and France, and fell into the arms of the most anti-Communist section of the international labour movement.

Besides the Social Democratic Executive, there were a number of other groups of German socialists which were, at first, prepared to contemplate joint action with the Communists. But their influence tended to decline as their German contacts were arrested and their finances gave out. They became more suspicious of the Communists, too, and less willing to co-operate with them, as reports and rumours reached them of purges in the Soviet Union between 1936 and 1938 and of conflicts in Spain between Trotskyists or anarchists on the one hand and Communists on the other. The

Spanish war, indeed, became a focal point of the national and class conflicts of the world. The effective and often heroic role played by Communists in the defence of Republican Spain enhanced the influence of Communism in many countries, while at the same time the growing economic and military strength of the Soviet Union impressed and frightened the middle classes in many countries, and caused a new wave of anti-Communism in the capitalist world, which was reflected in a falling away of some of the original supporters of a German People's Front.

Discussions similar to those in Paris and Prague were held in other countries where German *émigrés* had settled, and with similar, very limited results. At the beginning of 1936, for instance, an 'Askania Circle' was founded in Stockholm, which organised in October 1937 a conference of German anti-fascist refugees living in the Scandinavian countries. As a result, a Working Committee for the North was founded, with the aim of multiplying existing contacts with anti-Nazis in northern Germany.[10] In Switzerland there was some informal co-operation between the relatively few KPD exiles and individual left-wing Social Democrats in such activities as smuggling anti-Nazi literature over the frontier, holding discussion seminars on political subjects, and helping comrades threatened with expulsion.[11] More formal unity remained no more than an aspiration in all centres of the emigration where Sopade carried weight, and this was true in the more distant centres, too, such as Britain and the United States, and Mexico.

The most striking example of successful co-operation was in the German section of the International Mineworkers' Federation, whose head office in Amsterdam was run jointly by the Social Democratic trade unionist, Franz Vogt, and the Communist, Wilhelm Knöchel, who had also had experience as a Communist Party underground organiser,[12] had been elected to the Party's Central Committee at the Brussels Conference[13] and was later, thanks to this dual experience, to play a key role in the wartime activities of the Party.[14]

The organisation headed by Knöchel and Vogt was called a 'Working Committee'. It did not try to expand into a mass organisation or to undertake 'mass activities', but maintained a loose network of contacts with individual workers in a number of mines in the main coalfields.[15] The Committee issued a monthly paper in German, *Mineworkers' Information*,[16] for sale outside Germany, and the quarterly, *Mineworkers' News*,[17] for clandestine distribution within Germany. Their 'detailed and factual reports about wages and working conditions in the pits, about the policies of the German Labour Front, and about the various impulses of dissatisfaction and protest among the miners', Dr Peukert remarks, 'strongly suggest that the Committee must have had at its disposal very reliable connections within Germany'.[18] Knöchel seems to have pursued a flexible policy and to have made the sort of compromises necessary, so that the Joint Working Committee continued its activities until the Nazi invasion of the Netherlands in 1940.

As the Hitler government passed, in 1938, from war preparations and threats, to actual wars of conquest and territorial expansion, the German anti-fascists came to share a common interest with foreign victims of Nazi aggression. Those Germans who wished to overthrow Nazism in Germany had every reason to co-operate with those forces in the international field which were trying to maintain peace and prevent aggression, just as those forces had reason to join with one another. This meant, above all, co-operation with the USSR in defence of the Spanish Republic and Czechoslovakia, and this was the policy of the Popular Front movements in Germany as elsewhere. Those of the German anti-Nazis who rejected such co-operation out of fear of communism, as did the Social Democratic Party Executive and many bourgeois *émigrés*, could only adopt a waiting posture, while the Western powers tried to steer Hitler eastwards.

As Nazi Germany marched from victory to victory and the defeat of the Spanish Republic came nearer, a new situation developed. Despite much economic discontent, Hitler was succeeding in winning over, or at least neutralising, the greater part of the opposition, even among the workers. Among exiles, too, the People's Front committees were breaking up or becoming inactive, affected by the failure of the Popular Front movements in France and Spain, by the spread of pessimism about the inevitability of war, and by a growing anti-Communism which made many of the original supporters of the movement suspicious about the real intentions of the Communist Party and the probable consequences of a People's Front. At the same time the dismemberment of Czechoslovakia by the Munich settlement of September 1938 had disrupted the underground Party's communications with some of the most important regions of Germany, and this difficulty could only become more serious in the increasingly likely event of war.

It was to consider these developments, and to take appropriate measures, that another major Party conference, referred to then and since for security reasons as the 'Bern Conference', was held near Paris clandestinely at the end of January 1939.[19] 22 delegates were present, including 10 members of the existing Central Committee which had been elected at the Brussels Conference in 1935. The six Sector Leaders (Karl Mewis from Gothenburg, Paul Elias from Zürich, Josef Wagner from Paris for the Saar territory, Otto Niebergall from Brussels, Erich Gentsch from Amsterdam, and Heinrich Wiatrek from Copenhagen) were all present, and also several of the Instructors who had formed the main connection between the Sector Leaderships and the Communist underground in Germany during the previous three years. Among these were Artur Emmerlich, Elli Schmidt and Willy Seng. The delegates also included Wilhelm Knöchel from Amsterdam, whose trade union work in co-operation with Social Democrats had been outstanding; the editors of the Party's two central newspapers, Alexander Abusch and Gerhard Eisler; two representatives of the Young Communist League, Walter Hähnel and Erich Jungmann, and the leaders of the Austrian Communist Party, Johann Koplenig and Johann Mathieu. Of the Politburo members elected in 1935, Thälmann was, of course, still in prison and Heckert had died in 1936. Florin, Ulbricht and Wehner were not present, having remained in Moscow. Reports were made by Franz Dahlem, who headed the Central Committee's Secretariat at Paris, and by Anton Ackermann and Paul Merker. The main reports, however, were made by the acting Party chairman, Wilhelm Pieck, who had come from Moscow some weeks earlier to prepare and preside over the Conference.

The speakers at the Conference drew attention to the war preparations of the Hitler government and to the contradictory attitude of the German workers to them. On the one hand Hitler's nationalistic propaganda was not without effect; but on the other hand there was a widespead and growing fear of war. Yet there was disappointingly little action against the danger. Many workers had begun to think war inevitable and to sink into apathy and despair, seeing no way in which the Nazi régime could be overthrown except through war; a cure worse than the disease.

The Communists' answer, as the Conference proclaimed, was that the overthrow of Hitler *was* possible without war, but only if the different sections of the working class joined in a united struggle, together with anti-fascists of other classes. The call for unity issued from the Conference with a new urgency. Communists should now recognise, Pieck told the delegates, that the fatal division of the working class was not entirely the fault of the Social Democrats.[20] Communists, by their lingering sectarianism, had been partly to blame. Now they should make more vigorous efforts than ever before to reach agreement with other anti-fascist forces and to stop the Nazis from dragging the nation into war. They should fight against the idea that war was inevitable.

The Bern Conference not only repeated earlier calls for a United Front and a People's Front. It tried to develop these concepts further, stressing especially that the United Front should provide the basis of practical experience on which a united workers' party might be formed in course of time. The Conference further emphasised that the People's Front was not being put forward as a short-term expedient to be scrapped as soon as fascism was overthrown, but as a long-term class alliance through which the interests of peasantry, artisans, small traders and others, as well as those of the working class would be taken into account through the next historical stage.

At the same time, in case all attempts to prevent war should fail, the Bern Conference decided on a further reorganisation of the clandestine Party apparatus. In place of the relatively decentralised Sector system, it was planned to rebuild a network of KPD Instructors living in Germany, instead of merely making short visits. They would act as link between a new central internal leadership, which it was intended to establish, and a network of groups in important factories and work places. This type of tightened, centralised organisation was thought to be less likely to be cut off in wartime conditions; it was also argued, less realistically, that growing resistance activity was already providing a basis for such an organisation.

A considerable proportion of those present at the Conference had had recent experience of clandestine work, as Sector Leaders or Instructors, and a recurring theme of the speeches, as far as their content has survived, was the need to avoid wishful thinking and to base policy on sober factual experience.

The Conference assumed the status of a full Party Congress and elected a new Central Committee. This was reduced in size to fifteen members and in its composition a balance was struck between veterans of the pre-1933 leadership, including Dahlem, Florin, Merker, Pieck, Ulbricht, who had steered the Party through the transition from the old line to the new line of 1935, and younger members with recent experience of clandestine work in Germany, such as Anton Ackermann, Wilhelm Knöchel, Karl Mewis, Elli Schmidt, Herbert Wehner and Heinrich Wiatrek. The weight of the latter group, too, was to be increased by the co-option of up to three more underground activists. But, despite the introduction of new experience, the keynote was continuity. Wilhelm Pieck was re-elected as acting-chairman during Thälmann's continued imprisonment, and the leading positions in the two sections of the Politburo, to be situated at Moscow and Paris respectively, were assigned to Walter Ulbricht and Franz Dahlem; the latter, who remained at Paris as head of the Secretariat, being placed in charge of the Sector Leaderships and thus of the clandestine struggle in Germany.

The main outcome of the Bern Conference – apart from calls for a tightened organisation and increased 'mass activity' – was a renewed emphasis on the need for a united working-class front, leading towards a union of the working-class parties. In the following months the KPD leadership accordingly made further approaches to the Social Democratic Executive. On 3 April, for instance, Dahlem wrote to Hans Vogel, chairman of Sopade, proposing joint action or, failing that, parallel action by the two parties with a view to preventing war or, if war began, stopping it.[21] But these and other approaches elicited no response. Sopade maintained an ever more negative attitude, and some of those Social Democrats who had originally shown an interest in the People's Front movement were seriously affected by the change in the international atmosphere and by the purges in the USSR. The last remaining impulses were buried in the great explosion of anti-Communism which followed the conclusion of the German-Soviet Non-Aggression Pact on 24 August 1939.

War-Time

CHAPTER 12

The First Phase, 1939–41[1]

The diplomatic revolution of August 1939 placed the German Communists in a new situation. Up to that time their policy of building up a Popular Front aimed at the revolutionary overthrow of the Nazi régime and its replacement by a new type of democratic republic had fitted in with the Soviet Union's foreign policy aimed at the formation of an alliance with the bourgeois democracies for prevention of fascist agggression. But the negotiations between Britain, France and the USSR had finally petered out with the failure of the military talks on 21 August. Two days later Ribbentrop flew to Moscow and a Non-Aggression Pact between the Soviet Union and Germany was signed.

In retrospect it is not difficult to see that in view of the negative attitude of the British and French governments, not to mention the Poles, the government of the USSR had no real alternative but to come to terms with Germany if it wished to avert the danger that a victorious German army might arrive at the Soviet frontiers, freed, perhaps, by some new 'Munich' from effective restraint by the Western powers. In this sense the pact of 23 August represented no change of aim, but was a continuation in a new situation of the essentially defensive policy of the USSR. But at the time the news of the Pact came as a severe shock, not only to the world at large, but to the leaders of the German and other Communist parties, who had received no private warnings of the impending change of course, but had to form their own assessment of the new situation and of the conclusions to be drawn from it.[2]

Not surprisingly, there was some bewilderment and conflict of opinion. The international situation was complex and contradictory, and the full implications of so sudden and radical a realignment were not easily grasped, even by those, such as the leaders of the Communist International, who should have been comparatively well informed. For German Communists there was the additional difficulty that the outbreak of war cut most of the lines of communication between the membership in Germany and the leadership abroad, as well as between the two sections of the Politburo, in Moscow and Paris respectively, and German *émigrés* in other countries.

Among Communists in Germany there was much passionate argument and speculation about international events, as was reported to the Gestapo by its spies at the time and has since been noted in the recollections of surviving veterans. Some, misinterpreting the pact as a political alliance, could only imagine that Stalin had betrayed the cause. Others, realising that the Soviet Union had turned the tables on the 'Munichites' and gained time for her own defence, believed that she would ultimately emerge with enhanced power sufficient to bring about world revolution. Still others, shaken by Hitler's successive victories, could only fall back on their faith in the socialist state.[3]

The Non-Aggression Pact came as a complete surprise, and indeed as a shock, to the German Communist leadership. The Secretariat of the Central Committee, which operated clandestinely from Paris, and was responsible for the day-to-day operative leadership of the illegal Party organisations, discussed the new development on 24 August and issued a statement in the name of the Party on the following day.[4] This was to be, for all practical purposes the Party's effective reaction to the Pact, for it was the last statement to reach the Sector Leaderships before the breakdown of communications which followed the outbreak of war, and it may well have been, for many clandestine groups, the last policy document to reach them for a long time. The Secretariat's statement was issued after consultation with the leaders of the French Communist Party, and apparently with their approval, as also with that of Palmiro Togliatti who had been sent to Paris from Moscow to establish a West European Bureau of the Communist International for the event of war.[5]

It seems clear from their statements and actions that neither the French nor the German Communist Party leaders – nor perhaps at first even the International – were quick to grasp the full implications of the Non-Aggression Pact. They realised that the Soviet government had thwarted Chamberlain's clumsy efforts to steer Hitler's aggression towards conflict with the USSR. But they imagined that the result would be to increase the pressure of the peace forces on the British and French governments and to make them more willing, in their own interests, to enter into the sort of peace front with the Soviet Union which had been under discussion during the past few years and might still prevent Nazi aggression. On that basis it was possible to harbour the wishful thought that there was now more rather than less chance of preventing war – and therefore of rallying Germans for the overthrow of Hitler.

It was from such a standpoint that the KPD Secretariat viewed the consequences of the Pact in its statement of 25 August 1939. Greeting it as a 'blow for peace',[6] the statement called for renewed efforts to impose the will of the people for peace, and continued:

> The external and internal political situation created by the pact sets all anti-fascists, all peace and freedom-loving Germans, great tasks, which can only be carried out by an intensified struggle against the Nazi dictatorship . . .
>
> The German working people, and especially the German workers, must support the peace policy of the Soviet Union, must place themselves at the side of all peoples which are oppressed and threatened by the Nazis, and must now take up the fight as never before to ensure that peace pacts in the spirit of the pact which has just been concluded between the Soviet Union and Germany are also made with Poland and Romania, with France and England, and with all peoples which have reason to feel themselves threatened by Hitler's policy of aggression . . .[7]

The statement went on to demand: an end to predatory attacks on other peoples; protection of the independence and freedom of all peoples; freedom and national self-determination for the Austrian and Czechoslovak peoples; removal of German troops and Gestapo from those countries; 'Hands off Danzig!'; a peaceful understanding with Poland; peace and understanding with France and England; immediate reduction of the army to a peacetime level, and agreement with other peoples for general disarmament!

The Secretariat recognised that such a policy could only be imposed on the Nazis by a united working class, and the statement called for renewed efforts to overcome the divisions between Communists and Social Democrats in struggle against the Hitler dictatorship. If, despite all efforts to prevent it, the Nazis nevertheless plunged Europe into war, the Communist Party appealed to its members to work for their defeat, echoing

Liebknecht's words of 1915; 'The main enemy is at home!'

The analysis presented in the Secretariat's statement, and therefore the conclusions drawn, were in many respects unrealistic. Hopes for a continuation of the Anglo-Franco-Soviet negotiations quickly proved to be illusory, as did the calls for a union of German Communists and Social Democrats in the outburst of anti-Communism which followed the announcement of the Pact. Almost equally illusory was the belief that the Pact had created conditions in which German-Soviet friendship could be fostered. But if the line that was transmitted by the Secretariat to its subordinate organisations, and which continued in the main to form the basis of the policy proclaimed and followed by those organisations in the months ahead, was unrealistic, it was far removed from the co-operation with Nazism, of which the KPD has sometimes been accused.

For, although the KPD leaders, now established in the USSR, continued to express hostility to the Nazi régime after the conclusion of the German-Soviet Pact, they did not always give to that hostility the unambiguous priority which the Leninist doctrine of imperialist war might have seemed to dictate. The situation resulting from the division of Poland and from Hitler's 'peace offensive' in October 1939 was full of contradictions and posed harsh dilemmas for European Communist parties. Some of the statements which KPD leaders made at that time seemed, for instance, to express at least as much antagonism to British as to German imperialism and were later to be a source of embarrassment.[8]

A statement published in Stockholm on behalf of the KPD's Central Committee on 3 September, when the invasion of Poland had begun and the declaration of war by Britain and France was already imminent, continued to be primarily concerned with the need for working-class unity for the revolutionary overthrow of the Nazi dictatorship.[9] The same theme ran through the letter addressed by the KPD leadership in Moscow to Party members on 21 October,[10] and through the Political Platform worked out during the autumn and published at the end of December 1939.[11]

It is true that there was a change of emphasis, and in certain respects a revised analysis of the situation following the outbreak of war. The German Party's Secretariat at Paris, like the French and British Party leaderships, had at first been inclined to see the war as one of national defence on the part of Britain and France, and therefore as an anti-fascist struggle deserving of support. Because of this, Dahlem and his colleagues had emerged from clandestinity and had complied with the French government's registration requirements, as a result of which they were arrested and interned, together with other victims of the anti-Communist hysteria of the time.[12] This was only one of many incidents which helped to convert the leaders of Communist parties to the view that the war was in the main a conflict between two groups of imperialist powers for the redivision of the world. The KPD's 'Platform' of 30 December 1939 called on German Communists to make an effort to explain this to the German people and to try to mobilise them to bring the war to an end on the basis of the self-determination of the Austrian, Czech, Slovak and Polish peoples. The 'Germanisation' and plundering of the annexed territories, and the propaganda of 'Great German' chauvinism, it was argued, supplied grist to the mill of aggressive English and French imperialism and created only bitter enmity among the exploited peoples against the German people, thus hindering a common struggle of the German, Austrian, Czech, Slovak and Polish working class against imperialism. 'To promote that struggle,' the statement continued, 'Communists should continue to expose the falsity of National Socialist propaganda concerning so-called "German socialism" and should seek to organise all exploited classes to unite in defending their interests against the domination of monopoly capital.'[13]

This statement differed from those of August 1939, not only in its more hostile attitude to Britain and France, but in its formulations on inner-German affairs. For while it reiterated the call for united working-class struggle, it no longer described this in terms of the immediate revolutionary overthrow of the régime, but seemed to envisage a process by which the Nazi government would be forced, by popular pressure and the logic of the Pact with the USSR, to allow scope for legal or semi-legal activity.[14]

The situation in Germany itself following the Nazi conquest of Poland and the declaration of war by Britain and France seems to have been almost as contradictory as the international situation. There could be little doubt that the German people had a deeply-rooted fear of war which the lightning victory did little to dispel. Yet as Hitler marched from one success to another, this fear alternated with waves of chauvinistic euphoria, with grudging admiration for the Nazi leader's success, satisfaction at the humbling of the

Versailles powers, and illusions of easy victory. The right-wing opponents of the Nazis who feared Hitler's recklessness were silenced by his success, while the left-wing opposition was more divided than ever. The *émigré* Social Democrats and most other socialist groups, joining in the denunciation of the pact, broke off all remaining relations with representatives of the Communist Party and placed all their hopes on Britain and France.[15]

Yet there was another side to the situation. Ever since 1938 economic discontent had been growing, fostered by shortages of consumer goods and by a succession of measures for the conscription and direction of labour. Reports of the Labour Trustees and of the police spoke of worsening labour discipline and declining morale in the factories, of an increase of slacking, absenteeism and 'going sick', which some observers attributed to sheer physical exhaustion, others to political discontent expressing itself in disguised forms which often pointed to concerted action of a trade-union type.[16]

On the outbreak of war, on 1 September, more drastic labour legislation was introduced. Tighter control over the hiring and firing of workers was decreed, and on 4 September, by a War Economy Decree, the Labour Trustees were empowered to fix maximum wages and to determine working conditions in every branch of industry.[17] Employers were forbidden to attract workers by offering 'fringe benefits' or paying higher wages for Sunday work, night-work or overtime.[18] Paid holidays were suspended indefinitely. A few weeks later all wages were frozen.[19] In effect, the workers were deprived of their remaining rights.

These 'desperate measures', as Mason calls them,[20] were not described as temporary, but in the event they were almost immediately withdrawn.[21] On 16/17 November bonus rates for Sunday, holiday and night-work were restored and the previous holiday regulations were put into effect again with compensation for loss.[22] On 12 December limitations on hours of work, together with higher rates for overtime, were also restored.[23]

The reasons for this climb-down by the government of the Third Reich are clear from the minutes of a ministerial conference which recommended it. The simple fact was that the draconian 'war economy regulations' gave rise to 'a massive wave of indignation', resulting in an ominous fall in productivity.[24] Mason goes so far as to speak of a 'crisis' in the autumn of 1939, which drove the government on the one hand to 'back-pedal' in the economic sphere (thus probably saving itself, he thinks, from 'severe internal political disruptions')[25] while on the other hand it drove them into desperate plans to extend the war.

To speak of a crisis is perhaps to go too far. Nevertheless it is clear that the Nazi rulers were seriously concerned about the signs of growing working-class discontent in the autumn of 1939. Besides withdrawing or modifying some of the measures of economic mobilisation adopted during the previous summer, they took steps at the same time to strengthen the machinery of repression. The security departments of state and party were united on 27 September 1939 in a new Reich Head Security Office. At the same time the already savage penalties for political offences were increased by a great extension of the use of the death penalty and by the more and more frequent arbitrary interference of the SS and of Hitler personally in judicial matters, always in the direction of greater severity. So-called 'protective custody', i.e. imprisonment without trial, was used more frequently; the number of concentration camps was increased and conditions in them worsened, and it was laid down in principle that no prisoners should be released from them as long as the war lasted.[26] Already, too, in conjunction with the attack on Poland, and as a precaution against a possible resurgence of Communist activity, the Gestapo had arrested about 2,000 of the 'most dangerous' Communists, some of whom had only recently been released after long detention.[27]

Some Western writers assert that while the German-Soviet Non-Aggression Pact was in force, the German Communists ceased to resist the Nazi régime or even sought to find a place in it as a supposed 'ally' of the USSR. Sir John Wheeler-Bennett, for instance, wrote that 'Communist opposition to the Nazi régime had been "officially" called off from Moscow subsequent to the Nazi-Soviet Pact . . .'[28] while Terence Prittie alleged that '. . . in actual fact all Communist resistance to Hitler in Germany ended in September 1939 and had no faintest possibility of restarting until Hitler invaded the Soviet Union in May [*sic*] 1941.'[29] Professor H.R. Trevor-Roper[30] represents the KPD as having been 'for two vital years, the most shameless of Hitler's accomplices'.[31]

But these similar statements are inconsistent both with the Party's published policy documents and with police and trial records. There is, it is true, evidence, especially in the weeks immediately following the signature of the Pact, of some confusion among German Communists, both in emigration and in Germany, and it would not be difficult to find some contradictory or inconsistent utterances in newspapers or broadcasts, especially in the weeks following the collapse of Poland, when Hitler was posing as a seeker after peace, thwarted by the war-mongering Western powers and when the internment of the KPD Secretariat at Paris had temporarily disrupted the organisation at the top and increased its dependence on the Soviet government. In Germany many Communists undoubtedly imagined that the Pact would extend a certain protection to them and make it easier for them to carry out agitation and propaganda against the Nazis, since the authorities would be reluctant to prosecute them.[32]

This belief proved to be unfounded. Dr Duhnke, from his study of Gestapo situation reports in the autumn of 1939, concluded that attempts were being made by the leadership to give guidance and direction to the underground by sending Instructors, but that the clandestine struggle was at that time mainly conducted by individuals or small groups.[33] Both the Party leadership and the independent individuals and groups adhered, with little exception, to the line that the war was a war of imperialist powers, in which the duty of the revolutionary working-class party was to struggle for a just peace against its main enemy: its own government.[34]

This traditional Communist protest against militarism and imperialist war had been voiced already in the first days of the war. When workers in the Berlin suburbs of Neukölln and Tempelhof boarded their trams on the way to work in the early hours of 9 September 1939, they found on the seats leaflets headed: 'I call the youth of the world' – words reminiscent of the Olympic Games three years before – followed by a denunciation of the war and of those 'leaders' who were driving the people into another bloodbath like that of 1914–18. The leaflet recounted Hitler's lies and broken promises – on Spain and on Czechoslovakia – and listed the armament magnates whose pockets were being lined while German youth bled. And it called on young people to remember the two million German dead of the last war and to resist to the utmost to prevent that from happening again. 'Only the overthrow of Hitler and his band of warmongers,' the appeal concluded, 'can bring peace,' [signed:] 'Communist Youth League, South Berlin.'[35]

This was one of two such leaflets which are known to have been produced and distributed at that time by an anti-Nazi group led by a 27-year-old printer and Young Communist, Heinz Kapelle. He had already served a two-year prison sentence in 1934–36 for political activity, but had emerged with increased determination and had gradually built up an opposition group of some 60 young people, which is said to have included socialists and Christians as well as Communists. His courageous protest against the war was paid for dearly. Arrested with five others, Heinz Kapelle suffered the tortures of 'intensified interrogation' for many months. Finally, in February 1941, he was sentenced to death and executed in the following July. The police and prison records show that he steadily refused to betray others and died proclaiming his adherence to the Communist Party.[36]

During 1940 the policy statements issued by the KPD, while adhering to the general line that the main enemy was at home, laid increasing emphasis on the need, not simply for an early end to the war, but for a just peace without the subjection or plundering of any people. A statement issued by the Central Committee on 12 May 1940, two days after the German invasion of Belgium and Holland, expressed solidarity with the victims of war and repression in Denmark, Norway, Holland, Belgium and Luxembourg, as well as with the subject peoples of Austria, Czechoslovakia and Poland.[37] A further statement at the beginning of July condemned the 'brutal diktat' of Compiègne, and, declaring that the Nazi plans for 'a new Europe' meant nothing less than German domination of the continent, reiterated the demand for the immediate ending of the war by a peace without annexations or indemnities.[38]

As for the Non-Aggression Pact with the USSR, the German Communists called for its observance and warned of any extension of the war.[39] On 12 April 1941, after the invasion of Yugoslavia and Greece, they warned that in view of the superior resources of the 'Anglo-American bloc', and the growth of national liberation movements among the conquered peoples, Hitler's career of aggression was leading Germany to certain ruin, from which only a united front of all working people could save her.[40] From these and similar statements it is clear that the Communist Party leadership did not cease, during the period of the Pact, to call for resistance to the Nazi régime. They had therefore no need, when Hitler invaded the USSR, to make any fundamental change in their assessment of the international role of Nazism.

In addition to problems of policy and theory, the beginning of war in 1939 had confronted the Communist Party with difficult practical, organisational problems. At that time, as we have noted, while Pieck, Florin and Ulbricht represented the Party at the headquarters of the International in Moscow, the direction of operations was in the hands of a small Secretariat at Paris. Headed by Franz Dahlem, assisted by Paul Merker, Gerhart Eisler and Paul Bertz, this Secretariat worked through Sector Leaders in the countries bordering on Germany, who in turn kept in touch with their Sectors of Germany through Instructors who visited their allotted area periodically, keeping contact with representatives of clandestine groups.[41]

It appears that in many, perhaps most areas, there no longer existed a hierarchical system of Districts and Sub-districts, but only some loosely organised groups, each of them connected through one of its members with a visiting Instructor, so that a break of contact at one point might be difficult to repair. In some areas elements of the traditional structure had survived more than in others. In Berlin, notably, there were a number of area organisations, akin to the old Sub-districts, each linked independently through an Instructor with the Sector leadership for Central Germany, at that time based in Sweden.[42] In other cities, for example Augsburg in Bavaria, clandestine Communist groups existed without any connection to the *émigré* leadership.[43] The decision which had been taken at the Bern Conference to replace the Sector Leaderships by a new 'Central Operative Leadership' within Germany had not yet been put into effect when war began.[44]

The outbreak of war severely disrupted the Party's already fragmented illegal organisation. The members of the Secretariat at Paris were either interned or had to flee as a result of their decision to comply with the French government's decree requiring aliens to register – a decision which was disputed at the time and was later to be condemned as a grave error stemming from a mistaken assessment of the international situation. The leader of the Communist *émigrés* in France, Siegfried Rädel, and the Sector Leader for the South-West at Brussels, Otto Niebergall, were also arrested. Even the Sector leaders in Switzerland and Sweden were affected, since their Instructors were no longer able to cross the frontiers regularly, and although the German occupations of Denmark and Holland in April and May 1940 did not put an end to the operations of the Sector Leaders for Northern and Western Germany respectively, they were subject to increased difficulties and delays. The general effect of the transition from peace to war was to cut the connection of many clandestine groups within Germany with the Party leadership outside. At the same time the top political leadership was, by virtue of the course of events, no longer divided geographically but concentrated in Moscow where, inevitably, it was more directly subject to the influence of the Communist International and of the Soviet government.

For several practical reasons Moscow was not a centre from which clandestine operations in Germany could conveniently be directed. In the autumn of 1939, therefore, the Politburo decided to put into effect the decision of the Bern Conference to replace the Sector Leaderships by a new inner-German operative leadership (*Landesleitung*) at Berlin and, as far as possible, a new network of underground District Leaderships. This, however, in the conditions of even a 'phoney war', was easier said than done. A letter addressed by the Politburo to Party members on 21 October 1939[45] urged them to take every possible step to transform the often loose connections of clandestine Party groups into a firm organisation led by battle-tried comrades. But it was not until 11 December 1939 that a detailed plan of reorganisation was adopted by the Politburo,[46] and the putting of it into effect was to be attended by further delays and difficulties.

The first stage of the plan laid down in the Politburo's 'Platform' envisaged the setting up in Sweden of a new preparatory group or external leadership (*Auslandsleitung*). It was to consist of a small number of experienced younger members of the Central Committee, most of whom had taken part in underground work either as District Leaders before 1936 or as Sector Leaders since then. They included Karl Mewis, hitherto head of the Sector Leadership for Central Germany, including Berlin; Heinrich Wiatrek, Sector Leader for North Germany, based on Copenhagen; Herbert Wehner;[47] Richard Stahlmann; and Erich Glückauf.[48] Most of the group were intended ultimately to go to Berlin to form the new inner-German Operational Leadership (*Landesleitung*), together with Wilhelm Knöchel who, from his base at Amsterdam, had hitherto combined the function of joint-leader of the German Section of the International Mineworkers' Union with a share in the KPD's Sector Leadership for Western Germany.

The preparatory group was slow to assemble at Stockholm. Wiatrek appears to have been reluctant to leave Copenhagen, where he was involved in controversy with other Communist *émigrés*, arising from his belief that the Pact was something more than a mere tactical manoeuvre on Hitler's part, and that legal Communist activity was now possible; he was finally arrested by the Gestapo on 19 May 1941.[49] At the same time, Wehner's departure from Moscow was repeatedly postponed. Mewis and the others, however, who were already in Sweden from early 1940, took steps to prepare the ground for the intended move to Berlin.

The first step was to renew broken contacts with Party groups in Germany. At the outbreak of war, two of the Instructors on the staff of the Central German Sector had been in the Reich. One of them, Charlotte Krohne, had returned to Sweden on 9 September, bringing reports about the German people's reactions to the war and about the mood and activities of Communists.[50] The other Instructor, Willy Gall, had decided to remain in Berlin to try to further the process of reorganisation, but he had no means of communication with his base at Stockholm, and after some months was arrested before contact could be re-established.[51]

The Stockholm preparatory commission finally arranged to send to North Germany five further Instructors, whose task was to make contact with existing Communist groups and to make detailed preparations for the establishment at Berlin of the intended new Operative Leadership. The first of these Instructors, Rudolf Hallmeyer, reached Berlin from Sweden on 30 June 1940. He first attempted to contact Willy Gall, but found that not only he, but all the others who had been thought of as a new City Leadership had been arrested. Nevertheless, Hallmeyer made many contacts and was able to establish a new Berlin City Leadership, as well as to undertake much political discussion and propaganda. He had begun to extend his contacts to several other areas, including Magdeburg, Halle and Dresden, before he fell into the hands of the Gestapo on 24 August 1940. With exemplary heroism he gave nothing away and the network of contacts he had established remained to be built on by others.[52]

Meanwhile, during August 1940, the other four had also arrived in Germany by separate routes. One, Johannes Müller, was arrested at Hamburg docks soon after his arrival and before he could perform his task, which consisted of integrating into the proposed new Berlin

City organisation the contacts in a particular suburb which he had previously visited as Instructor. Another of the four, Heinrich Schmeer,[53] also a former Instructor for the Central German Sector, evaded arrest for the few weeks needed to pass on to the proposed new Berlin City Leadership his own contacts in another Berlin suburb, but was arrested in mid-September. A third, Georg Henke, visited groups in a number of North German coastal areas ranging from Lübeck to Königsberg and, having accomplished his mission, returned safely to Sweden.

The most important of the Instructor group was Arthur Emmerlich, who, alone of the five, was still at liberty in Germany after the middle of September 1940 and continued to be active there for a further eight months or more, until his arrest at Hamburg on or about 19 May 1941. Before this mission he had made several visits to Germany as the Central Sector Leadership's Instructor for a particular area of Berlin; and he had taken part in the Bern Conference. His mission of 1940, for which lengthy preparations had been made, consisted of making detailed arrangements for the setting up of the new Central Operative Leadership within Germany. In the event he did more than that, staying much longer than had orginally been envisaged and concentrating in his hands a whole network of contacts with Communist groups, not only in Berlin, but also along the Baltic coast, in Magdeburg, and in Central Germany and Saxony. He began, in effect, together with one or two of his long-standing Berlin contacts, such as Kurt Steffelbauer and Johannes Gloger, to perform some of the functions of the intended all-German Operative Leadership, including the publication of at least three numbers of *Rote Fahne* and other literature.[54] He is regarded by some GDR historians as representing the first provisional central leadership of the war period, even though his network seems to have included few if any contacts in Western or Southern Germany.

The task of the five Instructors sent from Sweden in 1940 was not confined to the linking up of those clandestine groups within Germany which had already been known to the Sector Leaderships through their Instructors. They were also required to seek out new underground groups which might be working independently, having either lost, or never had, connection with a Sector Leadership. The most important of such groups were those in Berlin which had gradually been brought together during the preceding period by Robert Uhrig. Uhrig, a toolmaker by trade and a Communist of long standing, had served a prison sentence followed by concentration camp for political activity after 1933. Released in 1936, he had found employment as a skilled craftsman at the Osram electricity works at Berlin, where he soon began to build up a clandestine anti-Nazi group. He was a talented organiser and by 1938, though living 'legally', he was at the head of an illegal organisation counting some 200 members. In the following years he had gradually and cautiously extended the network of factory cells, carrying out the oral propaganda and careful organisational work which were most characteristic of that period.[55]

Hallmeyer, during his stay in Berlin in the summer of 1940, came to the conclusion that Uhrig's organisation ought to be recognised as the new Communist Party leadership for Berlin and should receive corresponding help and encouragement.

In the course of 1940, Uhrig made contact with several other experienced Communists who had been carrying on political work independently or in small groups after release from prison or concentration camp. Among these were Herbert Grasse[56] and Otto Grabowski, who had already organised cells in a number of Berlin factories; and Wilhelm Guddorf and John Sieg, intellectuals and writers who had worked as journalists on the Party's papers before 1933. Sieg and Guddorf, for their part, were already in touch with the groupings of intellectuals and officials who had gathered round Arvid Harnack and Harro Schulze-Boysen. An equally significant addition was brought to Uhrig's almost exclusively working-class network when he made contact, early in 1940, with the former regular army captain and Freikorps leader Dr Josef ('Beppo') Römer. Römer, who had joined the Communist Party shortly before 1933, had an extensive acquaintance among military men, aristocrats and officials, and even industrialists, including some who were later to be involved in the July 1944 plot.[57]

The clandestine activities directed respectively by Uhrig and Römer, and by Sieg, Guddorf, Harnack and Schulze-Boysen, were to assume their full extent and effect only after the Nazi attack on the Soviet Union, when they were to form links with one another and with what was still a separate organisation in the Ruhr and Rhineland, directed by Wilhelm Knöchel from Amsterdam, where the activity of the Sector Leadership for Western Germany had continued despite the occupation of Holland in May 1940.[58]

Already in 1940 and the first half of 1941 there was a growing and active network centred in Berlin, which had the makings of a new internal German leadership, though its potential, as we now know, was undermined by the presence of one or two Gestapo agents in leading positions. More will be said in a later chapter about the activities of this organisation after the German attack on the USSR. Here it is enough to note that the organisation did not come into existence first in June 1941. Already then, it has been reckoned, there were Communist-led cells in 89 Berlin factories.[59] The network had been built up steadily during 1940 and early 1941 and had played what might have been a significant role in obtaining information and passing on warnings concerning the forthcoming attack in the East.

The outbreak of war in 1939 had the effect of isolating German Communist organisations, not only in Germany itself, but in the various centres of emigration in western and northern Europe. In France, which had been the most important centre,[60] many active Communists were interned, while others were forced into hiding. After the armistice in June 1940 some of the internees escaped and some of these, including the Politburo member Paul Merker, got away overseas.[61] Others, from hiding places in France, tried to organise the sending of Instructors into Western Germany, but they had little success in this and most of them eventually joined French partisan units. Of those who remained interned, many, including Franz Dahlem, were later handed over to the Gestapo when Vichy France was occupied in November 1942.

In Holland, while many German refugees fell into the hands of the German police in 1940, the KPD Sector leadership under Erich Gentsch and Wilhelm Knöchel remained undiscovered and continued to send Instructors, though on a very small scale, into the Ruhr and Lower Rhineland, and to make preparations for moving into Germany.

In Denmark the position was similar, except that dissensions broke out within the Sector Leadership. Wiatrek, who was head of it and a member of the Central Committee, had at first regarded the German-Soviet Pact as opening the way to legal Communist activity in Germany, and when this proved illusory, he became pessimistic. Even in Switzerland and Sweden the Communist *émigrés* were forced to operate in conditions of illegality or semi-illegality. The Party Leadership maintained the precarious links with the Berlin underground which have been described, while semi-

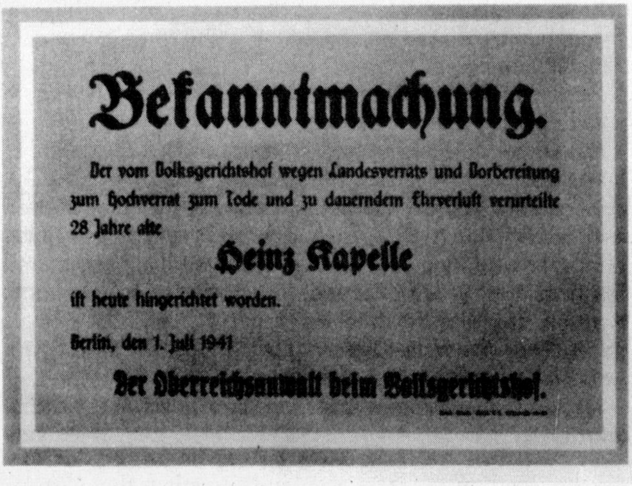

Bekanntmachung.

Der vom Volksgerichtshof wegen Landesverrats und Vorbereitung zum Hochverrat zum Tode und zu dauerndem Ehrverlust verurteilte 28 Jahre alte

Heinz Kapelle

ist heute hingerichtet worden.

Berlin, den 1. Juli 1941

Der Oberreichsanwalt beim Volksgerichtshof.

Heinz Kapelle, Communist activist in Berlin, and the official announcement of his execution, aged 28, for 'high treason', July 1941 independent groups like that of Schulze-Boysen made occasional *ad hoc* contacts across the frontiers.

In short, while the Party's top leadership persistently aimed, in the years 1939–41, at replacing the Sector organisation by a centralised leadership within Germany, and at keeping effective control of it, they made slow progress and experienced many difficulties, the results falling far short of the system which had been envisaged in the Central Committee's letters and instructions of 1939.[63]

Besides organisational measures, the Party leadership persistently called for more political action in these years, and there were Communists, especially in Austria – some of them with, some without regular contact – who answered these calls with a desperate, self-sacrificing heroism. Mention has already been made of the group of young people led by Heinz Kapelle, who denounced Hitler's war within a few days of the attack on Poland, and there was at least one other group of young people active in Berlin at this time, led by the Jewish Communist Herbert Baum. Of the less youthful groups, some of the most effective were led by experienced Communists who were released from concentration camps after the Nazi victory in Poland and who resumed resistance activities as soon as the clandestine Party's security procedures permitted, sometimes before.

One of the most widely-shared needs, once war had broken out – a need shared by Communists with many other sections of the people – was to find out what was really happening in the outside world, as distinct from the world of official propaganda, and it was this which led to the springing up of groups of neighbours and workmates for listening to radio-broadcasts from Moscow and London. How diverse the participation in such groups could be is well illustrated by the membership of one such group in a working-class suburb in the South German industrial city of Augsburg, which existed from the outbreak of war until May 1940 and included not only Communists and socialists, but also Catholics, Jehovah's Witnesses and even Nazis.[64]

One of the activities which a revived underground leadership of the German Communist Party was expected to undertake was the resumption of publication of the Party's national newspaper, *Rote Fahne*. This task was entrusted to Arthur Emmerlich when he went to Berlin in August 1940 and a news-sheet with that name was brought out at intervals of a month or six weeks until Emmerlich's arrest in the following May. There also appeared in the same period another illegal paper entitled *Berliner Rundbriefe*, as organ of the new Berlin City Leadership.

Considerable attention was paid by the leaders of the illegal groups to what may be broadly called 'educational activities'. Some of these were designed to convey knowledge and understanding of the Soviet Union through lectures given by comrades who had worked there or had been employed by Soviet trade delegations. This activity was intended to take advantage of the comparative lull in Goebbels's anti-Soviet propaganda which followed the conclusion of the Non-Aggression Pact as well as to clear up some of the confusions which it had caused. There was organised study of the Marxist classics, too, with special attention to imperialism, to the First World War, and to the monopoly-capitalist nature of national socialism; attention was also paid to the 'theoretical' aspects of Nazi propaganda.

From the beginning German Communist workers had been urged by the broadcasts of Party leaders and by visiting Instructors to look out for former Social Democrats and other colleagues of anti-Nazi views at their place of work, and to try to draw them into organised resistance activity. This was less difficult to achieve (despite the continued refusal of Sopade to countenance any collaboration) now that most Communist workers were in employment and that their resistance groups no longer corresponded so faithfully to the structure and personnel of the pre-1933 KPD. Thus, of the 80 or so works in Berlin in which resistance groups are known to have been active in May 1941 (before the invasion of the USSR), many included some non-Communists and a few were led by non-Communists, though the overwhelming majority were Communist-led.[65]

There was another direction, too, in which the Communists looked for allies. Prisoners-of-war of defeated and occupied countries, and foreign workers brought to the Reich either voluntarily or by compulsion, had been appealed to as allies in many KPD statements from September 1939. By October 1940 over 880,000 Poles were employed in Germany,[66] and, although most had at first been employed in agriculture, the proportion of Poles employed in industry was rapidly growing, while the ignominious treatment to which they were subjected made sabotage of German war production a patriotic duty for them.

The same was true for German Communists, who had done what they could, even before the war, to slow down and hold up the preparations for Nazi aggression. In the years leading up to the war there had been evidence of much minor sabotage in armament factories and similar enterprises and, if police reports are to be believed, it became more frequent when war started.[67] To combat it the security services were ordered to vet all personnel employed in munitions factories, but the task was beyond the resources of even the vast network of institutions newly united in the RSHA, in the pre-computer age, and no more than a beginning was made.

War also increased the importance of intelligence, and it was here that the resistance groups which included government officials and military officers had a key role to play. The best known of these were the groups led respectively by Arvid Harnack, an under-secretary (*Oberregierungsrat*) in the Ministry of Economics, and Harro Schulze-Boysen, a lieutenant in the Air Ministry. These two groups had existed for some years before the war, combining Marxist study and discussion with anti-Nazi political agitation. They were in contact with the Communist Party, though it is not clear whether they formed part of the KPD's formal structure. When war began, the two groups seem to have merged and also to have developed closer relations with those underground KPD leaders who, in 1941, were trying to rebuild a wider Party organisation based on Berlin.

From the beginning Harnack and Schulze-Boysen had often passed on to the USSR such information about Hitler's war preparations as was accessible to them. When war began, this aspect of their activity became more important. In the spring of 1941, when signs were multiplying of an imminent attack on the USSR, they developed a special section of their organisation, staffed largely by men and women employed in the forces, in industry, or in government departments, and got this integrated into the Soviet intelligence system in Europe. At the same time they consulted Guddorf and Sieg, as representatives of the Communist Party's Berlin Leadership, and it was agreed that those who were working in the intelligence section should be withdrawn from all other activity and should function independently of the Party as such.[68]

What is frequently overlooked is that this intelligence section represented only a part of the resistance organisation labelled *Rote Kapelle* (the Red orchestra) by the Gestapo. Moreover, to condemn this group as in some way uniquely treasonable or unpatriotic, as many Western writers have done, is to judge them by Nazi standards, or by a double standard; for many other anti-Nazis, Social Democrats and others, also viewed the Hitler régime as the enemy of the German people and thought themselves fully justified in passing what information they could to the British and French and other Western governments.[69]

The extent and effectiveness of Communist resistance during the first stage of the war are not easy to judge. Contrary to what is often alleged, and to what some Communists anticipated, the German-Soviet Non-Aggression Pact had not brought with it any fundamental change in the attitude either of the Communist Party to the Nazi régime or of the Nazi rulers to the Communists. There had, it is true, been a lull in the volume of Nazi propaganda against the Soviet Union and of Soviet propaganda against the Nazis, and this had bred among some German Communists the illusion that they could expect a loosening of the repression and even the opening of some opportunities for legal or semi-legal activity. But in fact the authorities had no more intention than before of tolerating Communist activity in Germany, while the Communist Party's continued calls for immediate peace without annexations and for the self-determination of all European peoples were tantamount to a demand for the condemnation of Nazism, even if, for a time, phrases like 'revolutionary overthrow' were dropped from the Party's vocabulary.

That the Nazi government continued, despite the superficial courtesies of the Pact and the weakened state of the Communist organisation, to take the illegal Party seriously as a potential threat is to be explained by the continued failure of the régime, despite its monopoly of the means of education and propaganda, to win the hearts and minds of the German workers. The outbreak of war only accentuated the already severe shortage of labour in the war-related industries and set bounds to the efficacy of repressive measures. There was chronic discontent among skilled workers and the increased proportion of women[70] and of foreign prisoners and conscript workers in the labour force made it more difficult to enforce work discipline. Moreover, as recent research has been bringing to light, the Nazis had failed to win working-class youth in any but a superficial, organisational sense, so that many of them were increasingly alienated and rebellious.[71] That all this amounted to a political crisis for the régime is open to debate, for there were other factors which appear to have worked in favour of the Nazis. Recurrent, if short-lived waves of patriotic elation swept through the population in the wake of Hitler's victories. In the factories, it has been suggested, a feeling of pride amounting to élitism was experienced by the remaining core of skilled men, as foreigners were recruited in increasing numbers and came to form a greater proportion of the labour force. In the minds of workers, national consciousness struggled with class consciousness and the Labour Front strove to combat the latter by cynical tricks of egalitarian demagogy which no doubt influenced the politically inexperienced.

Although the Gestapo was not inclined to treat the evidence of working-class discontent lightly, its reports suggested that these currents of dissatisfaction were not, at this period, reflected in any high level of Communist activity. The reason for this, if police spies are to be believed, was that the repeated calls for action emanating from the *émigré* leadership were received with reluctance by the Party's members in Germany. The heavy defeats of previous years were said to have left Party members in a cautious mood, unwilling to risk their lives unless they saw some prospect of achieving worthwhile results. Their conversation was reported to consist largely of rumours about the course of the war and of speculations about Nazi defeats, on which they were said to found all their hopes.[72]

No doubt many who still thought of themselves as Communists were affected by such feelings, as well as by political confusion, and there probably was, in consequence, a lower level of activity in terms of output of illegal literature. Established groups, too, were sometimes disrupted by the call-up of men to the forces and by transference of labour, though the fact that men with a 'criminal' record were excluded from service in the forces at this period will have worked the other way. On balance, the available evidence suggests that the Gestapo underestimated the extent of Communist or Communist-led activity at this period. Information continues to come to light showing the existence of independent Communist groups which had lost touch with the Party leadership. Their activity was often chiefly of the oral kind which was least open to detection and to quantitative assessment. At the same time attempts were constantly being made to link up these groups with a central leadership at Berlin and abroad, and slow progress (partly known and partly unknown to the Gestapo) was made toward the rebuilding of a centrally-directed movement.

The crux of the situation was that despite all the successes of National Socialism its hold on key sections of the working class was still insecure and the Communist Party, though fragmented and to some extent disorientated, still existed and was constantly reorganising itself. Hitler's war strategy consisted essentially of a series of risky gambles and he was conscious that if he were to suffer a serious setback there might be a rapid change in popular feeling; then the existence of an effective and centralised revolutionary organisation, however small, might assume decisive importance. This was a point which Georgi Dimitrov went out of his way to put to Karl Mewis and Herbert Wehner at the end of December 1939, just before Mewis left Moscow for Sweden, to arrange for the sending of Central Committee Instructors to Berlin. Despite the Nazi terror, Dimitrov observed, an active core of Communists had survived. Its effectiveness would depend on ability to combine tight organisation with flexibility in action and on the readiness of its leaders to set an individual example of firmness and confidence throughout the unexpected twists and turns to which historical events are subject.

CHAPTER 13

Inner-German Leaderships, 1941–43

The German invasion of the USSR on 22 June 1941 completed a change which was already becoming apparent in the character of the war. It was no longer predominantly a struggle of rival imperialisms, but of national defence and liberation of enslaved peoples from fascism. The broad anti-fascist coalition of powers at which Communists had aimed in the years 1935–39 had at last come into being. The ambiguities of the early war years had resolved themselves into a single issue on which the fate of all peoples, including the German people, depended.

In another way, too, the war underwent a change. With the failure of Hitler's blitz against Moscow in the autumn of 1941, and the entry of the United States, it became a total war, in which time and the balance of resources turned against the Nazis, and their ultimate defeat became ever more probable. They were forced to call up millions more men and to replace them in factories and on farms by prisoners-of-war and deportee labourers from occupied countries and client states. For the first time, too, arms production was maximised and production for civilian needs was drastically cut back; and although foreign workers and the populations of occupied countries were the first sufferers, German civilians also now experienced serious food shortages as well as the terrors and hardships of area bombing.

For German Communists the changing situation solved some problems but created others. The confusions and uncertainties of the pact period gave way to a new clarity. In the great struggle in the East all was now at stake. A Nazi victory would condemn both the people of Europe and the German working class to slavery for years, perhaps for generations, to come, while a Nazi defeat would open up prospects of a major advance. There was less justification than ever before for a policy of caution or hesitation. The interests of the working class, and of the German people as a whole, required the overthrow of the Third Reich and most German Communists recognised that they had a duty to help bring about its military defeat.

Yet this was not a message which it was easy to put across in Germany. At first the rapid advance of Hitler's armies in Russia infected many Germans with another attack of chauvinist fever, while some of those who understood the dangers of a Nazi victory were plunged into a despairing pessimism. And although the failure of the blitzkrieg in the East in the winter of 1941–42 shook many Germans' faith in victory, the news of the summer offensives of 1942 revived it, and it was not until the disaster at Stalingrad during the following winter that most Germans began to realise that the war might end in defeat.

Weakened faith in victory, together with increasing hardships at home and rumours of atrocities in the East, all helped to undermine the popularity of the Nazi régime and opened up possibilities of winning people in Germany for anti-fascist action. Yet these possibilities were not easily realised. Political activity was hindered, not only by police terror, but by the redistribution of the labour force which resulted from mass call-ups of men, including some categories previously exempt, and the mass recruitment of foreign workers, as well as the concentration of production in the larger enterprises. Equally important were what may be called psychological factors. The ill-defined fear of a total catastrophe, in which the whole German nation would perish, led to a certain closing of the ranks and to a sense of shared guilt for the atrocities committed against other peoples. Many who rejected and even hated Nazism felt hopelessly involved in its crimes and exposed to the indiscriminate vengeance which it was assumed that its victims – and especially a victorious Red Army – would take. And, while some dissociated themselves from the crimes of the Nazis by taking anti-fascist action, individually or in groups, many more were unable to break through the assumptions of traditional nationalist thought, with its horrified rejection of anything which might be interpreted as 'helping the enemy' or 'stabbing the German soldier in the back'.

Yet this was not the whole picture. The clandestine groups which had kept in touch with one another and maintained a certain level of anti-fascist activity during the previous two years reacted differently. They saw that the moment of supreme decision had come and that their previous activities made no sense unless they now threw their whole weight into the scales against the régime. These were not mere critics of Hitler's strategy: they were anti-fascists who rejected the aims of imperialism and thought that true German patriotism lay in joining hands with the oppressed peoples and the anti-fascist powers to bring about the political and military defeat of the Third Reich and a peace settlement based on the self-determination of peoples and the establishment of a truly democratic German state.

That opposition groups pursuing such aims as these greatly increased their activities after the invasion of the USSR is clear from the Gestapo's reports of the time. The monthly total of different leaflets found by the police, which had fluctuated between 62 and 519 during the first half of 1941, rose to 3,797 in July and remained at about that level until October, when it rose to a peak of 10,227.[1] At the same time the number of arrests for political offences rose sharply. The exact nature of these offences is not easy to determine with certainty, as the categories used in Gestapo statistics were legal rather than political, corresponding to the charge which could be or had been brought, rather than to the questions which the present-day historian is most likely to have in mind. In the Gestapo statistics for the later months of 1941[2], for instance, only some 5 per cent of these arrests were placed in the category 'Communism and Marxism', by which the Gestapo seems to have meant political activity organised by the Communist, Social Democratic or other socialist party. A much greater number were placed under the heading 'opposition', which apparently denoted a variety of more or less seditious activities, such as listening to foreign broadcasts, spreading rumours, or repeating political jokes – actions which might be merely individual expressions of protest. The most frequent of all reasons for arrest was participation in strikes or other forms of labour indiscipline; most of those concerned being foreign workers.

These statistics have sometimes been taken to show that the Communist Party played only a small part in such resistance as came to the notice of the police at this period. But care needs to be exercised in drawing such a conclusion. Many of the acts categorised by the Gestapo as 'opposition' or 'labour indiscipline' correspond closely to what the Communist Party was urging workers to do. How far the culprits acted under the influence or instructions of the Communist (or Social Democratic) Party might be virtually impossible to establish, and it was a connection they were likely to deny when questioned. It is therefore possible that the police, when they analysed the causes of the sharp increase in acts of political protest or resistance after the invasion of the USSR, may have tended to overestimate the element of individualism and spontaneity and to underestimate the influence of Communist resistance groups or Communist broadcasts.[3]

The groups which sprang into renewed activity at this time were in many cases not tightly organised Party formations of the traditional type. Their social composition might embrace a wide spectrum and it may sometimes have been difficult to say who was a Party member and who a sympathiser, if indeed the question was asked at all. In some groups left-wing intellectuals or professional men and women of outstanding ability and courage played a leading role. Yet on the whole the initiative was taken and the organising talent provided by experienced Communists with a long record of full-time Party work. Some of them had been released at various times in 1939 or early in 1940, after spending years in prisons and concentration camps, and had since been cautiously renewing their political contacts and laying the basis for action, conscious that they were under police observation and that too much haste might endanger others besides themselves. Now, with the attack on the USSR, they felt that the time for action had come.

The most extensive and effective of these Communist groups in 1941 was that led by Robert Uhrig, which was based on Berlin and had ramifications in many of the city's suburbs and in a considerable number of factories there.[4] At this time, moreover, Uhrig and one or two of his closest colleagues were beginning to develop links with resistance groups in other parts of the Third Reich.[5]

When news came of Hitler's attack on the USSR, Uhrig was quick to react to the challenge. His first step was to confer with nine or ten leading members of the organisation. The discussion took place in the Alexanderplatz in the very centre of Berlin on 24 June in a crowded bar where a waiter who was a member of the organisation had been able to arrange a suitable table.[6] All were agreed on the line to be taken: the USSR was the workers' fatherland and must be defended at all costs. In the following weeks this line was put forward by every available means, especially in factories where the group had members. Between 5 and 10 July 1941 the Berlin police found some 30 different wall-stickers bearing slogans calling on workers to express opposition to the war by slow work, resisting overtime, refusing to contribute to Nazi collections and in other ways.[7]

Uhrig and his comrades intensified their efforts to extend their organisation by finding new sympathisers and by linking up with other existing groups. In September 1941, for instance, they incorporated a group led by Walter Budeus, which had some 70 members in the big Berlin armament works *Deutsche Waffen- und Munitionsfabrik*.[8] At the same time Uhrig developed his collaboration with Josef Römer, whose numerous contacts with members of the Establishment enabled him to extend his organisation.[9]

The alliance with Römer gave the Uhrig organisation a new social dimension. At the same time Uhrig had been working to extend its connections geographically as well. During 1941 he undertook a number of journeys to make contact with clandestine resistance groups in other parts of Germany: in Hamburg and Hanover, for instance, in Vienna and Munich, and even in the Tyrol, where contacts had been supplied by a Social Democratic engineer who was a member of the group.[10] Uhrig and his associates aimed in this way at laying the foundations of a new, nation-wide, centrally directed resistance movement.

Another move in the same direction was made on 10 September 1941, when the new German *Volkssender* (People's Transmitter) which the Soviet government had put at the disposal of the German Communist leaders in the USSR began to broadcast. Besides publishing policy statements and news of the war and of Nazi crimes, the broadcasts gave practical directions and advice on methods of underground struggle. Uhrig was quick to make use of this new source of news and ideas. He established a regular monitoring service which produced transcripts of the broadcasts and he used these to produce a new illegal monthly news-sheet entitled *Informationsdienst* (Information Service).[11]

The issue of mid-December 1941, a copy of which has survived, is a six-page pamphlet.[12] After declaring that its purpose is to educate political fighters and calling for constructive criticism, the editors review in turn the military situation, the international situation, the economic situation and the internal political situation, and proceed to ask what the workers must do. The answer is, weaken Hitler's war potential at its most vulnerable points, above all, its petrol, rubber and steel supplies, by sabotage and slow work.

The group's plans for the next year included the setting up of a clandestine short-wave transmitter, with which to establish direct contact with the Party leadership, and the publication of a political manifesto.[13] According to one source,[14] Römer had agreed to participate in an officers' plot to assassinate Hitler; but if he did, he is unlikely to have acted with the approval of the Communist Party leaders. It is, indeed, uncertain whether the exiled leaders had any direct contact with the Uhrig group in the summer of 1941. Their main representative in Germany, Arthur Emmerlich, had been arrested in May and it was not until August that Alfred Kowalke arrived in Berlin from the Netherlands as an agent of the Central Committee, working closely with Uhrig.

Uhrig's organisation, though primarily a network of Berlin factory cells which was developing into a Berlin city organisation of the Communist Party, had a number of connections with other semi-independent groups. One of these was the group of former Communist editors and Marxist intellectuals who have come to be known as the *Innere Front* (Home Front) group, after the title of the clandestine newspaper which they produced in 1941–42.[15] The leaders of the group, Wilhelm Guddorf, John Sieg, Martin Weise and Jon Graudenz, had been on the editorial staff of the Communist Party's daily, *Rote Fahne*, before 1933, and had subsequently been in detention for some years. Released, like a number of other Communist Party officials, in 1939–40, they had resumed contact with one another and had gradually made the technical and other preparations for producing and circulating a clandestine paper. They began to bring it out, in 600 copies, soon after the invasion of the USSR, and maintained it on a fortnightly to monthly basis until the autumn of 1942. Drawing on the news broadcasts of the *Volkssender* and of Radio Moscow, and perhaps also of the BBC, they concentrated on exposing the falsity of Goebbels's propaganda and the probability of a German defeat. Given the primitiveness of the technical means available, the paper, which called itself 'a fighting sheet for a new, free Germany', achieved a high intellectual and journalistic level. In 1942 it began to appear in several non-German languages for distribution to foreign workers. The group's productions also included leaflets and pamphlets, such as John Sieg's 21-page pamphlet analysing the military situation after the initial German victories in Russia.[16]

Apart from such topical subjects, members of this group also undertook Marxist education through small classes and informal discussions on such themes as the monopoly-capitalist nature of fascism or the German revolution of 1918. The group's activities were not confined to Berlin: Guddorf in particular, had connections with Hamburg and maintained them through an underground activist there whom he knew from his concentration camp days.[17]

The *Innere Front* group, consisting as it did of Communist intellectuals with long experience of full-time Party work and a record of imprisonment, formed something of a bridge between Uhrig's organisation, composed overwhelmingly of industrial workers, and the more loosely defined circles of anti-Nazi professional people who had gathered round Arvid Harnack and Harro Schulze-Boysen. Among these were state officials, doctors, artists and architects, and even one or two military officers. Though many of them had been interested in Marxist ideas before 1933, and some, like Harnack, had visisted the USSR, they were not known as Communist Party members. But when Hitler came to power, and events confirmed the worst fears about his intentions, these men and women, unlike many other middle-class opponents of Nazism, were prepared to carry their opposition to its logical conclusion.

Already before the war, as has been noted in an earlier chapter,[18] the followers of the at first separate groups of Harnack and Schulze-Boysen had developed significant anti-fascist activity and had made contact with proletarian resistance organisations such as Uhrig's. They were relatively informally organised, meeting in each others' flats or on excursions and outings, and they recruited new members through personal friendships and through professional or family connections, until several hundred people were involved in their activities. These activities included the study of the Marxist classics and the reading and circulation of papers on the economic or military situation or on historical questions relevant to current events. Some of this material was published by the *Innere Front* group in its newspaper of that name or in its pamphlet series known as AGIS,[19] thanks to a personal connection which was established between the two groups after the outbreak of war.

As the members of the Schulze-Boysen-Harnack group had been less closely involved than others in inner-Party controversies, they seem to have been less affected by problems of adjustment to the German-Soviet Pact of 1939. Similarly, the invasion of the USSR did not take them by surprise and they had no hesitation about doing everything in their power to ensure Hitler's military as well as political defeat. They engaged in conventional forms of anti-war and anti-Nazi propaganda, by leaflets, stickers, chalking and oral dissemination of facts concealed by the authorities. The best known of such propaganda actions was the campaign which the group conducted against the anti-Soviet exhibition, 'The Soviet Paradise', which Goebbels's ministry arranged in the Lustgarten, a park in the centre of Berlin, in May 1942. Stickers were widely distributed by some sixty members of the group, bearing the slogan:

> Permanent Exhibition: The Nazi Paradise. War! Hunger! Lies! Gestapo! How much longer?[20]

The Schulze-Boysen-Harnack group was in a different position from most other clandestine anti-Nazi organisations, in that a number of its members were employed in ministries or in the armed forces and had access to secret information. At least one member, Horst Heilmann, worked in the radio counter-intelligence branch. When Hitler invaded the USSR the leaders of the group were in no doubt that the saving of the world from barbarism should take precedence over conventional nationalism, and that it was their duty to contribute to the defeat of the Nazi régime in any way they could. They therefore developed an intelligence branch of their organisation, which was integrated into the Soviet intelligence system in Western Europe and supplied information to the USSR by means of coded radio messages beamed from houses in Berlin to listening posts in Belgium and elsewhere.

Those who were drawn into the intelligence work, as radio operators, or as hosts who had lent their homes for the operators to work from, or in other ways, were withdrawn from the already long-established political and propaganda activities of the group, and it was intended to keep the two branches separate. But in practice this was difficult to achieve and there was a considerable overlap between the two. Partly for that reason historians have differed as to when the 'espionage' work began and how important a place it occupied in the group's activities. Horst Duhnke gives the impression that it began as early as 1936, or at least in 1939, but he seems to have been referring to personal social contacts with the Soviet embassy, which are unlikely to have been combined with

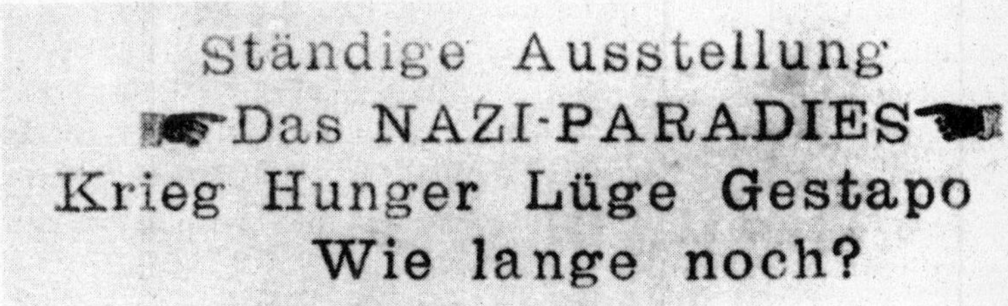

Harro Schulze-Boysen, executed in December 1942, and anti-Nazi sticker against an anti-Soviet exhibition in the Berlin Lustgarten flyposted by members of the Schulze-Boysen-Harnack group, armed and in uniform

espionage.[21] The first firm evidence that members of the group were transmitting secret information to the USSR seems to refer to either May or June 1941, that is, either just before or just after the attack on the Soviet Union. It would thus appear that the group had originated as a political resistance organisation and had continued to have that character even after the development of an intelligence branch.[22]

West German historians have commonly refused to accord to this group (to which the Gestapo investigators gave the nickname *Rote Kapelle* [Red Orchestra]) the honourable title of an anti-Nazi resistance organisation, on the ground that its main activity was espionage for the Soviet Union. How relatively important the group's intelligence branch was after June 1941 is difficult to estimate. Dr Duhnke maintains that the Schulze-Boysen group was primarily an espionage organisation, only secondarily a resistance group; but at the same time he points out the anomaly that some of the military conspirators against Hitler, who gave information to the Western powers, are not similarly denied the homage due to patriotism.

Another question which has been disputed concerning the Schulze-Boysen-Harnack group is whether it is to be counted as a Communist Party organisation. Certainly it had arisen independently of the Party leadership and it is not certain that all the group's leading members were members of the Party in the formal sense. Yet they made contact with the KPD organisation at an early date. At Easter 1939, for instance, they sent Dr Elfriede Paul, a member of the group and a doctor of medicine practising in Berlin, to Switzerland, where she contacted Wolfgang Langhoff, the former Düsseldorf theatre producer, and through him the KPD's Southern Sector Leadership.[23] In their thinking, too, Harnack and Schulze-Boysen and their friends had started from different points and in some cases had graduated by stages from 'national Bolshevism' or humanism or (as with Harnack) from the study of Soviet economic planning, towards Marxism-Leninism.[24] But what is significant is that it was in that direction that they were moving; this development was at once expressed and reinforced by their ever-closer collaboration with long-standing Marxists such as Wilhelm Guddorf and John Sieg and other members of the *Innere Front* group who, after the arrest of Uhrig, represented the Communist Party leadership in Berlin.

Another resistance group whose leaders at least were in contact with the Communist Party or its Youth League, and were possibly members of one or both, was the Baum group, so-called after its outstanding leader, Herbert Baum. This was the only specifically Jewish resistance group in Germany of which evidence has survived. It began about 1938–39 as a group of Jewish youth, most of whom worked in the Siemens works in Berlin.[25] They studied Marxist writings and conducted anti-Nazi propaganda, and after the outbreak of war their activities expanded and they made contact with other groups, such as the Schulze-Boysen-Harnack group, and with foreign workers at their places of employment. By the end of 1941 the group had come to number some 30 members, mostly between 20 and 30 years of age, and they had further contact with some 40 individuals. Something of their bold, uncompromising spirit is conveyed in the monthly news-sheet which they were issuing at that time, entitled *Der Ausweg* (The Way Out) and described as 'A paper of anti-fascist struggle' published by 'German Anti-Fascist Action'. The issue of December 1941, which has survived, was designated 'Frontline Edition' and addressed to German soldiers on all fronts, to be passed on 'to all your comrades who are ready to fight with us for the overthrow of the Hitler régime'.[26] The climax of the group's activities, and its end, came with a feat of striking élan on 18 May 1942, two days after the opening of Goebbels's anti-Soviet exhibition, already mentioned. Like the Schulze-Boysen group, though not, as far as is known, in concert with them, Baum and his comrades resolved that this incitement to hatred should not be allowed to go unanswered. Eleven members of the group invaded the exhibition and set fire to it at different points. Taking advantage of the surprise, they escaped, but only temporarily. A few days later arrests began and soon embraced the whole group, most of whose members, after appalling tortures, were sentenced to death and executed. Yet the incident had shaken the authorities, perhaps all the more because those who had dared to counter-attack so defiantly were Jews. Not content with the condemnation of those involved, the Nazis further arrested some 500 Jews as hostages and put them to death.[27]

This action of the Baum group had a quality similar to that of the Scholls at Munich a few months later and deserves to be no less well remembered. Both were gestures of moral protest and defiance which were bound to fail in the immediate sense, but contributed to a longer-term achievement by showing that Nazi barbarism did not represent the whole German nation.

The Schulze-Boysen-Harnack organisation was not the only group of middle-class intellectuals and professional people in Berlin who answered the supreme challenge of 1941 by coming out unequivocally on the side of the oppressed peoples and the Soviet Union. In that year another circle became active, including the distinguished medical professor Georg Grosscürth, the physicist Robert Havemann and the architect Herbert Richter-Luckian, who was on Goering's staff at the Air Ministry and had occasion to travel frequently both within and beyond the Reich for the assessment of bomb damage. There were others, too, who had access to confidential information by reason of their official positions or of their connections with well-placed and well-informed clients or patients.

At first this group's leaders had contact with Robert Uhrig and thus received a certain amount of guidance from a Communist Party viewpoint. But after Uhrig's arrest in February 1942, in which they escaped involvement, they continued independently. One of their activities had been to pass on information through Uhrig, and it appears that they continued to do this through a Soviet contact, although they did not become involved in the Soviet intelligence network in the way that Schulze-Boysen and Harnack did. The main emphasis of their illegal work, as it developed, seems to have been to give aid to foreign workers and Jews, and to carry on discreet propaganda. Their thinking diverged, after Uhrig's arrest, from the line of the Communist Party leaders in exile, for they envisaged as the outcome of the war not a new German democratic republic but a revolution of European peoples from which a European socialist union would emerge; their literature bore the signature, after which the group has since been named, of *Europäische Union* (European Union).[28]

While Berlin was unique in the social and political variety of its left-wing resistance groups at this time, there were also a number of provincial centres in which Communist resistance developed during the war, most of them – like the Uhrig organisation in Berlin – based on work-places and led by experienced Communist Party officials. Such was the Bästlein-Jacob-Abshagen organisation at Hamburg, whose leaders had been released from concentration camps in 1939–40. At first they had confined themselves to a cautious renewal of contacts, but from about December 1941 they began to build up an extensive organisation, which came to have cells in about 30 of the larger Hamburg factories and wharves.[29] The organisation followed a traditional Communist Party pattern, with a three-man leadership – political, organisational and propaganda secretaries – and a hierarchical structure of three-member cells which were designed as a security against betrayal, since each cell was meant to have only one link to the level above and no communication sideways – though in practice clandestine activists in a factory almost inevitably got to know one another.

The Hamburg factory groups not only came together under one leadership, but made contact with groups in other North German ports such as Bremen, Flensburg, Kiel, Lübeck and Rostock. They also achieved regular contact with Berlin through Wilhelm Guddorf, and through him obtained some of the publications of the Schulze-Boysen-Harnack and *Innere Front* groups. For here, as in Berlin, the group's activities embraced not only agitation round current issues at places of work, and broad anti-war propaganda, but also theoretical discussion and Marxist education.

The Hamburg group may have had at least spasmodic contact with the *émigré* Party leadership. In 1940–41, as has been noted above, one or two of the Central Committee's Instructors from Sweden passed through Hamburg, and in May 1942 Erna Eifler and Wilhelm Fellendorf, two representatives of the Party leadership who had flown from the USSR and parachuted into East Prussia, reached Hamburg and made contact with Wilhelm Guddorf. This incident ultimately proved disastrous, however, for the parachutists were under observation by the Gestapo, which thus got on to the track of both the Berlin *Innere Front* and the Hamburg group.[30]

One of the most important centres of German war production, with synthetic petrol and rubber plants, was the region round the industrial towns of Eisleben, Mansfeld and Halle-Merseburg, which was known as Mitteldeutschland (Central Germany) and had long been a stronghold of the working-class movement. Here, already in the autumn of 1940, a number of factory groups developed, whose main activity was listening to foreign radio broadcasts and spreading the news orally among fellow workers. In 1941 these groups were linked up into a wider, regional organisation which called itself 'The Anti-Fascist Workers' Group of Central Germany'.[31] It included some 70 or 80 Communist activists and a greater number of others, under the leadership of a former KPD functionary, Robert Büchner. In this case the three-man organisational structure seems to have been proof against Gestapo infiltration and the group continued to exist and to be active until 1945 when it played a significant role in the transfer of authority from the Nazis to the advancing American forces. As so often, the fact that the clandestine organisation escaped the Gestapo net makes it difficult for the historian to assess the extent of its activities.

Another centre of the war industries in which Communist influence among the working class had been strong before 1933 was Mannheim on the Upper Rhine, and here, too, a resistance organisation which had already existed at the beginning of the war sprang into new activity after June 1941. Its leader, Georg Lechleiter, was a former Communist editor and member of the Baden state parliament, and both he and his principal assistants had been a long time in detention but were subsequently released, subject to the usual police supervision. They built up cells in the main factories, recruited former members of workers' sports clubs, and tried to bring groups in neighbouring towns under the centralised control of a new provisional District Leadership, as well as to contact resistance groups among foreign workers. Among their propaganda activities was the production of leaflets and of a monthly paper, *Der Vorbote* (The Herald), the first number of which appeared in October 1941. This, however, proved to be a costly achievement. A copy of a later issue fell into the hands of the Gestapo and enabled it to begin arrests in February and March 1942, which led to the destruction of the group and the execution of nineteen of its members.[32]

In many other industrial areas and major cities of Germany there was evidence of discontent and opposition in the latter half of 1941 and the early months of 1942.[33] It was attributed by the Gestapo mainly to economic grievances, such as poor food and bad working conditions, and it manifested itself in slow work and minor sabotage, and in semi-political actions such as listening to foreign broadcasts and spreading the news derived from them; fraternisation with foreign workers and prisoners-of-war was also a growing form of opposition. But the extent to which these symptoms of discontent developed into overt political opposition depended very much on whether – and when – leadership was given to it by experienced Communist or socialist functionaries. In most cases in which small groups were developed into a wider and more active resistance

Underground Communist printing press and premises at Jena, used by the Neubauer-Poser group, 1943–44

movement, this will be found to have resulted from the initiative of Communist organisers who had been released from prisons or concentration camps. This happened earlier in some areas than in others, partly by chance, partly through the tactics of the Gestapo, which might, for instance, take steps to ensure that Communists released from detention were given employment in small firms, where they could be more easily supervised, rather than in large works, where they could do more damage. Thus at Frankfurt-am-Main, while there were many small resistance groups, no one seems to have been able to play the centralising and directing role assumed by Bästlein and Jacob at Hamburg or by Lechleiter at Mannheim.[34] In Thuringia, where there were many small industrial centres, widely separated from one another, the Communist editor and former Reichstag deputy, Dr Theodor Neubauer, from his home in the small country town of Tabarz, was able only gradually to develop connections between local groups. The Leipzig Communists also succeeded only gradually in welding the individual factory groups together. They had to overcome not only practical difficulties but a feeling of helplessness on the part of many workers who were bitterly opposed to the Nazi régime but had a despairing feeling that they could do little to hasten the military defeat from which alone, they felt, the liberation of Germany could come.

The left-wing resistance organisations which were active in the year-and-a-half after Hitler's invasion of the USSR differed from the bourgeois opposition groups of the period above all in the internationalism of their outlook. They understood the importance for the German people's own liberation of solidarity with the oppressed peoples of Europe and with the USSR, to the extent of taking part in the struggle to overthrow the Third Reich, not only by acts of fraternisation and ordinary humanity, but by active co-operation in the sabotaging of Nazi war production. Most of the groups, though led by German Communists, included socialists of other parties and anti-fascists of no party, and had much less of a formal Party structure than had been the case in the first years of the Third Reich. The mixture varied, as did the extent of the groups' co-operation with foreign workers and the degree of importance attached to propaganda aimed at the German soldier.

Most of the groups had developed more or less spontaneously, by local initiative, and some may have remained small, scattered and isolated. Others, however, grew into larger organisations by the deliberate efforts of experienced Communists who had emerged from detention or, in a few cases, had made their way back to Germany from centres of emigration abroad, How far the groups were effectively guided by the Party leaders in Moscow is a matter of controversy and difficult to assess with certainty. The Instructors who were smuggled into Germany with directives from the Central Committee were too few and came too infrequently to give anything like day-to-day guidance to most groups. The voice of the Party leadership is more likely to have reached clandestine activists through the broadcasts of Moscow radio and of the *Deutsche Volkssender*.[35] Professor Duhnke can hardly be right in concluding that the exiled leaders had no effective influence after the autumn of 1941 (when, as he reminds us, many of them were evacuated from Moscow to the Asian parts of the USSR),[36] for there is much evidence of organised listening and of dissemination of the news so obtained. Yet their influence must have varied greatly at different times and places. The policy changes decided on in 1935 only gradually became known in Germany and the thinking which underlay the propaganda of some underground groups continued, until 1944, or even later, to differ from the line of the exiled leadership.

The exiled leadership had foreseen that they would have difficulty, when war came, in maintaining communication with the membership in Germany, and they had decided, as early as the Bern Conference of January 1939, to wind up the Sector system and rebuild a Central Operative Leadership within the Reich, together with something like the traditional pattern of Regional or District leaderships.[37] Arthur Emmerlich, who, as we have seen, went to Berlin in September 1940 as a representative of the Central Committee to prepare the way for the new Operative Leadership, and who spent nine months in north Germany building a network of contacts, was finally arrested in May 1941. As he gave little or nothing away, his work was not wasted but remained to be built on by the new leaders, whenever they should arrive.

The arrival of the new Operative Leadership was, however, further delayed by various difficulties. One of its proposed members, Heinrich Wiatrek, who had been leading the Northern Sector from Copenhagen, and who was directed to join Karl Mewis in Sweden in preparation for the move to Berlin, was slow to leave

Denmark, even after the German occupation on 9 April 1940. According to some accounts he had become involved, as we have seen, in disagreements with other members of the Sector Leadership because he interpreted the Party's policy following the German-Soviet Non-Aggression Treaty as one of 'benevolent neutrality' towards the Nazi régime, whereas the others placed the main emphasis on calls to the masses to struggle for peace. Finally, before Wiatrek could leave Denmark, he was arrested in May 1941. This misfortune was bound to delay Mewis's preparations, for it had to be assumed – as in fact later turned out to be the case – that Wiatrek might be forced to reveal to his interrogators what he knew of the Party's plans.[38]

Meanwhile Herbert Wehner had joined Mewis in January 1941, bringing the latest instructions from the Party leadership at Moscow, and the planning of the move from Sweden to Berlin began again. As a preliminary step a new Instructor was sent: Charlotte Bischoff,[39] who crossed the Baltic disguised as a sailor on a Swedish ship and reached Germany on 25 July 1941. In Berlin she made contact with the Uhrig organisation, bringing instructions from the exiled leadership, but was then cut off from her base in Sweden by failure of radio communication. Nevertheless, having escaped the mass arrests which destroyed Uhrig's organisation, she stayed in Berlin, earning a living as a charwoman and working successfully with Knöchel and with the remnants of the *Innere Front*, whose paper continued until 1944. She was one of the few clandestine Instructors who survived to take part in the Liberation in 1945.

By the beginning of 1942 revised plans for Mewis's and Wehner's departure from Sweden were completed, when a new and decisive misfortune occurred. Wehner was arrested by the Swedish police on 18 February 1942. Mewis subsequently, and the KPD leadership too, came to the view that Wehner had 'played himself' into the hands of the police, either through fear of the all too obvious risks of the Berlin project or even as a result of some connection with British Intelligence.[40] But whether these suspicions were justified or not, it had in any case to be assumed that he might reveal Party secrets to the Swedish police, and that they, in the circumstances of that year, might pass them on to the Gestapo. Mewis's journey had, therefore, to be postponed again, and before new plans could be made and put into effect, he too fell into the hands of the Swedish police on 19 August 1942. His place, and those of Wiatrek and Wehner, were intended at first, to be taken by three other members of the Central Committee with experience of underground work who were then in Moscow: Anton Ackermann, Elli Schmidt and Walter Ulbricht. This plan too however, was short-lived.[41]

While successive plans to send a new collective leadership to Berlin from Sweden were thus repeatedly revised and finally abandoned, the Party leadership in Moscow made sporadic attempts to keep in touch with the underground by sending parachutists who landed behind the German lines and proceeded either to Berlin or to an area of Germany with which they had some previous connection. At least twelve such agents are known to have reached Germany. Several of them took with them radio apparatuses with which they themselves or an existing clandestine group might open up communication with Moscow. Some historians have denied these agents any political significance on the ground that their missions were directed predominantly, or even exclusively, to military espionage. But even if a clear distinction can be made – which is doubtful – the facts about the missions are by no means clear. According to Duhnke,[42] whose account is not without inconsistencies, Eifler and Fellendorf, who had parachuted into East Prussia in May 1942, went on to contact groups in Hamburg docks. Two more parachutists, Albert Hössler and Robert Barth reached Berlin at the beginning of August 1942,[43] contacted the Schulze-Boysen group and opened up radio communication with the USSR before they were involved at the end of September in the mass arrests of the group. Heinrich Koenen, son of the former Central Committee member, Wilhelm Koenen, who parachuted in October 1942 and also sought to contact the Schulze-Boysen-Harnack group, fell into the waiting arms of the Gestápo. All of these, and other parachutists, were eventually either executed or, like Hössler, simply murdered in prison.

Besides Mewis, Wiatrek and Wehner, the proposed Operative Leadership had been intended to include another member of the Central Committee, Wilhelm Knöchel, who had for several years, together with Erich Gentsch, taken part in directing the operations of the Western Sector from clandestine headquarters at Amsterdam, undetected by the police. Knöchel approached the task of moving to Germany with great caution and thoroughness.[45] He spent many months completing the technical preparations for the move, such as the forging of passports, identity cards and ration books, the planning of frontier crossings by road, rail or Rhine barge, and the making of arrangements for the reception and lodging of the members of his team. In August 1940 Knöchel sent one of his staff of Instructors ahead to Germany. This was Willy Seng, who established himself at Wuppertal and, during the following nine or ten months, built up an extensive network of some 33 contacts in the industrial cities of the Ruhr and Lower Rhine.[46] The exact nature of these contacts is not known, but they probably did not amount to a tightly-knit organisation of the old type, and some may have been no more than individuals whose names had been supplied by fugitives from the Reich.

In June 1941 another member of Knöchel's staff, Alfons Kaps, was sent to Düsseldorf, which he had visited as Instructor before the war, and where he now added further contacts to the network formed by Seng. These, and one or two other members of the 'Leadership for the West', taking their cue from Knöchel, seem to have pursued a cautious policy at this stage and did not call for immediate action at any cost.

Knöchel took a further step in August 1941, when he sent another of his staff of Instructors, Alfred Kowalke, to Berlin, where he contacted Uhrig and joined him in what some historians have termed 'the second provisional operative leadership':[47] a somewhat over-formal description, perhaps.

So far, Knöchel had been in no hurry to respond to the urgent calls for further action which issued from the Party leadership in the USSR after June 1941. But the repulse of the German armies before Moscow in December 1941 convinced him that the time had come to go over to the offensive. On 9 January 1942 he arrived in Berlin and established himself in lodgings which Kowalke had arranged with the help of the Uhrig group. Thanks to his careful preparatory work, Knöchel had left behind him, with the help of two Mitropa (Sleeping Car) employees and an Instructor at the inland port of Duisburg on the Rhine, a line of communication to two colleagues, Cilly Hansmann and Erich Gentsch, who had remained at Amsterdam, and through them and a Dutch Comintern agent, to Moscow. At the same time he instructed Seng and Kaps to tighten up the Ruhr-Rhine network, while other Instructors from his Sector staff, such as Wilhelm Beuttel[48] and Alfred Kamradt, were given the task of contacting and activating groups in other German regions.

Knöchel's aim was to unite the existing groups under a central leadership, of which, pending the arrival of Mewis and Wehner, the elements at least seemed to exist in the persons of Uhrig, Guddorf, Sieg and some others who, incidentally, had the advantage of living 'legally', whereas Knöchel and Kowalke had to exist clandestinely.

Knöchel was not content with merely establishing contact with existing underground groups. He tried to stimulate them into increased activity and to provide political guidance by issuing a number of different publications. Some of these were local or regional sheets, others were directed to a particular readership whose point of view they purported to take up: *Der patriotische SA-Mann* (The Patriotic Stormtrooper) for instance.[49] But the central organ of leadership was *Der Friedenskämpfer* (The Peace Fighter),[50] which gave the general political line.

Der Friedenskämpfer followed, in the main, the line laid down in the statements of the Party leadership broadcast over the *Deutsche Volkssender* in the USSR. It declared that the repulse of the German armies in the East in the winter of 1941–42 marked the turning-point of the war and that the end was approaching, and it called urgently for mass action by the German workers to overthrow Hitler by a people's revolution and thus preserve the nation's independence.

In some ways, as Dr Peukert has argued,[51] *Der Friedenskämpfer* differed in emphasis from other Party propaganda of the time. It laid greater emphasis on the national aspect of the approaching catastrophe, and insisted that the German workers had a moral as well as a political duty to act now and to free themselves, at however high a cost. It had, therefore, rather less to say about the liberating role of the Red Army than Uhrig had said or than the Party leadership was to say in 1943–44.

On some points, Peukert suggests, Knöchel may have been inclined to diverge from the line of the Moscow-based leadership. He appears to have thought that the Central Committee overestimated the extent of opposition to the Nazi régime among German workers, especially in the second half of 1942, when an increase in food rations caused – as the police also estimated – a decline of popular discontent.[52] He also criticised the Central Committee's call for the formation of worker-soldier committees as impracticable in the prevailing circumstances. But there was no question of a breach between Knöchel and the Moscow leadership, for it was moving in the same direction as he was, only more cautiously. The discussions which Politburo members held with German prisoners-of-war in camps in the USSR from October 1941 onwards impressed them, too, with the importance of the national question and with the strength of the hold which Nazi ideas still had on the mass of German soldiers. The information which reached them in Knöchel's reports not only provided material for the broadcasts of the *Volkssender*, but helped to influence the development of the leadership's policy. This can be seen in the Manifesto which it published on 6 December 1942, which sketched the outline of a national programme for peace, and anticipated the line to be taken later by the Free Germany movement.[53] It has been suggested, indeed, that it was from Knöchel's reports that the Moscow leadership first heard of the German officers' plots against Hitler, and that this may have helped to prompt them in the next year to found the German Officers' League.[54] The unreality which Knöchel sometimes complained of in the Central Committee's instructions was probably due, in part at least, to the slowness and uncertainty of communications. An attempt to improve them seems to have been contemplated at the end of 1942, when a Dutch radio technician, Jan Proosdy, was sent to Berlin to install, for Knöchel's use, a transmitting set which would have enabled him to communicate directly with Moscow.

It was at this point that the Gestapo stepped in, as it had done sometimes before at decisive turning-points. For the struggle to rebuild a central and regional Party apparatus in 1942 had not occurred in a political void, but had taken the form of a running fight between clandestine organisers and the police, in which the Gestapo sought to infiltrate the party organisations with spies and *provocateurs* and, if possible, to obtain control of them. In the latter part of 1941 the most extensive and effective Communist underground organisation, the Uhrig group, with its network of factory cells, had, unknown to its leaders, been fatally weakened when two former Communists, now in the service of the police, managed to occupy the key positions of organisation secretary and factory cell organiser respectively.[55] The Gestapo, as was its wont, did not strike at once, but used its advantage to probe further into the group's contacts and connections. Before they could uncover more than a part of these, however, something happened to interrupt their explorations. According to the most probable explanation, the two Gestapo 'confidence men' fell under suspicion because of their unhealthy curiosity and the whole group was reorganised so as to put them on ice. The Gestapo, then having no further reason for delay, began on 4 February 1942 the process of arrests and interrogations against Robert Uhrig, Josef Römer and the associates included in their organisation. By the spring there had been 150 arrests in Berlin, some 60 in Munich and 50 in the Tyrol, and a few more in other places such as Leipzig and Essen. Estimates of the number involved vary, depending on whom one counts as a member of the organisation. According to one reckoning, of some 200 members, 16 were murdered before trial and 36 sentenced to death and executed; according to another calculation there were from 60 to 120 executions.[56]

Those arrests seriously disrupted the Communist Party organisation in Berlin and one or two other places, but they did not eliminate all the clandestine cells and groups. Indeed, recent research seems to show that of 89 or so factory groups, which had had a connection with Uhrig, only 22 were destroyed, and although others were weakened, 67 were able to continue activity, though independently of one another, and thus preserved a basis on which renewed attempts at a co-ordinated movement were to be made at a later period. Meanwhile these groups worked individually, some of them making contact with foreign workers and collaborating with them in minor acts of sabotage.[57]

In the same month of February 1942, when the police action against Uhrig and his comrades began, but independently of that action, the Gestapo at the South-West German city of Mannheim arrested the Lechleiter group, as it was preparing the fifth issue of its publication, *Der Vorbote*. In this case, too, it was infiltration and betrayal which put the police on the track of the group, though as usual it was torture in interrogation which enabled them to follow up the first leads. Nineteen members of the group, most of them workers in Mannheim factories, were sentenced to death; two committed suicide.

The Schulze-Boysen-Harnack group, despite its many connections with Uhrig, had escaped involvement in the destruction of his organisation and continued its activities in the spring and summer of 1942. Its detection was not initially the result of betrayal, but of a technical slip or inadvertent mistake in its communications between Berlin and Brussels, which enabled the Nazi authorities to decode its secret messages. The police were thus enabled to intercept several representatives of the KPD Central Committee who came from Moscow by parachute with instructions and equipment for the clandestine operations of the group. After this, the police seem to have observed the movements of some members of the group for some time. Finally, having acquired a considerable knowledge of the workings of the organisation, they began, on 31 August 1942, the process of arrests and interrogations, and the members of the group began their long-drawn-out martyrdom. Altogether some 600 members were traced, mainly in Berlin (270), but also in Hamburg, Brussels and Paris. At least 55 to 58 executions were ultimately carried out in Germany, and many more elsewhere. It was by following up the connections of Schulze-Boysen-Harnack that the Gestapo were able also, in October 1942, to destroy the *Innere Front* group in Berlin and the Bästlein-Jacob group at Hamburg.

In the autumn of 1942, while the battle of Stalingrad was raging, a parallel battle of the underground was taking place in Germany, and the main Communist-led resistance organisations were being rounded up one after another by the Gestapo. Finally Knöchel himself, who, from his base in Berlin, had been gradually asserting control over groups in other areas and laying the basis for a new, centralised leadership, suffered a disaster. He had contracted tuberculosis and arrangements had to be made to evacuate him to Holland for treatment. In January 1943 a certain 'Hermann' arrived in Berlin to prepare the move. But it was already too late. Since November 1942 the Gestapo had somehow been uncovering Knöchel's Instructor network in the Ruhr and Rhineland. On 11 January they began arrests and interrogations, leading them to Berlin and to Knöchel himself on 30 January 1943, to Kowalke on 2 February and to Wilhelm Beuttel on 10 February. Knöchel made very full admissions, but he had little alternative in view of the very full knowledge which he found that the police already possessed. The interrogations were largely a matter of filling gaps and completing the picture which the Gestapo already had of the Communist Party's organisation and policies, both in Germany and in exile.

The arrest of Knöchel and his associates represented a serious defeat for the Communist Party. At the very time when the Nazis' military disaster at Stalingrad might have been expected to open up unprecedented opportunities for anti-fascist activity, the main illegal organisation had been put out of action and the developing central leadership in Germany had been destroyed. What remained in Berlin and in certain provincial centres were autonomous groups which had not been directly involved in the defeat of the Schulze-Boysen and *Innere Front* groups. The Communist resistance at Hamburg had been so seriously affected by the breaking of the Bästlein-Jacob group that it only slowly and partially recovered. The same was true of the Ruhr and Rhineland after the destruction of the Seng-Kaps network, and of Mannheim after the elimination of the Lechleiter group. In other provinces, however, such as Saxony, Thuringia and Sachsen-Anhalt (Magdeburg), there were incipient groups which had remained more independent of successive attempts to assert the central control of an Operative Leadership in Berlin, and were less directly affected by the successive defeats of those attempts. And in Berlin, too, there remained many autonomous factory and neighbourhood groups which survived the fall alike of Uhrig, Schulze-Boysen-Harnack and Guddorf-Sieg.

The task of reuniting these remaining groups into a wider organisation required above all leaders with experience and initiative, and there were some former Communist Party officials who immediately began to take the task in hand. One of these was Anton Saefkow, who before 1933 had been a Communist Party District Secretary at Hamburg and had then spent six years in prison and concentration camp. After his release in June 1939 he had gone to Berlin and obtained employment as a chauffeur for a care hire firm, which gave him opportunities for travel. From the beginning of 1941 he had begun cautiously to form contacts with Communist Party members whom he had known before 1933 or during his imprisonment. One of these was Uhrig, with whom Saefkow had begun to discuss collaboration in the autumn of 1941.[58] These plans had not come to fruition by the beginning of 1942, when the Uhrig group were arrested, and Saefkow had escaped involvement at that time. He continued to develop plans for further action, which apparently extended to acts of sabotage and storage of arms. He also entered into correspondence with Franz Jacob at Hamburg and when the Bästlein-Jacob group was broken in the autumn of 1942 and Jacob escaped to Berlin, Saefkow began a collaboration with him which was to bear fruit in the following two years.

When Knöchel and his associates were eliminated at the beginning of 1943, Saefkow and Jacob were thus to some extent ready to step into their shoes, having a considerable circle of contacts, both in

Berlin and with the leaders of certain regional organisations which, because of their comparative independence of successive Berlin leaderships, had not come under the observation of the police. The most important of these were the networks formed by Dr Theodor Neubauer and Magnus Poser in Thuringia, and by Georg Schumann at Leipzig. These contacts were far from amounting at that stage to a centralised all-German organisation, but they did represent beginnings from which a new attempt might be made to build such an organisation.

CHAPTER 14

'Free Germany' and the Generals' Plot 1943–44

After the German defeat at Stalingrad in the winter of 1942–43, a mood of pessimism, or at least scepticism, spread among the German people. Since the disaster could not be concealed, it was represented by Goebbels's propaganda machine as a heroic episode to be celebrated by a period of mourning followed by a new effort. But the effort failed. The much-heralded spring offensive ended in a further defeat in the great tank battle in the Kursk salient in July 1943. Meanwhile the Mediterranean had been the scene of a continuous retreat ending in the fall of Mussolini and the withdrawal of Italy from the war. For people steeped in Nazi-Fascist mythology and the leader cult, this was indeed the writing on the wall.

There were other causes of increasing discontent in Germany in 1943. Losses at the front had to be replaced by the calling-up of hitherto exempt workers while the need for the most efficient mobilisation of resources led to the closing down of hundreds of thousands of small businesses and the concentration of production in larger enterprises.[1] The bombing of German cities, too, though it did not produce the expected collapse of morale, gradually wore down the people's resistance and undermined their health. Even more important, perhaps, were food shortages which were now beginning to hit the German population and were repeatedly noted in the 'situation reports' of the police and other official agencies as a major cause of discontent. There were psychological factors, too, less easy to measure and less directly alluded to in official reports. As news filtered through of atrocities in occupied countries, especially in the East, there was a growing if ill-defined fear that a heavy price would ultimately have to be paid by the German people as a whole.

The prevailing mood of *malaise* and anxiety found many expressions, direct and indirect, open and disguised: in grumbling, especially about food, pessimistic or cynical talk about official corruption or memories of 1918, a tendency to omit the Hitler greeting, even in occasional brief strikes in industrial areas. More serious, perhaps, in the long run, was the ever more noticeable alienation of working-class youth in the big cities, whose reaction against the boredom and corruption of the Third Reich expressed itself in spontaneous movements of nonconformity. Teenage cliques or gangs such as the *Edelweisspiraten* (Edelweiss pirates) or *Kittelbachpiraten* of the Ruhr and Rhineland (so called after the badge they wore or their place of meeting) and the *Meute* (the Pack) of Leipzig had already been springing up in some cities in the later 1930s. They were mainly working class in social composition and drew to some extent on radical and Communist traditions. The police had cracked down on them in 1939 and it was only in the social disintegration of the later war years that they reappeared on a bigger scale. The groups varied in the degree of their political awareness. In many cases their reaction went no further than gang warfare, yet it always represented in some degree a rejection of the official ideology and the culture of the Hitler Youth. On occasion they came into direct conflict with the Hitler Youth, slipping over the border into overt protest against militarism and regimentation and joining hands, but not often, with Communist or socialist resistance. For it was a form of protest which did not coalesce easily with the anti-fascist resistance, which represented a different tradition and a different generation, as well as expressing its dissent in a different language.[2]

Yet despite failures and defeats, and grim omens of ultimate disaster, the Hitler régime maintained its grip on the German people. Gestapo statistics and reports of the judicial authorities seem to show that it was from the ever-growing army of foreign workers, now numbering millions, that the majority of those arrested and detained after 1942 were drawn. The number of political offences committed by Germans did not, according to these records, increase and may even have declined, at least in the Western provinces.[3]

One reason for this was the ever-growing ruthlessness of the repression. The subordination of the law and the courts to political expediency and arbitrariness entered a new stage on 26 April 1942, when Hitler explicitly arrogated to himself the title and power of Supreme Judge and began more and more often to interfere in individual cases, setting aside the decisions of courts and not infrequently substituting the death penalty for a sentence of imprisonment. The courts themselves, prodded by a new and fanatical Minister of Justice, Otto Thierack, were not slow to take the hint. Relatively trivial expressions of disillusionment or 'defeatism', no more perhaps than listening to foreign broadcasts or the repetition of political jokes and rumours, were punished by ferocious penalties, including death, even where no political organisation was suspected. During 1943 the number of death sentences pronounced by civil courts in Germany has been variously estimated at 5,336 and 5,684.[4] Neither figure includes sentences imposed by courts martial, which were probably at least as numerous, nor do they include murders by the SS in police stations or concentrations camps, nor the still more numerous deaths in the extermination camps.

Yet repression alone could hardly have ensured the continued survival of the Hitler dictatorship, if there had been a broadly based and united anti-fascist movement capable of mobilising the discontent of different sections of the people and offering a credible alternative to the existing régime. The Popular Front movement had tried to provide such an alternative in the 1930s, but had been unsuccessful, and the German-Soviet Non-Aggression Pact had deepened the division between the Communists and other anti-Nazi groups.

In the spring of 1943, however, as the forces of the anti-Nazi alliance gained ground on all fronts and the prospect of a military defeat of the Nazis came closer, conditions became more favourable for a new attempt to unite the anti-Nazi forces, both in Germany itself and among German *émigrés* and prisoners-of-war abroad. The Communist Party leadership therefore began to explore the possibility of a fresh initiative.

By 1943 the functions of Party leadership, as far as they could be exercised effectively, had come to be concentrated in those members of the Politburo and Central Committee who were living in the USSR. This had come about less by design than by force of events. In the first years of the war the Central Committee members who were not detained in Germany had come to be widely dispersed in many different countries, in most of which they were severely restricted in their activities and subject to varying difficulties of communication. The five-man[5] Politburo elected at the Bern Conference had originally been divided into two groups, centred in Paris and Moscow respectively. By the end of 1942, however, the two members who had headed the Operative Secretariat at Paris had long ceased to function effectively, Dahlem having first been interned and later handed over by the Vichy government to the Gestapo, and Merker having escaped to Mexico. The group in Moscow, therefore, which included the acting Party chairman, Wilhelm Pieck, and the other two Politburo members, Florin and Ulbricht, as well as the two candidate members, Ackermann and Wehner, had an indisputable claim to represent the leadership elected at the last Congress, and was also in a better position to exercise the functions of leadership than any other exile group, especially by 1943, when they received increasing material and moral support from the Soviet authorities.

The Moscow group, having obtained recognition as far as possible as the sole KPD leadership, had strengthened its position further in 1941 by co-opting several new members to the Central Committee from among refugees in the USSR and by making, or confirming, the appointment of leaders for Party groups in other lands of emigration or occupation, such as Britain (Wilhelm Koenen),[6] France and Belgium (Otto Niebergall).[7]

In 1943, therefore, it was this Moscow-based leadership which, recognising the decisive turn in the course of the war, took steps to try and unite a broader opposition in Germany.

The Communist Party leadership in exile in the USSR, despite the resources placed at its disposal by the Soviet government, was not well placed at this time to exert a direct influence on the situation in Germany. The arrest of the Schulze-Boysen-Harnack and *Innere Front* groups in the autumn of 1942 had destroyed the most extensive and effective Communist resistance organisations and the arrest of Wilhelm Knöchel and his Instructor group in January and February 1943 had removed the main link between the Central Committee and the surviving Party organisations in Germany. What remained of these organisations were scattered local groups which were largely isolated from one another. The Moscow leadership was occasionally able to send messages and instructions by volunteers who parachuted behind the German lines, but these came very rarely, and none of them returned.

On the other hand, the exiled leaders in Moscow had a new constituency and, it seemed at first sight, an unprecedented opportunity, in the growing number of German prisoners-of-war in Soviet camps. Already in the first autumn of the Soviet-German war, attempts had been made to win over captured German soldiers and persuade them to come out openly against Hitler. Communist *émigrés* were enabled by Red Army authorities to publish a paper in German, *Das freie Wort* (The Free Word), and to organise anti-fascist schools (*Antifaschulen*) at which volunteers from among the prisoners were put through an intensive and prolonged course of study. From time to time conferences were held at which graduates of these schools and Communist exiles discussed further action.

At one of the first of such conferences, which took place at a prisoner-of-war camp at Krasnogorsk near Moscow in October 1941, Walter Ulbricht presented an anti-Nazi *Appeal to the German People*. It called for the establishment of 'a free and independent Germany' and was signed by 158 soldiers.[8] Further conferences were held in December 1941 and in the first half of 1942, at which the Appeal was discussed by delegates elected by groups of prisoners. A considerable effort of propaganda and education was made in these months by an outstanding group of *émigrés* and by a small 'initiative group' of 22 officers headed by Captain Hadermann. Yet participation in the 'Antifa' schools and in the conferences remained relatively small, varying with the fortunes of the German armies on the Eastern Front. The response increased after the repulse before Moscow in December 1941, but fell off again in the summer and autumn of 1942, when the German drive to the Volga and the Caucasus revived German soldiers' hopes of victory. In the main, support for the Appeal remained very small. The overwhelming majority of German soldiers, and above all of officers, remained unconvinced. They had been strongly influenced by Nazi ideas and, at a deeper level still, by nationalist and militarist ideas, and they were unable to overcome the conviction that any form of co-operation with 'the enemy' was a betrayal of their nation. It may be, too, that the language of Marxism, in which the Communists at first tended to address them, was strange and even repellent to many of the soldiers. It needed an effort of imagination for Communists who had been in emigration for ten years to understand the thoughts and feelings of those who had grown up in Nazi Germany and to adapt their approach accordingly. Among those who made such an effort were the members of the Initiative Group, who strove to persuade their fellow officers in captivity that the salvation of Germany was a higher duty than loyalty to Hitler.

The long drawn-out battle for the Volga and the Caucasus marked a turning point, not only militarily, but morally too. While the outcome remained in the balance, the leaders of the anti-fascist

Walter Ulbricht (*left*) and Erich Weinert, calling by loudspeaker to German troops from a trench at Stalingrad, December 1942

movement, both among exiles and among prisoners, attempted to influence the course of the battle in key sectors in which German forces had been cut off, by going into front-line trenches and addressing the German troops by megaphone, urging them to surrender. But these appeals had very limited success: of the 330,000 troops surrounded at Stalingrad, only 91,000 survived into captivity.

It was in the months after the Stalingrad surrender that the effects on the German soldiery began to reveal themselves in an inevitable crisis of confidence. Many of the prisoners were deeply disillusioned and not a few were pessimistic about the outcome of the war, sceptical about Hitler's leadership and distrustful about Nazi propaganda. Yet they were slow to pursue their doubts to a logical conclusion. Many of them, believing that the defeat of Hitler would involve the total destruction of Germany, still saw no alternative but to fight on, however much they disliked the Nazi régime. In the minds of many, class and national loyalties conflicted, and traditional nationalist prejudices had become hardened through the experiences of the German-Soviet war – a war in which the Geneva Convention was not observed and the treatment of Red Army prisoners by the Germans amounted to murder on a mass scale.[9] The result was that the reports spread by the German Command that the Red Army shot their prisoners found credence among German soldiers and prevented them from surrendering. The authority of the officers in the German army continued unshaken, while among the officers themselves, the personal oath of loyalty and obedience which they had taken to Hitler still deterred many of those who came into captivity from coming out openly against the Führer, however disastrous they saw his leadership to be.

In this situation the German Communist leaders in the USSR drew the conclusion that if the crisis of confidence in the German army were to bring about a political crisis of the régime, some prospect beyond that of mere total defeat must be offered: some acceptable alternative, some new version of Germany's future after the overthrow of the Nazis.

The conception of an 'alternative Germany' in the form of a National Committee representing a broad coalition of anti-fascists pledged to found a new democratic republic without the weaknesses of the Weimar Republic had already been put forward and discussed by the German Communist Party's Central Committee in the USSR in the spring of 1942.[10] But at that time the preoccupation of both sides with military events and the very limited response among German prisoners-of-war had cut short its further development. In the months after Stalingrad, however, the Communists discovered among prisoners a new readiness to listen and discuss their ideas. The process was one, not so much of conversion as of negotiation, and it was to some extent a three-sided negotiation, for the Soviet authorities were, inevitably, directly concerned with its outcome.

The discussions resulted in the formation, on 12/13 July 1943, of a National Committee for a Free Germany (*Nationalkomitee 'Freies Deutschland'*) at a camp in the neighbourhood of Moscow. The Committee consisted initially of 38 members. 25 of them were soldiers and officers up to the rank of major, elected at meetings in prisoner-of-war camps, while the remainder were Communist *émigrés*, some of them leading Party functionaries of long standing, such as Pieck, Ulbricht and Ackermann, others Communist writers and cultural figures, such as the poet Erich Weinert who became chairman.

The National Committee was not, as has often been alleged, merely a group of Communist leaders and their dupes, together with opportunists who were prepared to swim with the tide. The idea of such a committee went back a year-and-a-half, but it could not be realised until a real change had taken place in the attitude of at least a significant minority of German prisoners-of-war. Although the key documents were no doubt drafted by leading Communists, the signatures obtained to them undoubtedly emerged from a genuine ferment of ideas, in which many soldiers and officers wrestled with the need to draw conclusions from painful experience,[11] while the Communist leaders sought to draw conclusions from their own experiences, including their encounters and discussions with prisoners. Thus the formation of the National Committee and its initial programme included modification of the Communists' own programme to meet objections raised by prisoners' delegates. It may also have been influenced by the Soviet government, for whom the development of an anti-fascist movement in the German army was an important and urgent objective at this stage of the war.

The foundation of the National Committee was the outcome of a many-sided discussion. The theoretical basis of the proposed 'Free Germany' movement from the Marxist viewpoint was laid down by the Party's Central Committee in a resolution of 16 June 1943.[12] Meanwhile a small preparatory committee on which both refugees and prisoners were represented had been set up in May. Yet the broadening of the Committee, so as to make it the basis of a possible alternative régime proved difficult to achieve. The Communist leaders set store by the recruitment to it of senior figures in the German army and Wilhelm Pieck spent much time in talks with Field Marshal Paulus and other generals in the second half of June.[13] But the gap remained wide and the Committee had to be set up with no officers above the rank of major.

The Manifesto which the National Committee adopted at its inaugural conference at Krasnogorsk near Moscow on 12/13 July 1943 was addressed to the German people and armed forces, and was designed to attract the broadest possible support, including that of Germans who were turning against the Nazi régime on purely national grounds.[14] Declaring that Hitler was leading the German people to destruction, the Manifesto called on leading men to follow the example of the Prussian liberal heroes Vom Stein, Yorck, Clausewitz and Arndt who, in 1813, when German armies had once before stood on Russian soil, had appealed from Russia over the heads of treacherous rulers to the people's conscience, calling them to a struggle for freedom. Since none of the Allied Powers would be prepared to make peace with Hitler, or even to negotiate with him, the most urgent need was to replace him by a new government, representative of the whole people which would stop the fighting, withdraw in orderly fashion to Germany's own frontiers, enter into peace negotiations, and renounce all conquests. What was meant by Germany's own frontiers was not clarified at this stage, though the adoption by the Committee of the old, imperial pre-Weimar colours was an indication that its programme was not meant to include total defeat, let alone 'unconditional surrender'.[15]

As for the character of the government which was to carry out this programme, the Manifesto made clear that it should be representative of all sections of the people and should be at once democratic and strong. One of its first tasks would be to liberate and compensate all victims of Nazi persecution, to confiscate war profits and to put on trial those guilty of war crimes, while extending an amnesty to those who dissociated themselves from the Nazi régime in good time. The new state would repudiate all forms of national and racial oppression. At the same time the Manifesto made no

Meeting of the National Committee for a Free Germany, 25 October 1944. Wilhelm Pieck (*foreground*), Erich Weinert (*in centre*) and Walter Ulbricht (*at back*), all in civilian clothes, and German officers.

mention of socialism, but explicitly guaranteed free enterprise in trade and industry.[16]

Although the German Communist leadership at Moscow went far along the road of compromise in its efforts to produce for the 'Free Germany' movement a programme which would be acceptable to the broadest circles in the army, they failed at first to win over any of the more senior officers. German generals had a strong *esprit de corps* and even those of them who saw that the war was irretrievably lost and that its continuation threatened ruin to the German people could not overcome their scruples about the 'treasonable' nature of appeals directed to German soldiers from enemy soil. They wrestled with their consciences about the sanctity of the military oath and feared that to break it might lead to the disintegration of military discipline and to social revolution. In the course of the summer of 1943, however, as a result of conversations between a number of generals and colonels headed by General Walther von Seydlitz on the one hand and Wilhelm Pieck and Erich Weinert together with representatives of the Red Army's political branch on the other, it was agreed to set up a German Officers' League, which would come out openly against the Hitler régime, but would not involve the officers in any more co-operation with Communists than they were prepared for. In effect, however, the League, which was founded on 11/12 September 1943, under the presidency of Seydlitz, proved to be a transitional stage, enabling its members to make a personal approach to other generals still serving on the other side. Conversation and co-operation in the following months created an atmosphere of greater confidence between the Communist refugees and the captured officers, and their activities eventually merged into those of the Committee.

The activities of the National Committee were of several kinds. A newspaper, *Freies Deutschland*, was produced under the editorship of Anton Ackermann, a member of the KPD Politburo, and was distributed by parachute behind the German lines. Representatives of the Committee were also appointed to the various fronts in the East, where they addressed the German troops from the trenches through loud-speakers, arranged for the firing of packages of pamphlets or newspapers into the opposite trenches and invited deserters. Desertion did not occur on a mass scale, but there was a continuous trickle. Some of the deserters volunteered for the perilous task of returning to the other side, in the hope of influencing others.

It was perhaps by radio that the Free Germany movement had most influence. Already in July 1943 the Soviet government put a further wireless transmitter at the disposal of the German emigration, in addition to the existing *Deutsche Volkssender*. The new transmitter was Radio Free Germany, the voice of the National Committee, and through its broadcasts the existence and programme of the Committee became widely known in Europe. They evoked a varying response in different German *émigré* communities, according to the varying conditions which prevailed in each. In countries occupied by German forces refugees could only live and act illegally; but this did not necessarily mean that it was impossible for them to organise anti-Nazi committees or resistance activities. In general, the more widespread native hostility to the occupying forces was, the more difficult it was for the Gestapo to apply its usual methods, which relied heavily on the use of informers.

The most important centre of German Communist emigration outside the USSR was France. The most senior of the Communist exiles there had been interned in camps or foreign labour companies in the south of France in 1939, either on their way from Spain at the end of the Civil War, or when they had registered with the authorities at the beginning of the Second World War. Others had gone into hiding with the help of French Communists and these had been joined later by others who had succeeded in escaping from the camps at the time of the fall of France in 1940. Those who had done so soon re-established contact with the leading members who had remained in the camps, and although attempts to organise the latter's escape failed, their approval was obtained for the setting up of a new KPD organisation at Toulouse, in Vichy France.[17]

During the winter of 1940–41, after discussions with the French Communist Party, a programme of political agitation among German soldiers and occupation officials was adopted, and Otto Niebergall was sent from the South to Paris as head of a 'Western Leadership' (*Westleitung*) to take charge of all such political work both in occupied France and in Belgium and Luxembourg. He suffered the considerable disadvantage of speaking no French; but others with him did, and although it is not easy to assess the results of their work, it is at least clear that it gave the Gestapo grounds for concern. They produced a lot of printed material, based on the broadcasts of the *Deutsche Volkssender*. Their products included papers such as *Wahrheit* (Truth) and *Soldat im Westen* (Soldier in the West) intended for distribution among the occupation forces; other papers were directed to readers in the western provinces of Germany, such as *Ruhr-Echo, Freiheit* (Freedom) or *Der Friedenskämpfer* (The Peace Fighter) and (for Belgians) *Le Drapeau Rouge*. These were distributed, as opportunity arose, by soldiers going home on leave or by Instructors posing as Frenchmen working in Germany.

This work of trying to influence Germans stationed in France, or of reaching across the border into the nearer parts of Germany, was known as *travail allemand* (TA). Meetings were occasionally held in Paris to assess the results: one, for instance, in May 1942, and another in the following November.[18] The *Westleitung's* contact with the Party's leadership at Moscow seems at first to have been largely or wholly confined to the monitoring of the broadcasts of the *Volkssender*. But on 15 December 1942 two-way contact was established by wireless (probably with the help of the French Communist Party), when Niebergall sent a report to Pieck on the contacts and activities of his organisation, informing him, among other things, that the *Westleitung* had made contact through foreign workers with a number of cities in Germany, including Berlin, Leipzig, Düsseldorf and Bremen.[19] Pieck replied on 30 December 1942, welcoming the report and asking both for more information and for more help in the political work directed to Germany.[20] At the same time, to make sure that the two KPD centres spoke with one voice, Pieck gave a brief statement of the Politburo's policy in these words:[21]

> Our policy is directed towards the creation of the broadest national peace movement, including all those persons and former parties who are against Hitler, not excluding the right-wing parties and the Nazi opposition, with the aim of overthrowing the Hitler government and the creation of a democratic peace régime. . .

This was followed, at infrequent intervals, by further wireless communications between Pieck and Niebergall, some 30 of which, varying in length from 2 to 40 lines, have so far been discovered, of dates between December 1942 and June 1945.[22]

News of the foundation of the National Committee on 12/13 July

1943 quickly reached Niebergall's group and prompted them to follow the Moscow example. A Committee with a similar programme was set up at Paris in September 1943 and enlarged in November after a conference in which representatives of the German armed forces and of the Todt labour organisation took part. It was thereafter commonly referred to, in order to distinguish it from the Moscow-based committee, by its French title CALPO (*Comité 'Allemagne Libre' pour l'Ouest*). Every attempt was made to widen the membership, following the policy defined in Pieck's letter, though the conditions of illegality and the necessity of suppressing the names of the Committee's members and supporters made the process a difficult one. CALPO came to be recognised by the French *Conseil National de la Résistance* as an organ of the French Resistance, and many of its members, some of them original *émigrés*, others escapers from Vichy internment camps or *Wehrmacht* deserters, fought with the French maquis[23] and in some cases rose to positions of command.

CALPO is reckoned to have had over 2,000 members. Its leaders in Paris maintained relations, through Major von Hofacker, with the army conspirators who later revolted against Hitler in July 1944. But CALPO explicitly recognised the authority of the National 'Free Germany' Committee at Moscow,[24] followed its political line and reprinted and disseminated many of its broadcast statements, though it is unlikely that there was anything more than a relatively infrequent contact between the CALPO leadership and Moscow.

In each of the countries to which German Communists had emigrated the situation was different. In Denmark, for instance, the occupying forces had initially allowed some scope for Danish political activity, and the Danish Communist Party, with a view to taking advantage of this, had abstained from activity among German soldiers; and the very small group of German Communist refugees had necessarily conformed to the same line. After Stalingrad, however, the attitude both of the Danish population and of the members of the occupying forces began to change. In July 1943 the Communist group began to issue a paper – at first monthly, later fortnightly – for distribution among Germans. It adopted the 'neutral' title *German News* and set itself the limited aim of satisfying the German soldier's thirst for reliable, factual information. It was not until the end of 1944 or the beginning of 1945 that the publishers of *German News* succeeded in overcoming the scruples and reservations of a sufficient number of conservative officers and officials to make possible the foundation of a Free Germany Committee in Denmark.[25]

In neutral countries bordering on Germany the situation was different again, and the restrictions imposed on German *émigrés* tended to be enforced with a rigour proportionate to the apparent likelihood of a German victory in the war. In Switzerland, though German refugees were required to abstain from political activities and were disturbed periodically by a wave of arrests, there had been a Communist organisation among them from the beginning of the war, headed after his escape from France in 1940 by Paul Bertz, a Central Committee member. In August 1943 a Free Germany movement was inaugurated under the sponsorship of the well-known theatrical producer and Communist exile, Wolfgang Langhoff. But the movement was slow to develop, partly because of the rivalry of an unusually strong Social Democratic movement, and its first delegate conference did not take place until May 1945, too late to have great effect.[26]

In Sweden there were some 800 German political refugees (as distinct from Jews who had emigrated because of racial persecution), and here, too, the government forbade them to engage in political activity. The ban was enforced strictly as long as there seemed to be a real danger of German military intervention. At times there seems to have been some co-operation between the Swedish police and the Nazi authorities and from time to time known Communists among the refugees, such as Herbert Wehner and Karl Mewis, were interned or forced to go underground. Nevertheless the *émigré* Communists managed to maintain occasional contact with the Party leadership in Moscow, as well as with resistance groups in Germany and with the Swedish Communist Party. But these contacts were not enough for the formation of a Free Germany movement in Sweden until the end of 1944, when an organisation of that type was set up, including not only Communists but exiled trade union leaders and Social Democrats too.[27] Despite the long period of preparation, the hopes of the founders were not fulfilled, for the Social Democratic Party Executive, now based mainly in London, forbade members of their party to participate and a split developed among the Social Democratic exiles in Sweden.[28]

In Britain and the Americas conditions were different again. In these countries Communist or Social Democratic officials formed only a small minority of the *émigrés* and found themselves competing for the support of the Jewish and cultural refugees – writers, artists, musicians, academics – who formed the great majority. A typical product of this struggle was the *Freie Deutsche Kulturbund* (Free German League of Culture) in London, founded on 1 March 1939 by some outstanding Communist functionaries such as Johannes Fladung, Kurt Hager and Wilhelm Koenen and other anti-Nazis such as the painter Kokoschka, Professor Alfred Meusel, Professor René Kuczynski and his son Jürgen. The League did not, however, succeed in uniting all German refugees in Britain, for it was boycotted by the followers of the Social Democratic Executive and subsequently weakened by the dissensions occasioned by the German-Soviet Non-Aggression Treaty and by the internment of 'enemy aliens' in Britain in 1940. The formation of the National Committee in the USSR led to an attempt to revive and broaden this pre-war *Kulturbund*. On 25 September 1943 a conference was held in London with the aim of uniting the different exile groups in Britain in a 'Free Germany' movement. An organisation was built up with about 1,000 members, but it was still not representative of all sections, for Sopade again refused to have anything to do with it – this time on the rather bizarre grounds that the Free Germany movement, both in Britain and in Moscow was too 'bourgeois' and was contaminated by co-operation with reactionary generals.[29]

In the United States the German refugees were, even more than in Britain, overwhelmingly Jewish or cultural and the Communists among them were few in number and were restrained from political activity by the restrictive conditions imposed on them as immigrants. Slow progress was made towards the organisation of a Free Germany movement and it was not until April 1944 that its equivalent, the Council for a Democratic Germany, was formed under the chairmanship of the theologian, Paul Tillich. This was a genuinely broad organisation, embracing most sections of refugee opinion and striking a compromise in its statements about a future German government, though even so the remaining fragment of the Social Democratic Executive, represented in the USA by Friedrich Stampfer, excluded itself.[30]

It was, somewhat surprisingly, in Latin America that the first initiatives towards the foundation of a Free Germany movement had been taken, even before the National Committee was formed in the USSR. There had been a strong left-wing cultural organisation of

German refugees in Mexico, headed by the Communist writers, Ludwig Renn, Bodo Uhse and Anna Seghers, and an attempt was made as early as December 1941 to extend its activities into the political field. A Free Germany movement was accordingly set up in Mexico in January 1942 and, after a long interval, probably due to intense internal discussions as well as to the international situation, a congress was held in May 1943 and an Executive elected, with Renn as president and the former KPD Politburo member, Paul Merker, as one of the secretaries.

Meanwhile, on the initiative of Merker and the Communist journalist, Alexander Abusch, who had also escaped from occupied France, a Free Germany committee for Latin America as a whole had been established in February 1943 and strenuous efforts were made to unite all sections of German exiles in the Latin American countries. There was, however, already an organisation in existence, *Das Andere Deutschland* (The Other Germany), with which *émigré* groups in some of the Latin American states were connected, but which did not recognise the leadership of the Moscow-based National Committee. This dualism, and the conflicts to which it led, absorbed much of the energy of the refugees in Latin America in the subsequent months.[31]

In the autumn of 1943 there was a fleeting prospect of the establishment of a world-wide organisation which might have been able to speak authoritatively for 'the other Germany' – for a 'Free Germany' – and have offered a convincing alternative régime capable of winning recognition by the German people and army and by foreign powers alike. But the prospect faded almost as soon as it was glimpsed, for several reasons.

One reason was that the remnants of social democracy, split as they were into many factions dispersed throughout the world, and lacking for the time being any considerable influence, still refused to co-operate with Communists and repulsed all overtures from the local representatives of the Free Germany movement for the formation of a united front against Nazism. Another reason is to be found in the changing international situation and the corresponding development of Soviet foreign policy. During the first stage of the Nazi invasion of the Soviet Union, Soviet pronouncements made a clear distinction between the Nazis and the German people – as in Stalin's remark in February 1942 that 'the Hitlers come and go; but the German people, the German state, remain'.[32] Similarly the

German Communist Party insisted that it lay within the power of the German people to save their country from destruction and dismemberment by overthrowing the Nazi régime. This, too, was the prospect held out by the National Committee and the Officers' League in the first months after their foundation. But it was an assurance which it became more and more difficult to entertain or to convey to others as events developed in the following year. The growth of the Free Germany movement was disappointingly slow and it became ever more certain that the future of Germany was not likely to be decided by the German people, but by the three great powers arrayed against Germany. This became finally clear when the policy of unconditional surrender, adopted by the Americans and British at Casablanca in January 1943, was agreed to by Stalin at the Teheran Conference in December 1943 and thus became the policy of the United Nations and the condition of their unity.

Unconditional surrender was not a platform from which it was likely to be easy to persuade German army leaders to withdraw their forces from foreign soil in defiance of orders from above. What did it mean in terms of post-war territorial settlement? The National Committee could say little on that score and the logic of events drove it inexorably to replace its original calls for ordered withdrawal by straightforward invitations to German soldiers to desert, individually or in groups, and to come over to the side of the Committee. That German soldiers and officers were slow to answer these calls was due not only to misguided patriotism but to the fear that surrender to the Red Army would mean exposure to revenge for the atrocities that the Nazi retreat was bringing more clearly to the knowledge of German as well as Soviet soldiers. The possibility that the Free Germany movement might develop into a credible alternative régime, with which the United Nations might at some stage negotiate, came to nothing and the development of the Committee and of its policies was cut short.

The National Committee's propaganda did not in 1943 lead to mass desertions nor to the surrender of large formations. But its effect, difficult as it is to measure, was certainly not negligible. Its representatives at the front showed much bravery in the dangerous task of addressing German units from front-line trenches, and they suffered many casualties in doing so. A fair number of individual deserters arrived, bringing with them leaflet-passes which had been scattered by shell-fire over the German positions. In 1944 the changing tone of German counter-propaganda testified to a growing concern at the influence of the Free Germany movement. More and more ferocious punishments were announced against soldiers who passed on Free Germany leaflets, including reprisals against their families. At the same time ridicule was no longer considered an adequate response and a serious attempt began to be made to answer the statements and arguments in the Committee's literature. In the summer of 1944, when the Central Army Group, with over 350,000 men in 28 divisions, was encircled in White Russia, the grim resistance of the Sixth Army was not repeated. Numerous officers, including 50 generals, ultimately joined the Committee and added their signatures to its calls to their comrades to abandon the Nazi cause. One of these, after a year-and-a-half's hesitation, was Field Marshal Paulus himself.[33] Yet it was the encirclements and consequent surrenders that swelled the ranks of the Free Germany movement, not the other way round. The German armed forces had not earned the right to decide Germany's future by overthrowing Hitler.

The National Committee's propaganda, and especially its broadcasts, combined with optimistic expectations of an early collapse of the Nazi régime, stimulated new efforts by underground Communist groups in Germany to unite the anti-fascist struggle there round a single centrally directed organisation with an agreed programme. But serious difficulties had to be overcome, both organisational and political.

When Wilhelm Knöchel's attempt to develop a central underground leadership in Berlin had been broken by the Gestapo in January 1943, the Communist who was best placed to renew the attempt was, as we have seen, Anton Saefkow.[34] Ever since his release in 1939 Saefkow, a machine-builder by trade and an experienced Party functionary, had acted with great caution. Although he had made contact with the Uhrig and *Innere Front* groups, he was not involved in their arrest and was able to some extent to reorganise what remained of the cells they had formed. In this he was joined by Franz Jacob after the KPD's organisation at Hamburg had been destroyed in November 1942. Jacob had fled to Berlin and had contacted Saefkow, who arranged for him to live illegally. The fact that Saefkow lived legally while Jacob lived illegally, and was therefore unable to appear in public without danger of arrest, led to a natural division of labour between the two,

Saefkow undertaking the main organisational work and cultivating outside contacts, while Jacob was responsible for much theoretical and propaganda work, such as the writing of leaflets and the drafting of political statements.[35]

Saefkow and Jacob built up a many-sided clandestine organisation. Its central feature and first priority was a network of factory groups in the main Berlin armament works, organised on the three-member cell system and engaging in anti-war propaganda and discreet forms of industrial sabotage. The organisation also had a number of specialist sections: a section for agitation among soldiers, including those on leave and those in the field, reached through field-post letters; an intelligence section which gathered information to be passed to the leadership in the USSR; a section which specialised in the forging of ration and identity-cards and other documents; a section for the 'servicing', for example with accommodation, of those living illegally, like Jacob; a section for the production of leaflets, pamphlets and other 'literature'; and a translation service.[36]

The numbers engaged in the various aspects of this work cannot be counted precisely. What does seem certain is that the organisation grew greatly in numbers and activity during the second half of 1943 and the first half of 1944. In the summer of 1943, according to one account,[37] it had 20 cells in Berlin. A year later it is said to have had members in almost all the larger Berlin enterprises, especially those concerned with war production, and to have had a considerable network of cells in some of them. In the two Askania works, for instance, 80 members were arrested at that time, and there were 40 members employed by Alfred Teves's machine and instrument factory.

All in all, Saefkow and Jacob built up a complex and ever-growing clandestine organisation, extending throughout the Berlin-Brandenburg region. But this was not the limit of their ambitions. They hoped to establish a nation-wide Free Germany movement, directed from one centre. This involved linking up with other existing Communist-led resistance groups, of which there were a number, some of them working in comparative isolation.

One of these groups was centred in the North German industrial city of Magdeburg, to the west of Berlin. Its leading figure, Martin Schwantes, a teacher by profession, had been a Communist Party organiser before 1933 and had then been in prison and in

Sachsenhausen concentration camp until 1941, when he was released. At the end of 1942 he had contacted Jacob in Berlin and subsequently met him, or Saefkow, at monthly intervals, discussing policy questions and receiving literature for distribution through a growing network of factory cells.[38]

Another notable Communist organisation was that which was being built up at the same time in the province of Thuringia which, though it was not one of the great centres of heavy industry, had many small and medium-sized industrial towns with secondary industries such as the Zeiss optical works at Jena, the small-arms manufacture at Suhl and many factories making components for armaments. It was a region, too, which had a long radical tradition going back to the medieval peasant wars.

In many of the Thuringian towns small Communist groups had survived the persecutions of the first seven years of the Third Reich and had carried on unco-ordinated opposition activities. Then, as the war developed, the co-ordination of these activities was taken in hand by two outstanding Communists, Magnus Poser and Dr Theodor Neubauer. Poser was a young man who had been imprisoned from 1933 to 1936 and had then got work as a carpenter at Jena, where he took part in reorganising the illegal Communist Party, Neubauer was an older man, a grammar school master by profession, who had entered the First World War as a volunteer and left it as a wounded officer and convinced Communist. He had then become editor of Communist newspapers in the Rhineland and subsequently a member of the Reichstag and the Communist fraction's spokesman on foreign affairs. After the Reichstag Fire the Nazis tried to bully him into giving evidence for the prosecution, but he resisted and thereby earned the praise of Dimitrov. As a result he was kept in concentration camps despite some international intervention on his behalf (including that of an imposing list of senior members of Oxford University)[39] until the summer of 1939, when he was released from Buchenwald and returned to his family, now living at Tabarz at the western end of Thuringia.

Although he had to reckon with police supervision, Neubauer seems to have lost little time in renewing contacts, though cautiously. He got in touch with old acquaintances (including former Social Democratic teaching colleagues) and with local KPD members, and it was through them that he was introduced to Magnus Poser, with whom he began a fruitful collaboration from the beginning of January 1942. They worked with scrupulous attention to the rules of conspiracy, linking up with existing groups or building new ones in the main arms factories, in the familiar form of three or five-member groups. They made contact, too, with Soviet, Polish, French and other foreign workers and issued some material in those languages. It was characteristic of their style of work that they set great store by Marxist education, arranging classes when they could; and since the classics were difficult to lay hands on, a primitive library was arranged.

Another of their activities was, of course, the monitoring of Moscow and other anti-Nazi news broadcasts and they were helped in this by the fact that one of the speakers from Moscow was Fritz Heilmann, who had once been Party organiser in Thuringia and whose voice was familiar to many of the clandestine listeners. Another circumstance favourable to the clandestine activities of the Thuringian Communists was that one of their members ran a fire-insurance office,[40] whose lively business and frequent callers provided cover for illegal contacts. In another town a group member managed a local *Ratskeller* hostelry[41] and could provide accommodation for illicit meetings, covered on occasion by simultaneous meetings of a Brownshirt unit in an adjacent room.

As the outcome of the war became clearer, the groups became bolder in the painting of slogans and the distribution of leaflets and pamphlets. The production of this literature posed difficult practical problems to the groups. They gradually acquired a number of typewriters and duplicating machines in different places and finally, by a remarkable feat of improvisation, succeeded in constructing an elementary printing press in Jena, enabling them to produce leaflets in small format in hundreds of copies. The texts were mostly written by Neubauer, the most familiar theme being that expressed in the title of a leaflet of September 1943: 'Hitler's war is lost!' 'Only simpletons are still dreaming of victory!'[42]

While Neubauer was building up this regional organisation in Thuringia, a somewhat similar process was taking place in the neighbouring province of Saxony. The leading figure here was the veteran Leipzig Communist, Georg Schumann, who, before 1933, had been full-time Party Secretary in more than one District and a member of the Party's Central Committee, as well as a member of the Reichstag. Arrested in 1933, he had spent six years in concentration camps until he was released in June 1939. Then, like

Neubauer, he had gradually and cautiously renewed contact with the underground groups which existed in the important industrial and commercial city of Leipzig and in other industrial centres of the region, such as Merseburg and Halle and, more distantly, Chemnitz and Dresden. In Leipzig itself there were at the beginning of 1943 Communist cells in some sixteen or seventeen of the larger factories, as well as contacts with some military institutions and a youth group with 120 members.[43]

In 1942 the Leipzig group appears to have been visited by Knöchel's Instructor, Alfred Kowalke, but the connection did not, as far as is known, continue after Kowalke's departure and arrest, and the Leipzig regional organisation apparently developed independently during 1943.

A striking feature of the Leipzig organisation was its close collaboration with the Soviet prisoners' and civilian workers' resistance movement, BSW, which not only helped the prisoners and workers to survive, but performed minor acts of sabotage and interfered with German war production. Similar co-operation, not only with Soviet prisoners, but also with Polish, French and other foreign workers, was also practised by the Berlin and Thuringian organisations, which helped foreign workers to obtain news and provided them with money and extra food as well as translating documents for them and exchanging propaganda.

In the course of 1943 the leaders of the main regional organisations began to make contact with one another. The connection between the Berlin and Magdeburg groups has already been noticed. In the autumn of 1943, or possibly earlier, Neubauer seems to have established regular co-operation with the Leipzig organisation.[44] At about the same time Saefkow, on behalf of the Berlin-Brandenburg organisation, also made contact with Leipzig and with Neubauer, and it was arranged that the leaders of the main regional networks – Saefkow, Neubauer, Schumann and Schwantes – should form a new, provisional, Central Operative Leadership for the direction of the struggle in Germany. Several of the leaders of this incipient nation-wide organisation had been in Sachsenhausen concentration camp and, as major problems of theory or policy arose, they sought and sometimes found means of consulting some of the senior Communists who were still imprisoned there.[45] They even attempted to consult Thälmann, though without success.[46] They were also, of course, concerned to achieve regular contact with the

KPD leadership in the USSR. This was no easy task after the Nazi invasion of the Soviet Union.

One means of contact between the *émigré* leadership and the clandestine groups in Germany was, after September 1941, the dropping of parachutists from Soviet aircraft behind the German lines. Sixteen such emissaries, four of them women, are known to have done this. Those who were not captured on landing made their way to important industrial areas such as Hamburg, the Ruhr and Upper Silesia; but almost all were quickly captured. Only one, Vinzent Porembka, sent to Upper Silesia, is known to have accomplished his mission of organising a local resistance group and to have survived the war.[47]

The landing of a parachutist was, however, a rare occurrence and it was also necessarily a one-way traffic. More fruitful, perhaps, in practice was the contact with Arvid Lundgren, a young Swedish Social Democrat who was employed as a chauffeur at the Swedish Legation in Berlin. From about May 1943 Lundgren acted as a link between Saefkow and Jacob on the one side and Karl Mewis, who was a member of the Central Committee elected at the Bern Conference and now a refugee in Sweden on the other. Mewis has described in his memoirs how in the latter half of 1943 he several times received reports and documents through Lundgren and sent advice and instructions in exchange.[48] But this was a slow, irregular and uncertain connection, and the subsequent stage, from Sweden to Moscow was no more certain.

The carrying out of clandestine operations on a nation-wide scale, involving co-operation with regional leaderships and the maintenance of links with imprisoned leaders in Germany and with an exiled leadership in the USSR: all this presented immense practical difficulties in the conditions of Nazi Germany at war, in 1943–44. But the difficulties were not only practical. It was also difficult to reach clarity about the sort of organisation which it was necessary to build up. In the early policy documents which Saefkow and Jacob drew up, such as the statement headed 'Material No. 1' of 1 October 1943,[49] they emphasised that the situation in Germany was now such that there could be no question of building mass movements of the traditional kind. Conditions demanded rather a tightly organised, centrally directed cadre organisation with a relatively small but experienced membership, run on semi-military lines. In one sense this was obvious and was dictated by the conditions of the struggle. Yet the programmatic documents continued to develop the conception of a broad political movement of a mass character.

These different concepts of organisation reflected more fundamental differences of political aim and programme between the exiled Party leadership and the underground Party groups within Germany. The members of some, perhaps of most of these groups had been struggling for many years in comparative isolation and were often very imperfectly informed of the important policy changes which had been made by the Party leadership, notably at the Brussels and Bern conferences in 1935 and 1939. Consequently, when the leaders of the main regional organisations got together in the latter part of 1943, they found that the programmatic documents which they had issued, or drafted for discussion, differed in political line both from one another and from the statements broadcast by the National Committee for a Free Germany, which represented an application and development of the Brussels-Bern line.

In August and September 1943, soon after the formation of the National 'Free Germany' Committee in the USSR, Saefkow and Jacob drafted two discussion documents on fundamental policy issues.[50] Nominally they accepted the programme of the National Committee, but in fact they differed from it in important respects and also contained some contradictions. The struggle against the Nazi dictatorship, as they envisaged it, would develop after the overthrow of Hitler into a revolutionary war, in which the German working class would fight side by side with the USSR for its own liberation from capitalism. They defined the new German democratic republic mentioned at 'Brussels' and 'Bern', and in the Free Germany programme, as a *socialist* democracy, equivalent to the dictatorship of the proletariat.

These conceptions, outdated from the KPD leadership's point of view, were most firmly entrenched in the thinking of the Leipzig group. They did not recognise the change which had taken place in the character of the war from an imperialist war to an anti-fascist war of national liberation and they failed to see the possibility and necessity of a really broad anti-Nazi front. Instead, they saw the war as a struggle of the working class, in alliance with the peasantry, to seize power and establish a proletarian dictatorship. Neubauer seems to have been quicker to grasp that such a conception could not be reconciled with the policies set out in the statements of the Free

Germany movement, and his 'Situation Report',[51] written in the late summer of 1943, represented a big step towards acceptance of the NKFD line, especially with regard to the breadth of the class alliance now seen to be required and the limitations of the new democratic state which this implied. For many months in the autumn of 1943 and the first months of 1944 the underground leaders wrestled with these issues, striving slowly and painfully to reach clarity and agreement. A big step was the drafting by Saefkow and Jacob of the document 'We Communists and the National "Free Germany" Committee' and its discussion at successive meetings of the group leaders,[52] who also consulted imprisoned Communists in Sachsenhausen.[53] By the spring of 1944 a final version was agreed,[54] representing a decisive acceptance of the NKFD line by the new Central Operative Leadership.

The aim of this new central leadership was to unite all sections of anti-Nazis on the basis of the Free Germany programme and by the early summer of 1944 they seemed to have taken some significant steps towards that goal. The next step was to make contact with the bourgeois-military opposition, which the disastrous turn of the war in 1943–44 had reactivated into successive plots for the assassination of Hitler and the overthrow of the Nazi government.

In this opposition two main trends could be distinguished: a reactionary trend which aimed at rescuing German imperialism, and even securing some of its expansionist aims, by a right-wing military *putsch* followed by a military-authoritarian régime; and a liberal-Christian and progressive trend which associated the overthrow of fascism with some sort of social regeneration. The leaders of the Communist groups in Berlin and Leipzig had had one or two contacts with representatives of these opposition trends but the tentative, exploratory conversations had come to nothing. For both trends in the bourgeois opposition were above all concerned that the overthrow of Hitler should be brought about in such a manner as to forestall the development of a popular revolutionary movement in Germany, and they gave much thought to the possibility of splitting the Allies, so that the Western powers would be able to enter Germany and prevent revolution, while the German armies concentrated on repulsing the Red Army from the eastern frontiers. Now, however, as the German armies were driven back, the bargaining strength not only of the Nazi régime but of any alternative German government became weaker and the matter became increasingly urgent if there was to be anything left to bargain with. Some of the conspirators therefore toyed with the idea of trying to squeeze concessions out of the Western powers by 'playing the Russian card' and entering into negotiations with the underground Communist Party.[55]

Meanwhile the Communist leaders had been trying, ever since the autumn of 1943, to make contact with leaders of the Social Democratic resistance in Germany and to win them for joint action in the spirit of the Free Germany movement. One of the tasks set to the factory cells which Saefkow and Jacob were establishing was to make contact with Social Democratic activists. Some such contact was made in October 1943 and led, according to one source,[56] to several discussions between Saefkow, Jacob and Neubauer on the Communist side and leading Social Democrats on the other. Another and perhaps more likely version is that the Social Democratic leaders declined the proposed discussions at that time because they were afraid of compromising their relations with middle-class and military opponents of the regime.[57]

The Communist leaders were aware in general of the activities of the middle-class and military plotters and had made some tentative contacts with them. In the same autumn of 1943 Jacob had had several talks with three women, including Walpurga Pechel, through whom he passed Free Germany literature to other middle-class opponents of the régime.[58] Through them, too, he made contact and had talks with other representatives of the bourgeois opposition, including the director of an important industrial enterprise and landowning circles in Pomerania and East Prussia who were opposed to the continuation of the war. At the end of 1943, too, he had talks with some Catholic priests and with leading members of the former Centre Party. Meanwhile the Leipzig group, which had finally come to accept the programme of the Free Germany movement, had made some contacts, through General Lindemann, with the Stauffenberg circle,[59] while Georg Schumann had had some exchange of views, through intermediaries, with Carl Goerdeler who had once been Oberbürgermeister of Leipzig and was now the bourgeois-military opposition's candidate for the Reich chancellorship.[60]

These various tentative contacts and probings in the winter of 1943–44 seem to have petered out without any definite result. But in the spring of 1944, as the situation became ever more serious and the need for action more urgent, the more progressive section of the conspirators, represented by Colonel Stauffenberg and by a section of the Social Democratic underground represented by Julius Leber and Professor Adolf Reichwein,[61] seem to have gained in influence and to have been able to insist on serious discussions with the Communists. It was with Leber and Reichwein that Saefkow and Jacob had what might have been a historic meeting in Berlin on 22 June 1944. What took place is not known in detail, but there is some evidence that steps towards joint action of the Saefkow organisation with the military conspiracy were agreed on. A confidant of Franz Jacob later quoted him as having said on 29 June that 'Things have now reached the point that we are to conclude a pact with the devil himself – in other words the generals – and to make a *putsch* together.'[62]

A further meeting had been arranged for 4 July. But before it could take place, Himmler intervened, arresting those who had taken part in the earlier meeting and all their contacts. He may well have known of both movements and have been holding his hand for tactical reasons, until the threatened union of the two wings of the Resistance, combined with fears of a fall in morale following the Normandy invasion (6 June), made it seem risky to wait any longer. The beginning of the arrests, in turn, may have pushed the military plotters into final, desperate action even though the political preparations had been cut short.

The repression of both wings of the Resistance, Communist and non-Communist, which followed, was carried through on a huge scale and with a ruthlessness born of fear. The members of the Communist Party's newly established Central Operational Leadership and almost all the other leading members of its clandestine organisations in Berlin, Saxony, Thuringia and Magdeburg were arrested, tried and executed, and others sentenced to long prison terms. Moreover many Communists and other anti-fascists already in custody, who might play a leading political role if the Nazi régime collapsed, were simply murdered by executive order, presumably emanating from Hitler. Ernst Thälmann, who had been in detention since March 1933, was shot at Buchenwald on 18 August 1944, and in the following October twenty-four leading Communists in the concentration camp at Sachsenhausen were killed in similar fashion.

Thus, as the retreating German armies were driven back to the old frontiers, the main anti-Nazi organisations again lay shattered, while the repressive apparatus of the Nazi state remained intact.

CHAPTER 15

The Absent Revolution, 1944–45

In the summer of 1944, with the advance of the Red Army to the Vistula and the Anglo-American invasion of France, the Third Reich appeared to be on the brink of military collapse. The destruction of the Communist-led Saefkow-Jacob organisation and its regional branches, and the failure of the Officers' Plot on 20 July, might have been expected to do no more than slow down momentarily a process of disintegration which had gathered so much momentum. Yet in the event the war was to drag on for a further nine months. Despite growing hopelessness and discontent neither the military fronts nor the home front collapsed, nor did the mass of the German people revolt. It was then and still is difficult to say how far the absence of popular uprisings like those of 1918 was the cause and how far the consequence of the prolongation of military resistance.

In the German-occupied countries and European satellite states, mass resistance movements against German occupation and its local agents had been increasing in scope and significance and in some cases had taken the form of partisan or guerrilla forces which made a major military contribution to the liberation of their country, as in Yugoslavia and Greece. In many countries the resistance forces were divided, one section being led by bourgeois nationalists, another section by Communists. In some a broad political alliance of patriotic forces emerged, under the leadership usually, though not always, of Communists.

In a number of these liberation movements German anti-fascists played a significant part. Some of them had fought in Spain and had subsequently either lived illegally in France or had been interned there and had later escaped to join the maquis. Others, again, deserted from the German armed forces either in an occupied country or at the front, especially in Russia, where leaflets disseminated by the 'Free Germany' Committee were put in the form of a safe-conduct, the bearer of which, on giving himself up to the Red Army, was promised good treatment and return home after the war.[1] Some of those who deserted were absorbed into political work in prisoner-of-war camps, others were trained and parachuted behind the German lines, either to join partisan units or to try to conduct political or propaganda activities as representatives of the Free Germany Committee.[2] In Poland many cases are known in which German deserters, either individually or in groups, joined left-wing partisan units and in a few cases even rose to command a Polish unit.[3] In other cases members of the German occupation forces (often in non-combatant units) are known to have given help to local resistance organisations in the form of supplies, money or information, or to have distributed propaganda to them. Most likely to aid local partisans or to go over to them were Germans with an anti-Nazi record who, in the final stages of the war, were sometimes enrolled in so-called '999 Punishment Units' and sent to the Balkans and certain other fronts.

The full story of the participation of German anti-fascists in foreign resistance movements and partisan units will probably never be known. Most of those concerned went by pseudonyms and many were killed. In France it has been estimated that by the summer of 1944, when the Resistance forces (FFI) reached their greatest extent, anti-Nazi Germans were enrolled in them in no less than 30 *départements*.[4]

In Germany there were no partisan movements or popular uprisings comparable to those that occurred in the USSR, Yugoslavia, Poland, Italy, Greece or France. In the autumn of 1944 remnants of Communist-led groups survived in a number of German cities, but they were widely scattered, politically comparatively isolated, and not co-ordinated by any central direction such as successive operative leaderships had tried in their time to provide. There was, consequently, some confusion or uncertainty among them as to what policy to follow in what seemed likely, to many Germans, to be the final months, or even weeks, of the war. To some it seemed vitally important that German anti-fascists should seize the initiative, at almost any cost. Others thought that to attempt desperate uprisings would be to incur heavy casualties without hope of success, and that the best course was to form broad anti-Nazi committees which might intervene to prevent the carrying out of Hitler's 'scorched earth' commands[5] and so save their own town from last-minute total destruction, while at the same time preparing to take over the local administration as the Nazi officials fled from the approaching Allied forces.

At first sight Germany might have seemed ripe for revolution in these months. The hardships of total war were now coming home to the German people themselves in the shape of food shortages and reduction of rations and the relentless toll of Anglo-American bombing raids.[6] Nazi demagogy could not disguise the inequality of sacrifice involved, as between workers and employers, between city and countryside, and even among the bourgeoisie, between big business, particularly the armament contractors, and the rest.

These increasing pressures caused contradictory reactions among German workers. Industrial unrest increased, expressed in absenteeism from work and in widespread sabotage, mainly by foreign workers and prisoners-of-war. Productivity in the war industries, which had actually risen from 1942 up to the middle of 1944 under the 'total war' régime,[7] now began to fall decisively as supplies of essential raw materials at last began to fail.[8] As the final catastrophe approached, and as Hitler issued frenzied orders for war to the end and for the total destruction of everything that might be of use to the enemy, it became increasingly clear that the very survival of the German people was at risk.

Yet this situation did not generate a revolutionary mood in Germany. There was no armed uprising, no revolt of the masses. Rather, as Hitler's infallibility wore thin, its place tended to be taken by anxiety, by hopelessness and despair, mixed in some cases with feelings of cynicism and apathy or self-pity. At the same time these negative reactions proved, paradoxically, not incompatible with dogged continuance of the hopeless struggle, nurtured by official propaganda campaigns about secret weapons and rumoured splits in the enemy alliance. And so, despite many desertions or attempted desertions, the armies held together and appeared to keep up their strength by statistical sleight of hand, when reserves and new recruits brought up to fill the yawning gap in shattered divisions were deceitfully described as new divisions.

There was thus no 'stab-in-the-back' of retreating armies, no collapse, no great explosion of discontent and disillusionment. How is this to be explained?

One reason was the almost unimaginable ferocity of the repression during the last winter of the war. Already in August and September 1944 existing penalties for political offences were sharpened and new penalties introduced. On 1 August an order was issued providing for the arrest and sending to a concentration camp of the relatives of officers who came out against the régime when taken prisoner or in other ways; this policy of making relatives into hostages was later applied to soldiers of any rank. On 6 August 1944 Goebbels, who had been appointed Reich Commissioner for Total War on 25 July 1944, took a further long step towards the militarisation of daily life by decreeing that absenteeism from work (or incitement to it) would in future be treated, and punished, in the same way as military desertion. In the following months a stream of threatening decrees poured out: no less than 42 from the Head of Reich Security (Kaltenbrunner) alone, between 20 September 1944 and 2 February 1945.[9]

These were in no way mere threats. On the contrary they represented, in many cases, a perfunctory gesture of legalisation covering an all too real régime of arbitrary terror. On 22 August, in a sudden blitz, the Gestapo arrested from 5,000 to 6,000 people who had once been active members of labour organisations or non-Nazi political parties and sent them to concentration camps as a cautionary measure.[10] Those who fell into the hands of the law courts could expect no better treatment under the merciless and sadistic rule of Freisler. Death sentences were freely imposed for quite trivial expressions of political criticism, and wide publicity was given them in the hope of stamping out defeatism. In the year 1944 alone 5,764 executions in civil prisons were registered in the Ministry of Justice and about 800 more probably took place in the first few months of 1945.[11] These figures exclude executions by military justice which, it has been estimated, increased from 4,000 up to1943 to some 12,000 in the final period of the war.[12]

Something of the inhuman spirit which animated Nazi 'justice' is conveyed by the statistics which Günther Weisenborn gives for the single prison of Brandenburg-Görden. Of the 1,807 people who were executed in that prison for political offences between 22 August 1940 and 20 April 1945 – most of them almost certainly in 1944–45 – one was blind, two were without legs, two were brothers and six were fathers and sons. 75 were under 21 years of age, the youngest being only 16 and several others only 17 or 18 while 78 were over 60. And this slaughter went on to the very end, with 28 executions taking place on 20 April 1945 in celebration of Hitler's last birthday.[13]

Yet terror cannot alone explain why the Nazis were able to retain to the end the obedience and the at least passive support of the great majority of Germans. Nor can it be explained purely by reference to the century-long tradition of militarism and acceptance of authority in Germany. The truth is that the German people, including a large part of the working class, had been profoundly corrupted by National Socialist ideas and practices and were demoralised by a sense of shared guilt. This had, indeed, been to some extent a deliberate aim of the Nazi government; for, when the blitzkrieg victories had come to an end and it had become necessary to call up further millions of Germans for military service and to replace them in the war industries by millions of foreigners, Hitler had chosen to do this, contrary to armament minister Speer's advice, by bringing the foreign workers to Germany and concentrating Europe's war industries there, rather than by developing the industries of the occupied and satellite countries. This was an uneconomic policy pursued for political reasons, and it had resulted in a hierarchical labour system in which German workers came to constitute a privileged élite who were kept away from foreign workers not only by better conditions, but by various forms of legal 'apartheid'.[14]

Many German workers, therefore, as the inevitable defeat could be seen approaching, lived in a state of anxiety, fearing that the millions of foreign workers in their midst would take the first opportunity of revenging themselves. They were afraid, above all, of the advance of the Red Army, partly because the treatment of Soviet workers and prisoners-of-war had been so unforgivable[15] and partly because twelve years of concentrated anti-Soviet propaganda had given currency to the most absurd beliefs and expectations. In the minds of many Germans, including some who had in past years longed for an end to the Hitler dictatorship, fear of defeat by the Russians loomed larger than hatred of Nazism, and it was widely believed that the victory of the anti-fascist powers would involve the total destruction of Germany, leaving nothing to work or hope for.

As the final defeat of the Hitler régime approached, most Germans could still see no acceptable alternative. This negative attitude may have been strengthened by the insistence of the Allied powers on unconditional surrender, but it was connected also with the continued disunity of the opposition forces in Germany. The negotiations aimed at a junction of the Communist and the bourgeois resistance movements had been cut short by the arrests of

July 1944. At the same time the incipient divisions in the ruling class which had been visible at the time of the unsuccessful *putsch* of that month did not develop. A few of the great capitalist magnates, such as Bosch of Stuttgart, Paul Reusch, Hjalmar Schacht and others, had formed tentative links with Carl Goerdeler's wing – the right wing of the bourgeois opposition[16] – partly, no doubt, by way of re-insurance and possible eventual link-up with the Western powers against the USSR. But the feelers put out by that section of Big Business – which never represented more than a minority – were quickly withdrawn after the failure of the plot. The leading figures of the German capitalist class, realistic as ever, had few doubts that their interests were best served by a policy of holding out to the end, so that, in as large a part of Germany as possible, the authority of Hitler might be replaced by that of the Anglo-American armies, with as little intermission as possible in which revolutionary mass movements could develop, as they had done in Italy in 1943.

Some hints of such an alternative, revolutionary development can be glimpsed in events at Cologne in the autumn of 1944. In September, as the American armies reached the German frontier to the west and the fall of the city seemed imminent, something like guerrilla warfare developed in the ruined cellars, especially of some working-class suburbs. According to Gestapo reports there were up to 24 resistance groups, numbering from 3 to 20 members each and in one case up to 120 members.[17] The groups were said to be of mixed composition, including not only deserters from the German army and youth protest groups (*Edelweisspiraten* or *Kittelbachpiraten*), but also Soviet and other foreign deportee workers and prisoners-of-war. In order to live without identity papers and ration cards they had to procure food illegally and were branded by the police as criminals and looters, but there can be little doubt that the great majority of them were politically motivated. Some of the groups maintained contact through a Communist named Jansen with a People's Front Free Germany Committee which had been established by the Communist Party in March 1944 and had built up a broadly-based organisation of some 200 members which might take over the government of the city on the overthrow of the Nazi rulers.[18]

The collapse of Nazi authority in Cologne seemed very close at times during October and November 1944. In addition to numerous acts of sabotage, there were quite frequent armed engagements of a partisan type, in which the dead on the government side included not only SA and SS men and soldiers, but several Gestapo men, including SS-Sturmbannführer (Colonel) Hoffmann himself, head of the Cologne Gestapo. It was not until December, when the military front became established to the west of the city, that the Nazi authorities recovered full control in the course of a series of police and military operations against the underground groups.

The Cologne 'uprising' was, as Dr Peukert has remarked,[19] the nearest thing in Germany to the Italian partisan operations. If the military front had not settled down to a long period of winter immobility broken only by the Ardennes offensive, the outcome at Cologne might have been different and resistance might have taken on a new dimension in other cities too. For Cologne was not the only part of Germany in which there was collaboration between foreign workers and German anti-fascists during the final stage of the war. The presence of foreign workers and prisoners-of-war could not but be of crucial significance in deciding the outcome of the anti-Nazi struggle. There was a growing number of strikes and labour disputes involving foreign workers. In the first six months of 1944, according to police statistics quoted by Günter Weisenborn,[20] 193,024 foreign workers were arrested for taking part in strikes, while in the second quarter of 1944 alone 49,958 foreigners were arrested for other reasons. During the same three months 4,310 Germans were arrested for consorting illegally with foreign workers or prisoners-of-war. These figures, which continued to grow, give evidence of the fear which the millions of foreign workers inspired in the minds of the Nazi authorities and German industrialists. Nor was this fear groundless. The Soviet workers and prisoners in particular had built secret organisations in many parts of Germany and had developed ambitious plans for uprisings. The biggest of these organisations, Brotherly Co-operation of Prisoners of War (BSW),[21] originally centred in Bavaria, stretched as far as the Rhineland and Westphalia and formed contact with German anti-fascist groups which still survived in some regions, such as the Anti-Nazi German People's Front (ADV) in southern Germany,[22] and the International Anti-Fascist Committee (IAK) in the Leipzig area.[23]

The far-reaching plans that were made for joint action between these foreign and German organisations were largely frustrated by police actions after the suppression of the July Plot and again at the turn of the year. Mass resistance of the kind envisaged could only have succeeded if the repressive apparatus had first been decisively weakened or confused, allowing the revolutionary forces to seize the initiative. The repressive apparatus no doubt was temporarily shaken by the military defeats and political confusion of the summer of 1944, but it had recovered quickly and regained full control. Despite widening cracks in the Nazi state, the strength of the German anti-fascists was not sufficient – even in conjunction with foreign workers' organisations – to lead a full-scale armed uprising. There remained to them the possibility only of a more limited role: that of preserving the elements of the people's livelihood and existence from the total destruction which Hitler was now ordering. What this meant, in most cases, was that anti-fascists should combine to arrange for a timely and peaceful surrender to the approaching Soviet or Anglo-American forces. Sometimes the initiative could be taken by an existing illegal Free Germany Committee in which, in the East, parachutists might play a part. Elsewhere the lead might be taken, as at Greifswald in Pomerania, by a local garrison commander,[24] or, as at Düsseldorf, by a group of leading citizens, including in that particular instance the chief of the ordinary police.[25] Such initiatives sometimes succeeded, as at Greifswald, and sometimes failed, as at Düsseldorf, in both cases by the narrowest of margins.

Such local actions could only have assumed a revolutionary character if a considerable section of German workers had been prepared to take a political initiative. Because German revolutionaries had been forestalled by the security authorities, the future of Germany was left to be decided from outside, by the great powers of the anti-Hitler coalition. The first stage of the settlement mirrored the compromise formulae of the wartime conferences: banning of Nazism, prosecution of war criminals and the setting up of democratic institutions by a coalition of anti-fascist parties. The second and more lasting settlement mirrored the Cold War division of the wartime allies in a corresponding political and territorial division.

For the German Communists, as for other anti-fascists, the defeat of the plot of July 1944 proved decisive, in one sense at least. It precluded the development in the immediate future of a mobile situation in which new class alignments and a revolutionary initiative might have been possible. The exiled Party leadership did make renewed efforts to stir the working class into action, by radio appeals and by parachuting Instructors behind the front in eastern Germany.[26] Many of these fell into Nazi hands, but others were able to make contact with existing anti-fascist committees, especially in the region of Greater Berlin, where the Red Army's advance from one suburb to another in April 1945 was facilitated in some cases by help from small groups of German anti-fascists, including some individual Soviet workers who escaped from their camps and were hidden by Germans. Evidence which has accumulated in recent years suggests that these anti-fascist committees of 1944–45, however modest their achievements, may nevertheless have been more numerous than used to be thought, especially in the eastern parts of Germany.[27] They issued leaflets, conducted sabotage, sometimes even acquired arms and tried above all to arrange for the peaceful surrender of towns. Yet the record of events and the recollections of survivors alike suggest that conditions were largely lacking for successful uprisings against the Nazi tyranny on any significant scale, and that a concerted attempt by anti-fascists to seize control of a town was rarely made until the Allied forces were in the immediate vicinity and the Nazi power structure had already begun to crumble.

In the early months of 1945 most of those who might have had the experience and ability necessary to lead an anti-fascist uprising or liberation struggle in Germany – that is, in the main, the surviving cadres of the Communist Party – were in prisons or concentration camps. These camps changed greatly during the war (quite apart from the specialised extermination camps) with the enormous growth in their numbers and population and the international character which they assumed with the growing preponderance of non-German prisoners. More than ever it was only through self-organisation and self-discipline that prisoners were able to survive and more than ever, too, it was only by involving prisoners in the various administrative functions that the SS were able to keep the camps going. At first they had tried to employ common criminals in these functions, but experience had usually convinced them that, although criminals might be useful as spies and informers, efficiency was best served by employing political prisoners to keep order among their fellows in the responsible positions of *Kapo* (hut leader) and *Lagerälteste* (camp senior), not to mention such key departments as the camp office, where records were kept and jobs allocated, the kitchens, the camp library and above all the sick bay, scene of some memorable manipulations by which the identity of a prisoner who had died was transferred to one who was threatened.[28] When a new camp was set up, it was not long before the Communist prisoners had a working organisation. In some of the main camps in Germany itself, such as Sachsenhausen (1936), Buchenwald (1937) and Mauthausen in Austria (1938), the camp administration at prisoner level became virtually identical with the Communist Party leadership in the camp.[29] When the conclusions of the Brussels Conference had become known to the leading Communists in a camp, they began to try to form People's Front committees, including Social Democrats and other anti-fascists; as the number of non-German prisoners grew, clandestine international committees were formed.

The first aim of these committees, and of the prisoner-officials who tried to follow their instructions, was to save the lives of especially vulnerable prisoners (such as new arrivals) by complicated manipulations of the administrative machinery. Another of their activities was to set up a radio monitoring apparatus, so that the latest news could be ascertained and spread through the camp. Another function was that of countering the SS spy system in the camp by discovering and eliminating informers. In some camps, too, draft policy documents drawn up by an underground organisation outside the camp, such as those of the Central Operative Leadership in 1943–44, were smuggled in, discussed by leading Communist prisoners and returned with comments. This was part of a more general process of theoretical preparation for the post-war period.

As the Allied forces advanced into Germany in 1945, the balance of power in the concentration camps changed, but only gradually. The authority of the guards weakened, but did not collapse, and while the prisoners gained influence, they faced increasing danger of desperate measures such as forced evacuation or deliberate massacre. The clandestine international prisoners' committees which existed in most if not all camps gained in authority, but not decisively enough for them to seize control of the camp and liberate themselves. Their first objective had to be to try to prevent forced evacuation or mass murder of prisoners. The struggle took a different course in each camp. The best known case, and that in which the prisoners were most successful, was that of Buchenwald camp near Weimar, where the underground international committee, led by a German Communist, Walter Bartel, seized control when the American forces were still two days away.

The KPD leaders had given much thought, over a considerable period of time, to the problems that would face them when the Hitler dictatorship finally collapsed. As early as February 1944 Pieck and the other Politburo members in Moscow had set up a commission of 20 members to study such questions as the Party's tasks in the period leading up to the overthrow of Hitler; the political leadership during the overthrow of the Nazis and in the New Germany; the role of the Soviet Union after the war and the national question in Germany; the new trade unions; the economy in the new Germany; the agrarian problem and the peasantry. The commission sat regularly from the beginning of March until the end of August 1944, referring specific topics to expert working parties for further elaboration. The result was the drafting of a number of programmes, guidelines and other documents, the most important of which was the 'Programme of Action for the creation of a Bloc of Militant Democracy' produced by the Party leadership in October 1944.[30]

The 'Bloc' itself was a development of the pre-war conception of a Popular Front. Its programme was not a programme for socialism, but for an 'Anti-fascist Democracy'. There was to be universal suffrage with proportional representation, and the economy, after the seizure of the property of war criminals and monopolists, was to be one of private enterprise controlled by the democratic state and the trade unions, while wages, it was specified, were to be fixed by agreement between employers and workers endorsed by the state. A key feature of the 'Militant Democracy' proposed by the Programme was the destruction of the social and economic roots of militarism and fascism, and not only of their constitutional superstructure, as had happened in 1918. This would require a thorough purge of 'anti-popular elements' from all organs of state power.

What this would mean in detail was shown in subsequent documents, such as the 'Guidelines for the work of anti-fascists in areas occupied by the Red Army', which were drawn up by the KPD leadership on 5 April 1945.[31] These guidelines were notable for their wide scope and for the sensible, practical thinking embodied in them. They showed few illusions about the state of mind of the German population and gave priority to measures designed to change it. These included the foundation of an anti-fascist newspaper and other forms of propaganda. More remarkable, however, were the policies designed to reform the educational system.[32] In each locality a School Board composed of proven anti-Nazis was to be appointed and charged with such matters as the appointment of teachers and the approval of syllabuses. Only anti-Nazis or non-Nazis were to be appointed to teaching posts, though purely formal and passive membership of the Nazi Party was not necessarily to be a disqualification in all cases. In order that the vacancies left by the dismissal of Nazi teachers might be filled, working people without previous teaching qualifications might be appointed as probationary teachers and required to take a three-month crash course. Special care was to be taken in the choice of teachers of history, politics (*Staatskunde*) and geography. Textbooks, not only of the Nazi period, but of all previous periods, were to be scrapped and replaced by new ones. Finally, to give time for the carrying-out of these measures, all schools were to be closed for three months.

The Guidelines proposed a similar radical reform of local government, with a purge of Nazi officials to be carried out by a Personnel Office headed, it was recommended, by a returning anti-fascist exile. Here again, however, care was to be taken to distinguish between professional people who had been active Nazis and those who had been mere card-holding conformists, the latter being not necessarily debarred from professional employment.[33]

As for the economy, the Guidelines were conspicuously practical. There was no talk of socialisation and a serious attempt was to be made to distinguish the small business man or peasant from the big capitalist or estate-owner. All stock or machinery or land was to be used by someone, whatever the ultimate decision about ownership, and landless agricultural labourers or peasants without enough land were to have first claim on unused land.

Another question to which the Communist leaders had been concerned to work out a clear answer before events overtook them was that of the character, role and strategy of their party. Already in a broadcast from Moscow on 29 January 1945 Pieck had outlined the leadership's view. They should not plan for a small 'cadre party', but should aim at becoming a 'mass party',[34] and the gates should be opened to new recruits, despite the risk that the experienced few might be diluted, or inundated, by a big influx.

On the issue of working-class unity, Pieck argued that, however strong the tide in that direction, the first task must be to rebuild the Communist Party, leaving the question of a united party of the working class to a later stage. Meanwhile the Party must learn to think of itself, not as a party of opposition, but as a party destined to play a leading part in the reconstruction of the country. But he emphasised that this leading role must not be taken for granted – it must be *earned* in action. The Party would also have to resume in the post-war period the processes of democratic centralism, such as the election and accountability of functionaries, which it had not been possible to observe fully in conditions of illegality; but this might have to wait until the return to legality was completed. Until then it was proposed that in each Party District (*Bezirk*) there should be a commission nominated by the Central Committee to control such things as recruitment and the appointment of functionaries.[35]

While this work of theoretical clarification and detailed planning was going on at Party Centre in the last months of 1944 and the first months of 1945, Communists within Germany were making their own plans for the future and taking such steps as they could to influence the course of events. Numerous local committees are known to have been active in these months, usually on the initiative of old Communist Party members. They took various names – 'Anti-fascist Committees' or 'Free Germany Committees' – and there was a good deal of variation in their programmatic statements. Some groups knew through Moscow broadcasts of the developments which had taken place in KPD policy at the Brussels and Bern conferences and in the Free Germany movement and were familiar with the concept of a new democratic republic based on an anti-fascist class alliance which had been worked out at those conferences and subsequently accepted by the Central Operative Leadership under Saefkow and Jacob as well as by the regional underground organisations which had come under their influence.

Others, however, who had remained in isolation from these influences, whether in German civilian life or in the forces, seem to have thought in rather general terms of taking up the struggle again from the point which they imagined it to have reached in 1933: they expected, that is, that the collapse of the Third Reich would quickly bring about a revolutionary situation in which the proletariat could take power. Gustav Sobottka, who had been co-opted to the Central Committee while an *émigré* in the USSR and was sent to Pomerania and Mecklenburg at the time of their liberation, wrote to Wilhelm Pieck that he found 'political confusion' and that even the most progressive comrades in the region know hardly anything about the NKFD [i.e. National Free Germany Committee] or its policy'. Ignorance was one thing, but real sectarianism was another, and Sobottka considered that those who clung to sectarian views were a small minority.[36]

Nevertheless, such differences of view as there were among Communists in Germany in the last months of the war might have posed a threat to the unity of the Party, and have prevented it from acting effectively in the critical days and weeks of the Third Reich's collapse, if steps had not been taken to bring those who lagged behind in their thinking quickly up to date. As far as senior Party leaders were concerned, the persistent supporters of the ultra-left line had been excluded from the leadership at the Brussels Conference and every effort had been made since then to ensure that the main policy decisions reached by the Moscow-based leadership were communicated to, and concurred in by, leading Communists in other centres of emigration.

There was little reason to doubt that leading Communists who had taken refuge in Britain and the Americas were aware, through radio broadcasts, of the policy being followed by the Free Germany movement in the USSR and that they agreed with it in the main. What was more doubtful was when the leaders now dispersed in the Western world would be able to return to Germany as the war drew to a close. Pieck was evidently afraid – justifiably, as it turned out – that their return from exile might be delayed by the Western governments and that this might leave an opening for differences to develop among anti-fascists generally and perhaps also among Communists. It was with this eventuality in mind, with a view to having more leading Communists on the spot when the time came, that Pieck, already on 4 August 1944, had discussed with Georgi Dimitrov the possibility of arranging to bring to Moscow Paul Merker, a Politburo member, and Erich Jungmann, a leader of the Young Communist League, who were both in Mexico, and Wilhelm Koenen, leader of the Communist emigrants in Britain.[37] Nothing came of this particular suggestion, but the thought behind it – that leading Communists ought to be on the spot as promptly as possible in the hour of Germany's defeat, bore ample fruit.

As soon as parts of Germany began to be liberated from the Nazis, local anti-fascist committees began to appear and to take control of local government affairs, as far as the Allied authorities would permit. There is no doubt that individual Communists, and in some places Communist groups, played a leading part in this, but how far they did this by way of spontaneous local initiative and how far in fulfilment of leads and instructions transmitted by leaflets or radio broadcasts from party headquarters has been much disputed. A West German historian, Professor Lutz Niethammer, who has investigated the question, argues that there is a lack of evidence to show that the local groups were centrally directed from KPD headquarters in the final chaotic months of the Third Reich. They acted rather, he concludes, independently and spontaneously.[38] Most GDR historians, on the other hand, emphasise the part played by guidance from the Centre at this, as at other periods. This is, indeed, partly a question of dates. However much or little effective direction there was through the last winter and up to April 1945, the situation then changed decisively in the East. On 30 April 1945 – the day of Hitler's suicide, as it happens – the KPD was able to send three high-powered 'Initiative Groups' from Moscow to areas newly occupied by the Red Army, and there can be little doubt that they played a crucial role in the following weeks.

The first group, led by Walter Ulbricht, a senior member of the Politburo, was assigned to the Berlin-Brandenburg region; a second group, led by Anton Ackermann, also a Politburo member,[39] was to operate in Saxony from a base in Dresden; and the third group, headed by the Central Committee member Gustav Sobottka, was sent to the northern coastal region of Western Pomerania and Mecklenburg.[40] Their function – subject of course to the authority of the Soviet military government – was to supervise the first steps towards the normalisation of life, including the setting up of new local government institutions and trade unions. They were also able to control the resumption of legal activity by the Party, as soon as this was permitted, which turned out to be very soon after the end of the war.

There can be no doubt that the prompt arrival of the three Initiative Groups had an important effect on political developments in the eastern provinces, the future Soviet occupation zone and later German Democratic Republic.[41] They came with the full authority of the Party Chairman and Politburo, and with a clear and comprehensive programme worked out in very many months of intensive discussion, giving unambiguous answers to the most urgent questions of the present. Because of that they were quickly able to overcome the remaining differences of view and to unite the Party membership round the policies worked out at the Brussels and Bern conferences and in the Free Germany movement. Moreover, the comprehensiveness and clarity of detail with which the principles of those policies had been applied in more recent documents to the circumstances of 1945 made it easier to develop united action with the Social Democratic and other anti-fascist groups in the East. Such united action had gone so far in some localities that an alternative anti-fascist administration was ready to step into the place of the deposed Nazi authority – if, that is, the approval of the Occupying Power could be obtained. And when, on 10 June 1945, the Soviet occupation authorities announced the legalisation of non-fascist political parties in the Eastern zone, the KPD was able to publish on the following day a coherent programme[42] which was to be the first step on the road to a working-class state and a socialist society in that part of Germany then occupied by the Red Army.

The programme which the German Communists had worked out from the experience of the twelve years 1933–1945 did not envisage so rapid an advance to socialism as was actually to occur. It sketched out for the immediate future a 'militant' or 'anti-fascist' democracy which was intended to be valid for the whole of Germany. That development was frustrated when the Western Powers divided Germany and drove the Communists out of the state governments in the Western zones. The authorities of the Soviet zone were forced, in self-defence, to take steps which led to an accelerated movement towards socialism.

The KPD had taken time to learn the lessons of its defeat of 1933; but its reaction to the crisis of 1945 and the sureness with which it charted its course in the following years showed that it had learned those lessons thoroughly.

CHAPTER 16

The Heritage of Communist Resistance

This book has shown that resistance by Germans to the Nazi tyranny did not begin in 1936 with church leaders or in 1938 with generals. It began in 1933, and the great majority of those who took part in it were manual workers and Communists. For the Communist Party did not collapse in 1933, but recovered from the first shock and rallied something like a quarter to a third of its members in a desperate struggle to continue or resume its normal activities, in the belief that an impending crisis of the National Socialist régime would open the way to proletarian revolution, provided that the revolutionary party, schooled in Marxist theory, was there to play its leading role. In the eyes of the Communists their movement was the only alternative to National Socialism and was destined sooner or later, by historical necessity, to supersede it.

For three years the Party threw its cadres into an unequal battle of a scope and intensity to which few Western writers have done justice. By 1935 a large part of the original mass membership were either dead, imprisoned or in exile, and it was no longer possible to fill the widening gaps in the ranks. A new perspective and a new strategy had to be adopted. Nevertheless, the struggle was never abandoned, but was continued on a reduced scale, and to some extent in new forms, until 1945.

The Communists who resisted at such heavy cost in the early years, 1933 to 1935, at first underestimated National Socialism. Drawing on traditions of the Bismarck era and of the revolution of 1918–23, they tended to see the Third Reich as just another reactionary régime and failed to appreciate fully the peculiar and deadly force of its new combination of limitless state power with a fanatical mass movement. As a result they overestimated the strength of their own position and the scope which was left for opposition. They sought to combat the fascist state by methods more appropriate in some cases to the struggle in a democratic republic or in a more conventional type of authoritarian régime.[2]

Deterred by Leninist doctrine from fighting terror with counter-terror, they answered mass murder by mass leafletting and fell victim too easily to a political police whose powers had acquired a new dimension by the systematic use of torture.

The Communists acted in this way because they expected an early crisis of the régime. And for the same reason they pursued with something less at times than the maximum urgency and persistence the aim of overcoming the divisions in the working class and achieving that unity which they rightly and repeatedly stated to be the essential condition of an effective anti-fascist struggle. Admittedly the Social Democratic leadership bears a heavy responsibility for its typically negative attitude to practical unity proposals, but the Communists, for their part, were slow to perceive the full implications of the priority which now needed to be given to the struggle for unity.

The continuing ultra-leftist mistakes of the German Communist leadership were not forced on it from outside. Indeed the Executive Committee of the Communist International and the Soviet government had already adopted policies of Popular Front and international anti-fascist alliance at a time when the majority of the German Party's Political Bureau were still stubbornly resisting this new line. The evidence which has been reviewed in this book points to the conclusion that ultra-left sectarianism was not peculiar to a leading group, but had deep roots in the history and experience of the revolutionary section of the German working class.

The losing battle which the German Communists waged at such cost in the years from 1933 to 1935, in order to keep their party alive, should not be judged a waste of effort or of lives, given the situation in 1933 and what had gone before; nor, though it ended in defeat in the short run, was it without positive effect in the long run. The working class, as Dr Mason has said,[3] played, despite all appearances, a decisive role in the history of the Third Reich, as an object alike of repression and of fear. Research continues to bring to light evidence showing how keenly aware Hitler was of the danger of working-class unrest and how radically this consideration influenced his war preparations, limiting the extent of mobilisation of resources which he thought it safe to carry out and so affecting the course and outcome of the war.[4] And in this connection it is clear that in the eyes of the Gestapo the mere survival of a Marxist revolutionary organisation, however restricted its activities, represented a real danger in the event of a weakening of Nazi influence on the people's minds.[5] The notion that the Nazi state was safe against all opposition except that of discontented generals, though taken for granted by many post-war historians, was not shared by the Gestapo.

Some historians have characterised Communist Resistance in the Third Reich as a moral triumph but a political disaster.[6] True, the sacrifices which were made may seem out of proportion to the immediate results, for they failed to achieve the liberation of the German people from fascism. But there are situations in history in which refusal to acknowledge defeat and the continuation of a hopeless struggle at whatever cost amount, not only to a moral triumph, but to a real political achievement with long-term consequences.[7] Some have criticised the German Communists for not having taken up arms in 1933. But they did not fail to fight back, as this book has attempted to show, in their own fashion. Armed struggle would have been no less unsuccessful, but far more costly.

Some writers, again, have been inclined to contrast the almost military-style discipline of the Communist Party apparatus with the spontaneous heroism shown by so many rank-and-file members, sometimes implying that the leaders insisted on iron discipline and a rigid organisational structure because they mistrusted the ordinary members. But this is to give a misleading picture of the Party. The division between leaders and led was not so sharp: of the mass membership in 1933, as many as 50 per cent were, as we have seen, *Funktionäre* (office-holders).[8] It was not blind obedience that John Schehr, the first leader of the underground Party, demanded of his colleagues in 1933, but 'initiative and imagination' to which, he said, 'no limits are set'.[9] And if there was distrust of the rank-and-file, it proved to be without justification in very many cases in which the constraints of Party discipline, dissolved by arrests, were replaced by self-discipline and individual initiative. The 'spontaneous heroism' of so many individual German workers was a very disciplined kind of behaviour, directed as it often was to the preservation or restoration and reactivation of the party apparatus. Rank-and-file German Communists were, after all, German workers and had the virtues of their nation and their class. Their struggle against Nazi tyranny after 1933 was a true 'mass heroism',[10] as Franz Dahlem called it at the Seventh World Congress, claiming, not without reason, that it was unequalled in the history of the workers' movement in capitalist countries.

The Brussels Conference of October 1935 was a turning-point in the history of the KPD. It marked the final abandonment by the party leadership of 'ultra-leftism' and the adoption of a new conception of the transition to socialism by way of a new type of democratic republic, which in turn implied a basic modification of strategy and tactics.

The Conference began with a far-reaching, self-critical review of the Party's mistakes in the recent past. It was recognised that insufficient attention had been paid to the changes which had taken place in Germany with the rise of fascism after 1930, and that as a result the Party had fallen behind events. In particular the Communists' attitude to Social Democracy had ceased to correspond to realities. The notion that Social Democracy was the main enemy, expressed in the concept 'social fascism', was rejected, as was the ultra-left idea that left-wing Social Democracy was especially dangerous. It was recognised, too, that the policy of working-class unity, to which the KPD had been committed for many years, had been interpreted in such a way as to mean little more than an attempt to recruit Social Democrats to the Communist Party in the name of 'unity from below'. A new kind of working-class unity was now required: joint action on equal terms, from above and below, which could form the basis of a broader class alliance with sections of the middle and lower-middle class against fascism. The possibility of such an alliance was implied in the new definition of fascism formulated by Georgi Dimitrov at the Seventh World Congress of the International. If fascism was 'the open, terrorist dictatorship of the most reactionary, most chauvinist and most imperialist elements of finance capital',[11] it followed that whatever mass following it might for the time being win among other classes, its objective class basis was narrow and the possibility of a very broad anti-fascist alliance must always exist.

The Popular Front conception involved not only a broad class alliance, but a longer time-scale than Communists had recently thought in terms of. After 'Brussels'[12] they no longer envisaged an imminent seizure of power and the immediate building of socialism by a proletarian revolutionary government. They had to begin thinking in terms of a more protracted development, best described as 'anti-fascist democratic revolution', the exact nature of which remained to be clarified.

The Brussels Conference brought to an end a year-long ideological and political struggle within the KPD Politburo. For many months the adherents of the new line, Wilhelm Pieck and Walter Ulbricht, had remained an isolated minority, despite increasing signs of change in the policies of the International under the influence of Dimitrov and of the Soviet government in the international field. Pieck and Ulbricht only finally prevailed when the ECCI intervened with all its weight, amid growing evidence of demand for change on the part of leading underground activists in Germany. Even so, there was no abrupt change of leadership. The unrepentent 'Leftists', Schubert and Schulte, were removed from the Central Committee, but an influential group who held the balance – Dahlem, Heckert, Florin, Merker – accepted the new line and retained their places in the Politburo, whose membership reflected the importance attached to continuity and to collective leadership. That Pieck and Ulbricht were ultimately to attain such predominance was at least partly due to accidents of death (Heckert 1936, Florin 1944) and of war (Dahlem and Merker, caught in France 1939).

The Brussels Conference, besides changing policy, brought into a new and smaller Central Committee some younger men with lively minds and recent experience of clandestine work. The most notable of these was Wilhelm Knöchel[13] who, in the later 1930s, from his base at Amsterdam, was to combine the joint-chairmanship of the Working Committee of German Mineworkers with a share in the direction of the KPD's Western sector.[14] On the trade union side he set a striking example of successful co-operation with a Social Democratic counterpart, Franz Vogt, while the activity of the KPD's Western sector also furnished examples of new methods of political work, such as semi-legal activity in Nazi institutions. When Knöchel moved from Amsterdam to Berlin in January 1942, he was able to apply in a wider field the lessons thus gained.

The war-time propaganda put out by Knöchel and his Instructors struck what Dr Peukert calls a 'national communist' note, emphasising strongly the need to overthrow the Nazi dictatorship from within and viewing the prospect of the liberation of the German people by foreign powers as a national disaster.

Knöchel was also struck by the key role played by terror and the apparatus of terror in the Nazi state and he proposed the use of counter-terror, directed in particular against police agents and informers.[15] Yet this was contrary to the traditions of the German Communist movement and was not taken up by the party leadership. Nor does the KPD's Central Operative Leadership appear to have concerned itself, either before or during the war, with plans for the assassination of Hitler,[16] although arguments might have been advanced for it, since he enjoyed an unprecedented and crucial combination of powers and his removal might have brought about a destabilisation capable of setting in motion a process of revolutionary change. For the Third Reich was not as stable as it looked at first sight: it went through many crises and came near to disaster on more than one occasion. The presence or absence of an alternative was inevitably a factor in these crises, determining the extent of Hitler's room for manoeuvre. The Communist Party did not, in the event, play an important part in any of these crises, but the fact that it maintained an organisation and a degree of activity throughout the period gave it a certain credibility as a potential alternative.[17] The stereotyped organisational pattern, which made the Party vulnerable and was a weakness in one sense, was in another sense a strength, for it enabled rank-and-file members to take over the work of arrested functionaries without delay. The reality of this appeared clearly in 1945, when in many factories, prisoner-of-war and concentration camps, and working-class suburbs, KPD organisations sprang almost immediately into action, conducting political and educational activity with a self-confidence derived from the consciousness of an unbroken twelve-year struggle.

Communist resistance to the Third Reich exceeded that of all other parties and groups. It never ceased altogether, even in the period of the Pact. Wherever events had brought Communists together – in factories, in working-class suburbs, in army units, in prisons and concentration camps – they had formed groups and tried to organise political resistance, and they had fought side by side with the Spanish Republicans, with the partisans of many European freedom movements, and with the Red Army. The human cost was enormous. Of the 300,000 party members of 1932, an estimated 150,000 had been arrested and persecuted; some 25,000 or 30,000 had been murdered, executed or had died of ill-treatment in concentration camps: losses far exceeding those of any other German resistance group or party. Even the bitterest critics of the KPD's policies have paid tribute to the spirit of self-sacrifice, adherence to principle and loyalty to their cause which its members showed.

The Communists were convinced that if they were to present an effective alternative to the Nazi régime, their resistance activities in Germany must be centrally organised. The story of their fight against the Nazis is the story of successive attempts to build up a national resistance organisation directed from a single centre either within Germany or outside, according to circumstances. There were times when the destruction of a directing centre left the clandestine groups without central guidance,[18] and it is difficult to be certain when and where such a situation prevailed. The Party itself attached the greatest importance to central direction, and its historians today insist that the multifarious resistance activities which are known to have been carried out by Commmunists were, in the main, effectively directed by the Central Committee through its broadcasts, leaflets, and visiting Instructors.[19] This remains, however, a question on which further research is needed.

The younger activists who had led the underground struggle in Germany during the war did not exercise a decisive influence on the course followed by the Party at the end of the war, for most of them were dead. The line which had been laid down at the Brussels and Bern Conferences was interpreted and applied to the circumstances of 1945 by surviving veterans of the pre-1933 leadership returning, like Pieck and Ulbricht, from Moscow, or, like Merker, from Western exile,[20] or, like Dahlem, from a concentration camp. Wherever they had been – and their individual fates had been various and often governed by chance – they had fanatically cherished and preserved the unity of the Party and the continuity of its policy and organisation. That was one of the chief lessons they had learnt from the twelve-year experience of fascism. The other was the necessity of achieving working-class unity and a broader democratic alliance under the leadership of a united working class.

Fascism suffered a defeat in 1945, but its seeds remained. The Communists learned from their long struggle against Hitlerism that in certain circumstances, when the working class was divided, an extremist section of the monopoly bourgeoisie might resort to fascism and war, not scrupling to put the survival of humanity at risk. Only anti-fascist unity could prevent that, and the time to unite against fascism was at its beginnings, before its ideas had got a firm hold on any considerable numbers of the workers or the lower middle class.

In the event, it was not only to the struggle for peace and against fascism that the German Communists were to apply the lessons of their anti-fascist struggle, but to the building of socialism too: a task which history imposed on the eastern parts of Germany. To ignore or underestimate the Communist Resistance against the Third Reich is to distort one's understanding of the GDR, to be blind to its historical roots and to present it as a mere rootless imposition of Soviet military occupation – as it has been taken to be in the West until recently. Readers of this book will surely conclude on the contrary, that the GDR has roots in the experience of the German working class, and especially in the experience of the working-class resistance against the Nazi tyranny. Yet the GDR represents more than the straightforward putting into effect of the programme adopted by the KPD at its conferences of 1935 and 1939. For the German people did not free itself from fascism, but was liberated by foreign powers. The German Communists had to carry out their programme in conditions created for them by others, and above all in a divided Germany. The fateful division in the working class had taken a new form. As a result the 'broad democratic anti-fascist front envisaged in the Brussels and Bern resolutions could not be realised literally in either part of Germany. In the West it was ruled out by the pressure of the British and American authorities, who would not allow the unification of the working-class parties which was the first stage of the programme. In the East, as a result of the division of Germany and the Cold War, the application of the KPD programme was speeded up, so that the transition from anti-fascist democracy to socialism was shorter and more direct than had been envisaged earlier. In the unexpected situations that resulted, the Communists would surely have made many more mistakes than they did, if they had not learnt from the experiences of 1933–45. Nor is it likely that the unification of the two working-class parties would have been achieved so quickly and successfully as it was in the East, but for the experience which many Social Democrats and Communists had shared in the underground struggle and in Nazi prisons and concentration camps – an experience which dissolved much ancient prejudice and created a new mutual respect.

The full story of the Communist Resistance will never be known. But enough is now known to make clear that it was no epic of a few heroes and heroines (though there was much heroism), but an unbroken, twelve-year struggle of many thousands of ordinary working people, in which the Party not only created a moral heritage (which even its enemies have come to recognise) but perseveringly grappled with past errors and outdated conceptions and so acquired a theoretical and political heritage which was to make it possible to turn a catastrophe in one generation into a great constructive achievement in the next.

Notes

Chapter 1. Introduction

[1]*Wiener Library Bulletin*, Vol. XIX, No. 2, April 1965.
[2]Gerhard Ritter, *The German Resistance. Carl Goerdeler's Struggle Against Tyranny* (London: George Allen & Unwin, 1958), Chapter 3.
[3]Ibid., p. 46.
[4]Hans Rothfels, *The German Opposition. An assessment* (London: Oswald Wolff, 1961).
[5]Sir John Wheeler-Bennett, *The Nemesis of Power. The German Army in Politics, 1918–1945* (London: Macmillan, 1961).
[6]Encounter, June 1969.
[7]Alan Bullock, 'The German Communists and the Rise of Hitler' in Maurice Baumont et al. (eds), *The Third Reich* (London: Weidenfeld & Nicolson, 1955), pp. 504–21.
[8]W.L. Shirer, *The Rise and Fall of the Third Reich* (London: Secker & Warburg, 1960).
[9]Wheeler-Bennett, op. cit.
[10]Richard Grunberger, *A Social History of the Third Reich* (London: Weidenfeld & Nicolson, 1971) in his chapter on 'The Workers' overemphasises their conversion to the Nazi way of life.
[11]Hutchinson of London, 1964.
[12]*New Statesman*, 24 July 1964.
[13]Published in 1953 by Rowohlt Verlag (Hamburg). No English translation.
[14]Prittie, op. cit., pp. 277–80.
[15]See Gerhard Förster, Bruno Löwel, Wolfgang Schumann (eds), 'Forschungen zur deutschen Geschichte 1933–45' in *Historische Forschungen in der DDR, 1960–1970. Analysen und Berichte* (Berlin: VEB Deutscher Verlag der Wissenschaften, 1970), pp. 552–89.
[16]Lehrbuch der deutschen Geschichte (Beiträge) (Berlin: VEB Deutscher Verlag der Wissenschaften, 1969): Vol. 11: E. Paterna et al., *Deutschland 1933–1939*; Vol. 12: W. Bleyer et al., *Deutschland 1939–1945*.
[17]This tendency has continued: see especially Klaus Mammach, *Widerstand 1933–1939* (Berlin: Akademie-Verlag, 1984).
[18]See especially Hans-Josef Steinberg, *Widerstand und Verfolgung in Essen, 1933–1945, Schriftenreihe des Forschungsinstituts der Friedrich-Ebert-Stiftung* (Hanover: Verlag für Literatur und Zeitgeschehen, 1969).
[19]Horst Duhnke, *Die KPD von 1933 bis 1945* (Cologne: Kiepenheuer & Witsch, 1972), p. 11. Regrettably there is no English translation of this work.
[20]T.W. Mason, 'Labour in the Third Reich, 1933–1939' in *Past & Present*, No. 33, April 1966, pp. 112–141; also 'Workers' Opposition in Nazi Germany' in *History Workshop Journal*, No. 11, 1981; see also his *Arbeiterklasse und Volksgemeinschaft* (Opladen: Westdeutscher Verlag, 1975) and 'Der

antifaschistische Widerstand im Spiegel der SED-Historiographie' in *Das Argument*, No. 43, July 1967, Heft 2/3, pp. 144–153. For a similar conclusion, see also Hermann Weber, 'Die KPD in der Illegalität' in Richard Löwenthal and P. von zur Mühlen (eds), *Widerstand und Verweigerung in Deutschland, 1933 bis 1945* (Bonn: Verlag J.H.W. Dietz Nachf, 1982), pp. 83–101 (referred to hereafter as *Widerstand und Verweigerung*).

[21]Ian Kershaw, *Popular Opinion and Political Dissent in the Third Reich: Bavaria, 1933–1945* (Oxford: Clarendon Press, 1983).

[22]Detlev Peukert, 'Protest und Widerstand von Jugendlichen im Dritten Reich' in *Widerstand und Verweigerung*, pp. 177–201.

[23]Martin Broszat et al (eds), *Bayern in der NS-Zeit*, Vol. I, *Soziale Lage und politisches Verhalten der Bevölkerung im Spiegel vertraulicher Berichte*. (Munich: R. Oldenbourg, 1977); also Vol. III, *Herrschaft und Gesellschaft in Konflikt*, (1981) (referred to hereafter as *Bayern in der NS-Zeit*, Vol. . .).

[24]D. Peukert, *Die KPD im Widerstand. Verfolgung und Untergrundarbeit an Rhein und Ruhr, 1933 bis 1945* (Wuppertal: Peter Hammer Verlag, 1980) (referred to hereafter as *Die KPD im Widerstand*).

[25]Rudi Goguel, *Antifaschistischer Widerstand und Klassenkampf. Bibliographie deutschsprachiger Literatur, 1945–1973* (Berlin: Militärverlag der DDR, 1976). Another useful reference work is Heinz Gittig's *Illegale antifaschistische Tarnschriften* (Leipzig: VEB Bibliographisches Institut, 1972).

[26]*Beiträge zur Geschichte der deutschen Arbeiterbewegung* (referred to hereafter as *BzG*).

[27]'Dokumente illegaler Leitungen der KPD' in *BzG*, 4/1978 (1933); 5/1978 (1934); 1/1979 (1936); 4/1979 (1937).

[28]Margot Pikarski and Günter Uebel (eds), *Der antifaschistische Widerstandskampf der KPD im Spiegel des Flugblattes 1933–1945* (Berlin: Dietz. 1978) (referred to hereafter as *Antifaschistische Widerstandskampf*). A shorter, paperback version by the same editors was published by Dietz in 1980 under the title *Die KPD Lebt!*

[29]Richard Löwenthal, 'Widerstand im totalen Staat' in *Widerstand und Verweigerung*, pp. 11–24.

[30]T.W. Mason, 'Arbeiteropposition im nationalsozialistischen Deutschland' in Peukert and Reulecke (eds), *Die Reihen fast geschlossen*, Beiträge zur Geschichte des Alltags unterm Nationalsozialismus. (Wuppertal: Peter Hammer Verlag, 1981), pp. 293–313. Wheeler-Bennett makes the same distinction in *The Nemesis of Power*, op. cit., p. 385. See also T.W. Mason's 'The Workers' Opposition in Nazi Germany' in *History Workshop Journal*, No. 11, 198.

[31]Some limitations of access are said to be due to the fragile condition of many documents surviving from the period of illegality. In West Germany I have sometimes been allowed to see, but not to copy or quote from records of public proceedings, for example court cases.

[32]This is the gist of Duhnke's remarks, op. cit., p. 11.

[33]Many such texts have been published in the section 'Dokumente und Materialien' in *BzG*.

[34]Duhnke, op. cit.

[35]*The Times Literary Supplement*, 2 June 1972, p. 636.

[36]T.W. Mason in *Das Argument*, No. 43, July 1967, p. 147, reviewing *Geschichte der deutschen Arbeiterbewegung in acht Bänden, Vol. 5. Von Januar 1933 bis Mai 1945*

(Berlin: Dietz, 1966) (referred to hereafter as *GddA*).

[37]For the use of interviews as a source, see Peukert, *Die KPD im Widerstand*, p. 441.

[38]Die Vereinigung der Verfolgten des Nazi-Régimes (VVN) has much biographical material in its archives and has published some of it.

[39]Karl Mewis, *Im Auftrag der Partei* (Berlin: Dietz, 1971); Bruno Retzlaff-Kresse, *Illegalität-Kerker-Exil. Erinnerungen* (Dietz, 1980) (referred to hereafter as *Illegalität-Kerker-Exil*); Jürgen Kuczynski, *Memoiren* (Berlin and Weimar: Aufbau Verlag, 1981). Among other interesting recent memoirs are: Lucie Suhling, *Der Unbekannte Widerstand. Erinnerungen* (Frankfurt-am-Main: Röderberg, 1980); Elfriede Paul, *Ein Sprechzimmer der Roten Kapelle* (Berlin: Militärverlag der DDR, 1981). Of earlier memoirs, Werner Eggerath, *Nur ein Mensch* (Berlin: Dietz, 1961) should not be missed.

[40]T.W. Mason, 'Der antifaschistische Widerstand der Arbeiterbewegung im Spiegel der SED-Historiographie' in *Das Argument*, No. 43, July 1967, Heft 2/3, p. 147.

Chapter 2. The German Communist Party.

[1]A good account is given by Ben Fowkes, *Communism in Germany under the Weimar Republic*, (London: Macmillan, 1984). See also Chris Harman, *The Lost Revolution. Germany 1918 to 1923* (London: Bookmarks, 1982).

[2]The Spartacist uprising in Berlin and the Bavarian Soviet Republic.

[3]The Kapp *putsch* in Berlin and the Red Army of the Ruhr.

[4]The 'March Action' (*März-Aktion*) in Central Germany.

[5]Fowkes, op. cit., Chapter 5; Harman, Chapters 11–13. For the Communist International's estimate, see extracts from an ECCI statement of 19 January 1924 in Jane Degras (ed), *The Communist International 1919–43. Documents* (London: Frank Cass & Co., 1971), Vol. II, pp. 68–78 (referred to hereafter as Degras, Vol. . .).

[6]Degras, Vol. II, pp. 471 ff. Programme of the Communist International adopted at its Sixth Congress, 1 September 1928.

[7]Fowkes, op. cit., pp. 145–71.

[8]See Fowkes, Chapter 8, pp. 172–98: 'Some structural features of the KPD'.

[9]Zygmunt Paterczyk, 'Dokumente der KPD in Pila aufgefunden' (*BzG*, 4/1973, pp. 691–3); and, more generally, Peukert, *Die KPD im Widerstand*, pp. 44–58.

[10]Arnold Sywotteck in *Deutsche Volksdemokratie. Studien zur politischen Konzeption der KPD, 1939–1946* (Düsseldorf: Bertelsmann, 1971) remarks on the stability of the KPD cadres in the 1920s. Both M. Pikarski in 'Umstellung der KPD auf die Illegalität, 1932–1934' (*BzG*, 5/1978, p. 721 (referred to hereafter as 'Umstellung')) and H. Kühnrich, *Die KPD im Kampf gegen die faschistische Diktatur, 1933–1945* (Berlin: Dietz Verlag, 1983), p. 35, give a registered membership of 360,000 at the beginning of 1933. Pieck, speaking in 1935, said 'over 300,000' (*Der neue Weg zum gemeinsamen Kampf für den Sturz der Hitlerdiktatur* (Berlin: Dietz Verlag, 1954) p. 12 (referred to hereafter as *Der neue Weg*).

[11]See, for example, Peukert, *Die KPD im Widerstand*, p. 45.

[12]On the other hand, where these subsidiary organisations had Social

Democratic as well as Communist members, they formed a basis on which political unity might be built. The sectarian or ultra-left tendency involved further splitting these organisations along party lines.
[13]Figures taken from Peukert, *Die KPD im Widerstand*, pp. 55–6.
[14]Ibid., p. 56.
[15]J. Kuczynski, *Memoiren* (Berlin: Aufbau Verlag, 1981), p. 228.
[16]Lucie Suhling, *Der unbekannte Widerstand* (Frankfurt: Röderberg Verlag, 1980), p. 18.
[17]Gustav Noske was a right-wing Social Democrat; Minister of Defence in Ebert's government, 1919–20.
[18]An especially bitter memory for the Communists was the suppression with many casualties of their May Day demonstration in Berlin in 1929 on the orders of the Social Democratic police president, Zörgiebel, and the subsequent banning of the *Rote Frontkämpferbund* by the Social Democratic Minister of the Interior in Prussia, Carl Severing.
[19]See Programme of the Communist International adopted at its Sixth Congress, 1 September 1928 (Degras, Vol. II, pp. 471 ff.). Non-Communist historians generally write this off as being no genuine forecast, but an *ex post facto* justification of a change of policy decided on other grounds.
[20]Figures taken from M. Pikarski, 'Umstellung der KPD auf die Illegalität, 1932–1934' in *BzG*, 5/1978, pp. 721–2; Peukert, *Die KPD in Widerstand*, p. 53. The membership in January 1933 is given sometimes as 300,000, sometimes as 360,000. Siegfried Vietzke in *Die KPD auf dem Wege zur Brüsseler Konferenz* (Berlin: Dietz Verlag, 1966) (referred to hereafter as Brüsseler Konferenz), p. 47n, refers to a document in the records of the financial department of the KPD headed 'State of the organisation on the accession to power of Hitler in January 1933', according to which 299,219 members were paid up. Previous experience, Vietzke says, suggests that that was likely to have represented about four-fifths of the registered membership, which he therefore estimates as about 360,000.
[21]Pikarski, 'Umstellung', p. 721.
[22]Of 2,825 recruits to the KPD in the Ruhr District in December 1931, only two were recorded as having previously been in the Nazi Party. In the Lower Rhine District the figure was nil out of 824 (Peukert, *Die KPD im Widerstand*, pp. 54–5).
[23]Between 80 and 90 per cent according to Peukert, ibid., p. 34.
[24]Alfred Milatz, 'Das Ende der Parteien im Spiegel der Wahlen, 1930 bis 1933' in E. Matthias and R. Morsey (eds), *Das Ende der Parteien 1933* (Düsseldorf: Droste Verlag, 1960), pp. 777–8 (referred to hereafter as *Das Ende der Parteien*).
[25]Peukert, *Die KPD im Widerstand*, p. 50.
[26]Ibid, p. 47.
[27]Ibid, p. 39.
[28]Siegfried Bahne, 'Sozialfaschismus in Deutschland. Zur Geschichte eines politischen Begriffs' in *International Review of Social History*, No. 10, 1965, pp. 211–244; John M. Cammett, 'Communist Theories of Fascism, 1920–1935' in *Science and Society*, 1967, No. 2, p. 160.
[29]See Pieck's analysis in *Der neue Weg*, pp. 32–51; also G. Dimitrov, 'For the Unity of the Working Class against Fascism', Report to the Seventh Congress of the Communist International, 1935 (Degras, Vol. III, pp. 350 ff.).
[30]Pieck analysed the weaknesses and mistakes of KPD policy before 1933 in his

opening speeches at both the Seventh World Congress of the International and the 'Brussels' Conference of the KPD, both in 1935 (Degras, Vol. III, pp. 350 ff.; Pieck, *Der neue Weg*, pp. 14–31).

[31]Pieck later acknowledged that the KPD had underestimated the fascist danger – *Der neue Weg*, p. 24.

[32]Some of the blame for the underestimation of the Nazi danger was later to be attributed to Heinz Neumann (see Pieck, *Der neue Weg*, p. 25); his role, however, has never been fully clarified.

[33]See Pikarski, 'Umstellung', pp. 721–2.

[34]An apposite saying of Lenin is quoted by Fernando Claudín: 'Our tactical and strategical methods (if we take them on an international scale) still lag behind the excellent strategy of the bourgeoisie, which has learned from the example of Russia and will not let itself be "taken by surprise".' See *The Communist Movement from Comintern to Cominform* (Harmondsworth: Penguin Books, 1975), p. 126.

[35]The leadership, for example, called for a united front policy, but criticised attempts by local party units to apply the policy (Pieck, *Der neue Weg*, pp. 26–7); Heinz Karl and Walter Wimmer (eds), *Ernst Thälmann, Ausgewählte Reden und Schriften in zwei Bänden* (Frankfurt-am-Main, 1976/7), Vol. 2, pp. 236–62.

[36]Documents and extracts continue to be published in *BzG*.

[37]*GddA*, Vol. 4, pp. 312–4. For a different assessment of Neumann's role, see Duhnke, op. cit., pp. 36–7.

[38]Quoted by Peukert, *Die KPD im Widerstand*, p. 29.

[39]Peukert describes them as 'dilletantisch'.

[40]For the AM-Apparat in western Germany, see Peukert, *Die KPD im Widerstand*, pp. 73–5.

[41]Duhnke describes the KPD's supposed 'uprising plan' as more myth than reality: (*Die KPD von 1933 bis 1945*, pp. 13–14). He prints an anonymous police report which reaches the same conclusion, ibid., pp. 531–3. The Party's conception of revolution was explained by Thälmann in a letter to the Examining Magistrate, *BzG*, 3/1964, pp. 464–7; *GddA*, Vol. 5, pp. 455–6.

[42]Pikarski, 'Umstellung', p. 720.

[43]Ibid.

[44]Ibid., pp. 720–3. In order to get these preparations for illegality understood and applied, a Reich conference was held from 15 to 18 October 1932, followed by District Congresses in November and December.

[45]Ibid., p. 720.

[46]Ibid.

[47]Ibid., p. 721.

[48]Max Spangenberg, 'Antifaschistischer Kampf deutscher Kommunisten in Dänemark' in *BzG*, 4/1977, p. 618. See also M. Pikarski, 'Zur Hilfe der KI und der kommunistischen Bruderparteien beim Übergang der KPD in die Illegalität im Jahre 1933' (*BzG*, 5/1974, pp. 838–47) and Klaus Mammach, 'Zum gemeinsamen Kampf deutscher und polnischer Kommunisten und anderer Antifaschisten 1933 bis 1939' (Ibid., pp. 848–61).

[49]Duhnke, op. cit., pp. 531–3.

[50]Kuczynski, op. cit., p. 241.

[51]Duhnke, op. cit., pp. 13–15, 531–3.

[52]Resolution of the ECCI praesidium on the situation in Germany, 1 April 1933 in Degras, III, pp. 261–2.
[53]L.J. Edinger, *German Exile Politics* (Berkeley and Los Angeles: University of California Press, 1956), p. 9.
[54]For a self-critical analysis of the reasons for the failure of the KPD to prevent the assumption of power by Hitler, see Pieck's opening report at the 'Brussels Conference of 1935,' *Der neue Weg*, pp. 21–31.

Chapter 3. Defeat and Recovery, February–June 1933.

[1]Details from Heinz Kühnrich, *Die KPD im Kampf gegen die faschistische Diktatur, 1933–1945* (Berlin: Dietz, 1983), p. 23 (referred to hereafter as *Die KPD im Kampf*).
[2]Peukert emphasises the element of spontaneity in many of these demonstrations in the Ruhr and Lower Rhine districts (*Die KPD im Widerstand*, pp. 32–3); GDR authors generally insist on the Party's leading role.
[3]See above, Chapter 2, p. 316, note 23.
[4]This leaflet is reproduced in full-size facsimile in Pikarski and Uebel (eds), *Antifaschistischer Widerstandskampf*; also, in reduced format, *Die KPD lebt!*, pp. 125–6.
[5]*Antifaschistischer Widerstandskampf*, p. 36.
[6]The percentage of valid votes cast for the SPD and KPD respectively in the Reichstag elections of 6 November 1932 and 5 March 1933 were:

	6 November 1932	5 March 1933
SPD:	20.4%	18.3%
KPD:	16.9%	12.3%

Figures from Matthias and Morsey (eds), *Das Ende der Parteien*, pp. 777–8.
[7]See leaflets produced by the KPD in Leipzig now in the Institut für Marxismus-Leninismus, Zentrales Parteiarchiv Ref. I2/8/40 (referred to hereafter as 1ML/ZPA).
[8]*Illegalität-Kerker-Exil*, pp. 37–8. The demonstration was on 5 February.
[9]Edinger, op. cit., pp. 8–9.
[10]W. Pieck, *Der neue Weg*, pp. 15 ff. analysed the Party's mistakes in his speech at the Brussels Conference of 1935.
[11]These judgements were prominent in the reports sent up from District leaderships to the Secretariat in the early months of the new régime, according to Peukert, *Die KPD im Widerstand*, p. 110.
[12]Ibid., p. 112.
[13]Printed in *Die Illegale Tagung des Zentralkomitees der KPD am 7 Februar 1933 in Ziegenhals bei Berlin* (Berlin: Dietz, 1981) (referred to hereafter as *Die Illegale Tagung*), together with biographical notes on participants.
[14]E. Paterna et al, *Deutschland von 1933 bis 1939* (Berlin: VEB Deutscher Verlag der Wissenschaften, 1969), p. 24.
[15]*Die KPD im Kampf*, p. 28, quoting W. Pieck, *Gesammelte Reden und Schriften*, Vol. 5 (Berlin, 1972), pp. 6–15.
[16]Martin Broszat, *Der Staat Hitlers* (Munich: Deutscher Taschenbuch Verlag,

1969) p. 88.
[17]Jürgen Stroech, 'Zur Herstellung und Verbreitung der illegalen "Rote Fahne", 1933–1939' in *BzG*, 1/1977, pp. 81–2.
[18]Hans-Peter Görgen, *Düsseldorf und der Nationalisozialismus* (Düsseldorf: Schwann, 1969), p. 35.
[19]Printed in English translation in J. Noakes and G. Pridham, *Documents on Nazism, 1919–1945* (London: Jonathan Cape, 1974), p. 169 (referred to hereafter as *Documents on Nazism*).
[20]Ibid.
[21]'Höhere Formen der wehrhaften Massennotwehr'. The phrase, defined as 'die geschlossene aktive Verteidigung des Arbeiterlebens und Arbeitereigentums', occurs in Thälmann's speech at Ziegenhals on 7 February 1933, printed in *Die Illegale Tagung*, p. 38.
[22]Peukert, *Die KPD im Widerstand*, pp. 110–3.
[23]See M. Pikarski, 'Umstellung', pp. 724–5.
[24]For the different views see: Karl-Heinz Biernat, *Der Reichstag brennt. Hintergründe und Auswirkungen* (Berlin: Dietz, 1960); Hans Mommsen, 'Der Reichstagsbrand und seine politischen Folgen' (*Vierteljahreshefte für Zeitgeschichte* No. 12, 1965, pp. 351–413); Walther Hofer (ed), *Der Reichstagsbrand. Eine wissenschaftliche Dokumentation*, Vol. I (West Berlin: Arani, 1972).
[25]Duhnke, *Die KPD von 1933 bis 1945*, p. 46, quoting Winzer, *Zwölf Jahre Kampf Gegen Faschismus und Krieg* (Berlin: Dietz, 1957), p. 30. Kühnrich, *Die KPD im Kampf*, p. 30, gives the same figure as inclusive of Social Democrats.
[26]Both were later arrested: Beimler in April; Horn, after transfer to Berlin, in November.
[27]Communist candidates were allowed lest otherwise their supporters should vote for Social Democrats. See also S. Bahne, 'Die Kommunistische Partei Deutschlands' in *Das Ende der Parteien*, p. 696.
[28]Kurt Werner and Karl Heinz Biernat, *Die Köpenicker Blutwoche 1933* (Berlin: Dietz, 1960). One of the victims, Johannes Stelling, was a member of the Executive Committee of the SPD.
[29]Figures from *Das Ende der Parteien*, p. 778.
[30]*The Times Literary Supplement*, 7 May 1982, p. 513.
[31]Peukert, *Die KPD im Widerstand*, p. 107.
[32]Ibid.
[33]Ibid, pp. 107–8.
[34]Peukert, *Die KPD im Widerstand*, p. 97; Duhnke, op cit., p. 108; H. Weber in Löwenthal and von zur Mühlen (eds), *Widerstand und Verweigerung*, p. 89.
[35]For example, Arthur Menzel a Düsseldorf sympathiser joined the KPD after February 1933 and became leader of its factory group in the Schiess de Fries works, was arrested at the end of June 1933 and died in custody (GStA Hamm, OJ 779/33, pp. 80–1, Vol. iii, pp. 3 ff; and author's interview with A. Götschenberg, 5 January 1972).
[36]For this reorganisation see M. Pikarski, 'Umstellung', pp. 719–32.
[37]Gerhard Hetzer, 'Die Industriestadt Augsburg' in *Bayern in der NS-Zeit, Vol. III*, p. 154.
[38]See below, Chapter 6.
[39]See, for example, the Resolution of the Praesidium of ECCI on the Situation

in Germany, April 1933, in Degras, Vol. III, p. 257.
[40]Chapter 6.
[41]*Illegalität-Kerker-Exil*, pp. 48–50.
[42]Degras, Vol. III, pp. 249–51; Peukert, *Die KPD im Widerstand*, pp. 110–1.
[43]Peukert, *Die KPD im Widerstand*, p. 108.
[44]Ibid.
[45]Ibid, p. 113.
[46]Ibid, pp. 97–8 for rejection of this assertion.
[47]T.W. Mason, 'Resistance in the Ruhr' in *The Times Literary Supplement*, 7 May 1982, p. 513.
[48]*Die KPD im Widerstand*, p. 108.
[49]See note 47.
[50]K.H. Biernat et al., 'Über den Beitrag der KPD zur Vorbereitung des VII Weltkongresses der K.I.' in *BzG*, 4/1965, pp. 610–11.
[51]Translated by the author from a photocopy made of the original in GStA Hamm, OJ 779/33, Vol. iii, fo. 465, for which thanks are due to the State Attorney at the Oberlandesgericht. Underlining reproduced from the original.
[52]Reading uncertain.
[53]See Pieck's remarks of 1935 in *Der neue Weg*, pp. 22ff.

Chapter 4. State and Opposition

[1]For one view see Allan Merson, 'Nazis and Monopoly Capital,' *Our History*, pamphlet 57, summer 1973.
[2]See Noakes and Pridham (eds), *Documents on Nazism*, pp. 421–38; Richard Grunberger, *A Social History of the Third Reich* (London: Weidenfeld & Nicolson, 1971), pp. 185–202.
[3]National Socialist Factory-Cell Organisation.
[4]*Documents on Nazism*, pp. 425–6.
[5]See Peukert, *Die KPD im Widerstand*, pp. 89–90.
[6]*Documents on Nazism*, pp. 205–6. For Düsseldorf see H-P. Görgen, *Düsseldorf und der Nationalsozialismus* (Düsseldorf: Schwann, 1969), p. 36.
[7]H. Buchheim, *Anatomie des SS-Staates*, Vol. I (Munich: Deutscher Taschenbuch Verlag, 1967) p. 162.
[8]At Düsseldorf this role was played by *Kriminalsekretär* Max Brosig, an anti-Communist expert of Section IA, who had been a Social Democrat; W. Eggerath, *Nur Ein Mensch* (Berlin: Dietz, 1961), pp. 63 ff.
[9]For example, on 22 February 1935, when the Düsseldorf Gestapo was ready to round up the KPD organisation in the suburb of Gerresheim, a large part of the county criminal police (99 officers) were ordered to report at 6.00 a.m. to assist about twenty members of the Gestapo itself.
[10]'Confidential persons' or secret agents.
[11]For V-persons at Düsseldorf see below, Chapter 6, pp. 34–6.
[12]For a Düsseldorf example, see below, Chapter 6, Wilhelm Gather.
[13]The 'rules of conspiracy' forbade the resumption of contact with released prisoners, at least for a long time, but shortage of cadres led to frequent disregard of this precaution. See, for example, the evidence of R. Goguel in Chapter 6, p.

137.

[14]Albrecht Wagner, 'Die Umgestaltung der Gerichtsverfassung . . .' in *Die deutsche Justiz und der Nationalsozialismus*, Vol. 16/1 (Stuttgart: Deutsche Verlags-Anstalt, 1968), pp. 296, 303.

[15]HDG (Hauptstaatsarchiv-Düsseldorf-Gestapo) 25316 Rübesamen, fos. 178v–179v. The nature of the obstacle to more violent methods in this instance is not clear.

[16]See the account of his experiences published after the war by Dr Walter Hensel, later *Oberstadtdirektor* of Düsseldorf, quoted in Görgen, op cit., p. 174.

[17]In HDG 49174, pp. 1–3, a prisoner who had refused to incriminate any associate at his trial was later induced to do so; and in HDG 53684 another prisoner, re-interrogated after two years in prison, attempted suicide to avoid incriminating comrades.

[18]In one Düsseldorf case the deposition was signed 'at pistol point' at the end of a six-hour interrogation, according to a survivor (VVN (Dü) 2092, Tibulsky).

[19]For an example, see HDG 22781 Benden.

[20]E. Gritzbach, *Hermann Goering, Werk und Mensch*, 9/10 edition (1938), p. 35; Reinhard Heydrich, 'Politisches Soldatentum in der Polizei' in *Der Generalanzeiger der Stadt Frankfurt-am-Main*, 17 February 1941. Seen in HDG Generalakten, file No. 1 (2303).

[21]Ibid. (HDG. Generalakten).

[22]*Untersuchungsrichter.*

[23]*Voruntersuchung*. This was dispensed with in treason cases from February 1933; in Speial Court proceedings from their inauguration in March 1933; and in all other proceedings from 1935 (Albrecht Wagner, op. cit., pp. 257, 259, 262).

[24]*Verordnung des Reichspräsidenten zum Schutz von Volk und Staat.*

[25]*Sondergerichte.*

[26]Treason was at once more serious and more elastic than *Heimtücke*, which might require evidence of an overt act of 'malicious opposition'. Charges of breaking a specific law might also stimulate dormant legal scruples, as in a case of 1934 (GStA Hamm, OJ 693/34) when a charge based on the presidential ordinance of 4 February 1933 gave rise to a division between the judges as to whether the ordinance applied to possession of single copies of a leaflet or only to stocks of it.

[27]*Volksgerichtshof.*

[28]For example, in the People's Court case 14a/8J 796/3 [1H 31/34] against Johannes Fladung (B[erlin] D[ocument] C[enter], VGH F 116).

[29]A judgement of 27 February 1936 included the following: '. . . There is no need of further demonstration that the aims of the illegal KPD are of a treasonable nature. At least since the Reichstag Fire and the subsequent official enlightenment of the German people, everyone knows that the illegal KPD wants to attain power in Germany by means of force and by unleashing a civil war. . .' (Translated from judgement in 6 OJs 710/35). See also judgement in OJ 779/33 (BDC/VGH H 606).

[30]See judgement in GStA Hamm, OJ 779/33. Vol [III], fos. 74r–75r.

[31]*Machtübernahme*. The terms National Revival, National Revolution and National-Socialist Revolution occur with the same meaning in other judgements.

[32]This implication seems to be contained in the judgement of the Higher Regional Court at Hamm on W.A. Albrecht of Neuss, who was charged with preparation of treason for having supplied the KPD with reports on the mood of the SA and SS up to the beginning of 1933. He was acquitted, but only on grounds of doubt, mixed motives, and his plea that he had remained a Nazi at heart – not because of the invalidity of the charge itself (GStA Hamm, OJ 779/33, Bd.[II?], fos. 82–84).

[33]By 1935 members merely receiving literature or paying dues were liable to hard labour for from one to ten years, while the minimum sentence for being a functionary was two years' hard labour (*Zuchthaus*). See judgement in GStA Hamm, 6 OJs 128/35, pt. vi (in BDC/VGH R 398. Rübesamen).

[34]Judgement in GStA Hamm, OJ 178/34, 18.8.34. (BDC/VGH, Sch 507).

[35]Judgement in GStA Hamm, OJ 789/34, fos. 8–13 (also BDC/VGH K 251 Klemm). It was in fact a time when (as the judges might have noted, if their justice had not been deaf as well as blind) Hitler himself had proclaimed a serious political crisis justifying emergency measures.

[36]See VVN–Dü 1152 for photocopy of judgement in People's Court case: 9J 710/35 [2H 42/35].

[37]The court duly acquitted the two, but expressed its protest (and at the same time made its confession) in the words of the chairman to the two acquitted, that they should not imagine that they had been any less guilty than the others. An account by a survivor, dated 23 October 1964 is in VVN-Dü 2092.

[38]The Gestapo file HDG 17720 Fonk, fos. 258–60 contains a draft memorandum, probably prepared by the chief of the Düsseldorf Gestapo for submission to his Berlin HQ, bitterly complaining about a senior judge who had closely interrogated Gestapo secretary Brosig about the methods used to obtain depositions for a treason trial.

[39]Wagner, op. cit., pp. 207–8.

[40]For example, GStA Hamm, OJs 249/35 (BDC/VGH B 209) in which Hans F., a Düsseldorf Communist, was acquitted because the only witness against him, another alleged Communist, withdrew his deposition in court, as having been taken in an interrogation in which he was 'exceptionally nervous'.

[41]In the trial of Communists in the Düsseldorf suburb of Zooviertel in August 1935, the Higher Regional Court at Hamm accepted the evidence of the *agent provocateur* Nosbüsch, although fully informed of the role he had played, and further accepted his hearsay account of the alleged statements of a 'V-man', whose identity, presumably, the police did not wish to reveal by allowing him to appear in the witness box. Although the accused flatly denied Nosbüsch's allegations, the court judged that 'no ground has been shown for doubting the credibility of the witness Nosbüsch'.

[42]Preussisches Geheimes Statsarchiv, Berlin-Dahlem, rep. 90, Abt. P. nr. 78, Heft 5.

[43]*Untersuchungshaft*.

[44]*Zuchthaus*, as distinct from the lighter and usually shorter detention in an ordinary prison (*Gefängnis*).

[45]Hugo Paul, Instrukteur for Düsseldorf until June 1933, was sentenced by the People's Court on 26 November 1934 to 2½ years (17J 617/33, reported in VVN-Dü 2005).

[46]The law read: '. . . by death or, insofar as a more severe penalty has not hitherto been applicable, by life imprisonment or hard labour up to fifteen years. . .' (Reichsgesetzblatt, I, p. 723, printed in extract form in *Gesetze des NS-Staates*, Bd. 2, West Berlin: Gehlen Verlag, 1968.)
[47]See, for example, HDG 49174, W[ ], Josef.
[48]In the case of the Communist security officer and Ruhr miner, Karl Tuttas (HDG 49665, fo. 5), the Gestapo renounced its claim to punish the prisoner for his 'slander', leaving appropriate action to the prison authorities.
[49]So much so that some Communists probably owe their survival to a sentence of life imprisonment under the new treason law of October 1933.
[50]For example, Hugo Paul, in a concentration camp since the completion of his prison sentence in 1936, was provisonally released from Sachsenhausen on 20 April 1939 under the 'birthday amnesty', thanks in part to his wife's persistent lobbying (interview with Frau Luise Paul, 17 April 1971).
[51]Figures from G. Weisenborn, *Der lautlose Aufstand* (Hamburg: Rowohlt, 1962) p. 133, quoting an article by Max Braun in the French periodical *L'Ordre*, 12 August 1939. Kühnrich also gives a round figure of 300,000 (*Die KPD im Kampf*, p. 147).
[52]*GddA*, Vol. 5, p. 235.
[53]Described in M. Pikarski, 'Umstellung', pp. 719–32.
[54]Chapter 2, pp. 24–5.
[55]The phrase, referring to 1934, is from Rudolf Goguel's *Es war ein langer Weg* (Cologne: Komet Verlag, 1947; 2nd edition, Singen: Volks Verlag, 1948).
[56]Penetration of the Labour Front was a waste of time, a senior KPD organiser told Goguel in 1934, in view of the imminence of revolutionary crisis (ibid.)
[57]When the KPD's Lower Rhine District Secretary, Otto Hertel, was arrested in August 1934, his lodging contained a veritable archive, partly inherited from his predecessor. It included information and directives relating to recent events such as the 30 June massacre, the Austrian *putsch* of 25 July and the anniversary of the outbreak of the First World War. For a list of the material see: HDG 23040 Hertel, fos. 64r–65v (deposition of 10 September 1934), annexes iii–vi.
[58]See judgement of People's Court in 9 J 151/35 [1 H 31/36] dated 5.2.36 against Wilhelm Paulick and others, in HDG 23099; also HDG 30512, Dahlhaus, M.
[59]See, for example, W. Eggerath, *Nur ein Mensch* (Berlin: Dietz, 1961), pp. 90–1.
[60]For a vivid account see Karl Mewis, *Im Auftrag der Partei* (Berlin: Dietz, 1971), pp. 13–46.
[61]One such case was that of Karl Düllgen and his circle of friends in Düsseldorf who remained for years a thorn in the flesh of police and employers. (HDG 54512 fos. 71 ff.)

Chapter 5. The Underground Struggle

[1]For the KPD's underestimation of the strength of the Nazi régime and its reluctance to recognise that the working class had suffered a serious defeat, see *GddA*, vol. 5, p. 40; also Kühnrich, *Die KPD im Kampf*, pp. 36–7.
[2]For the expected speeding-up of the revolutionary process, see Thälmann's report in *Die illegale Tagung*, pp. 24–5, 28, 37, 39.

[3]Ibid.
[4]Theses referring to Germany printed in extract form in Degras, Vol. III, pp. 210–7.
[5]Ibid, pp. 248–63.
[6]Extracts from this correspondence (between 20 June 1933 and 1 October 1937) under the heading 'Dokumente und Materialien; Die KPD – führende Kraft im antifaschistischen Widerstand. Aus der Tätigkeit illegaler Leitungen im Lande' are printed by Gerhard Nitzsche and Günter Uebel in *BzG*, 4/1978, pp. 528–539; 5/1978, pp. 691, 702; 1/1979, pp. 72–83; 4/1979, pp. 543–556.
[7]*BzG*, 4/1978, pp. 531–3.
[8]*BzG*, 4/1978, pp. 537–8.
[9]Duhnke, *Die KPD von 1933 bis 1945*, pp. 105–6.
[10]Letter dated 6 September 1933 from Inlandleitung to Auslandsleitung concerning a proposed month-long party school (*BzG*, 4/1978, pp. 537–8); also, on District schools in 1934, Bahne in *Das Ende der Parteien*, p. 701; also *re* memo on policy towards officials and white-collar workers, see Schehr's letter of 2 September 1933 (*BzG* 4/1978, p. 534).
[11]Letter dated 1 August 1933 in *BzG*, 4/1978, pp. 530–1.
[12]See Vietzke, *Brüsseler Konferenz*, p. 96, where Remmele is said to have held an ultra-left 'all-or-nothing conception' and to have been guilty of factionalism. He was removed from the Politburo on 25 April 1933 and transferred to Comintern headquarters in the USSR, where he later fell victim to the great purges. The same fate was to befall many other German Communist refugees, including some prominent ultra-leftists such as Heinz Neumann, who had been removed from the KPD leadership in 1932, and Hermann Schubert and Fritz Schulte, who were to be excluded in 1935. The facts are only partly known (See Duhnke, op. cit., pp. 278, 295; Mammach, op. cit., p. 234).
[13]Peukert, *Die KPD im Widerstand*, pp. 109–11; Bahne in *Das Ende der Parteien*, pp. 710–11. GDR writers present this differently: Vietzke, for instance, draws attention to a directive sent out to KPD Districts on 23 February 1933, emphasising that the government change of 30 January had brought about 'a basic change in the situation' which called for an equally basic change in the Party's policy. See *Brüsseler Konferenz*, p. 38, quoting IML/ZPA 3/19/385, B1.46.
[14]Degras, Vol. III, p. 297; Extracts from Theses of Thirteenth ECCI Plenum, December 1933; Duhnke, op. cit., pp. 122–3.
[15]The 1928 line was confirmed in essentials at the Thirteenth ECCI Plenum: see commentary and extracts in Degras, Vol. III, pp. 285–306.
[16]Degras, loc. cit.; but see note 13 above.
[17]This is briefly referred to in the Theses of the Thirteenth Plenum: Degras, Vol. III, pp. 297–8.
[18]Kühnrich quotes Dimitrov's words summarising the 'alpha and omega of Communist policy' as: 'Massenarbeit, Massenkampf, Massenwiderstand', *Die KPD im Kampf*, p. 69.
[19]See the political letter to members reproduced in Chapter 3 above.
[20]See Chapter 4, note 55 for Goguel's comment on 'an intoxication of optimism'.
[21]*GddA*, Vol. 5, pp. 40–1.

[22]For the New Beginning movement, see Edinger, op. cit., pp. 83ff.
[23]These were Siegfried Aufhäuser and Karl Böchel.
[24]Originally printed in *Neuer Vorwärts*; discussed in Edinger, op. cit., pp. 42–8.
[25]Degras, Vol. III, pp. 285–306.
[26]Resolution of the ECCI Praesidium on the situation in Germany, 1 April 1933, Degras, Vol. III, pp. 254–63.
[27]Ibid, p. 297.
[28]Ibid, p. 303.
[29]KPD organisation at this period is described in Duhnke, op. cit., pp. 109–16; Vietzke, *Brüsseler Konferenz*, pp. 46–54; Kühnrich, *Die KPD im Kampf*, pp. 35–47; Pikarski, 'Umstellung', pp. 719–32; H. Weber, 'Die KPD in der Illegalität', *Widerstand und Verweigerung*, pp. 83–101.
[30]Pikarski, 'Umstellung', p. 722.
[31]Ibid.
[32]Ibid., p. 721. Recruitment had been suspended on 25 July 1932.
[33]See Stefan Weber, 'Nach der Verhaftung Ernst Thälmanns leitete John Schehr die illegale KPD', *BzG*, 4/1982, pp. 483–98; G. Nitzsche and G. Uebel (eds), 'Die KPD – Führende Kraft im antifaschistischen Widerstand. Aus der Tätigkeit illegaler Leitungen der KPD im Lande', (I), *BzG*, 4/1978, pp. 528–39.
[34]*Polleiter*.
[35]'Umstellung', p. 722.
[36]Ibid., pp. 721–2.
[37]Nitzsche and Uebel (eds), op. cit., (II), *BzG*, 5/1978, pp. 695–6.
[38]Peukert, *Die KPD im Widerstand*, p. 49; Peukert, 'Der deutsche Arbeiterwiderstand, 1933–1945' (*das parlament* (supplement), 14 July 1979, p. 28).
[39]On 4 August 1933, for example, the Home Leadership instructed the North Bavarian district to make preparations to influence the Nazis attending the forthcoming Nazi Party rally at Nuremberg (*BzG*, 4/1978, pp. 531–2).
[40]See Berta Karola Karg, 'Mein Kampf gegen die braune Diktatur' in Löwenthal and von zur Mühlen (eds), *Widerstand und Verweigerung*, pp. 102–111.
[41]Pikarski and Uebel, *Antifaschistische Widerstandskampf*, p. 11; Dokumente 37, 47.
[42]On *Rote Hilfe* at Augsburg see Gerhard Hetzer, 'Die Industriestadt Augsburg. Eine Sozialgeschichte der Arbeiteropposition' in *Bayern in der NS-Zeit*, Vol. III, (1981), pp. 168–73.
[43]*Antifaschistische Widerstandskampf*, Dokument No. 47.
[44]Peukert, *Die KPD im Widerstand* pp. 104, 137.
[45]Pikarski, 'Umstellung', p. 720.
[46]Vietzke, *Brüsseler Konferenz*, p. 48; Peukert, *Die KPD im Widerstand*, pp. 137–8; see also Kühnrich, *Die KPD im Kampf*, pp. 46–7, who puts the division at summer 1933.
[47]From a report of the Landesleitung, November 1933 to March 1934, printed in *BzG*, 5/1978, p. 692.
[48]*BzG*, 5/1978, p. 692; *BzG*, 1/1981 p. 91.
[49]See above Chapter 4, p. 64.
[50]Above, Chapter 3, p. 29.
[51]See 'Unbekannte Dokumente Ernst Thälmanns aus dem faschistischen

Kerker', *BzG*, 3/1964, pp. 462–73; 'Berichte des Thälmann-Kuriers, Walter Trautsch (Ibid., 5/1965, pp/ 849–75).

[52]After having been removed from the Politburo on 25 April 1933. Vietzke, *Brüsseler Konferenz*, p. 96.

[53]For a selection of these reports see *BzG*, 4/1978, pp. 528 ff.

[54]For the latter arrangement see K. Mammach, op. cit., p. 48.

[55]*BzG*, 5/1978, p. 695.

[56]For accounts of this sector organisation: Kühnrich, *Die KPD im Kampf*, p. 91–4; Mammach, *Widerstand, 1933–1939*, p. 170.

[57]Bruno Retzlaff-Kresse, *Illegalität-Kerker-Exil*, pp. 122–205. See also Mammach, *Widerstand 1933–1939*, pp. 169–70.

[58]Chapter 3, p. 35 above.

[59]D. Peukert, 'Der deutsche Arbeiterwiderstand 1933–1945' in *das parlament* (supplement) B 28–29/79, 14 July 1979, p. 28.

[60]A. Ackermann, 'Erinnerungen' in *BzG*, 5/1965, p. 827.

[61]Peukert, *Die KPD im Widerstand*, pp. 153–4.

[62]This was Hans Pfeiffer: see below, Chapter 6, pp. 127–8; above Chapter 4, n. 57; also HDG 17720 F[ ]k, fos. 1–8; GStA Hamm OJ 779/33, F[ ]k, H.

[63]See Chapter 6 below (Otto Hertel). Detail in HDG 23040, fos. 1–173.

[64]Hugo Paul (see Chapter 6 below) rented a flat from a non-Communist Jew, who emigrated.

[65]Peukert in *das parlament* (supplement) 14 July 1979, p. 28.

[66]Peukert, *Die KPD im Widerstand*, p. 151.

[67]Vietzke, *Brüsseler Konferenz*, p. 181.

[68]Ibid., pp. 178–9.

[69]See Hanna Eling, *Frauen im deutschen Widerstand, 1933–45* (Frankfurt-am-Main: Röderberg Verlag, 1978).

[70]Translated from quotation in K.H. Biernat, K. Mammach, G. Nitzsche (eds), 'Über den Beitrag der KPD zur Vorbereitung des VII Weltkongresses der Kommunistischen Internationale, (*BzG*, 4/1965, p. 611n.).

[71] *The Times Literary Supplement*, 7 May 1982.

[72]Peukert, *Die KPD im Widerstand*, p. 225.

[73]See plan outlined by Schehr in *BzG*, 4/1978, pp. 537–8.

[74]See letter dated end of June 1934 from Home Leadership to Districts, printed in *BzG*, 5/1978, p. 697.

[75]*Bayern in der NS-Zeit*, Vol. I, p. 212.

[76]G. Hetzer, 'Die Industriestadt Augsburg' in *Bayern in der NS-Zeit*, Vol. III, p. 160.

[77]'Aus der Tätigkeit illegaler Leitungen der KPD im Lande (I)' in *BzG*, 4/1978, pp. 537–8.

[78]Ibid.

[79]Memoranda from Schehr, 1 August 1933 and 2 September 1933 printed in 'Dokumente illegaler Leitungen der KPD (I)' *BzG*, 4/1978, pp. 530–1, 534–5.

[80]See above, n. 40.

[81]See Karl Schabrod, *Widerstand an Rhein und Ruhr, 1933–1945*, p. 29, for a case in which ten RFB men of Düsseldorf-Gerresheim were sentenced to death in September 1933 in connection with a clash with the local SS in June 1932.

[82]See the Gerresheim case, above, Chapter 4, p. 58, in which SA men joined in

protests which secured a reprieve for seven of those condemned to death. See also *BzG*, 5/1978, p. 693.

[83]Letters of 26 August 1933 and 5 September 1933 in *BzG*, 4/1978, pp. 533, 535.

[84]Ibid.

[85]See Thälmann's definition of revolution as a mass movement in his letter to the examining judge in *BzG*, 3/1964, pp. 464–7.

[86]See 'Bericht über die Tätigkeit der Landesleitung der KPD, November 1933 bis März 1934' *BzG*, 5/1978, pp. 692–4.

[87]Görgen, op. cit., p. 43 (see pp. 126–7 below for Schlageter cult).

[88]See *BzG*, 4/1978, pp. 531–3.

[89]A Ackermann, 'Ich kam aus der illegalen Arbeit in Berlin', *BzG* 5/1965, pp. 827–30. Klaus Mammach (ed), *Die Brüsseler Konferenz der KPD* (Frankfurt-am-Main: Verlag Marxistische Blätter, 1975), p. 29.

[90]IML/ZPA I 2/8/29.

[91]Ibid. concerning D-Werke, Berlin-Spandau.

[92]Ibid.

[93]*BzG*, 5/1978, pp. 695–7.

[94]Ibid., p. 696.

[95]Ibid.

[96]IML/ZPA I 2/8/29.

[97]Ibid.

[98]*BzG*, 4/1978, pp. 533–4.

[99]*Die KPD im Widerstand*, p. 107.

[100]*Illegalität-Kerker-Exil*, pp. 106–115.

[101]Interview with the late Fritz Sbozny, 21 April 1971.

[102]Pieck gave the number as 35 in a report to the ECCI in November 1933 – see *BzG*, 4/1982, p. 490; in his opening report to the Brussels Conference he gave a total of 37 dailies, including local editions – see Mammach, *Die Brüsseler Konferenz der KPD*, p. 69.

[103]Erich Glückauf, editor of the Lower Rhine District paper, *Freiheit*, took over the political secretaryship in May 1933 when Lambert Horn was moved to Berlin.

[104]See Karl-Egon Lönne, 'Thesen zum publizistischen Tageskampf der KPD gegen den Faschismus. Die "Rote Fahne" – Zentralorgan der KPD' in *Gesellschaftliche Beiträge zur Marxschen Theorie*, Vol. 6, 1976, pp. 242–91; M. Pikarski and G. Uebel, *Antifaschistische Widerstand*; Pikarski and Uebel, *Die KPD lebt*; Jürgen Stroech, *Die illegale Presse. Eine Waffe im Kampf gegen den deutschen Faschismus* (Diss. IML, Berlin, 1974; shortened, printed, version: Leipzig, 1979); Stroech, 'Zur Herstellung und Verbreitung der illegalen *Rote Fahne* 1933 bis 1939' in *BzG*, 1/1977, pp. 81–91; Liselotte Maas, *Handbuch der deutschen Exilpresse* (Munich/Vienna: Carl Hauser Verlag, 1976).

[105]See Stroech in *BzG*, 1/1977, p. 82; also Duhnke, op. cit., p. 117.

[106]Duhnke, pp. 116–7.

[107]The 'Black Forest' pamphlet, of which a copy is included in a pocket of Pikarski and Uebel's book, contained an appeal by Dolores Ibarruri for aid to Republican Spain. For a full treatment of disguised pamphlets and brochures, see Heinz Gittig, *Illegale antifaschistische Tarnschriften, 1933–1945* (Leipzig: VEB Bibliographisches Institut, 1972).

[108]Duhnke, op. cit., p. 116, note 67.
[109]Ibid.
[110]'Der deutsche Arbeiterwiderstand 1933–1945' in *das parlament* (supplement), B 28–29/79, 14 July 1979, p. 28.
[111]Duhnke, op. cit., p. 117.
[112]Peukert, *Die KPD im Widerstand*, p. 189.
[113]The paper produced by the exiled SPD for clandestine circulation in Germany, *Sozialistische Aktion*, is said at its peak to have been produced in 30,000 copies (*BzG*, 1/1977, p. 91); it ceased publication in 1938.
[114]Duhnke, op. cit., p. 117.
[115]Ibid., pp. 117–8.
[116]*BzG*, 4/1978, pp. 529–30.
[117]J. Stroech, 'Zur Herstellung und Verbreitung der illegalen *Rote Fahne*, 1933–1939' (*BzG*, 1/1977, pp. 89–90).
[118]Ibid. pp. 86 ff.
[119]Stroech, ibid., pp. 87–9.
[120]Stroech (*BzG*, 1/1977, p. 91) gives the print of RF as 300,000 in March 1933; 100,000 in July/August 1933; then 52,000 until 1935 and subsequently 30,000.
[121]Stroech in *BzG*, 1/1977, p. 88; also Peukert, *Die KPD im Widerstand*, pp. 184–6.
[122]Peukert, p. 186; for a local leaflet said to have been distributed in some 20,000 copies, see H-P. Görgen, *Düsseldorf und der Nationalsozialismus*, p. 43.
[123]In March 1935, for example, Hans Knodt was superseded as editor of *Rote Fahne* by Alexander Abusch (*BzG*, 2/1979, p. 265).
[124]Cf. the leaflet of July 1934, printed in Solingen and containing the text of a resolution of the Central Committee, proclaiming: 'All power to the Councils [i.e. Soviets] – Long Live Soviet Germany'; Peukert, *Die KPD im Widerstand*, p. 200; Vietzke, *Brüsseler Konferenz*, p. 252.
[125]'Kommunismus – der einzige Ausweg! Das soziale und nationale Befreiungsprogramm der Werktätigen Deutschlands. Aufruf des ZK der KPD' (May 1934). Vietzke, *Brüsseler Konferenz*, p. 252.
[126]This tiny booklet is included in the pocket of Pikarski and Uebel's *Antifaschistischer Widerstand*.
[127]Probably Wilmersdorf and Zehlendorf. Originals in IML/ZPA I 2/8/29.
[128]*GddA*, Vol. 5; Hans Teubner, 'Der deutsche Freiheitssender 29,8 als Führungsorgan der KPD im antifaschistischen Kampf' in *Militärwesen* 9, 1965, pp. 176–88.

Chapter 6. A Closer Look

[1]Rheinmetall-Borsig AG, for example, soon to play an important part in the Nazi re-armament programme.
[2]Figures from H.P. Görgen, op. cit., p. 244.
[3]Ibid., p. 35. This was in the Phönix-Rheinrohr-Werke (steel tubes).
[4]Görgen (p. 36) gives 350 as the number of KPD and SPD officials arrested on or immediately after 28 February. Most of them will have been Communists. By

4 March it was reported that 1,000 leading Communists had been arrested in the Düsseldorf administrative county (*Regierungsbezirk*) (*Essener Volkszeitung*, quoted by H-J. Steinberg, *Widerstand und Verfolgung in Essen 1933–1945*, Schriftenreihe des Forschungsinstituts der Friedrich-Ebert-Stiftung [Hanover: Verlag für Literatur und Zeitgeschehen, 1969] p. 38.)

[5]Friedrich Fränken, then a full-time functionary in the District, told the author (27 December 1970) that very few convinced Communists went over. He could only remember two of any prominence, both Sub-district leaders. See also Peukert, *Die KPD im Widerstand*, p. 107.

[6]Author's interview with Frau Luise Paul, 17 April 1971; obituary brochure, 1962.

[7]280, according to the contemporary Communist leaflet, quoted in Görgen, op. cit., p. 42. See also Karl Schabrod (ed), *Widerstand gegen Flick und Florian. Düsseldorfer Antifaschisten über ihren Widerstand 1933–1945* (Frankfurt-am-Main: Röderberg Verlag, 1978), p. 14 (referred to hereafter as *Flick und Florian*).

[8]For this pamphlet see Schabrod, *Widerstand an Rhein und Ruhr 1933–1945* (Düsseldorf: Landesvorstand der VVN, 1969), pp. 26–7; Görgen, pp. 42–3. The title page and pages 1 and 2 are reproduced in *Flick und Florian*, pp. 76–9.

[9]*Das Kreuz auf der Heide*. See *Widerstand an Rhein und Ruhr*, pp. 25–26; *Flick und Florian*, pp. 67, 81, where the print run is said to have amounted to 20,000 copies; also VVN Dü 1567.

[10]GStA Hamm, OJ 779/33, fos. 1–8.

[11]Text and commentary by Günter Plum, headed: 'Die KPD in der Illegalität. Rechenschaftsbericht einer Bezirksleitung aus dem Jahre 1934' in *Vierteljahreshefte für Zeitgeschichte* No. 97, pp. 219–235.

[12]*BzG*, 5/1978, pp. 697–700.

[13]Plum, op. cit., p. 221.

[14]Phönix-Röhrenwerke. Mannesmann also produced steel tubes. Rheinmetall produced railway engines and wagons; it acquired the Berlin firm Borsig in 1933.

[15]Plum, op. cit., p. 234.

[16]Ibid., pp. 334–335.

[17]For an account of KPD resistance in this ward, 1933–34, see Allan Merson, 'Erfolgreiche Arbeit in Friedrichstadt' in *Flick und Florian*, pp. 107–12.

[18]GStA Hamm, 6 OJs 133/34 Becker, pp. 1–27; VVN Dü 845 (pp. 1–3).

[19]Ludwig Koerner, in an interview of 31 August 1963 (VVN Dü 1509).

[20]GStA Hamm, 6 OJ 133/134 Becker.

[21]VVN Dü 797, 1509.

[22]In an interview with K. Schabrod (VVN Dü 845); see also L. Koerner in VVN Dü 797.

[23]For the text of these pamphlets, see VVN Dü 1119; for Barth's recollections, ibid, 971.

[24]Above p. 131

[25]GStA Hamm, OJ 741/34, Felix, P. und Genossen, pp. 1–177.

[26]GStA Hamm, OJ 133/34 Becker H., deposition of 13 November 1934.

[27]Ibid.

[28]*Flick und Florian*, p. 120.

[29]For a similar case see GStA, OJ 713/34, W. Schmitz und Genossen.

[30]Alwin Ramme, *Der Sicherheitsdienst der SS* (Deutsche Akademie der Wissenschaften zu Berlin: Deutscher Militärverlag, 1969), pp. 45, 274.
[31]GStA Hamm, OJ 713/34 Schmitz.
[32]Klara Schneider: see GStA Hamm, 6 OJs 560/35.
[33]*Der rote Grossvater erzählt. Berichte und Erzählungen von Veteranen der Arbeiterbewegung aus der Zeit von 1914 bis 1945* (Frankfurt-am-Main: Fischer, Taschenbuch Verlag, 1974), pp. 137–63.
[34]*Es war ein langer Weg* (Cologne: Komet Verlag, 1947; 2nd edition, Singen: Volks Verlag, 1948).
[35]Above, Chapter 4, p. 89.
[36]Rudolf Goguel, 'Nach dem KZ – weiter in der Gewerkschaftsarbeit,' in *Flick und Florian*, pp. 112–22.
[37]Ibid.
[38]Peukert, *Die KPD im Widerstand*, p. 126, citing IML/ZPA St 3/40/111, Blatt 694 f.
[39]Schabrod, *Flick und Florian*, pp. 93–4.
[40]*Deutsche Widerstandskämpfer 1933–1945. Biographien und Briefe* (Berlin: Dietz, 1970), Vol. 1, pp. 500–2; *Flick und Florian*, pp. 39–40.
[41]Hermann Laupsien, 'Sportler gegen Missbrauch der Olympiade' in *Flick und Florian*, pp. 95–107.
[42]*Die Illegalen*: a play by Günther Weisenborn (Leipzig: Reclam, 1955).
[43]*Nur ein Mensch* (Berlin: Dietz, 1961) pp. 90–1.
[44]Jürgen Kuczynski, op. cit., p. 271.
[45]Peukert, *Die KPD im Widerstand*, pp. 153–5.
[46]Ibid., p. 153; also p. 428.

Chapter 7. A Losing Battle

[1]*Die KPD im Widerstand*, p. 145.
[2]By the murder of Röhm, Schleicher and others.
[3]On 9 June 1934: see above, Chapter 6, note 30.
[4]*Documents on Nazism*, p. 270.
[5]The first authentic account was Hans Beimler's *Im Mörderlager Dachau* (Moscow, August 1933). Beimler, after 14 days in the camp, had escaped on 9 May.
[6]'Die Industriestadt Augsburg' in *Bayern in der NS-Zeit*, Vol. III, pp. 168, 199.
[7]Ibid., p. 173.
[8]*Die KPD im Widerstand*, p. 150.
[9]Ibid.
[10]Ibid.
[11]Ibid.
[12]Ibid.
[13]Hetzer, op. cit., p. 142.
[14]Ibid.
[15]*Die KPD im Widerstand*, p. 159.
[16]Ibid., p. 148.

[17]For examples, see Klaus Mammach, *Die deutsche antifaschistische Widerstandsbewegung, 1933–1939* (Berlin: Dietz, 1974), pp. 80–2.
[18]Ibid., for written exchanges between Pieck and Ulbricht for the KPD and the left-socialists, Aufhäuser and Böchel. For a joint proclamation of KPD and SPD district leaders in Hessen on 5 September 1934, see *GddA*, Vol. 5, pp. 465–7, document No. 19.
[19]For this much disputed episode, see: Duhnke, *Die KPD von 1933 bis 1945*, pp. 137–62; Edinger, *German Exile Politics*, pp. 148–53; Vietzke, Brüsseler Konferenz, pp. 131–62, pp. 182 ff.
[20]Pikarski and Uebel, *Antifaschistische Widerstandskampf*, No. 37.
[21]Ibid., No. 47.
[22]For co-operation between Communist and Catholic youth leaders in 1933–35, see: Berta Karg, 'Mein Kampf gegen die braune Diktatur' in *Widerstand und Verweigerung*, pp. 102–10; also Peukert, op. cit., pp. 246–9.
[23]Merson, 'High Treason in Düsseldorf' (MS), Chapter X, pp. 30–34.
[24]Peukert, *Die KPD im Widerstand*, p. 225.

Chapter 8. The Crisis of Policy

[1]HDG Hertel, 0, 23040, pp. 121, 168; R. Goguel, *Es war ein langer Weg*. For the KPO, Hermann Weber, 'Die KPD in der Illegalität in Löwenthal and von zur Mühlen (eds), *Widerstand und Verweigerung*, p. 94.
[2]Otto Winzer, *Zwölf Jahre Kampf gegen Faschismus und Krieg* (Berlin: Dietz, 1957), p. 53. Dimitrov's final speech to the court is reprinted in *Report to the 7th Congress of the Communist International, 1935* (London: Red Star Press, 1975) pp. 17–38. See also *BzG*, 1/1965, p. 613.
[3]The letter is printed in *BzG*, 2/1963, pp. 282–4; also (extracts) in *GddA*, Vol. 5, pp. 462–3; for comment, see Vietzke, *Brüsseler Konferenz*, p. 119 ff.
[4]'Kommunismus – der einzige Ausweg! Das soziale und nationale Befreiungsprogramm der Werktätigen Deutschlands', *Aufruf des Zentralkomitees der Kommunistischen Partei Deutschlands* (Mai 1934), Printed in *Rundschau* (Basel), No. 36, pp. 1405 ff.
[5]Duhnke, *Die KPD von 1933 bis 1945*, p. 90.
[6]Ibid.
[7]Sozialistische Arbeiterpartei: a left-wing group which had broken away from the SPD in 1931.
[8]Vietzke, p. 124.
[9]Ibid., pp. 125–130.
[10]Resolution of the Central Committee of the KPD, 1 August 1934, printed in extract form in *GddA*, Vol. 5, document No. 18, pp. 463 ff., where the source is given as *Rundschau* (Basel), 1934, No. 45, p. 1867.
[11]*BzG*, 4/1965, p. 617; *Brüsseler Konferenz*, pp. 134–5, 42n. Text of the joint appeal, dated 5 September 1934, printed in Biernat et al., op. cit., pp. 50–2; extracts in *GddA*, Vol. 5, pp. 465–7.
[12]W. Pieck, 'Aktionseinheit gegen den Faschismus. Ein Feind: ein gemeinsamer Kampf aller Antifaschisten' in *Rundschau*, 1934, No. 48, pp. 2021; W. Ulbricht,

'Der Prager Emigrantenvorstand der SPD und die Ereignisse des 30 Juni,' in *Rundschau*, 6 September 1934, reprinted in Ulbricht, *Zur Geschichte der deutschen Arbeiterbewegung*, Vol. 2, pp. 31–5. Ulbricht, on the instructions of the Politburo, had held preliminary discussions with Aufhäuser in Prague in August.

[13]Duhnke, pp. 143–4; Vietzke *Brüsseler Konferenz*, pp. 139–41, 149–50; for Ulbricht's view, see his article, 'Schmiedet die Aktionseinheit gegen den Hitlerfaschismus' in *Rundschau*, No. 55, 18 October 1934, reprinted in *Zur Geschichte der deutschen Arbeiterbewegung*, Vol. II, pp. 36–41.

[14]Vietzke, op. cit. pp. 149–53.

[15]*BzG*, 4/1975, pp. 638–40.

[16]*Rundschau*, 8 November 1934, pp. 2588–9., cited in *BzG*, 4/1965, p. 620.

[17]*BzG*, 4/1965, p. 619.

[18]*BzG*, 5/1978, p. 700. Document of 8 December 1934 headed 'Richtlinien zur Durchführung des Beschlusses des P[olit] B[uros] über die Diskussion zum 7 Weltkongress der Komintern'.

[19]'Der Weg zur Aktionseinheit' in W. Ulbricht, *Zur Geschichte der deutschen Arbeiterbewegung*, Vol. II, (Berlin: Dietz 1963), pp. 50–6.

[20]Among these were Dimitrov, Togliatti, Manuilski and Wan Min. The KPD was represented by all the Politburo members and some members of the underground Landesleitung, the Berlin leadership and the Communist Youth League. Vietzke, *Brüsseler Konferenz*, pp. 164–5.

[21]*BzG*, 4/1965, p. 621. See also Vietzke, pp. 163 ff, 175.

[22]*GddA*, Vol. 5, p. 143; Peukert, *Die KPD im Widerstand*, pp. 236–40, 302–4.

[23]Extracts in *GddA*, Vol. 5, pp. 468–71.

[24]Duhnke, op. cit., p. 191; Peukert, *Die KPD im Widerstand*, pp. 224–5.

[25]*GddA*, Vol. 5, pp. 96–7; L.J. Edinger, *German Exile Politics*, pp. 155, 168.

[26]*BzG*, 4/1965, pp. 623–4; Vietzke, pp. 176–89.

[27]On the frontier conferences at Easter and Whitsuntide, see Vietzke, *Brüsseler Konferenz*. 176–89; *BzG*, 5/1965, pp. 831–3.

[28]The Seventh World Congress lasted from 25 July to 20 August 1935, the KPD's 'Brussels Conference' from 3 to 15 October following. On the former, see Degras Vol. III, pp. 350–78; a full account of the latter is in Klaus Mammach, *Die Brüsseler Konferenz der Kommunistischen Partei Deutschlands* (Frankfurt-am-Main: Verlag Marxistische Blätter, 1975).

[29]Details in Mammach, op. cit., also *GddA*, Vol. 5, pp. 113–128. For a non-Communist interpretation: Hermann Weber, 'Die KPD in der Illegalität' in *Widerstand und Verweigerung*, pp. 90–3.

[30]Togliatti's speech is printed in Mammach, op. cit., pp. 511–31.

[31]Knöchel's speech is not included in Mammach's selection, but extracts are printed in *BzG*, 5/1965, pp. 894–6, and it is mentioned in *GddA*, Vol. 5, p. 117.

[32]The new Central Committee was to comprise fifteen full members (Anton Ackermann, Paul Bertz, Franz Dahlem, Leo Flieg, Wilhelm Florin, Walter Hähnel, Fritz Heckert, Paul Merker, Willi Münzenberg, Wilhelm Pieck, Elli Schmidt, Ernst Thälmann, Walter Ulbricht, Herbert Wehner, Heinrich Wiatrek) and three candidate members (Wilhelm Knöchel, Wilhelm Kowalski, Karl Mewis). The Politburo was to consist of seven full members (Dahlem, Florin, Heckert, Merker, Pieck, Thälmann, Ulbricht) and two candidates

(Ackermann and Wehner). The Operative Leadership for the conduct of the underground struggle, though from outside the Reich, was to consist of Ackermann, Dahlem, Merker, Ulbricht and Wehner, led by Ulbricht. Pieck was elected acting Party chairman during the imprisonment of Thälmann.
[33]For the sector organisation, see Kühnrich, *Die KPD im Kampf*, pp. 91–3; Duhnke, pp. 189–94; Mammach, *Die deutsche antifaschistische Widerstandsbewegung* (Berlin: Dietz, 1974), pp. 128–9.
[34]Mammach, *Die Brüsseler Konferenz der KPD*, pp. 27–42.

Chapter 9. Changing Conditions

[1]For this chapter, see: T.W. Mason, 'Labour in the Third Reich 1933–1939', (*Past and Present*, No. 33, April 1966); also Mason, *Arbeiterklasse und Volksgemeinschaft. Dokumente und Materialien zur deutschen Arbeiterpolitik 1936–1939* (Opladen: Westdeutscher Verlag, 1975) (referred to hereafter as *A und V*).
[2]The monthly total had fallen from 6,013,612 in January 1933 to 2,520,499 in January 1936 and in the following September (usually the month of lowest unemployment) to 1,035,237, then in September 1937 to 469,053 and in September 1938 to 156,000. These figures are from a useful table in Noakes and Pridham (eds), *Documents on Nazism*, p. 383.
[3]Mason, *A und V*, p. 111.
[4]Ibid., p. 112.
[5]Tim Mason, 'Resistance in the Ruhr' in *The Times Literary Supplement*, 7 May 1982, p. 513, quoting Peukert, *Die KPD im Widerstand*.
[6]Johannes Bech *et al.*, *Terror und Hoffnung in Deutschland, 1933–1945* (Hamburg: Rowohlt, 1980), pp. 222 ff.
[7]Mason, *A und V*, p. 114.
[8]Ibid.
[9]*BzG*, 1/1979, p. 81: report from a Dortmund mine, 5 November 1936; G. Hetzer, 'Industriestadt Augsburg' in *Bayern in der NS-Zeit*, Vol. III, pp. 117–9.
[10]Ian Kershaw, 'Alltägliches und Ausseralltägliches: ihre Bedeutung für die Volksmeinung 1933–1939' in D. Peukert and J. Reulecke (eds), *Die Reihen fast geschlossen* (Wuppertal: Peter Hammer Verlag, 1981), p. 283.
[11]Ibid.
[12]Ibid.
[13]Hetzer, op. cit., pp. 131–2.
[14]Hetzer, pp. 115–7, 119–22.
[15]Ibid.
[16]Ibid., pp. 118–9.
[17]Ibid., p. 121.
[18]D. Peukert, *Alltag unterm Nationalsozialismus: Beiträge zum Thema Widerstand*, No. 17 (West Berlin: Informationszentrum, 1981), p. 29.
[19]Mason, *A und V*, p. 110.
[20]An account of the Plan, with Hitler's memorandum and Goering's decree, is in *Documents on Nazism*, pp. 398–411.
[21]Ibid.

[22]In his memoirs Speer remarks that 'in private conversations Hitler indicated that after the experience of 1918 one could not be cautious enough. In order to anticipate any discontent, more effort and money was expended on consumer goods and on military pensions or compensation to women . . . than in countries with democratic government: (*Inside the Third Reich*, London: Sphere Books, 1971). See also Christian Streit, *Keine Kameraden* (Stuttgart: dva, 1978) pp. 191, 193; Mason, *A und V*, p. xxi.
[23]Mason, *A und V*, p. xxi.
[24]*Documents on Nazism*, pp. 398–411; Mason, *A und V*, pp. 124–5.
[25]Mason, *A und V*, pp. 125, 129.
[26]Ludolf Herbst, (*Vierteljahreshefte für Zeitgeschichte*, Vol. 26, 197, pp. 347–92) criticises Mason's concept of a 'general crisis' of the Nazi régime in 1937–39: see especially page 361.
[27]Mason, *A und V*, p. 103.
[28]Ian Kershaw, op. cit., pp. 290–1.

Chapter 10. Resistance in Lower Key

[1]90.76 per cent of the electorate voted for union with Germany.
[2]See *GddA*, Vol. 6, pp. 96–8.
[3]Pieck, *Der neue Weg*, p. 80. For the conference, K. Mammach, *Die Brüsseler Konferenz der KPD*, especially p. 131.
[4]Figures given in Heinz Kühnrich, *Die KPD im Kampf*, p. 58.
[5]Extracts from some of these reports are in *BzG*, 1/1979, pp. 72 ff.
[6]*BzG*, 1/1979, p. 76 (Würtemberg, February 1936).
[7]The division of Berlin District into seven small Districts was reported by Elli Schmidt, returning from the Brussels Conference (*BzG*, 5/1965, pp. 835–6); see also proposed division in Würtemberg (*BzG*, 1/1979, pp. 75–7).
[8]Figure from Duhnke, *Die KPD von 1933 bis 1945*, p. 201, citing Gestapo records.
[9]Figures for 1936–1938 from Duhnke (p. 201), quoting Heinz Schumann, 'Die Behandlung des antifaschistischen Widerstandskampfes in der westdeutschen Geschichtsschreibung' in L. Stern (ed), *Probleme der Geschichte des Zweiten Weltkrieges*, (Berlin: Akademie-Verlag, 1958), p. 343. Mason, *A und V* (p. 123) gives 15,000 for 1936; a figure which may include Social Democrats.
[10]Löwenthal and von zur Mühlen (eds), *Widerstand und Verweigerung*, p. 96; *BzG*, 1/1979, p. 78.
[11]E. Aleff et al., 'Terror und Widerstand 1933–1945. Dokumente aus Deutschland und dem besetzten Europa (West Berlin: 1966), pp. 222–30 (MS).
[12]E.g. *BzG*, 1/1979, p. 83. (Bremen, 14 November 1936).
[13]For proposed conference of representatives of Siemens cells, including Social Democrats, at Easter 1936, see *BzG*, 1/1979, p. 75.
[14]See report from Stuttgart, February 1936 (*BzG*, 1/1979, p. 77).
[15]Peukert, *Die KPD im Widerstand*, p. 273.
[16]Ibid., p. 262.
[17]*BzG*, 1/1979, p. 78.

[18]G. Hetzer, 'Die Industriestadt Augsburg' in *Bayern in der NS-Zeit*, Vol. III, pp. 173–4.

[19]Extracts published so far by Nitzsche and Uebel: *BzG* 4/1978, pp. 528–39 (1933); 5/1978, pp. 691–701 (1933–4); 1/1979, pp. 72–83 (1936); 4/1979, pp. 543–56 (1937).

[20]See above, note 7.

[21]*BzG*, 1/1979, p. 74.

[22]Ibid.

[23]*BzG*, 4/1979, p. 545.

[24]See Luise Kraushaar, *Berliner Kommunisten im Kampf gegen den Faschismus* (Berlin: Dietz, 1981) pp. 74–6 (referred to hereafter as *Berliner Kommunisten*).

[25]Ibid.

[26]Ibid.

[27]*BzG*, 1/1979, p. 78 (report of 10 February 1936).

[28]Ibid.

[29]*BzG*, 4/1979, pp. 548–9.

[30]Ibid., p. 554.

[31]Ibid.

[32]See, for example, *BzG*, 1/1979, p. 72.

[33]Mason, *A und V*, p. 123.

[34]*BzG*, 1/1979, pp. 82–3.

[35]*BzG*, 4/1979, p. 555–6 (1 October 1937).

[36]Peukert, *Die KPD im Widerstand*, p. 288.

[37]See above, Chapter 4, note 61.

[38]J. Bech et al., *Terror und Hoffnung in Deutschland, 1933–1945*, pp. 222–30.

[39]Otto Winzer (*Zwölf Jahre Kampf gegen Faschismus und Krieg*, 1955, pp. 93 f.) briefly surveys the conclusions of Gestapo 'situation reports' for 1935–36. See also report of January 1938 by the Düsseldorf District Gestapo on the illegal 'Marxist' and Communist movement for the year 1937 (BA Koblenz, R. 58 457).

[40]*BzG*, 1/1979, p. 77.

[41]Hetzer, op. cit., pp. 174–5.

[42]*BzG*, 4/1979, pp. 554–5.

[43]*BzG*, 1/1979, pp. 73–4.

[44]Ibid., pp. 74–5.

[45]See Luise Kraushaar, *Berliner Kommunisten*, p. 69.

[46]Ibid. pp. 68–70 for other examples of a Trojan Horse situation.

[47]*BzG*, 1/1979, p. 80 (East Saxony, 31 March 1936).

[48]The result was a genuine political discussion: see *BzG*, 1/1979, p. 82 (Dortmund, 29 October 1936).

[49]*BzG*, 1/1979, pp. 73–5 (January 1936).

[50]*BzG*, 1/1979, p. 73 ('Mix und Genest', end of January 1936).

[51]Schabrod, *Flick und Florian*, pp. 39 f.

[52]See K. Mammach, *Widerstand 1933–1939* (Berlin: Akademie-Verlag, 1984) pp. 171–2.

Chapter 11. Popular Front Politics

[1]See the Resolution of the Brussels Conference: 'Der neue Weg zum gemeinsamen Kampf aller Werktätigen für den Sturz der Hitlerdiktatur' in Mammach, *Die Brüsseler Konferenz der KPD*, p. 610.
[2]L.J. Edinger, op. cit., p. 144.
[3]Ibid., pp. 156–7.
[4]Ulbricht's speech is printed in *BzG*, 1/1963, pp. 75 ff. See also Edinger, pp. 157–9.
[5]See Otto Findeisen, 'Zu den Einheitsfrontverhandlungen am 23 November 1935 in Prag, *BzG*, 4/1966, pp. 676–94; Edinger, pp. 157–9.
[6]See *GddA*, Vol. 5, pp. 144–5.
[7]Facsimile in Pikarski and Uebel (eds), *Antifaschistische Widerstandskampf*, No. 74. Text (without signatures) also in *GddA*, Vol. 5, pp. 489–91.
[8]K. Mammach (ed), *Die Berner Konferenz der KPD (30 Januar – 1 Februar 1939)*, (Berlin: Dietz. 1974), p. 29.
[9]See *GddA*, Vol. 5, pp. 148–9; also pp. 482–4, where extracts of the Guidelines are printed as document No. 29.
[10]*GddA*, Vol. 5, p. 178.
[11]See Hans Teubner, *Exilland Schweiz, 1933–1945* (Berlin: Dietz, 1975), pp. 67–73.
[12]Peukert, *Die KPD im Widerstand*, p. 253.
[13]Mammach, *Die Brüsseler Konferenz der KPD*, pp. 21, 28–9.
[14]Peukert, op. cit., pp. 253, 342 ff.
[15]Peukert, pp. 308–11.
[16]*Bergarbeitermitteilungen.*
[17]*Bergarbeiterzeitung.*
[18]Peukert, op. cit., pp. 309–10.
[19]For an account of the proceedings, see Klaus Mammach (ed), *Die Berner Konferenz der KPD.*
[20]Ibid., p. 83.
[21]See Erich Paterna, 'Zum Kampf der KPD gegen die Vorbereitung des zweiten Weltkrieges durch das Naziregime (Februar bis August 1939)', *BzG*, 4/1964, p. 589.

Chapter 12. The First Phase, 1939–41

[1]For GDR views see Klaus Mammach and Gerhard Nitzsche, 'Zum antifaschistischen Kampf der KPD in den Jahren von 1939 bis 1941', *BzG*, 6/1971, pp. 911–35; Heinz Kühnrich, 'Einige Fragen des Kampfes der KPD in der ersten Periode des zweiten Weltkrieges', *BzG*, 1/1982, pp. 25–39.
[2]For a detailed account by a KPD leader, see Franz Dahlem, *Am Vorabend des zweiten Weltkrieges. Erinnerungen* (Berlin: Dietz, 1977) Vol. 2, pp. 335–439.
[3]See, for example, Dahlem, Vol. 2, pp. 349, 351; Duhnke, *Die KPD von 1933 bis 1945*, p. 334; Karl Mewis, *Im Auftrag der Partei*, p. 214; J. Kuczynski, *Memoiren*, p. 354.
[4]The original 'Declaration of the KPD on the conclusion of the Non-Aggression

Pact between the Soviet Union and Germany' was published in the Basel *Rundschau*, No. 46 (variously dated 27 and 31 August) and is reproduced in Dahlem, op. cit., Vol. 2, pp. 357–61; extracts in *GddA*, Vol. 5, doc. no. 56, pp. 520–1; also in T. Pirker, *Komintern und Faschismus* (Stuttgart: dva, 1965) doc. no. 34, pp. 200–1.

[5]Dahlem, Vol. 2, pp. 355–6.

[6]'Eine erfolgreiche Friedenstat' (Dahlem, Vol. 2., p. 357).

[7]Translated from Dahlem, Vol. 2, p. 358.

[8]See Duhnke, *Die KPD von 1933 bis 1945*, pp. 337–351.

[9]*GddA*, Vol. 5, No. 59, pp. 524–5; Kühnrich, 'Einige Fragen. . .' in *BzG*, 1/1982, p. 28; Peukert *Die KPD im Widerstand*, pp. 327–8.

[10]*GddA*, Vol. 5, No. 64, pp. 530–1; also *BzG*, 6/1971, p. 912.

[11]*GddA*, Vol. 5, No. 66, pp. 532–5 (extracts); *Die KPD im Widerstand*, p. 328.

[12]Dahlem, Vol. 2, pp. 376–409.

[13]On the 'Platform' see also: *BzG*, 1/1982, pp. 34–5; *BzG*, 6/1971, pp. 912–3.

[14]See *Die KPD im Widerstand*, pp. 326–30.

[15]For the reactions of the socialist groups to the German-Soviet Pact, see Edinger, *German Exile Politics*, pp. 222–8.

[16]T.W. Mason, 'Labour in the Third Reich, 1933–39' in *Past and Present*, No. 33, April 1966; also above, Chapter 9.

[17]Mason, 'Labour in the Third Reich', p. 139. Extracts in Mason, *A und V*, No. 185, pp. 1077–83 and of subordinate regulations in Nos. 187–202, pp. 1086–1135.

[18]Mason, 'Labour in the Third Reich', pp. 139–40.

[19]Ibid.

[20]Ibid, p. 140.

[21]Ibid, pp. 140–1.

[22]Ibid.

[23]Ibid. Fuller details in Mason, *A und V*, No. 235, pp. 1212, 'Verordnung über den Arbeitsschutz'.

[24]T.W. Mason, 'Arbeiteropposition im nationalsozialistischen Deutschland' in D. Peukert and J. Reulecke (eds), *Die Reihen fast geschlossen* (Wuppertal: Peter Hammer Verlag, 1981), p. 309.

[25]Ibid., p. 312.

[26]Martin Broszat, 'Nationalsozialistische Konzentrationslager 1933–1945' in M. Broszat (ed), *Anatomie des SS-Staates*, Vol. 2, p. 92 ff. (Munich: dtv, 1967).

[27]H. Kühnrich, *Die KPD im Kampf*, p. 147.

[28]*The Nemesis of Power* (London: Macmillan, 1961), p. 481n.

[29]*Germans Against Hitler* (London: Hutchinson, 1964) p. 207.

[30]Now Lord Dacre.

[31]In his foreword to Prittie's *Germans Against Hitler*, p. 13. The remark may refer to the alleged handing over of German Communists by the NKVD to the Gestapo in 1939–40 (Duhnke, pp. 347–8 n. 175, referring to the memoirs of Wehner and Buber-Neumann.) There is no evidence of any political agreement by which the KPD would acquire any scope for activity in Germany.

[32]Duhnke, pp. 336, 350; Peukert, *Die KPD im Widerstand*, p. 328.

[33]Duhnke, pp. 457–8.

[34]*GddA*, Vol. 5, pp. 244 ff.

[35]See Kühnrich, *Die KPD im Kampf*, p. 144. A facsimile is reproduced in Pikarski and Uebel, *Antifaschistische Widerstandskampf*, doc. no. 138; original in ZPA/IML St3/1047.
[36]For Kapelle (1913–41) see *Die KPD im Kampf*, p. 144; Luise Kraushaar in Karl Heinz Biernat et al. (eds), *Deutsche Widerstandskämpfer* (Berlin: Dietz, 1970), Vol. I, p. 474.
[37]Extracts in *GddA*, Vol. 5., No. 68, pp. 537–8.
[38]Ibid., No. 70, pp. 539–41.
[39]*Die KPD im Kampf*, p. 172.
[40]See *GddA*, Vol. 5, No. 74, pp. 545–547.
[41]Above, Chapter 10.
[42]Luise Kraushaar, *Berliner Kommunisten*, pp. 100 ff.
[43]Hetzer, 'Die Industriestadt Augsburg' in *Bayern in der NZ-Zeit*, Vol. 3, pp. 175–6.
[44]K. Mammach, *Die Berner Konferenz der KPD*, pp. 144–5; *Die KPD im Kampf*, pp. 131, 133.
[45]Above, note 10; *GddA*, Vol. 5, doc. no. 64.
[46]Above, note 11. The draft was confirmed by ECCI on 30 December (*Die KPD im Kampf*, p. 158).
[47]Wehner had been a member of the underground *Landesleitung* in 1935 and had been elected to the Central Committee at the Brussels Conference and to the Politburo as a candidate member at the Bern Conference.
[48]Glückauf had been Political Secretary of the Lower Rhine District in 1933–34 and later editor of the 29,8 short-wave broadcasts.
[49]I.e. soon after the German occupation of Denmark on 9 April 1940.
[50]Her other task had been to take KPD policy statements to Heinz Kapelle and his group (Mammach, *Widerstand 1933–1939*, pp. 197–8).
[51]He was arrested in December 1939 and executed on 25 July 1941.
[52]He was executed 8 September 1943.
[53]He and Müller were sentenced to life imprisonment.
[54]*Berliner Kommunisten*, p. 126.
[55]For Uhrig's organisation see *Berliner Kommunisten*, passim.
[56]Grasse (1910–42) was a book-printer.
[57]On Römer see *Berliner Kommunisten*, pp. 164–6; Duhnke, *Die KPD von 1933 bis 1945*, pp. 460–1.
[58]*Die KPD im Widerstand*, p. 336.
[59]*Berliner Kommunisten*, pp. 146–51.
[60]Above, p. 220.
[61]Merker reached Mexico, where he played a leading part in founding the 'Free Germany' movement. On emigration to the USA, see J. Kuczynski, *Memoiren*, p. 368; for Instructors *Die KPD im Widerstand*, p. 337; E. Zorn, *BzG*, 2/1965, pp. 298 ff.
[62]The relations of Schulze-Boysen and the KPD are discussed in Duhnke, pp. 464–8; also in *Berliner Kommunisten*, pp. 139–44.
[63]For polemic about the extent to which anti-Nazi activities were directed by the KPD leadership, see Mammach and Nitzsche in *BzG*, 6/1971, pp. 932–4; also Duhnke, pp. 366–8.
[64]Hetzer, in *Bayern in der NS-Zeit*, Vol. III, pp. 175–6.

[65]*Berliner Kommunisten*, pp. 145, 278, also above, p. 187.
[66]Edward L. Homze, *Foreign Labor in Nazi Germany* (Princeton New Jersey: Princeton University Press, 1967), p. 37.
[67]*Berliner Kommunisten*, pp. 151–5, 160; Mason, *A und V*, p. 111.
[68]*Berliner Kommunisten*, pp. 142–4.
[69]For example, there are grounds for thinking that Colonel Hans Oster conveyed detailed warnings of Hitler's aggressive intentions to the Scandinavian and Dutch, and possibly also the Yugoslav, governments; see Gerhard Ritter, *The German Resistance* (London: Allen & Unwin, 1958), p. 167.
[70]When war began, the number of women employed fell, but their proportion in the labour force rose: see Ludwig Eiber, 'Frauen in der Kriegsindustrie, Arbeitsbedingungen, Lebensumstände und Protestverhalten' in *Bayern in der NS-Zeit*, Vol. III, pp. 569–87.
[71]D. Peukert, 'Protest und Widerstand von Jugendlichen im Dritten Reich' in Löwenthal and von zur Mühlen (eds), *Widerstand und Verweigerung*, pp. 177–201.
[72]H. Boberach (ed), *Meldungen aus dem Reich* (West Berlin: Luchterhand, 1965), pp. 20, 23, etc.
[73]*Berliner Kommunisten*, p. 119.

Chapter 13. Inner-German Leaderships, 1941–43.

[1]Figures from Duhnke, *Die KPD von 1933 bis 1945*, p. 457n.
[2]RSHA statistics quoted by Peukert, *Die KPD im Widerstand*, p. 335 from: BA, R 58, Bd. 198, Bl. 68–72, Bd. 200, Bl. 58–62.; Kühnrich, *Die KPD im Kampf*, p. 181.
[3]Peukert on the other hand argues that if a case had any recognised political background, it would be placed in a distinctively political category (Ibid., p. 335).
[4]There were 89 Berlin factory groups in Uhrig's connection at the beginning of 1942, according to Kraushaar, *Berliner Kommunisten*, p. 278. See above, Chapter 12.
[5]Ibid., op. cit., pp. 173 ff.
[6]Ibid., p. 192.
[7]Ibid., p. 194.
[8]Ibid., pp. 147, 153, 185.
[9]Ibid. pp. 164–9.
[10]Ibid., pp. 181–2.
[11]The earliest number to have survived is of the first half of October 1941 (Ibid., p. 214).
[12]For a facsimile of this issue, see *Berliner Kommunisten*, pp. 208–13; also Pikarski and Uebel (eds), *Antifaschistische Widerstandskampf*, doc. no. 154.
[13]Kraushaar, *Berliner Kommunisten*, p. 221.
[14]See Fabian von Schlabrendorff, *Offiziere gegen Hitler* (Frankfurt-am-Main: Fischer, 1959) pp. 76–7, referred to in Duhnke, pp. 460–1.
[15]See Charlotte Bischoff, 'Die Innere Front – ein Beispiel des Kampfes der deutschen Arbeiterklasse unter Führung der KPD gegen Militarismus und Faschismus' in *Der deutsche Imperialismus und der zweite Weltkrieg* (Berlin: Rütten

& Loening, 1959), Vol. 4, pp. 415–6. Facsimile of number dated August 1942 in Pikarski and Uebel, op. cit., doc. no. 170 [variously described as issue no. 1 (Kraushaar and Pikarski/Uebel) and issue no. 15 (Bischoff and Biernat/ Kraushaar)].

[16]Bischoff, loc. cit., pp. 415–6, 418.

[17]For Guddorf, see *Berliner Kommunisten*, pp. 134–6; Ursula Puls, *Die Bästlein-Jacob-Abshagen-Gruppe* (Berlin: Dietz, 1959), pp. 187–91.

[18]See Karl-Heinz Biernat and Luise Kraushaar, *Die Schulze-Boysen-Harnack Organisation im antifaschistischen Kampf* (Berlin: Dietz, 1970, also above, Chapter 12, pp. 224–5.

[19]For titles of AGIS pamphlets see Bischoff, loc. cit., p. 418.

[20]Facsimile in Biernat and Kraushaar, op. cit., p. 160; also Duhnke, p. 470; and above Chapter 12, p. 229.

[21]See Duhnke, pp. 465–6.

[22]On this controversial topic see, e.g., Biernat and Kraushaar, op. cit., pp. 37–41; *Berliner Kommunisten*, pp. 142–4; on the other side, Duhnke, pp. 457, 467–9, 472–9.

[23]See Dr Elfriede Paul's autobiograhy, *Ein Sprechzimmer der Roten Kapelle*, (Berlin: Militärverlag der DDR, 1981), pp. 113–20.

[24]Biernat and Kraushaar give brief biographies of 52 members of the group.

[25]Kraushaar (*Berliner Kommunisten*, pp. 14, 15, 148) and *GddA*, Vol. 5 (pp. 313–4) describe Baum as a long-standing member of the Young Communist League; but Duhnke (pp. 479–80) questions this.

[26]For a facsimile of the title page, see Pikarski and Uebel, *Antifaschistische Widerstandskampf*, No. 156. This was the second monthly issue; it ran to fourteen sides.

[27]Duhnke, p. 480; also M. Pikarski, *Jugend im Berliner Widerstand* (Berlin. 1978).

[28]Duhnke, pp. 480–1; *Berliner Kommunisten*, pp. 224–6, where the list of names noticeably omits Havemann.

[29]Ursula Puls, *Die Bästlein-Jacob-Abshagen-Gruppe*, pp. 50–100; Ursel Hochmuth and Gertrud Meyer, *Streiflichter aus dem Hamburger Widerstand 1933–1945. Berichte und Dokumente*. (Frankfurt: Röderberg Verlag. 1969), pp. 341–86.

[30]For Eifler and Fellendorf, see Duhnke, pp. 367 ff, 485; for Eifler *GddA*, Vol. 5, p. 303.

[31]Duhnke, pp. 462–3; *GddA*, Vol. 5, pp. 283, 432.

[32]Facsimile of title page dated December 1941 is reproduced in Pikarski and Uebel, document no. 157. Five numbers appeared between the beginning of October 1941 and beginning of 1942. See also Max Oppenheimer, *Der Fall Vorbote* (Frankfurt: Röderberg Verlag, 1969).

[33]See, for example, the SD report of 22 January 1942 printed in Noakes and Pridham (eds) *Documents on Nazism*, pp. 660–2, under the heading: 'Disillusionment and concern among the population'.

[34]See Barbara Mausbach-Bromberger, *Arbeiterwiderstand in Frankfurt-am-Main gegen den Faschismus 1933–1945* (Frankfurt: Röderberg, 1976).

[35]The *Volkssender* began broadcasting in German from the USSR on 10 September 1941, as the voice of the KPD. See L. Kraushaar, 'Zur Tätigkeit und Wirkung des deutschen Volkssenders' in *BzG*, 1/1964, pp. 116–33; R. Gyptner in *BzG*, 5/1964, pp. 881 ff.

[36]Duhnke, pp. 366–7.
[37]*GddA*, Vol. 5, pp. 223, 282; *Die KPD im Widerstand*, p. 335–6.
[38]He was later expelled from the Party for allegedly betraying it in the interrogations following his arrest. Even before his arrest he had disagreed sharply over policy with other leading members of the KPD *émigré* colony in Denmark: see Mewis, *Im Auftrag der Partei*, pp. 268–9; *GddA*, Vol. 5, p. 313; Peukert, *Die KPD im Widerstand*, p. 342.
[39]*GddA*, Vol. 5, p. 308; *Berliner Kommunisten*, pp. 224, 231–2. Her safe arrival in Berlin was reported by the insertion of an agreed advertisement in the Nazi paper *Völkischer Beobachter* (Mewis, p. 280).
[40]This allegation is made by Mewis in *Im Auftrag der Partei*, p. 319. See also, ibid, pp. 282, 315–320.
[41]Duhnke, p. 358; *Die KPD im Widerstand*, p. 342n.
[42]Duhnke, pp. 367–8, 485.
[43]Ibid., p. 367.
[44]Ibid.
[45]*Die KPD im Widerstand*, p. 336.
[46]Ibid., pp. 336–7, 339, 343.
[47]*Berliner Kommunisten*, p. 276; also pp. 130–131, 232–233, 248–249, 257. But see Peukert's warning: *Die KPD im Widerstand*, p. 340.
[48]Beuttel covered parts of South and South-Western Germany, including Cologne, where he was executed in 1944.
[49]A facsimile of the first page is reproduced in Pikarski and Uebel, document no. 178. It was of 6 pages and circulated in the Ruhr district. Addressed to national-socialist working people.
[50]See facsimile of the front page of the final issue in Pikarski and Uebel, doc. no. 180. Several issues were circulated in Berlin and the Rhine-Ruhr region from the beginning of 1942 to January 1943.
[51]*Die KPD im Widerstand*, pp. 348 f.
[52]Ibid., 345n, 346.
[53]'Friedensmanifest an das deutsche Volk und an die deutsche Wehrmacht . . . vom 6 Dezember 1942' in *Zur Geschichte der deutschen antifaschistischen Widerstandsbewegung 1933 bis 1945*. (Berlin: Verlag des Ministeriums der Nationalen Verteidigung, 1958) pp. 174–180. Extracts also in *GddA*, Vol. 5, doc. no. 91.
[54]*Die KPD im Widerstand*, p. 352n.
[55]Ibid., p. 337.
[56]Estimates from Duhnke, p. 461; *GddA*, Vol. 5, p. 309; Günther Weisenborn, *Der lautlose Aufstand* (Hamburg: Rowohlt, 1953), p. 159.
[57]*Berliner Kommunisten*, pp. 278–9.
[58]Ibid., p. 234.

Chapter 14. 'Free Germany' and the Generals' Plot, 1943–44.

[1]Noakes and Pridham, *Documents on Nazism*, p. 643; A.S. Milward, *The German Economy at War* (London: Athlone Press, 1965); Bleyer et al., *Lehrbuch der*

deutschen Geschichte, Vol. 12, 1939–45 (Berlin: VEB Deutscher Verlag der Wissenchaften, 1969) pp. 255–6.

[2]Above, Chapter 12, pp. 230–1, D. Peukert, 'Protest und Widerstand von Jugendlichen im Dritten Reich' in Löwenthal and von zur Mühlen (eds), *Widerstand und Verweigerung*; also Peukert, *Die Edelweisspiraten. Protest-bewegung jugendlicher Arbeiter im Dritten Reich* (Cologne, 1980).

[3]Peukert, *Die KPD im Widerstand*, pp. 385–6.

[4]Günther Weisenborn, *Der lautlose Aufstand* (Hamburg: Rowohlt, 1953), p. 240, gives this as the number registered at the Ministry of Justice for 1943.

[5]Not counting Thälmann, still in captivity, or the two candidate members. Florin died in 1944 (Details in Mammach, *Die Berner Konferenz der KPD*, p. 1974).

[6]See Emmy Koenen, 'Exil in England. Erinnerungen', *BzG*, 4/1978, p. 545.

[7]For an autobiographical sketch by Niebergall, see Dora Schaul (ed), *Résistance. Erinnerungen deutscher Antifaschisten* (Berlin: Dietz, 1975) pp. 25–69.

[8]The text of the Appeal is printed in *Sie Kämpften für Deutschland* (Berlin: Verlag des Ministeriums der Nationalen Verteidigung, 1959), pp. 113–21; and a shortened version in *GddA*, doc. no. 80, pp. 553–5. The date of the conference is given in these publications and in Ulbricht's *Zur Geschichte der deutschen Arbeiterbewegung* (Vol. 2, pp. 269–70), and in some other GDR works, as 9/10 October 1941; but Erich Weinert in *Das Nationalkomitee Freies Deutschland* (Berlin: Rütten & Loening, 1957) gives the date as December 1941 – that is, after the failure of the German attack on Moscow; and other Western writers have accepted the later date. Arguments for the earlier date are given by Bruno Löwel in *BzG*, 4/1963, p. 615, n.7. See also Duhnke, p. 371.

[9]See Christian Streit, *Keine Kameraden* (Stuttgart: dva, 1978).

[10]See statement of 3 April 1942 by KPD Politburo (*GddA*, Vol. 5, doc. no. 85, pp. 559–62).

[11]An example of re-thinking is *Der schwere Entschluss* (The difficult decision) by Wilhelm Adam, who had been First Adjutant of the Sixth Army and thus closely associated with Field-Marshal Paulus (Berlin: Verlag der Nation, 1965).

[12]Bruno Löwel, 'Die Gründung des NKFD im Lichte der Entwicklung der Strategie und Taktik der KPD' in *BzG*, 4/1963, p. 619.

[13]Löwel, op. cit.; A.S. Blank, 'Die Zusammenkunft Wilhelm Piecks mit kriegsgefangenen Generälen und Offizieren der Hitlerwehrmacht in Susdal' in *BzG*, 4/1963, p. 675. For a Western account see Duhnke, *Die KPD von 1933 bis 1945*, pp. 375–8.

[14]Text in Erich Weinert, *Das Nationalkomitee 'Freies Deutschland' 1943–1945. Bericht über seine Tätigkeit und seine Auswirkung* (Berlin: Rütten & Loening, 1957) pp. 19–22.

[15]'Unconditional surrender' as an Allied war aim had been announced by President Roosevelt on behalf of the USA and Britain at the Casablanca conference in January 1943, but had not yet been formally adopted by the USSR.

[16]'. . . The aim is a Free Germany. That means . . . a free economy, free trade and free enterprise'.

[17]See Otto Niebergall, 'Der antifaschistische deutsche Widerstandskampf in Frankreich – seine Leitung und Entwicklung', in Dora Schaul (ed), *Résistance. Erinnerungen deutscher Antifaschisten* (Berlin: Dietz, pp. 28–35).

[18]Ibid., pp. 45, 47.
[19]See Edith Zorn, 'Einige neue Forschungsergebnisse zur Tätigkeit deutscher Antifaschisten die an der Seite der französischen Résistance kämpften' in *BzG*, 2/1965, p. 307.
[20]Ibid.
[21]Ibid(translated by the author).
[22]Zorn, loc. cit., p. 298.
[23]In at least 25 departments, according to E. Zorn in *BzG*, 5–6/1963.
[24]Edith Zorn, 'Zeugnisse der illegalen Wehrmachtpropaganda deutscher Antifaschisten und der Bewegung "Freies Deutschland" für den Westen in Frankreich aus den Jahren 1943 und 1944' in *BzG*, 5–6/1963, p. 975n. 7.
[25]See Max Spangenberg, 'Antifaschistischer Kampf deutscher Kommunisten in Dänemark. Erinnerungen' in *BzG*, 4/1977, pp. 617–35.
[26]The delay was also due to the opposition of the Swiss authorities, concerned to preserve their neutrality (Duhnke, pp. 413–6).
[27]Ibid., pp. 416–7.
[28]On the German exiles in Sweden, see also K. Mewis, *Im Auftrag der Partei*, pp. 262 ff.
[29]Duhnke, pp. 406–7.
[30]Ibid., pp. 417–31.
[31]Ibid., pp. 403–5.
[32]In his order of 23 February 1942, quoted in Ilse Krause, *die Schumann-Engert-Kresse-Gruppe* (Berlin: Dietz, 1960), p. 18. See also Duhnke, p. 432.
[33]W. Bleyer et al., *Lehrbuch der deutschen Geschichte (Beiträge)*, Vol. 12, 1939–45 (Berlin: VEB Deutscher Verlag der Wissenschaften 1969), pp. 343–44.
[34]Above, Chapter 13, p. 257.
[35]Gerhard Nitzsche, *Die Saefkow-Jacob-Bästlein-Gruppe. Dokumente und Materialien des illegalen antifaschistischen Kampfes (1942 bis 1945)* (Berlin: Dietz, 1957); also Bärbel Schindler-Saefkow, 'Biographische Skizze über A. Saefkow' in *BzG*, 4/1978; also Duhnke, pp. 485–8.
[36]Nitzsche, pp. 28–35.
[37]By the end of 1943 the organisation embraced cells in 30 or more of the larger Berlin factories, according to Winzer (*Zwölf Jahre Kampfes*, p. 213) and Duhnke, p. 486. Rossmann, *Der Kampf der KPD um die Einheit aller Hitlergegner* (Berlin: Dietz, 1963) speaks of 25 cells in Berlin and 25 firm connections to factory workers (p. 74).
[38]Rossmann puts the first contact at autumn 1943 (ibid., p. 81).
[39]See G. Glondajewski and H. Schumann, *Die Neubauer-Poser-Gruppe* (Berlin: Dietz, 1957) pp. 91–3. The 28 signatories included 12 heads of colleges and 9 university professors.
[40]Ibid., p. 27.
[41]Ibid.
[42]Facsimile in Pikarski and Uebel (eds), *Antifaschistische Widerstandskampf*, doc. no. 187.
[43]See Duhnke, pp. 490–2; Ilse Krause, *Die Schumann-Engert-Kresse-Gruppe. Dokumente und Materialien des illegalen antifaschistischen Kampfes (Leipzig – 1943 bis 1945)* (Berlin: Dietz, 1960).
[44]Ibid., p. 21; Duhnke, pp. 492–3.

[45]Winzer, p. 221; Rossmann, pp. 98, 105–6, 114, 116.
[46]Winzer, loc. cit.; Rossmann, p. 98.
[47]For his account of his mission, see V. Porembka, 'Als Fallschirmspringer im illegalen Einsatz' in Heinz Vosske (ed), *Im Kampf bewährt* (Berlin: Dietz, 1969), pp. 105–41. Another woman Communist, Charlotte Bischoff, had entered by sea from Sweden, as mentioned above.
[48]Mewis, *Im Auftrag der Partei*, pp. 302–4; see also Report of Arvid Lundgren in G. Nitzsche, *Die Saefkow-Jacob-Bästlein-Gruppe*, pp. 204–7 (translated from the Swedish paper *Ny Tid* of 28 May, 5 and 9 June 1947).
[49]Printed in Nitzsche, op. cit., pp 137–49.
[50]See Rossmann, op. cit., pp. 51 ff.; Nitzsche, op. cit., 137–49.
[51]Rossmann, p. 83
[52]Ibid.
[53]Ibid., p. 98.
[54]Ibid., pp. 99 ff.
[55]Duhnke, pp. 506–7; Nitzsche, op. cit., pp. 68–9.
[56]Rossmann, p. 191; Nitzsche, p. 69.
[57]Rossmann, p. 191n. 152.
[58]Rossmann, p. 219. Walpurga's husband, Rudolf Pechel the editor, was imprisoned.
[59]Rossmann, pp. 221–2; *GddA*, Vol. 5. p. 408.
[60]*GddA*, Vol. 5, p. 408; Rossmann, p. 222.
[61]Both Leber and Reichwein have been described as members of the 'Kreisau Circle'.
[62]Rudolf Pechel, *Deutscher Widerstand* (Erlenbach-Zürich: Rentsch 1947), p. 70, quoted in Duhnke, p. 508n. 190.

Chapter 15. The Absent Revolution, 1944–45

[1]*For facsimiles see E. Weinert, Das Nationalkomitee 'Freies Deutschland'*, appendix of illustrations; Pikarski and Uebel, *Antifaschistische Widerstandskampf*, doc. no. 177; *Sie kämpften für Deutschland* (Berlin: 1959), pp. 425 ff.
[2]For examples of 'Rückkehrer', *Sie kämpften fur Deutschland*, pp. 547 ff., 555.
[3]Instances are given in Stanislaw Okecki, 'Die Teilnahme deutscher Antifaschisten an der polnischen revolutionären Widerstandbewegung' in *Der deutsche Imperialismus und der zweite Weltkrieg*, Vol. 4 (Berlin: Rütten & Loening, 1961), pp. 521–7.
[4]H. Kühnrich, *Der Partisanenkrieg in Europa, 1939–1945* (Berlin: Dietz, 1965), p. 339.
[5]For Hitler's 'scorched earth' decree of 19 March 1945, see Noakes and Pridham (eds), *Documents on Nazism*, p. 676.
[6]See Bleyer et al., *Lehrbuch der deutschen Geschichte (Beiträge)*, Vol. 12, 1939–1945 (Berlin: VEB Deutscher Verlag der Wissenschaften, 1969), pp. 283–4, 373–4.
[7]See A.S. Milward, *The German Economy at War*, p. 72.
[8]Ibid., pp. 162–3.
[9]Bleyer et al., op. cit., p. 370.
[10]Ibid.

[11]Figures from G. Weisenborn, *Der lautlose Aufstand*, p. 240.
[12]Bleyer et al., p. 371.
[13]Weisenborn, p. 240.
[14]Edward L. Homze, 'The foreign worker's life in the Reich', Chapter 12 in his *Foreign Labor in Nazi Germany* (Princeton University Press, 1967).
[15]C. Streit, *Keine Kameraden* (Stuttgart: dva, 1978).
[16]For the so-called 'Bosch circle' and 'Reusch circle' in heavy and electrical industry and their relations with Goerdeler, see *GddA*, Vol. 5, p. 343; also W. Bleyer et al., op. cit., p. 367.
[17]See Kühnrich, *Der Partisanenkrieg*, p. 346; Peukert, *Die KPD im Widerstand*, pp. 396–400.
[18]Peukert, *KPD im Widerstand*, pp. 406–7; J. Zanders, 'Der antifaschistische Widerstandskampf des Volksfrontkomitees "Freies Deutschland" in Köln im Jahre 1943–4' in *BzG*, 1960, pp. 720–41.
[19]Peukert, op. cit., p. 400.
[20]From *Der lautlose Aufstand*, pp. 133–4, quoting an internal Ministry of Justice information sheet, *Die Lage*.
[21]For an account of these organisations see: E.A. Brodski, 'Die Teilnahme Sowjetischer Patrioten an der antifaschistischen Widerstandsbewegung in Süddeutschland (1943–1944)' in *Der deutsche Imperialismus und der zweite Weltkrieg*, vol. 4, pp. 489–520; also Duhnke, p. 512.
[22]e.g. 'Die antinazistische deutsche Volksfront', described by Brodski, op. cit., pp. 511 ff.
[23]'Das internationale antifaschistische Komitee', mentioned in Ilse Krause, *Die Schumann-Engert-Kresse-Gruppe*, pp. 43–52, 144–5.
[24]Colonel Rudolf Petershagen, for whose memoirs see *Gewissen in Aufruhr* (Berlin: Verlag der Nation, n.d.).
[25]Described in H-P. Görgen, *Düsseldorf und der Nationalsozialismus* (Düsseldorf: L. Schwann Verlag, 1969), pp. 234–7.
[26]Duhnke, p. 512.
[27]See Franz Peplinski, 'Kämpfer an der illegalen Front. Erinnerungen', in *BzG*, 3/1980, pp. 383–93. Peukert suggests that conditions may have been far less favourable for attempts to seize control of towns in Western than in Central Germany, because the Gestapo may have been more reluctant to release top Communists in the former (*Die KPD im Widerstand*, p. 410).
[28]Duhnke, p. 514.
[29]Duhnke, pp. 512–22.
[30]For extracts see *GddA*, Vol. 5, No. 119, pp. 607–9; also ibid., pp. 420–1. For the third draft, see: *BzG*, 2/1965, pp. 259–63.
[31]Text in *BzG*, 2/1965, pp. 263–8; also (extracts) in *GddA*, Vol. 5, No. 128, pp. 618–23.
[32]*BzG*, 2/1965, p. 267; *GddA*, Vol. 5, pp. 622–3.
[33]*BzG*, 2/1965, pp. 265–6.
[34]See Günter Benser, 'Kurs auf die legale kommunistische Massenpartei. Die Parteifrage in den konzeptionellen Überlegungen der KPD (Dezember 1944 bis Juni 1945)' in *BzG*, 3/1980, pp. 334–48.
[35]Benser, p. 341.
[36]Sobottka to Pieck, 30 May 1945, quoted by Benser in *BzG*, 3/1980, pp. 346–7.

[37]Benser in *BzG*, 3/1980, p. 340.

[38]Lutz Niethammer in Niethammer, Borsdorf and Brandt (eds), *Arbeiterinitiative 1945. Antifaschistische Ausschüsse und Reorganisation der Arbeiterbewegung in Deutschland* (Wuppertal: Peter Hammer Verlag, 1976), pp. 179 ff., 182 ff.

[39]Elected as a candidate member at the Bern Conference.

[40]See Heinz Vosske, 'Über die Initiativgruppe des Zentralkomitees der KPD in Mecklenburg-Vorpommern [Mai bis Jul 1945]' in *BzG*, 3/1964, pp. 424–37.

[41]See G. Benser, 'Das Jahr 1945. Vom antifaschistischen Widerstand zur antifaschistisch-demokratischen Umwälzung' in *Zeitschrift für Geschichtswissenschaft* 4/1980. Parts of these provinces were at first occupied by the Americans.

[42]This manifesto, *Aufruf der Kommunistischen Partei Deutschlands*, dated Berlin, 11 June 1945, was signed on behalf of the Central Committee by Pieck, Ulbricht, Dahlem, Ackermann and twelve other prominent members. Full text in Pikarski and Uebel, document no. 240.

Chapter 16. The Heritage of Communist Resistance

[1]Quoted from Peukert, *Die KPD im Widerstand*, p. 422.

[2]Ibid., p. 423.

[3]T.W. Mason, *A und V*, p. xx.

[4]Tim Mason, 'The Workers' Opposition in Nazi Germany' in *History Workshop Journal*, No. 11, Spring 1981, pp. 132–3.

[5]See, for example, Gestapo Situation Report (*Lagebericht*) of January 1936 printed in *GddA*, document no. 26, pp. 477–9.

[6]Dr Peukert emphasises this point: *Die KPD im Widerstand*, pp. 23, 338.

[7]Peukert, op. cit., p. 352.

[8]See above, Chapter 5, pp. 81–2.

[9]*BzG*, 4/1978, p. 534, letter of 2 September 1933.

[10]*BzG*, 4/1975, p. 642.

[11]Printed in Degras, Vol. III, p. 296.

[12]The KPD's 'Brussels Conference' was held near Moscow in October 1935.

[13]Wilhelm Knöchel (1899–1944) is portrayed by Dr Peukert as a man of independent ideas whose radicalism might, but for his arrest, have led him into disagreement with the Party leadership (*Die KPD im Widerstand*, pp. 342 ff.).

[14]In conjunction with Erich Gentsch, the Sector Leader.

[15]See Peukert, op. cit., p. 358.

[16]Saefkow and Jacob's discussions with Leber and Reichwein in June 1944 might have led to their participation in the Stauffenberg plot (see Chapter 14 above; also Duhnke, p. 508n. 190).

[17]Peukert, op. cit., pp. 428–9.

[18]See, e.g., *GddA*, Vol. 5, p. 326.

[19]See Duhnke, p. 494n.

[20]In Mexico.

Appendix on Sources

A. *Manuscript sources* used for this study (especially for Chapter 6) include:

1 *Hauptstaatsarchiv Nord-Rhein-Westfalen at Düsseldorf.*
Includes some 73,000 Gestapo personal files.

2 *Archive of the North-Rhine-Westphalian office of the VVN, at Düsseldorf.*
Includes much personal testimony offered by victims of Nazi persecution.

3 *Bundesarchiv (West German Federal Archive) at Koblenz.*
Especially Gestapo situation reports.

4 *Oberlandesgericht* (Regional Court) at Hamm in Westphalia.
Records of treason cases referred by the People's Court at Berlin.

5 *The Prussian Secret State Archive at West Berlin* (Geheimes Staatsarchiv).
Especially Gestapo situation reports.

6 *The Berlin Document Center at West Berlin.*
Especially records of People's Court cases.

7 *Institute for Marxism-Leninism: Central Party Archives in Berlin.*
Contains what remains of KPD records.

B. *Personal recollections of survivors.*
The author is indebted, among others, to the following – some alas no longer living – who deepened his understanding by talking to him about their personal experiences of persecution and resistance:

Berlin: Prof. Walter Bartel, Rudi Goguel, Prof. Ernst Hoffmann, Oskar and Raja Hoffmann, Bruno Retzlaff-Kresse, Prof. Heinrich Scheel, Friedel Schirm, Walter

Vesper, Rudolf Welskopf and Frau Prof. Welskopf.
Düsseldorf: Friedrich Fränken, Anton Götschenberg, Hans Heinen, Augusta Joschonnek, Willy Kutz, Hermann Laupsien, Hans Pumpat, Fritz Sbozny, Karl und Klara Schabrod.
Hamm: Walter Günter.
Neuss: Josefine Hollmann.
Krefeld: Aurel Billstein.
Wermelskirchen near Remscheid: Luise Paul.

C. *Publications mentioned in the text.*
[and in no way intended to represent a comprehensive list of works on the subject]

1 *Bibliographies.*

Förster, Gerhard et al. (eds), 'Forschungen zur deutschen Geschichte 1933–45' in *Historische Forschungen in der DDR, 1960–1970. Analysen und Berichte* (Berlin: Deutscher Verlag der Wissenschaften, 1970).

Gittig, Heinz, *Illegale antifaschistische Tarnschriften* (Leipzig: VEB Bibliographisches Institut, 1972) [List of disguised pamphlets].

Goguel, Rudi (ed), *Antifaschistischer Widerstand und Klassenkampf.* Bibliographie deutschsprachiger Literatur, 1945–1973 (Berlin: Militärverlag der DDR, 1976).

Maas, Liselotte, *Handbuch der deutschen Exilpresse* (Munich/ Vienna: Carl Hauser, 1976).

— *Persecution and Resistance under the Nazis.* The Wiener Library. Catalogue Series No. 7 (London: Institute of Contemporary History, 1978).

2 *Other publications.*

— *Beiträge zur Geschichte der deutschen Arbeiterbewegung* (Published by the Institute for Marxism-Leninism in Berlin).

— 'Berichte des Thälmann-Kuriers, Walter Trautsch' (*BzG*, 5/1965, pp. 849–875).

— *Deutsche Widerstandskämpfer 1933–1945. Biographien und*

Briefe, 2 vols. (Berlin: Dietz, 1970).

— *Die illegale Tagung des Zentralkomitees der KPD am 7 Februar 1933 in Ziegenhals bei Berlin* (Berlin: Dietz, 1981).

— *Report to the 7th Congress of the Communist International, 1935* (London: Red Star Press, 1975).

— *Gesetze des NS-Staates*, 2 vols (West Berlin: Gehlen Verlag, 1968).

— *Sie kämpften für Deutschland. Zur Geschichte des Kampfes der Bewegung "Freies Deutschland" bei der 1 Ukrainischen Front der Sovietarmee* (Berlin: Verlag des Ministeriums der Nationalen Verteidigung, 1959).

— 'Unbekannte Dokumente Ernst Thälmanns aus dem faschistischen Kerker' (*BzG*, 3/1964).

— *Zur Geschichte der deutschen antifaschistischen Widerstandsbewegung 1933 bis 1945* (Berlin: Verlag des Ministeriums der Nationalen Verteidigung, 1958).

Adam, Wilhelm, *Der schwere Entschluss* (Berlin: Verlag der Nation, 1965).

Aleff, Eberhard, et al. (eds), *Terror und Widerstand 1933–1945.* Dokumente aus Deutschland und dem besetzten Europa (West Berlin: 1966).

Bahne, Siegfried, 'Die Kommunistische Partei Deutschlands' in Matthias and Morsey (eds), *Das Ende der Parteien 1933* (Düsseldorf: Droste Verlag, 1960).

Bahne, S., 'Sozialfaschismus in Deutschland. Zur Geschichte eines politischen Begriffs' in *International Review of Social History*, No. 10 (1965, pp. 211–244).

Beck, Johannes et al., *Terror und Hoffnung in Deutschland, 1933–1945* (Hamburg: Rowohlt, 1980).

Benser, G., 'Das Jahr 1945. Vom antifaschistischen Widerstand zur antifaschistisch-demokratischen Umwälzung' in *Zeitschrift fur Geschichtswissenschaft*, 4/1980.

Biernat, Karl-Heinz, *Der Reichstag brennt. Hintergründe und Auswirkungen* (Berlin: Dietz, 1960).

Biernat, K-H. et al., 'Uber den Beitrag der KPD zur Vorbereitung des VII Weltkongresses der KI' in *BzG*, 4/ 1965.

Biernat, K-H. et al. (eds), *Die KPD und der VII Weltkongress der KI. Dokumente und Materialien* (Berlin, 1966).

Biernat, K–H. and Kraushaar, Luise, *Die Schulze-Boysen-Harnack-Organisation im antifaschistischen Kampf* (Berlin: Dietz, 1970).

Billstein, Aurel, *Der eine fällt, die anderen rücken nach.* Dokumente des Widerstandes und der Verfolgung in Krefeld 1933–1945 (Frankfurt-am-Main: Röderberg Verlag, 1973).

Bischoff, Charlotte, 'Die Innere Front: ein Beispiel des Kampfes der deutschen Arbeiterklasse unter Führung der KPD gegen Militarismus und Faschismus' in *Der deutsche Imperialismus und der zweite Weltkrieg*', Vol. 4 (Berlin: Rütten & Loening, 1959).

Bleyer, W. et al., *Deutschland 1939–1945. Lehrbuch der deutschen Geschichte*, Vol. 12 (Berlin: VEB Deutscher Verlag der Wissenschaften, 1969).

Boberach, Heinz, *Meldungen aus dem Reich* (West Berlin: Luchterhand, 1965).

Broszat, Martin, 'Nationalsozialistische Konzentrationslager 1933–1945' in M. Broszat (ed), *Anatomie des SS-Staats*, Vol. 2 (Munich: dtv, 1967).

Broszat, M., *Der Staat Hitlers* (Munich: dtv, 1969).

Broszat M. et al. (eds), *Bayern in der NS-Zeit. Soziale Lage und politisches Verhalten im Spiegel vertraulicher Berichte* (Munich: R. Oldenbourg, 1977).

Broszat, M., et al. (eds), *Bayern in der NS-Zeit*, Vol. III. *Herrschaft und Gesellschaft in Konflikt* (Munich: R. Oldenbourg, 1981).

Buchheim, H., *Anatomie des SS-Staats*, Vol. I (Munich: dtv, 1967).

Bullock, Alan, 'The German Communists and the rise of

Hitler' in M. Baumont et al. (eds), *The Third Reich* (London: Weidenfeld & Nicolson, 1955).

Cammett, John M., 'Communist Theories of Fascism, 1920–1935' in *Science and Society* (1966–7).

Claudin, Fernando, *The Communist Movement from Comintern to Cominform* (Harmondsworth: Penguin Books, 1975).

Dahlem, Franz, *Am Vorabend des zweiten Weltkrieges. Erinnerungen*, 2 vols (Berlin: Dietz, 1977).

Degras, Jane (ed), *The Communist International 1919–43. Documents.* Vol. II, 1923–28, Vol. III, 1928–43 (London: Frank Cass & Co, 1960, 1965).

Duhnke, Horst, *Die KPD von 1933 bis 1945* (Cologne: Kiepenheuer & Witsch, 1972).

Edinger, L.J., *German Exile Politics. The Social Democratic Executive Committee in the Nazi era* (Berkeley and Los Angeles: University of California Press, 1956).

Eggerath, Werner, *Nur ein Mensch* (Berlin: Dietz, 1961).

Eiber, Ludwig, 'Frauen in der Kriegsindustrie, Arbeitsbedingungen, Lebensumstände und Protestverhalten' in M. Broszat (ed), *Bayern in der NS-Zeit*, Vol. III, pp. 569–87.

Eling, Hanna, *Frauen im deutschen Widerstand 1933–45* (Frankfurt-am-Main: Röderberg, 1978).

Findeisen, Otto, 'Zu den Einheitsfrontverhandlungen am 23 November 1935 in Prag' (*BzG*, 4/1966).

Fowkes, Ben, *Communism in Germany under the Weimar Republic* (London: Macmillan, 1984).

Glondajewski, G. and Schumann, H., *Die Neubauer-Poser-Gruppe* (Berlin: Dietz, 1957).

Görgen, Hans-Peter, *Düsseldorf und der Nationalsozialismus* (Düsseldorf: Schwann, 1969).

Goguel, Rudi, *Es war ein langer Weg* (Cologne: Komet Verlag, 1947).

Grunberger, Richard, *A Social History of the Third Reich* (London: Weidenfeld & Nicolson, 1971).

Harman, Chris, *The Lost Revolution. Germany 1918 to 1923* (London: Bookmarks, 1982).

Hetzer, Gerhard, 'Die Industriestadt Augsburg' in *Bayern in der NS-Zeit*, Vol. III (Munich: Oldenbourg, 1981).

Hochmuth, Ursel and Meyer, Gertrud, *Streiflichter aus dem Hamburger Widerstand, 1933–1945, Berichte und Dokumente* (Frankfurt: Röderberg, 1969).

Hofer, Walther (ed), *Der Reichstagsbrand. Eine wissenschaftliche Dokumentation* (West Berlin: Arani, 1972).

Homze, Edward, *Foreign Labor in Nazi Germany* (Princeton, New Jersey: Princeton University Press, 1967).

Jahnke, Karl-Heinz, *Jungkommunisten im Widerstandskampf gegen den Hitlerfaschismus* (Berlin: Verlag Neues Leben, 1977).

Karg, Berta Karola, 'Mein Kampf gegen die braune Diktatur' in Löwenthal and von zur Mühlen (eds), *Widerstand und Verweigerung in Deutschland 1933 bis 1945* (Bonn, 1982).

Kershaw, Ian, *Popular Opinion and Political Dissent in the Third Reich: Bavaria 1933–1945* (Oxford: Clarendon Press, 1983).

Kershaw, Ian, 'Alltägliches und Ausseralltägliches: ihre Bedeutung für die Volksmeinung 1933–1939' in Peukert and Reulecke (eds), *Die Reihen fast geschlossen* (Wuppertal: Peter Hammer Verlag, 1981).

Kettenacker L., (ed), *'The Other Germany' in the Second World War. Emigration and Resistance in International Perspective.* Publications of the German Historical Institute in London, No. 2 (Stuttgart: Ernst Klett, 1977).

Koenen, Emmy, 'Exil in England. Erinnerungen' (*BzG*, 4/1978).

Krause, Ilse, *Die Schumann-Engert-Kresse-Gruppe* (Berlin: Dietz, 1960).

Kraushaar, Luise, 'Zur Tätigkeit und Wirkung des deutschen

Volkssenders' in *BzG*, 1/1964 [see also R. Gyptner in *BzG*, 5/1964].

Kraushaar, L., *Berliner Kommunisten im Kampf gegen den Faschismus, 1936–1942* (Berlin: Dietz, 1981).

Kuczynski, Jürgen, *Memoiren* (Berlin and Weimar: Aufbau Verlag, 1981).

Kühnrich, Heinz, *Der Partisanenkrieg in Europa, 1939–45* (Berlin: Dietz, 1965).

Kühnrich, H., 'Einige Fragen des Kampfes der KPD in der ersten Periode des zweiten Weltkrieges' (*BzG*, 1/1982, pp. 25–39).

Kühnrich, H., *Die KPD im Kampf gegen die faschistische Diktatur, 1933–1945* (Berlin: Dietz, 1983).

Lönne, Karl-Egon, 'Thesen zum publizistischen Tageskampf der KPD gegen den Faschismus: Die "Rote Fahne", Zentralorgan der KPD' in *Gesellschaftliche Beiträge zur Marxchen Theorie*. Vol. 6 (Frankfurt-am-Main: 1976).

Löwel, Bruno, 'Die Gründung des NKFD im Lichte der Entwicklung der Strategie und Taktik der KPD' in *BzG*, 4/1963.

Löwenthal, R., 'Widerstand im totalen Staat' in Löwenthal and von zur Mühlen (eds), *Widerstand und Verweigerung in Deutschland 1933 bis 1945* (Bonn: Verlag J.H.W. Dietz Nachf, 1982).

Mammach, Klaus and Nitzsche, Gerhard, 'Zum antifaschistischen Kampf der KPD in den Jahren von 1939 bis 1941' (*BzG*, 6/1971, pp. 911–35).

Mammach, K., (ed), *Die Berner Konferenz der KPD* (30 Januar-1 Februar 1939) (Berlin: Dietz, 1974).

Mammach, K. 'Zum gemeinsamen Kampf deutscher und polnischer Kommunisten und anderer Antifaschisten 1933 bis 1939' (*BzG, 5/1974).*

Mammach, K., (ed), *Die Brüsseler Konferenz der KPD* (Frankfurt-am-Main: Verlag Marxistische Blätter, 1975).

Mammach, K., *Widerstand 1933–1939* (Berlin: Akademie Verlag, 1983).

Mason, T.W. 'Labour in the Third Reich' in *Past and Present*, No. 33, April 1966.

Mason, Timothy, W., 'Der antifaschistische Widerstand im Spiegel der SED-Historiographie' in *Das Argument*, No. 43, July 1967.

Mason, Timothy W., *Arbeiterklasse und Volksgemeinschaft. Dokumente und Materialien zur deutschen Arbeiterpolitik 1936–1939* (Opladen: Westdeutscher Verlag, 1975).

Mason, T.W., 'Workers' Opposition in Nazi Germany' in *History Workshop Journal*, No. 11, 1981.

Mason, T.W., 'Resistance in the Ruhr' in *The Times Literary Supplement*, 7 May 1982 [review of Peukert's *Die KPD im Widerstand*].

Mausbach-Bromberger, Barbara, *Arbeiterwiderstand in Frankfurt-am-Main gegen den Faschismus 1933–1945* (Frankfurt: Röderberg, 1976).

Merson, Allan, 'High Treason in Düsseldorf' (Unpublished MS).

Merson, Allan, 'Nazi and Monopoly Capital', *Our History*, pamphlet 57, summer 1973.

Mewis, Karl, *Im Auftrag der Partei* (Berlin: Dietz, 1971).

Milatz, Alfred. 'Das Ende der Parteien im Spiegel der Wahlen, 1930 bis 1933' in E. Matthias and R. Morsey (eds), *Das Ende der Parteien 1933* (Düsseldorf: Droste Verlag, 1960).

Milward, A.S. *The German Economy at War* (London: Athlone Press, 1965).

Mommsen, Hans, 'Der Reichstagsbrand und seine politischen Folgen' (*VfZ*, No. 12, 1965).

Niethammer, Lutz et al. (eds), *Arbeiterinitiative 1945. Antifaschistische Ausschüsse und Reorganisation der Arbeiterbewegung in Deutschland* (Wuppertal: Peter Hammer

Verlag, 1976).

Nitzsche, Gerhard, *Die Saefkow-Jacob-Bästlein-Gruppe. Dokumente und Materialien des illegalen antifaschistischen Kampfes (1942 bis 1945)* (Berlin: Dietz, 1957).

Nitzsche, G. and Uebel, Günter (eds), 'Aus der Tätigkeit illegaler Leitungen im Lande' in *BzG*, 4/78, 5/78, 1/79, 4/79.

Noakes, J. and Pridham, G. (eds), *Documents on Nazism 1919–1945* (London: Jonathan Cape, 1974).

Oppenheimer, Max, *Der Fall Vorbote* (Frankfurt-am-Main: Röderberg, 1969).

Paterczyk, Zygmunt, 'Dokumente der KPD in Pila aufgefunden' in *BzG*, 4/1973, pp. 691–693.

Paterna, Erich, 'Zum Kampf der KPD gegen die Vorbereitung des zweiten Weltkrieges (Februar bis August 1939)' (*BzG*, 4/1964).

Paterna, E. et al., *Deutschland 1933–1939. Lehrbuch der deutschen Geschichte*, Vol. 11 (Berlin: Deutscher Verlag der Wissenschaften, 1969).

Paul, Elfriede, *Ein Sprechzimmer der Roten Kapelle* (Berlin: Militärverlag der DDR, 1981).

Pechel, Rudolf, *Deutscher Widerstand* (Zürich: 1947).

Peplinski, Franz, 'Kämpfer an der illegalen Front. Erinnerungen.' in *BzG*, 3/1980, pp. 383–93.

Petershagen, Colonel Rudolf, *Gewissen in Aufruhr* (Berlin: Verlag der Nation, n.d.).

Peukert, Detlev, 'Der Arbeiterwiderstand 1933–1945', in *das parlament* (supplement), B 28–29/79, 14 juli 1979.

Peukert, D., *Die KPD im Widerstand. Verfolgung und Untergrundarbeit an Rhein und Ruhr, 1933 bis 1945* (Wuppertal: Peter Hammer Verlag, 1980).

Peukert, D., *Die Edelweisspiraten. Protestbewegung jugendlicher Arbeiter im Dritten Reich* (Cologne: 1980).

Peukert, D., *Alltag unterm Nationalsozialismus. Beiträge zum Thema Widerstand*, No. 17 (West Berlin: Informationszentrum, 1981).

Pieck, Wilhelm, *Gesammelte Reden und Schriften*, Vol. 5 (Berlin, 1972).

Pieck, W., *Der neue Weg zum gemeinsamen Kampf für den Sturz der Hitlerdiktatur* (Berlin: Dietz, 1954).

Pikarski, Margot, 'Zur Hilfe der KI und der kommunistischen Bruderparteien beim Übergang der KPD in die Illegalität im Jahre 1933 (*BzF*, 5/1974).

Pikarski, Margot and Uebel, Günter (eds), *Der antifaschistische Widerstandskampf der KPD im Spiegel des Flugblattes 1933–1945* (Berlin: Dietz. 1978) [paperback version entitled *Die KPD lebt*].

Pikarski, M., 'Die Umstellung der KPD auf die Illegalität, 1932–1934' (*BzG , 5/1978)*.

Pirker, T., *Komintern und Faschismus* (Stuttgart: dva, 1965).

Plum, Günter, 'Die KPD in der Illegalität. Rechenschaftsbericht einer Bezirksleitung aus dem Jahre 1934' (*VfZ* No. 97, pp. 219–235).

Prittie, Terence, *Germans Against Hitler* (London: Hutchinson, 1964).

Puls, Ursula, *Die Bästlein-Jacob-Abshagen-Gruppe* (Berlin: Dietz, 1970).

Ramme, Alwin, *Der Sicherheitsdienst der SS* (Berlin: Deutsche Akademie der Wissenschaften, 1969).

Reichhardt, Hans J., 'Möglichkeiten und Grenzen des Widerstandes der Arbeiterbewegung' in Schmitthenner and Buchheim (eds), *Der deutsche Widerstand gegen Hitler* (Cologne: Kiepenheuer & Witsch. 1966).

Retzlaff-Kresse, Bruno, *Illegalität-Kerker-Exil* (Berlin: Dietz. 1980).

Ritter, Gerhard, *The German Resistance. Carl Goerdeler's struggle against tyranny*. (London: Allen & Unwin, 1958.)

Rossmann, G., *Der Kampf der KPD um die Einheit aller Hitlergegner* (Berlin: Dietz, 1963).

Rothfels, Hans, *The German Opposition*. An assessment (London: Oswald Wolff, 1961).

Schabrod, Karl, *Widerstand an Rhein und Ruhr 1933–1945* (Düsseldorf: 1969).

Schabrod, K. (ed), *Widerstand gegen Flick und Florian*. Düsseldorfer Antifaschisten über ihren Widerstand 1933–45 (Frankfurt-am-Main: Röderberg, 1969).

Schabrod, K. (ed), *Der rote Grossvater erzählt*. Berichte und Erzählungen von Veteranen der Arbeiterbewegung aus der Zeit von 1914 bis 1945 (Frankfurt-am-Main: Fischer Taschenbuch, 1974).

Schaul, Dora (ed), *Resistance*. Erinnerungen deutscher Antifaschisten (Berlin: Dietz, 1975).

Schlabrendorf, Fabian von, *Offiziere gegen Hitler* (Frankfurt-am-Main: Fischerbücherei, 1959).

Schumann, Heinz, 'Die Behandlung des antifaschistischen Widerstandskampfes in der westdeutschen Geschichtsschreibung' in L. Stern (ed), *Probleme der Geschichte des Zweiten Weltkrieges* (Berlin: Akademie-Verlag, 1958).

Shirer, W.L., *The Rise and Fall of the Third Reich* (London, 1960).

Spangenberg, Max, 'Antifaschistischer Kampf deutscher Kommunisten in Dänemark' in *BzG*, 4/1977.

Steinberg, Hans-Josef, *Widerstand und Verfolgung in Essen, 1933–1945*. Schriftenreihe des Forschungsinstituts der Friedrich-Ebert-Stiftung (Hanover: Verlag für Literatur und Zeitgeschehen, 1969).

Streit, Christian, *Keine Kameraden* (Stuttgart: dva, 1978) [on treatment of Soviet P.O.W's].

Stroech, Jürgen, 'Zur Herstellung und Verbreitung der illegalen "Rote Fahne", 1933–1945' (*BzG*, 1/1977, pp. 81 ff).

Stroech, J. 'Die illegale Presse. Eine Waffe im Kampf gegen

den deutschen Faschismus' (Diss. IML, Berlin 1974: gekürzte Druckfassung: Leipzig, 1979).

Suhling, Lucie, *Der Unbekannte Widerstand. Erinnerungen* (Frankfurt-am-Main: Röderberg, 1980).

Sywotteck, Arnold, *Deutsche Volksdemokratie*. Studien zur politischen Konzeption der KPD, 1939–1946 (Düsseldorf: Bertelsmann, 1971).

Teubner, Hans, *Exilland Schweiz, 1933–45* (Berlin: Dietz, 1975).

Teubner, Hans, 'Der deutsche Freiheitssender 29,8 als Führungsorgan der KPD im antifaschistischen Kampf' in *Militärwesen* No. 9 (1965), pp. 176–188.

Thälmann, Ernst, *Ausgewählte Reden und Schriften*, Vol. II. (Frankfurt-am-Main, 1977)

Ulbricht, Walter, *Zur Geschichte der deutschen Arbeiterbewegung*, Vol. II, 1936–1946 (Berlin: Dietz, 1955).

Ulbricht, Walter et al. (eds), *Geschichte der deutschen Arbeiterbewegung*, Vol. V, Jan. 1933 bis Mai 1945 (Berlin: Dietz, 1966).

Vietzke, Siegfried, *Die KPD auf dem Wege zur Brüsseler Konferenz* (Berlin: Dietz, 1966).

Vosske, Heinz, 'Über die Initiativgruppe des Zentralkomitees der KPD in Mecklenburg-Vorpommern, Mai bis Juli 1945' (*BzG*, 3/1964).

Vosske, H. (ed), *Im Kampf bewährt* (Berlin: Dietz, 1969) [a collection of short biographies].

Wagner, Albrecht, 'Die Umgestaltung der Gerichtsverfassung . . .' in *Die deutsche Justiz und der Nationalsozialismus*, Vol. 16/1 (Stuttgart: dva, 1968).

Weber, Hermann, 'Die KPD in der Illegalität' in R. Löwenthal and P. von zur Mühlen (eds), *Widerstand und Verweigerung in Deutschland 1933 bis 1945* (Bonn: Verlag J.H.W. Dietz Nacht., 1982).

Weber, Stefan, 'Nach der Verhaftung Ernst Thälmanns leitete John Schehr die Illegale KPD' (*BzG*, 4/1982, pp. 483–498).

Weinert, Erich, *Das Nationalkomitee 'Freies Deutschland'* (Berlin: Rütten & Loening, 1957).

Weisenborn, Günther, *Die Illegalen* (Reclam, 1955) [a one-act play].

Weisenborn, G., *Der lautlose Aufstand* (Hamburg: Rowohlt, 1953).

Werner, Kurt and Biernat, K-H., *Die Köpenicke Blutwoche*, 1933 (Berlin: Dietz, 1960).

Wheeler-Bennett, Sir John, *The Nemesis of Power.* The German Army in Politics, 1918–1945 (London: Macmillan, 1961).

The Wiener Library Bulletin.

Winzer, Otto, *Zwölf Jahre Kampf gegen Faschismus und Krieg.* Ein Beitrag zur Geschichte der KPD, 1933 bis 1945 (Berlin: Dietz, 1957).

Zanders, J., 'Der antifaschistische Widerstandskampf des Volksfrontkomitees "Freies Deutschland" in Köln im Jahre 1943–4' (*BzG*, 1960, pp. 720–741).

Zorn, Edith, 'Einige neue Forschungsergebnisse zur Tätigkeit deutscher Antifaschisten die an der Seite der französischen Résistance kämpften' (*BzG*, 2/1965).

Zorn, Edith, 'Zeugnisse der illegalen Wehrmachtpropaganda deutscher Antifaschisten und der Bewegung "Freies Deutschland für den Westen" in Frankreich aus den Jahren 1943 und 1944' (*BzG*, 5–6/1963).

Glossary and Abbreviations

ADV	*Antinazistische Deutsche Volksfront*	Anti-Nazi German People's Front
BA	*Bundesarchiv*	Federal Archive (at Koblenz)
BDC		Berlin Document Center (West Berlin)
BL	*Bezirksleitung*	District Leadership (of KPD)
BRD	*Bundesrepublik Deutschland*	The Federal Republic of Germany (West)
BSW		Resistance organisations of Soviet POW
BzG	*Beiträge zur Geschichte der Arbeiterbewegung*	Periodical publication of the Institute for Marxism-Leninism
CI		Communist International
CALPO	*Comité Allemagne Libre pour l'Ouest*	'Free Germany' Committee for the West
ECCI		Executive Committee of the Communist International
GddA	*Geschichte der deutschen Arbeiterbewegung*	History of the German Workers' Movement
GDR	*Deutsche Demokratische Republik*	German Democratic Republic
Gestapa	*Geheime Staatspolizeiamt*	Gestapo head office in Berlin
Gestapo		Secret State Police
GStA	*Generalstaatsanwalt*	Public Prosecutor at regional level
HDG	*Hauptstaatsarchiv-Düsseldorf-Gestapo*	Gestapo records in the North-Rhine-Westphalian state archives at Düsseldorf

IAD	*Internationale Arbeiterhilfe*	International Workers' Aid
IAK	*Internationales Antifaschistisches Komitee*	
IML	*Institut für Marxismus-Leninismus beim Zentralkomite der SED*	Institute attached to the Socialist Unity Party in Berlin
KgF	*Kampfbund gegen den Faschismus*	League of Struggle against Fascism
KJVD	*Kommunistischer Jugendverband Deutschlands*	Communist Youth League of Germany
KPD	*Kommunistische Partei Deutschlands*	Communist Party of Germany
KPO	*Kommunistische Partei Opposition*	A right-wing breakaway group
RFB	*Roter Frontkämpferbund*	Red Front-Line Fighters' League (Communist paramilitary organisation)
RGO	*Revolutionäre Gewerkschafts-opposition*	Revolutionary Trade Union Opposition
NKFD	*Nationalkomitee 'Freies Deutschland'*	National 'Free Germany' Committee (1943)
RHD	*Rote Hilfe Deutschlands*	Red Aid (Germany)
RSHA	*Reichssicherheitshauptamt*	Reich Security Headquarters (1939-)
SA	*Sturmabteilung*	Storm Troops (i.e. brownshirts)
SAPD	*Sozialistische Arbeiterpartei Deutschlands*	Socialist Workers' Party of Germany (left-wing breakaway from SPD, 1931)
SD	*Sicherheitsdienst der SS*	Security service of the SS
SED	*Sozialistische Einheitspartei Deutschlands*	Socialist Unity Party of Germany (founded April 1946)
Sopade		Social Democratic Party Executive
SPD	*Sozialdemokratische Partei Deutschlands*	Social Democratic Party of Germany
SS	*Schutzstaffel*	Defence squad (Nazi blackshirts)

VEB	*Volkseigener Betrieb*	Publicly owned enterprise (in GDR)
	Vertrauensrat	Councillor of Trust (shop-steward chosen by the employer)
V-Mann	*Vertrauensmann*	'Confidence man', i.e. police spy
VfZ	*Vierteljahreshefte für Zeitgeschichte*	
VGH	*Volksgerichtshof*	People's Court (1934)
VVN (Dü)	*Vereinigung der Verfolgten des Nazi-Regimes* (Düsseldorf branch)	Association of victims of the Nazi-regime
ZK	*Zentralkomite*	Central Committee
ZPA	*Zentrales Parteiarchiv*	Central KPD archive, now in the IML, in Berlin

Note: In references in this book to works published since 1946 'Berlin' means East Berlin unless otherwise stated.

Index